D0025863

Welcome!

Thank you for joining us! As you explore this book, you will find a number of active learning components that help you learn the material at your own pace.

1. **CODE CHALLENGES** ask you to implement the algorithms that you will encounter (in any programming language you like). These code challenges are hosted in the "Bioinformatics Textbook Track" location on Rosalind (http://rosalind.info), a website that will automatically test your implementations.

2. **CHARGING STATIONS** provide additional insights on implementing the algorithms you encounter. However, we suggest trying to solve a Code Challenge before you visit a Charging Station.

3. **EXERCISE BREAKS** offer "just in time" assessments testing your understanding of a topic before moving to the next one.

4. **STOP and Think** questions invite you to slow down and contemplate the current material before continuing to the next topic.

5. **DETOURS** provide extra content that didn't quite fit in the main text.

6. **FINAL CHALLENGES** ask you to apply what you have learned to real experimental datasets.

This textbook powers our popular online courses on Coursera. We encourage you to sign up for a session and learn this material while interacting with thousands of other talented students from around the world. You can also find lecture videos and PowerPoint slides at the textbook website, http://bioinformaticsalgorithms.org.

Bioinformatics Algorithms:
An Active Learning Approach
2nd Edition, Vol. I

Phillip Compeau & Pavel Pevzner

http://bioinformaticsalgorithms.org

Active Learning
Publishers

© 2015

Copyright © 2015 by Phillip Compeau and Pavel Pevzner. All rights reserved.

This book or any portion thereof may not be reproduced or used in any manner whatsoever without the express written permission of the publisher except for the use of brief quotations in a book review.

Printed in the United States of America

Third Printing, 2016

ISBN: 978-0-9903746-1-9

Library of Congress Control Number: 2015945208

Active Learning Publishers, LLC
9768 Claiborne Square
La Jolla, CA 92037

To my family. — P. C.

To my parents. — P. P.

Volume I Overview

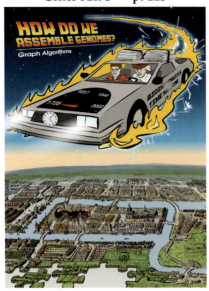

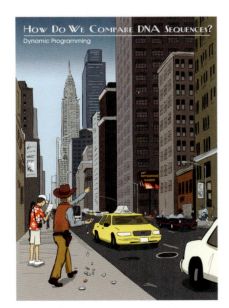

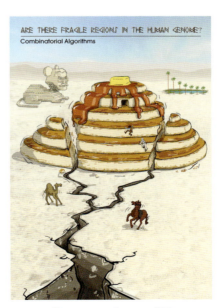

What To Expect in Volume II...

CHAPTER 7

CHAPTER 8

CHAPTER 9

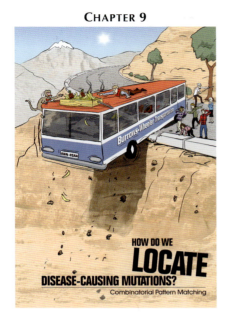

CHAPTER 10

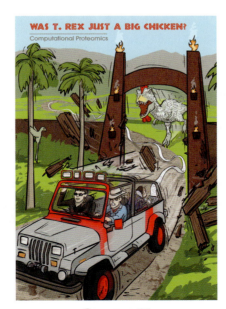

CHAPTER 11

Contents

List of Code Challenges

About the Textbook

Meet the Authors

PHILLIP COMPEAU is an Assistant Teaching Professor in the Computational Biology Department at Carnegie Mellon University. He is a former postdoctoral researcher in the Department of Computer Science & Engineering at the University of California, San Diego, where he received a Ph.D. in mathematics. He is passionate about the future of both offline and online education, having cofounded Rosalind with Nikolay Vyahhi in 2012. A retired tennis player, he dreams of one day going pro in golf.

PAVEL PEVZNER is Ronald R. Taylor Professor of Computer Science at the University of California, San Diego. He holds a Ph.D. from Moscow Institute of Physics and Technology, Russia and an Honorary Degree from Simon Fraser University. He is a Howard Hughes Medical Institute Professor (2006), an Association for Computing Machinery Fellow (2010), and an International Society for Computational Biology Fellow (2012). He has authored the textbooks *Computational Molecular Biology: An Algorithmic Approach* (2000) and *An Introduction to Bioinformatics Algorithms* (2004) (jointly with Neil Jones).

Meet the Development Team

OLGA BOTVINNIK is a Ph.D. candidate in Bioinformatics and Systems Biology at the University of California, San Diego. She holds an M.S. in Bioinformatics from University of California, Santa Cruz and B.S. degrees in Mathematics and Biological Engineering from the Massachusetts Institute of Technology. Her research interests are data visualization and single-cell transcriptomics. She enjoys yoga, photography, and playing cello.

SON PHAM is a postdoctoral researcher at Salk Institute in La Jolla, California. He holds a Ph.D. in Computer Science and Engineering from the University of California, San Diego and an M.S. in Applied Mathematics from St. Petersburg State University, Russia. His research interests include graph theory, genome assembly, comparative genomics, and neuroscience. Besides research, he enjoys walking meditation, gardening, and trying to catch the big one.

NIKOLAY VYAHHI coordinates the M.S. Program in Bioinformatics in the Academic University of St. Petersburg, Russian Academy of Sciences. In 2012, he cofounded the Rosalind online bioinformatics education project. He recently founded the Bioinformatics Institute in St. Petersburg as well as Stepic, a company focusing on content delivery for online education.

KAI ZHANG is a Ph.D. candidate in Bioinformatics and Systems Biology at the University of California, San Diego. He holds an M.S. in Molecular Biology from Xiamen University, China. His research interests include epigenetics, gene regulatory networks, and machine learning algorithms. Besides research, Kai likes basketball and music.

Acknowledgments

This textbook was greatly improved by the efforts of a large number of individuals, to whom we owe a debt of gratitude.

The development team (Olga Botvinnik, Son Pham, Nikolay Vyahhi, and Kai Zhang), as well as Laurence Bernstein and Ksenia Krasheninnikova, implemented coding challenges and exercises, rendered figures, helped typeset the text, and offered insightful feedback on the manuscript.

Glenn Tesler provided thorough chapter reviews and even implemented some software to catch errors in the early version of the manuscript!

Robin Betz, Petar Ivanov, James Jensen, and Yu Lin provided insightful comments on the manuscript in its early stages. David Robinson was kind enough to copy edit a few chapters and palliate our punctuation maladies.

Randall Christopher brought to life our ideas for illustrations in addition to the textbook cover.

Andrey Grigoriev and Max Alekseyev gave advice on the content of Chapter 1 and Chapter 6, respectively. Martin Tompa helped us develop the narrative in Chapter 2 by suggesting that we analyze latent tuberculosis infection.

Nikolay Vyahhi led a team composed of Andrey Balandin, Artem Suschev, Aleksey Kladov, and Kirill Shikhanov, who worked hard to support an online, interactive version of this textbook used in our online course on Coursera.

Our students on Coursera, especially Mark Mammel and Dmitry Kuzminov, found hundreds of typos in our preliminary manuscript.

Mikhail Gelfand, Uri Keich, Hosein Mohimani, Son Pham, and Glenn Tesler advised us on some of the book's "Open Problems" and led Massive Open Online Research projects (MOORs) in the first session of our online course.

Howard Hughes Medical Institute and the Russian Ministry of Education and Science generously gave their support for the development of the online courses based on this textbook. The Bioinformatics and Systems Biology Program and the Computer Science & Engineering Department at the University of California, San Diego provided additional support.

Finally, our families gracefully endured the many long days and nights that we spent poring over manuscripts, and they helped us preserve our sanity along the way.

P. C. and P. P.
San Diego
July 2015

Algorithmic Warmup

A Journey of a Thousand Miles...

Genome replication is one of the most important tasks carried out in the cell. Before a cell can divide, it must first replicate its genome so that each of the two daughter cells inherits its own copy. In 1953, James Watson and Francis Crick completed their landmark paper on the DNA double helix with a now-famous phrase:

> *It has not escaped our notice that the specific pairing we have postulated immediately suggests a possible copying mechanism for the genetic material.*

They conjectured that the two strands of the parent DNA molecule unwind during replication, and then each parent strand acts as a template for the synthesis of a new strand. As a result, the replication process begins with a pair of complementary strands of DNA and ends with two pairs of complementary strands, as shown in Figure 1.1.

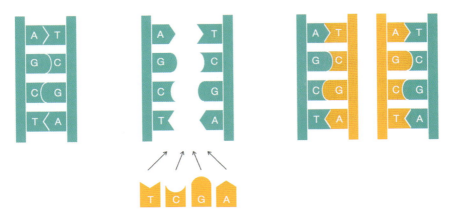

FIGURE 1.1 A naive view of DNA replication. Nucleotides adenine (A) and thymine (T) are complements of each other, as are cytosine (C) and guanine (G). Complementary nucleotides bind to each other in DNA.

Although Figure 1.1 models DNA replication on a simple level, the details of replication turned out to be much more intricate than Watson and Crick imagined; as we will see, an astounding amount of molecular logistics is required to ensure DNA replication.

At first glance, a computer scientist might not imagine that these details have any computational relevance. To mimic the process in Figure 1.1 algorithmically, we only need to take a string representing the genome and return a copy of it! Yet if we take the time to review the underlying biological process, we will be rewarded with new algorithmic insights into analyzing replication.

Replication begins in a genomic region called the **replication origin** (denoted *oriC*) and is performed by molecular copy machines called **DNA polymerases**. Locating *oriC* presents an important task not only for understanding how cells replicate but also for various biomedical problems. For example, some gene therapy methods use genetically engineered mini-genomes, which are called **viral vectors** because they are able to penetrate cell walls (just like real viruses). Viral vectors carrying artificial genes have been used in agriculture to engineer frost-resistant tomatoes and pesticide-resistant corn. In 1990, gene therapy was first successfully performed on humans when it saved the life of a four-year-old girl suffering from Severe Combined Immunodeficiency Disorder; the girl had been so vulnerable to infections that she was forced to live in a sterile environment.

The idea of gene therapy is to intentionally infect a patient who lacks a crucial gene with a viral vector containing an artificial gene that encodes a therapeutic protein. Once inside the cell, the vector replicates and eventually produces many copies of the therapeutic protein, which in turn treats the patient's disease. To ensure that the vector actually replicates inside the cell, biologists must know where *oriC* is in the vector's genome and ensure that the genetic manipulations that they perform do not affect it.

In the following problem, we assume that a genome has a single *oriC* and is represented as a **DNA string**, or a string of nucleotides from the four-letter alphabet {A, C, G, T}.

Finding Origin of Replication Problem:

> **Input**: A DNA string *Genome*.
> **Output**: The location of *oriC* in *Genome*.

STOP and Think: Does this biological problem represent a clearly stated computational problem?

Although the Finding Origin of Replication Problem asks a legitimate biological question, it does not present a well-defined computational problem. Indeed, biologists would immediately plan an experiment to locate *oriC*: for example, they might delete various short segments from the genome in an effort to find a segment whose deletion stops replication. Computer scientists, on the other hand, would shake their heads and demand more information before they can even start thinking about the problem.

Why should biologists care what computer scientists think? Computational methods are now the only realistic way to answer many questions in modern biology. First, these methods are much faster than experimental approaches; second, the results of many experiments cannot be interpreted without computational analysis. In particular, existing experimental approaches to *oriC* prediction are rather time consuming. As a result, *oriC* has only been experimentally located in a handful of species. Thus, we would like to design a computational approach to find *oriC* so that biologists are free to spend their time and money on other tasks.

Hidden Messages in the Replication Origin

DnaA boxes

In the rest of this chapter, we will focus on the relatively easy case of finding *oriC* in bacterial genomes, most of which consist of a single circular chromosome. Research has shown that the region of the bacterial genome encoding *oriC* is typically a few hundred nucleotides long. Our plan is to begin with a bacterium in which *oriC* is known, and then determine what makes this genomic region special in order to design a computational approach for finding *oriC* in other bacteria. Our example is *Vibrio cholerae*, the bacterium that causes cholera; here is the nucleotide sequence appearing in its *oriC*:

```
atcaatgatcaacgtaagcttctaagcatgatcaaggtgctcacacagtttatccacaac
ctgagtggatgacatcaagataggtcgttgtatctccttcctctcgtactctcatgacca
cggaaagatgatcaagagaggatgatttcttggccatatcgcaatgaatacttgtgactt
gtgcttccaattgacatcttcagcgccatattgcgctggccaaggtgacggagcgggatt
acgaaagcatgatcatggctgttgttctgtttatcttgttttgactgagacttgttagga
tagacggtttttcatcactgactagccaaagccttactctgcctgacatcgaccgtaaat
tgataatgaatttacatgcttccgcgacgatttacctcttgatcatcgatccgattgaag
atcttcaattgttaattctcttgcctcgactcatagccatgatgagctcttgatcatgtt
tccttaaccctctattttttacggaagaatgatcaagctgctgctcttgatcatcgtttc
```

How does the bacterial cell know to begin replication exactly in this short region within the much larger *Vibrio cholerae* chromosome, which consists of 1,108,250 nucleotides? There must be some "hidden message" in the *oriC* region ordering the cell to begin replication here. Indeed, we know that the initiation of replication is mediated by **DnaA**, a protein that binds to a short segment within the *oriC* known as a **DnaA box**. You can think of the *DnaA* box as a message within the DNA sequence telling the

DnaA protein: "bind here!" The question is how to find this hidden message without knowing what it looks like in advance — can you find it? In other words, can you find something that stands out in *oriC*? This discussion motivates the following problem.

Hidden Message Problem:
Find a "hidden message" in the replication origin.

    Input: A string *Text* (representing the replication origin of a genome).
    Output: A hidden message in *Text*.

STOP and Think: Does this problem represent a clearly stated computational problem?

Hidden messages in "The Gold-Bug"

Although the Hidden Message Problem poses a legitimate intuitive question, it again makes absolutely no sense to a computer scientist because the notion of a "hidden message" is not precisely defined. The *oriC* region of *Vibrio cholerae* is currently just as puzzling as the parchment discovered by William Legrand in Edgar Allan Poe's story "The Gold-Bug". Written on the parchment was the following:

```
53++!305))6*;4826)4+.)4+);806*;48!8'60))85;1+(;:+*8
!83(88)5*!;46(;88*96*?;8)*+(;485);5*!2:*+(;4956*2(5
*-4)8'8*;4069285));)6!8)4++;1(+9;48081;8:8+1;48!85:4
)485!528806*81(+9;48;(88;4(+?34;48)4+;161;:188;+?;
```

Upon seeing the parchment, the narrator remarks, "Were all the jewels of Golconda awaiting me upon my solution of this enigma, I am quite sure that I should be unable to earn them". Legrand retorts, "It may well be doubted whether human ingenuity can construct an enigma of the kind which human ingenuity may not, by proper application, resolve". He reasons that the three consecutive symbols ";48" appear with surprising frequency on the parchment:

```
53++!305))6*;4826)4+.)4+);806*;48!8'60))85;1+(;:+*8
!83(88)5*!;46(;88*96*?;8)*+(;485);5*!2:*+(;4956*2(5
*-4)8'8*;4069285));)6!8)4++;1(+9;48081;8:8+1;48!85:4
)485!528806*81(+9;48;(88;4(+?34;48)4+;161;:188;+?;
```

Legrand had already deduced that the pirates spoke English; he therefore assumed that the high frequency of ";48" implied that it encodes the most frequent English word, "THE". Substituting each symbol, Legrand had a slightly easier text to decipher, which would eventually lead him to the buried treasure. Can you decode this message too?

```
53++!305))6*THE26)H+.)H+)TE06*THE!E'60))E5T1+(T:+*E
!E3(EE)5*!TH6(TEE*96*?TE)*+(THE5)T5*!2:*+(TH956*2(5
*-H)E'E*TH0692E5)T)6!E)H++T1(+9THE0E1TE:E+1THE!E5TH
)HE5!52EE06*E1(+9THET(EETH(+?3HTHE)H+T161T:1EET+?T
```

Counting words

Operating under the assumption that DNA is a language of its own, let's borrow Legrand's method and see if we can find any surprisingly frequent "words" within the *oriC* of *Vibrio cholerae*. We have added reason to look for frequent words in the *oriC* because for various biological processes, certain nucleotide strings often appear surprisingly often in small regions of the genome. For example, **ACTAT** is a surprisingly frequent substring of

ACA**ACTAT**GCAT**ACTAT**CGGGA**ACTAT**CCT.

We use the term **k-mer** to refer to a string of length k and define COUNT(*Text, Pattern*) as the number of times that a k-mer *Pattern* appears as a substring of *Text*. Following the above example,

COUNT(ACA**ACTAT**GCAT**ACTAT**CGGGA**ACTAT**CCT, **ACTAT**) = 3.

Note that COUNT(CG**ATA**TA**TA**TCC**ATA**G, **ATA**) is equal to 3 (not 2) since we should account for overlapping occurrences of *Pattern* in *Text*.

To compute COUNT(*Text, Pattern*), our plan is to "slide a window" down *Text*, checking whether each k-mer substring of *Text* matches *Pattern*. We will therefore refer to the k-mer starting at position i of *Text* as *Text*(i, k). Throughout this book, we will often use **0-based indexing**, meaning that we count starting at 0 instead of 1. In this case, *Text* begins at position 0 and ends at position $|Text| - 1$ ($|Text|$ denotes the number of symbols in *Text*). For example, if *Text* = GACCATACTG, then *Text*$(4, 3)$ = ATA. Note that the last k-mer of *Text* begins at position $|Text| - k$, e.g., the last 3-mer of GACCATACTG starts at position $10 - 3 = 7$. This discussion results in the following pseudocode for computing COUNT(*Text, Pattern*).

```
PATTERNCOUNT(Text, Pattern)
    count ← 0
    for i ← 0 to |Text| − |Pattern|
        if Text(i, |Pattern|) = Pattern
            count ← count + 1
    return count
```

The Frequent Words Problem

We say that *Pattern* is a **most frequent k-mer** in *Text* if it maximizes COUNT(*Text, Pattern*) among all *k*-mers. You can see that **ACTAT** is a most frequent 5-mer for *Text* = ACA**ACTAT**GCAT**ACTAT**CGGGA**ACTAT**CCT, and **ATA** is a most frequent 3-mer for *Text* = CG**ATATAT**CC**ATA**G.

STOP and Think: Can a string have multiple most frequent *k*-mers?

We now have a rigorously defined computational problem.

Frequent Words Problem:
Find the most frequent k-mers in a string.

> **Input**: A string *Text* and an integer *k*.
> **Output**: All most frequent *k*-mers in *Text*.

A straightforward algorithm for finding the most frequent *k*-mers in a string *Text* checks all *k*-mers appearing in this string (there are |*Text*| − *k* + 1 such *k*-mers) and then computes how many times each *k*-mer appears in *Text*. To implement this algorithm, called **FREQUENTWORDS**, we will need to generate an array COUNT, where COUNT(*i*) stores COUNT(*Text, Pattern*) for *Pattern* = *Text*(*i, k*) (see Figure 1.2).

Text	A	C	T	G	A	C	T	C	C	C	A	C	C	C	C
COUNT	2	1	1	1	2	1	1	3	1	1	1	3	3		

FIGURE 1.2 The array COUNT for *Text* = ACTGACTCCCACCCC and *k* = 3. For example, COUNT(0) = COUNT(4) = 2 because ACT (shown in boldface) appears twice in *Text* at positions 0 and 4.

FREQUENTWORDS(*Text*, *k*)
    FrequentPatterns ← an empty set
    for *i* ← 0 to |*Text*| − *k*
        Pattern ← the *k*-mer *Text*(*i*, *k*)
        COUNT(*i*) ← **PATTERNCOUNT**(*Text*, *Pattern*)
    maxCount ← maximum value in array COUNT
    for *i* ← 0 to |*Text*| − *k*
        if COUNT(*i*) = *maxCount*
            add *Text*(*i*, *k*) to *FrequentPatterns*
    remove duplicates from *FrequentPatterns*
    return *FrequentPatterns*

STOP and Think: How fast is **FREQUENTWORDS**?

Although **FREQUENTWORDS** finds most frequent *k*-mers, it is not very efficient. Each call to **PATTERNCOUNT**(*Text*, *Pattern*) checks whether the *k*-mer *Pattern* appears in position 0 of *Text*, position 1 of *Text*, and so on. Since each *k*-mer requires |*Text*| − *k* + 1 such checks, each one requiring as many as *k* comparisons, the overall number of steps of **PATTERNCOUNT**(*Text*, *Pattern*) is (|*Text*| − *k* + 1) · *k*. Furthermore, **FREQUENTWORDS** must call **PATTERNCOUNT** |*Text*| − *k* + 1 times (once for each *k*-mer of *Text*), so that its overall number of steps is (|*Text*| − *k* + 1) · (|*Text*| − *k* + 1) · *k*. To simplify the matter, computer scientists often say that the runtime of **FREQUENTWORDS** has an upper bound of |*Text*|² · *k* steps and refer to the **complexity** of this algorithm as $\mathcal{O}(|Text|^2 \cdot k)$ (see **DETOUR: Big-O Notation**).

PAGE 52

CHARGING STATION (The Frequency Array): If |*Text*| and *k* are small, as is the case when looking for *DnaA* boxes in the typical bacterial *oriC*, then an algorithm with running time of $\mathcal{O}(|Text|^2 \cdot k)$ is perfectly acceptable. But once we find some new biological application requiring us to solve the Frequent Words Problem for a very long *Text*, we will quickly run into trouble. Check out this Charging Station to learn about solving the Frequent Words Problem using a frequency array, a data structure that will also help us solve new coding challenges later in the chapter.

PAGE 39

Frequent words in Vibrio cholerae

Figure 1.3 reveals the most frequent *k*-mers in the *oriC* region from *Vibrio cholerae*.

k	3	4	5	6	7	8	9
count	25	12	8	8	5	4	3
***k*-mers**	tga	atga tgatc	gatca	tgatca	atgatca	atgatcaa	atgatcaag cttgatcat tcttgatca ctcttgatc

FIGURE 1.3 The most frequent *k*-mers in the *oriC* region of *Vibrio cholerae* for *k* from 3 to 9, along with the number of times that each *k*-mer occurs.

STOP and Think: Do any of the counts in Figure 1.3 seem surprisingly large?

For example, the 9-mer **ATGATCAAG** appears three times in the *oriC* region of *Vibrio cholerae* — is it surprising?

```
atcaatgatcaacgtaagcttctaagcATGATCAAGgtgctcacacagtttatccacaac
ctgagtggatgacatcaagataggtcgttgtatctccttcctctcgtactctcatgacca
cggaaagATGATCAAGagaggatgatttcttggccatatcgcaatgaatacttgtgactt
gtgcttccaattgacatcttcagcgccatattgcgctggccaaggtgacggagcgggatt
acgaaagcatgatcatggctgttgttctgtttatcttgttttgactgagacttgttagga
tagacggtttttcatcactgactagccaaagccttactctgcctgacatcgaccgtaaat
tgataatgaatttacatgcttccgcgacgatttacctcttgatcatcgatccgattgaag
atcttcaattgttaattctcttgcctcgactcatagccatgatgagctcttgatcatgtt
tccttaaccctctattttttacggaagaATGATCAAGctgctgctcttgatcatcgtttc
```

We highlight a most frequent 9-mer instead of using some other value of *k* because experiments have revealed that bacterial *DnaA* boxes are usually nine nucleotides long. The probability that there exists a 9-mer appearing three or more times in a randomly **PAGE 52** generated DNA string of length 500 is approximately 1/1300 (see **DETOUR: Probabilities of Patterns in a String**). In fact, there are four different 9-mers repeated three or more times in this region: **ATGATCAAG**, CTTGATCAT, TCTTGATCA, and CTCTTGATC.

The low likelihood of witnessing even one repeated 9-mer in the *oriC* region of *Vibrio cholerae* leads us to the working hypothesis that one of these four 9-mers may represent a potential *DnaA* box that, when appearing multiple times in a short region, jump-starts replication. But which one?

STOP and Think: Is any one of the four most frequent 9-mers in the *oriC* of *Vibrio cholerae* "more surprising" than the others?

Some Hidden Messages are More Surprising than Others

Recall that nucleotides **A** and **T** are complements of each other, as are **C** and **G**. Having one strand of DNA and a supply of "free floating" nucleotides as shown in Figure 1.1, one can imagine the synthesis of a **complementary strand** on a **template strand**. This model of replication was confirmed by Meselson and Stahl in 1958 (see **DETOUR: The Most Beautiful Experiment in Biology**). Figure 1.4 shows a template strand **AGTCGCATAGT** and its complementary strand **ACTATGCGACT**. **PAGE 57**

At this point, you may think that we have made a mistake, since the complementary strand in Figure 1.4 reads out **TCAGCGTATCA** from left to right rather than **ACTATGCGACT**. We have not: each DNA strand has a direction, and the complementary strand runs in the opposite direction to the template strand, as shown by the arrows in Figure 1.4. Each strand is read in the 5′ → 3′ direction (see **DETOUR: Directionality of DNA Strands** to learn why biologists refer to the beginning and end of a strand of DNA using the terms 5′ and 3′). **PAGE 59**

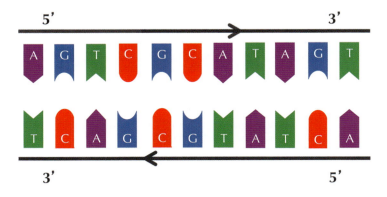

FIGURE 1.4 Complementary strands run in opposite directions.

Given a nucleotide p, we denote its complementary nucleotide as $\overline{p}$. The **reverse complement** of a string $Pattern = p_1 \cdots p_n$ is the string $\overline{Pattern} = \overline{p_n} \cdots \overline{p_1}$ formed by taking the complement of each nucleotide in *Pattern*, then reversing the resulting string. We will need the solution to the following problem throughout this chapter.

Reverse Complement Problem:

Find the reverse complement of a DNA string.

> **Input**: A DNA string *Pattern*.
> **Output**: $\overline{Pattern}$, the reverse complement of *Pattern*.

STOP and Think: Look again at the four most frequent 9-mers in the *oriC* region of *Vibrio cholerae* from Figure 1.3. Now do you notice anything surprising?

Interestingly, among the four most frequent 9-mers in the *oriC* region of *Vibrio cholerae*, **ATGATCAAG** and **CTTGATCAT** are reverse complements of each other, resulting in the following six occurrences of these strings.

```
atcaatgatcaacgtaagcttctaagcATGATCAAGgtgctcacacagtttatccacaac
ctgagtggatgacatcaagataggtcgttgtatctccttcctctcgtactctcatgacca
cggaaagATGATCAAGagaggatgatttcttggccatatcgcaatgaatacttgtgactt
gtgcttccaattgacatcttcagcgccatattgcgctggccaaggtgacggagcgggatt
acgaaagcatgatcatggctgttgttctgtttatcttgttttgactgagacttgttagga
tagacggtttttcatcactgactagccaaagccttactctgcctgacatcgaccgtaaat
tgataatgaatttacatgcttccgcgacgatttacctCTTGATCATcgatccgattgaag
atcttcaattgttaattctcttgcctcgactcatagccatgatgagctCTTGATCATgtt
tccttaaccctctattttttacggaagaATGATCAAGctgctgctCTTGATCATcgtttc
```

Finding a 9-mer that appears six times (either as itself or as its reverse complement) in a DNA string of length 500 is far more surprising than finding a 9-mer that appears three times (as itself). This observation leads us to the working hypothesis that **ATGATCAAG** and its reverse complement **CTTGATCAT** indeed represent *DnaA* boxes in *Vibrio cholerae*. This computational conclusion makes sense biologically because the *DnaA* protein that binds to *DnaA* boxes and initiates replication does not care which of the two strands it binds to. Thus, for our purposes, both **ATGATCAAG** and **CTTGATCAT** represent *DnaA* boxes.

However, before concluding that we have found the *DnaA* box of *Vibrio cholerae*, the careful bioinformatician should check if there are other short regions in the *Vibrio cholerae* genome exhibiting multiple occurrences of **ATGATCAAG** (or **CTTGATCAT**). After all, maybe these strings occur as repeats throughout the entire *Vibrio cholerae* genome, rather than just in the *oriC* region. To this end, we need to solve the following problem.

Pattern Matching Problem:

Find all occurrences of a pattern in a string.

> **Input**: Strings *Pattern* and *Genome*.
> **Output**: All starting positions in *Genome* where *Pattern* appears as a substring.

After solving the Pattern Matching Problem, we discover that **ATGATCAAG** appears 17 times in the following positions of the *Vibrio cholerae* genome:

116556, 149355, **151913**, **152013**, **152394**, 186189, 194276, 200076, 224527, 307692, 479770, 610980, 653338, 679985, 768828, 878903, 985368

With the exception of the three occurrences of **ATGATCAAG** in *oriC* at starting positions **151913**, **152013**, and **152394**, no other instances of **ATGATCAAG** form **clumps**, i.e., appear close to each other in a small region of the genome. You may check that the same conclusion is reached when searching for **CTTGATCAT**. We now have strong statistical evidence that **ATGATCAAG**/**CTTGATCAT** may represent the hidden message to *DnaA* to start replication.

> **STOP and Think:** Can we conclude that **ATGATCAAG**/**CTTGATCAT** also represents a *DnaA* box in other bacterial genomes?

An Explosion of Hidden Messages

Looking for hidden messages in multiple genomes

We should not jump to the conclusion that **ATGATCAAG**/**CTTGATCAT** is a hidden message for all bacterial genomes without first checking whether it even appears in known *oriC* regions from other bacteria. After all, maybe the clumping effect of **ATGATCAAG**/**CTTGATCAT** in the *oriC* region of *Vibrio cholerae* is simply a statistical fluke that has nothing to do with replication. Or maybe different bacteria have different *DnaA* boxes ...

Let's check the proposed *oriC* region of *Thermotoga petrophila*, a bacterium that thrives in extremely hot environments; its name derives from its discovery in the water beneath oil reservoirs, where temperatures can exceed 80° Celsius.

```
aactctatacctccttttttgtcgaatttgtgtgatttatagagaaaatcttattaactga
aactaaaatggtaggtttggtggtaggttttgtgtacattttgtagtatctgatttttaa
ttacataccgtatattgtattaaattgacgaacaattgcatggaattgaatatatgcaaa
acaaacctaccaccaaactctgtattgaccattttaggacaacttcagggtggtaggttt
ctgaagctctcatcaatagactattttagtctttacaaacaatattaccgttcagattca
agattctacaacgctgttttaatgggcgttgcagaaaacttaccacctaaaatccagtat
ccaagccgatttcagagaaacctaccacttacctaccacttacctaccacccgggtggta
agttgcagacattattaaaaacctcatcagaagcttgttcaaaaatttcaatactcgaaa
cctaccacctgcgtcccctattatttactactactaataatagcagtataattgatctga
```

This region does not contain a single occurrence of **ATGATCAAG** or **CTTGATCAT**! Thus, different bacteria may use different *DnaA* boxes as "hidden messages" to the *DnaA* protein.

Application of the Frequent Words Problem to the *oriC* region above reveals that the following six 9-mers appear in this region three or more times:

AACCTACCA	AAACCTACC	ACCTACCAC
CCTACCACC	GGTAGGTTT	TGGTAGGTT

Something peculiar must be happening because it is extremely unlikely that six different 9-mers will occur so frequently within a short region in a random string. We will cheat a little and consult with Ori-Finder, a software tool for finding replication origins in DNA sequences. This software chooses **CCTACCACC** (along with its reverse complement **GGTGGTAGG**) as a working hypothesis for the *DnaA* box in *Thermotoga petrophila*. Together, these two complementary 9-mers appear five times in the replication origin:

```
aactctatacctccttttttgtcgaatttgtgtgatttatagagaaaatcttattaactga
aactaaaatggtaggtttGGTGGTAGGttttgtgtacattttgtagtatctgatttttaa
ttacataccgtatattgtattaaattgacgaacaattgcatggaattgaatatatgcaaa
acaaaCCTACCACCaaactctgtattgaccattttaggacaacttcagGGTGGTAGGttt
ctgaagctctcatcaatagactattttagtctttacaaacaatattaccgttcagattca
agattctacaacgctgttttaatgggcgttgcagaaaacttaccacctaaaatccagtat
ccaagccgatttcagagaaacctaccacttacctaccactaCCTACCACCcgggtggta
agttgcagacattattaaaaacctcatcagaagcttgttcaaaaatttcaatactcgaaa
CCTACCACCtgcgtcccctattatttactactactaataatagcagtataattgatctga
```

The Clump Finding Problem

Now imagine that you are trying to find *oriC* in a newly sequenced bacterial genome. Searching for "clumps" of **ATGATCAAG**/**CTTGATCAT** or **CCTACCACC**/**GGTGGTAGG** is unlikely to help, since this new genome may use a completely different hidden message! Before we lose all hope, let's change our computational focus: instead of finding clumps of a specific *k*-mer, let's try to find *every k*-mer that forms a clump in the genome. Hopefully, the locations of these clumps will shed light on the location of *oriC*.

Our plan is to slide a window of fixed length L along the genome, looking for a region where a k-mer appears several times in short succession. The parameter value $L = 500$ reflects the typical length of *oriC* in bacterial genomes.

We defined a k-mer as a "clump" if it appears many times within a short interval of the genome. More formally, given integers L and t, a k-mer *Pattern* forms an **(L, t)-clump** inside a (longer) string *Genome* if there is an interval of *Genome* of length L in which this k-mer appears at least t times. (This definition assumes that the k-mer *completely* fits within the interval.) For example, **TGCA** forms a $(25, 3)$-clump in the following *Genome*:

gatcagcataagggtccC**TGCA**A**TGCA**TGACAAGCC**TGCA**GTgttttac

From our previous examples of *oriC* regions, **ATGATCAAG** forms a $(500, 3)$-clump in the *Vibrio cholerae* genome, and **CCTACCACC** forms a $(500, 3)$-clump in the *Thermotoga petrophila* genome. We are now ready to formulate the following problem.

Clump Finding Problem:
Find patterns forming clumps in a string.

> **Input**: A string *Genome*, and integers k, L, and t.
> **Output**: All distinct k-mers forming (L, t)-clumps in *Genome*.

CHARGING STATION (Solving the Clump Finding Problem): You can solve the Clump Finding Problem by simply applying your algorithm for the Frequent Words Problem to each window of length L in *Genome*. However, if your algorithm for the Frequent Words Problem is not very efficient, then such an approach may be impractical. For example, recall that **FREQUENTWORDS** has $\mathcal{O}(L^2 \cdot k)$ running time. Applying this algorithm to each window of length L in *Genome* will result in an algorithm with $\mathcal{O}(L^2 \cdot k \cdot |Genome|)$ running time. Moreover, even if we use a faster algorithm for the Frequent Words Problem (like the one described when we introduce a frequency array on page 39), the running time remains high when we try to analyze a bacterial — let alone human — genome. Check out this Charging Station to learn about a more efficient approach for solving the Clump Finding Problem.

PAGE 44

Let's look for clumps in the *Escherichia coli* (*E. coli*) genome, the workhorse of bacterial genomics. We find hundreds of different 9-mers forming $(500, 3)$-clumps in the *E. coli* genome, and it is absolutely unclear which of these 9-mers might represent a *DnaA* box in the bacterium's *oriC* region.

STOP and Think: Should we give up? If not, what would you do now?

At this point, an unseasoned researcher might give up, since it appears that we do not have enough information to locate *oriC* in *E. coli*. But a fearless veteran bioinformatician would try to learn more about the details of replication in the hope that they provide new algorithmic insights into finding *oriC*.

The Simplest Way to Replicate DNA

We are now ready to discuss the replication process in more detail. As illustrated in Figure 1.5 (top), the two complementary DNA strands running in opposite directions around a circular chromosome unravel, starting at *oriC*. As the strands unwind, they create two **replication forks**, which expand in both directions around the chromosome until the strands completely separate at the **replication terminus** (denoted *terC*). The replication terminus is located roughly opposite to *oriC* in the chromosome.

An important thing to know about replication is that a DNA polymerase does not wait for the two parent strands to completely separate before initiating replication; instead, it starts copying *while* the strands are unraveling. Thus, just four DNA polymerases, each responsible for one half-strand, can all start at *oriC* and replicate the entire chromosome. To start replication, a DNA polymerase needs a **primer**, a short complementary segment (shown in red in Figure 1.5) that binds to the parent strand and jump starts the DNA polymerase. After the strands start separating, each of the four DNA polymerases starts replication by adding nucleotides, beginning with the primer and proceeding around the chromosome from *oriC* to *terC* in either the clockwise or counterclockwise direction. When all four DNA polymerases have reached *terC*, the chromosome's DNA will have been completely replicated, resulting in two pairs of complementary strands (Figure 1.5 (bottom)), and the cell is ready to divide.

Yet while you were reading the description above, biology professors were writing a petition to have us fired and sent back to Biology 101. And they would be right, because our exposition suffers from a major flaw; we only described the replication process in this way so that you can better appreciate what we are about to reveal.

The problem with our current description is that it assumes that DNA polymerases can copy DNA in *either* direction along a strand of DNA (i.e., both $5' \to 3'$ and $3' \to 5'$).

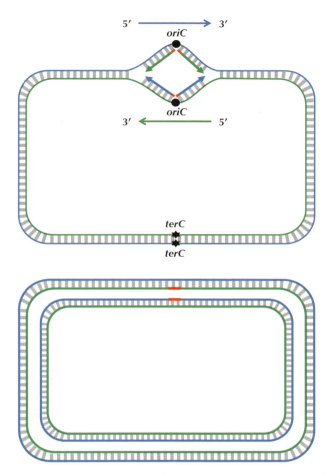

FIGURE 1.5 (Top) Four imaginary DNA polymerases at work replicating a chromosome as the replication forks extend from *oriC* to *terC*. The blue strand is directed clockwise, and the green strand is directed counterclockwise. (Bottom) Replication is complete.

However, nature has not yet equipped DNA polymerases with this ability, as they are **unidirectional**, meaning that they can only traverse a template strand of DNA in the $3' \to 5'$ direction. Notice that this is opposite from the $5' \to 3'$ direction of DNA.

STOP and Think: If you were a unidirectional DNA polymerase, how would you replicate DNA? How many DNA polymerases would be needed to complete this task?

The unidirectionality of DNA polymerase requires a major revision to our naive model of replication. Imagine that you decided to walk along DNA from *oriC* to *terC*. There are four different half-strands of parent DNA connecting *oriC* to *terC*, as highlighted in Figure 1.6. Two of these half-strands are traversed from *oriC* to *terC* in the $5' \rightarrow 3'$ direction and are thus called **forward half-strands** (represented by thin blue and green lines in Figure 1.6). The other two half-strands are traversed from *oriC* to *terC* in the $3' \rightarrow 5'$ direction and are thus called **reverse half-strands** (represented by thick blue and green lines in Figure 1.6).

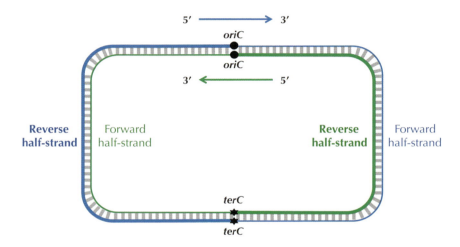

FIGURE 1.6 Complementary DNA strands with forward and reverse half-strands shown as thin and thick lines, respectively.

Asymmetry of Replication

While biologists will feel at home with the following description of DNA replication, computer scientists may find it overloaded with new terms. If it seems too biologically complex, then feel free to skim this section, as long as you believe us that the replication process is **asymmetric**, i.e., that forward and reverse half-strands have very different fates with respect to replication.

Since a DNA polymerase can only move in the reverse ($3' \to 5'$) direction, it can copy nucleotides non-stop from *oriC* to *terC* along reverse half-strands. However, replication on forward half-strands is very different because a DNA polymerase cannot move in the forward ($5' \to 3'$) direction; on these half-strands, a DNA polymerase must replicate *backwards* toward *oriC*. Take a look at Figure 1.7 to see why this must be the case.

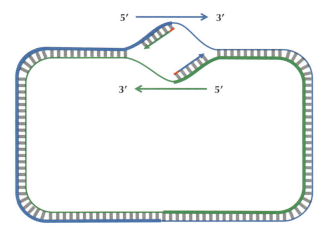

FIGURE 1.7 Replication begins at *oriC* (primers shown in red) with the synthesis of fragments on the reverse half-strands (shown by thick lines). A DNA polymerase must wait until the replication fork has opened some (small) distance before it starts copying the forward half-strands (shown by thin lines) back toward *oriC*.

On a forward half-strand, in order to replicate DNA, a DNA polymerase must wait for the replication fork to open a little (approximately 2,000 nucleotides) until a new primer is formed at the *end* of the replication fork; afterwards, the DNA polymerase starts replicating a small chunk of DNA starting from this primer and moving *backward* in the direction of *oriC*. When the two DNA polymerases on forward half-strands reach *oriC*, we have the situation shown in Figure 1.8. Note the contrast between this figure and Figure 1.5.

After this point, replication on each reverse half-strand progresses continuously; however, a DNA polymerase on a forward half-strand has no choice but to wait again until the replication fork has opened another 2,000 nucleotides or so. It then requires a new primer to begin synthesizing another fragment back toward *oriC*. On the whole, replication on a forward half-strand requires occasional stopping and restarting, which

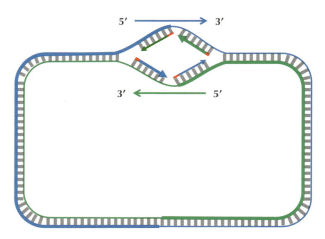

FIGURE 1.8 The daughter fragments are now synthesized (with some delay) on the forward half-strands (shown by thin lines).

results in the synthesis of short **Okazaki fragments** that are complementary to intervals on the forward half-strand. You can see these fragments forming in Figure 1.9 (top).

When the replication fork reaches *terC*, the replication process is almost complete, but gaps still remain between the disconnected Okazaki fragments (Figure 1.9 (middle)).

Finally, consecutive Okazaki fragments are sewn together by an enzyme called **DNA ligase**, resulting in two intact daughter chromosomes, each consisting of one parent strand and one newly synthesized daughter strand, as shown in Figure 1.9 (bottom). In reality, DNA ligase does not wait until after all the Okazaki fragments have been replicated to start sewing them together.

Biologists call a reverse half-strand a **leading half-strand** since a single DNA polymerase traverses this half-strand non-stop, and they call a forward half-strand a **lagging half-strand** since it is used as a template by many DNA polymerases stopping and starting replication. If you are confused about the differences between the leading and lagging half-strands, you are not alone — we and legions of biology students are also confused. The confusion is exacerbated by the fact that different textbooks use different terminology depending on whether the authors intend to refer to a leading *template* half-strand or a leading half-strand *that is being synthesized* from a (lagging) template half-strand. You hopefully see why we have chosen the terms "reverse" and "forward" half-strands in an attempt to mitigate some of this confusion.

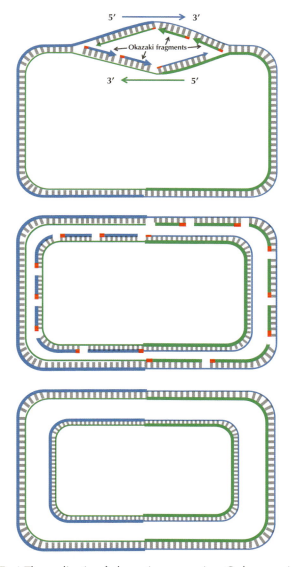

FIGURE 1.9 (Top) The replication fork continues growing. Only one primer is needed for each of the reverse half-strands (shown by thick lines), while the forward half-strands (shown by thin lines) require multiple primers in order to synthesize Okazaki fragments. Two of these primers are shown in red on each forward half-strand. (Middle) Replication is nearly complete, as all daughter DNA is synthesized. However, half of each daughter chromosome contains disconnected Okazaki fragments. (Bottom) Okazaki fragments have been sewn together, resulting in two intact daughter chromosomes.

Peculiar Statistics of the Forward and Reverse Half-Strands

Deamination

In the last section, we saw that as the replication fork expands, DNA polymerase synthesizes DNA quickly on the reverse half-strand but suffers delays on the forward half-strand. We will explore the asymmetry of DNA replication to design a new algorithm for finding *oriC*.

How in the world can the asymmetry of replication possibly help us locate *oriC*? Notice that since the replication of a reverse half-strand proceeds quickly, it lives double-stranded for most of its life. Conversely, a forward half-strand spends a much larger amount of its life single-stranded, waiting to be used as a template for replication. This discrepancy between the forward and reverse half-strands is important because single-stranded DNA has a much higher mutation rate than double-stranded DNA. In particular, if one of the four nucleotides in single-stranded DNA has a greater tendency than other nucleotides to mutate in single-stranded DNA, then we should observe a shortage of this nucleotide on the forward half-strand.

Following up on this thought, let's compare the nucleotide counts of the reverse and forward half-strands. If these counts differ substantially, then we will design an algorithm that attempts to track down these differences in genomes for which *oriC* is unknown. The nucleotide counts for *Thermotoga petrophila* are shown in Figure 1.10.

	#C	#G	#A	#T
Entire strand	427419	413241	491488	491363
Reverse half-strand	219518	201634	243963	246641
Forward half-strand	207901	211607	247525	244722
Difference	+11617	-9973	-3562	+1919

FIGURE 1.10 Counting nucleotides in the *Thermotoga petrophila* genome on the forward and reverse half-strands.

STOP and Think: Do you notice anything interesting about the nucleotide counts in Figure 1.10?

Although the frequencies of A and T are practically identical on the two half-strands, C is more frequent on the reverse half-strand than on the forward half-strand, resulting in a difference of 219518 − 207901 = +11617. Its complementary nucleotide G is less frequent on the reverse half-strand than on the forward half-strand, resulting in a difference of $201634 - 211607 = -9973$.

It turns out that we observe these discrepancies because cytosine (C) has a tendency to mutate into thymine (T) through a process called **deamination**. Deamination rates rise 100-fold when DNA is single-stranded, which leads to a decrease in cytosine on the forward half-strand, thus forming mismatched base pairs T–G. These mismatched pairs can further mutate into T–A pairs when the bond is repaired in the next round of replication, which accounts for the observed decrease in guanine (G) on the reverse half-strand (recall that a forward parent half-strand synthesizes a reverse daughter half-strand, and vice-versa).

STOP and Think: If deamination changes cytosine to thymine, why do you think that the forward half-strand still has some cytosine?

The skew diagram

Let's see if we can take advantage of these peculiar statistics caused by deamination to locate *oriC*. As Figure 1.10 illustrates, the difference between the total amount of guanine and the total amount of cytosine is negative on the reverse half-strand $(211607 - 207901 = 3706)$ and positive on the forward half-strand $(201634 - 219518 = -17884)$. Thus, our idea is to traverse the genome, keeping a running total of the difference between the counts of G and C. If this difference starts *increasing*, then we guess that we are on the forward half-strand; on the other hand, if this difference starts *decreasing*, then we guess that we are on the reverse half-strand. See Figure 1.11.

STOP and Think: Imagine that you are reading through the genome (in the $5' \rightarrow 3'$ direction) and notice that the difference between the guanine and cytosine counts just switched its behavior from decreasing to increasing. Where in the genome are you?

Since we don't know the location of *oriC* in a circular genome, let's linearize it (i.e., select an arbitrary position and pretend that the genome begins here), resulting in a linear string *Genome*. We define $\text{SKEW}_i(Genome)$ as the difference between the total number of occurrences of G and the total number of occurrences of C in the first i nucleotides of *Genome*. The **skew diagram** is defined by plotting $\text{SKEW}_i(Genome)$ as i ranges from 0 to $|Genome|$, where $\text{SKEW}_0(Genome)$ is set equal to zero. Figure 1.12 shows a skew diagram for a short DNA string.

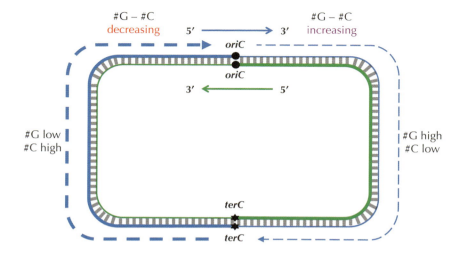

FIGURE 1.11 Because of deamination, each forward half-strand has a shortage of cytosine compared to guanine, and each reverse half-strand has a shortage of guanine compared to cytosine. The dashed blue line illustrates an imaginary walk along the outer strand of the genome counting the difference between the counts of G and C. We assume that the difference between these counts is positive on the forward half-strand and negative on the reverse half-strand.

Note that we can compute $\text{SKEW}_{i+1}(Genome)$ from $\text{SKEW}_i(Genome)$ according to the nucleotide in position i of *Genome*. If this nucleotide is **G**, then $\text{SKEW}_{i+1}(Genome) = \text{SKEW}_i(Genome) + 1$; if this nucleotide is **C**, then $\text{SKEW}_{i+1}(Genome) = \text{SKEW}_i(Genome) - 1$; otherwise, $\text{SKEW}_{i+1}(Genome) = \text{SKEW}_i(Genome)$.

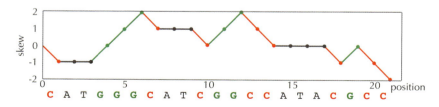

FIGURE 1.12 The skew diagram for *Genome* = CATGGGCATCGGCCATACGCC.

Figure 1.13 depicts the skew diagram for a linearized *E. coli* genome. Notice the very clear pattern! It turns out that the skew diagram for many bacterial genomes has a similar characteristic shape.

STOP and Think: After looking at the skew diagram in Figure 1.13, where do you think that *oriC* is located in *E. coli*?

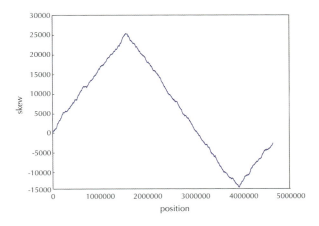

FIGURE 1.13 The skew diagram for *E. coli* achieves a maximum and minimum at positions 1550413 and 3923620, respectively.

Let's follow the $5' \rightarrow 3'$ direction of DNA and walk along the chromosome from *terC* to *oriC* (along a reverse half-strand), then continue on from *oriC* to *terC* (along a forward half-strand). In Figure 1.11, we saw that the skew is decreasing along the reverse half-strand and increasing along the forward half-strand. Thus, the skew should achieve a minimum at the position where the reverse half-strand ends and the forward half-strand begins, which is exactly the location of *oriC*! We have just developed an algorithm for locating *oriC*: it should be found where the skew attains a minimum.

Minimum Skew Problem:
Find a position in a genome where the skew diagram attains a minimum.

   Input: A DNA string *Genome*.
   Output: All integer(s) *i* minimizing $\text{SKEW}_i(Genome)$ among all values of *i* (from 0 to $|Genome|$).

STOP

STOP and Think: Note that the skew diagram changes depending on where we start our walk along the circular chromosome. Do you think that the minimum of the skew diagram points to the same position *in the genome* regardless of where we begin walking to generate the skew diagram?

Some Hidden Messages are More Elusive than Others

Solving the Minimum Skew Problem now provides us with an approximate location of *oriC* at position 3923620 in *E. coli*. In an attempt to confirm this hypothesis, let's look for a hidden message representing a potential *DnaA* box near this location. Solving the Frequent Words Problem in a window of length 500 starting at position 3923620 (shown below) reveals no 9-mers (along with their reverse complements) that appear three or more times! Even if we have located *oriC* in *E. coli*, it appears that we still have not found the *DnaA* boxes that jump-start replication in this bacterium ...

```
aatgatgatgacgtcaaaaggatccggataaaacatggtgattgcctcgcataacgcggt
atgaaaatggattgaagcccgggccgtggattctactcaactttgtcggcttgagaaaga
cctgggatcctgggtattaaaaagaagatctatttatttagagatctgttctattgtgat
ctcttattaggatcgcactgccctgtggataacaaggatccggcttttaagatcaacaac
ctggaaaggatcattaactgtgaatgatcggtgatcctggaccgtataagctgggatcag
aatgaggggttatacacaactcaaaaactgaacaacagttgttctttggataactaccgg
ttgatccaagcttcctgacagagttatccacagtagatcgcacgatctgtatacttattt
gagtaaaattaacccacgatcccagccattcttctgccggatcttccggaatgtcgtgatc
aagaatgttgatcttcagtg
```

STOP

STOP and Think: What would you do next?

Before we give up, let's examine the *oriC* of *Vibrio cholerae* one more time to see if it provides us with any insights on how to alter our algorithm to find *DnaA* boxes in *E. coli*. You may have noticed that in addition to the three occurrences of **ATGATCAAG** and three occurrences of its reverse complement **CTTGATCAT**, the *Vibrio cholerae oriC* contains additional occurrences of **ATGATCAAC** and **CATGATCAT**, which differ from **ATGATCAAG** and **CTTGATCAT** in only a single nucleotide:

```
atca**ATGATCAAC**gtaagcttctaagc**ATGATCAAG**gtgctcacacagtttatccacaac
ctgagtggatgacatcaagataggtcgttgtatctccttcctctcgtactctcatgacca
cggaaag**ATGATCAAG**agaggatgatttcttggccatatcgcaatgaatacttgtgactt
gtgcttccaattgacatcttcagcgccatattgcgctggccaaggtgacggagcgggatt
acgaaag**CATGATCAT**ggctgttgttctgtttatcttgttttgactgagacttgttagga
tagacggttttttcatcactgactagccaaagccttactctgcctgacatcgaccgtaaat
tgataatgaatttacatgcttccgcgacgatttacct**CTTGATCAT**cgatccgattgaag
atcttcaattgttaattctcttgcctcgactcatagccatgatgagct**CTTGATCAT**gtt
tccttaaccctctattttttacggaaga**ATGATCAAG**ctgctgct**CTTGATCAT**cgtttc
```

Finding eight *approximate* occurrences of our target 9-mer and its reverse complement in a short region is even more statistically surprising than finding the six *exact* occurrences of **ATGATCAAG** and its reverse complement **CTTGATCAT** that we stumbled upon in the beginning of our investigation. Furthermore, the discovery of these approximate 9-mers makes sense biologically, since *DnaA* can bind not only to "perfect" *DnaA* boxes but to their slight variations as well.

We say that position i in k-mers $p_1 \cdots p_k$ and $q_1 \cdots q_k$ is a **mismatch** if $p_i \neq q_i$. The number of mismatches between strings p and q is called the **Hamming distance** between these strings and is denoted HAMMINGDISTANCE(p, q).

Hamming Distance Problem:
Compute the Hamming distance between two strings.

> **Input**: Two strings of equal length.
> **Output**: The Hamming distance between these strings.

We say that a k-mer *Pattern* appears as a substring of *Text* with at most d mismatches if there is some k-mer substring *Pattern'* of *Text* having d or fewer mismatches with *Pattern*, i.e., HAMMINGDISTANCE(*Pattern*, *Pattern'*) $\leq d$. Our observation that a *DnaA* box may appear with slight variations leads to the following generalization of the Pattern Matching Problem.

Approximate Pattern Matching Problem:
Find all approximate occurrences of a pattern in a string.

> **Input**: Strings *Pattern* and *Text* along with an integer d.
> **Output**: All starting positions where *Pattern* appears as a substring of *Text* with at most d mismatches.

Our goal now is to modify our previous algorithm for the Frequent Words Problem in order to find *DnaA* boxes by identifying frequent *k*-mers, possibly with mismatches. Given strings *Text* and *Pattern* as well as an integer *d*, we define $\text{COUNT}_d(Text, Pattern)$ as the number of occurrences of *Pattern* in *Text* with at most *d* mismatches. For example,

$$\text{COUNT}_1(\textbf{AACAA}\text{GC}\textbf{ATAAACATTAAAGA}\text{G}, \textbf{AAAAA}) = 4$$

because **AAAAA** appears four times in this string with at most one mismatch: **AACAA**, **ATAAA**, **AAACA**, and **AAAGA**. Notice that two of these occurrences overlap.

EXERCISE BREAK: Compute $\text{COUNT}_2(\text{AACAAGCATAAACATTAAAGAG}, \text{AAAAA})$.

Computing $\text{COUNT}_d(Text, Pattern)$ simply requires us to compute the Hamming distance between *Pattern* and every *k*-mer substring of *Text*, as follows.

APPROXIMATEPATTERNCOUNT(*Text, Pattern, d*)
    count ← 0
    for *i* ← 0 to |*Text*| − |*Pattern*|
        Pattern' ← *Text*(*i*, |*Pattern*|)
        if HAMMINGDISTANCE(*Pattern, Pattern'*) ≤ *d*
            count ← *count* + 1
    return *count*

EXERCISE BREAK: Implement **APPROXIMATEPATTERNCOUNT**. What is its running time?

A **most frequent *k*-mer with up to *d* mismatches** in *Text* is simply a string *Pattern* maximizing $\text{COUNT}_d(Text, Pattern)$ among all *k*-mers. Note that *Pattern* does not need to actually appear as a substring of *Text*; for example, as we saw above, **AAAAA** is the most frequent 5-mer with 1 mismatch in **AACAA**GC**ATAAACA**TT**AAAGA**G, even though it does not appear exactly in this string. Keep this in mind while solving the following problem.

Frequent Words with Mismatches Problem:
Find the most frequent k-mers with mismatches in a string.

    Input: A string *Text* as well as integers *k* and *d*.
    Output: All most frequent *k*-mers with up to *d* mismatches in *Text*.

CHARGING STATION (Solving the Frequent Words with Mismatches Problem): One way to solve the above problem is to generate all 4^k k-mers *Pattern*, compute $\text{COUNT}_d(Text, Pattern, d)$ for each k-mer, and then output k-mers with the maximum number of approximate occurrences. This is an inefficient approach in practice, since many of the 4^k k-mers that this method analyzes should not be considered because neither they nor their mutated versions (with up to d mismatches) appear in *Text*. Check out this Charging Station to learn about a better approach that avoids analyzing such hopeless k-mers.

PAGE 47

We now redefine the Frequent Words Problem to account for both mismatches and reverse complements. Recall that $\overline{Pattern}$ refers to the reverse complement of *Pattern*.

Frequent Words with Mismatches and Reverse Complements Problem:

Find the most frequent k-mers (with mismatches and reverse complements) in a string.

Input: A DNA string *Text* as well as integers k and d.
Output: All k-mers *Pattern* that maximize the sum $\text{COUNT}_d(Text, Pattern) + \text{COUNT}_d(Text, \overline{Pattern})$ over all possible k-mers.

A Final Attempt at Finding *DnaA* Boxes in *E. coli*

We now make a final attempt to find *DnaA* boxes in *E. coli* by finding the most frequent 9-mers with mismatches and reverse complements in the region suggested by the minimum skew as *oriC*. Although the minimum of the skew diagram for *E. coli* is found at position 3923620, we should not assume that its *oriC* is found exactly at this position due to random fluctuations in the skew. To remedy this issue, we could choose a larger window size (e.g., $L = 1000$), but expanding the window introduces the risk that we may bring in other clumped 9-mers that do not represent *DnaA* boxes but appear in this window more often than the true *DnaA* box. It makes more sense to try a small window either starting, ending, or centered at the position of minimum skew.

Let's cross our fingers and identify the most frequent 9-mers (with 1 mismatch and reverse complements) within a window of length 500 starting at position 3923620 of the *E. coli* genome. Bingo! The experimentally confirmed *DnaA* box in *E. coli* (**TTATCCACA**) is a most frequent 9-mer with 1 mismatch, along with its reverse complement **TGTGGATAA**:

```
aatgatgatgacgtcaaaaggatccggataaaacatggtgattgcctcgcataacgcggt
atgaaaatggattgaagcccgggccgtggattctactcaactttgtcggcttgagaaaga
cctgggatcctgggtattaaaaagaagatctatttatttagagatctgttctattgtgat
ctcttattaggatcgcactgcccTGTGGATAAcaaggatccggcttttaagatcaacaac
ctggaaaggatcattaactgtgaatgatcggtgatcctggaccgtataagctgggatcag
aatgaggggTTATACACAactcaaaaactgaacaacagttgttcTTTGGATAActaccgg
ttgatccaagcttcctgacagagTTATCCACAgtagatcgcacgatctgtatacttattt
gagtaaattaacccacgatcccagccattcttctgccggatcttccggaatgtcgtgatc
aagaatgttgatcttcagtg
```

You will notice that we highlighted an interior interval of this sequence with darker text. This region is the experimentally verified *oriC* of *E. coli*, which starts 37 nucleotides after position 3923620, where the skew reaches its minimum value.

We were fortunate that the *DnaA* boxes of *E. coli* are captured in the window that we chose. Moreover, while TTATCCACA represents a most frequent 9-mer with 1 mismatch and reverse complements in this 500-nucleotide window, it is not the only one: GGATCCTGG, GATCCCAGC, GTTATCCAC, AGCTGGGAT, and CTGGGATCA also appear four times with 1 mismatch and reverse complements.

STOP and Think: In this chapter, every time we find *oriC*, we seem to find some other surprisingly frequent 9-mers. Why do you think this is?

We do not know what purpose — if any — these other 9-mers serve in the *E. coli* genome, but we do know that there are *many different types* of hidden messages in genomes; these hidden messages have a tendency to cluster within a genome, and most of them have nothing to do with replication. One example is the regulatory DNA motifs responsible for gene expression that we will study in Chapter 2. The important lesson is that existing approaches to *oriC* prediction remain imperfect and sometimes inconclusive. However, even providing biologists with a small collection of 9-mers as candidate *DnaA* boxes is a great aid as long as one of these 9-mers is correct.

Thus, the moral of this chapter is that even though computational predictions can be powerful, bioinformaticians should collaborate with biologists to verify their computational predictions. Or improve these predictions: the next question hints at how *oriC* predictions can be carried out using **comparative genomics**, a bioinformatics approach that uses evolutionary similarities to answer difficult questions about genomes.

STOP and Think: *Salmonella enterica* is a close relative of *E. coli* that causes typhoid fever and foodborne illness. After having learned what *DnaA* boxes look like in *E. coli*, how would you search for *DnaA* boxes in *Salmonella enterica*?

You will have an opportunity to look for *DnaA* boxes in *Salmonella enterica* in the epilogue, which will feature a "Challenge Problem" asking you to apply what you have learned to a real dataset. Some chapters also have an "Open Problems" section outlining unanswered research questions.

Epilogue: Complications in *oriC* Predictions

In this chapter, we have considered three genomes and found three different hypothesized 9-mers encoding *DnaA* boxes: **ATGATCAAG** in *Vibrio cholerae*, **CCTACCACC** in *Thermotoga petrophila*, and **TTATCCACA** in *E. coli*. We must warn you that finding *oriC* is often more complex than in the three examples we considered. Some bacteria have even fewer *DnaA* boxes than *E. coli*, making it difficult to identify them. The *terC* region is often located not directly opposite to *oriC* but may be significantly shifted, resulting in reverse and forward half-strands having substantially different lengths. The position of the skew minimum is often only a rough indicator of *oriC* position, which forces researchers to expand their windows when searching for *DnaA* boxes, bringing in extraneous repeated substrings. Finally, skew diagrams do not always look as nice as that of *E. coli*; for example, the skew diagram for *Thermotoga petrophila* is shown in Figure 1.14.

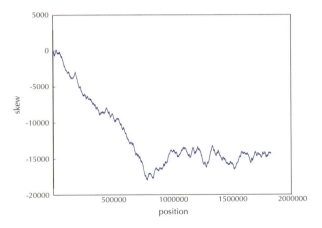

FIGURE 1.14 The skew diagram for *Thermotoga petrophila* achieves a minimum at position 787199 but does not have the same nice shape as the skew diagram for *E. coli*.

STOP and Think: What evolutionary process could possibly explain the shape of the skew diagram for *Thermotoga petrophila*?

Since the skew diagram for *Thermotoga petrophila* is complex and the *oriC* for this genome has not even been experimentally verified, there is a chance that the region predicted by Ori-Finder as the *oriC* region for *Thermotoga petrophila* (or even for *Vibrio cholerae*) is actually incorrect!

You now should have a good sense of how to locate *oriC* and *DnaA* boxes computationally. We will take the training wheels off and ask you to solve a challenge problem.

CHALLENGE PROBLEM: Find *DnaA* boxes in *Salmonella enterica*.

Open Problems

Multiple replication origins in a bacterial genome

Biologists long believed that each bacterial chromosome has only one *oriC*. Wang et al., 2011 genetically modified *E. coli* by inserting a synthetic *oriC* a million nucleotides away from the bacterium's known *oriC*. To their surprise, *E. coli* continued business as usual, starting replication at both locations!

Following the publication of this paper, the search for naturally occurring bacteria with multiple *oriC*s immediately started. In 2012, Xia raised doubts about the "single *oriC*" postulate and gave examples of bacteria with highly unusual skews. In fact, having more than one *oriC* makes sense in the light of evolution: if the genome is long and replication is slow, then multiple replication origins would decrease the amount of time that the bacterium must spend replicating its DNA.

For example, *Wigglesworthia glossinidia*, a symbiotic bacterium living in the intestines of tsetse flies, has the atypical skew diagram shown in Figure 1.15. Since this diagram has at least two pronounced local minima, Xia argued that this bacterium may have two or more *oriC* regions.

We should be careful with Xia's hypothesis that this bacterium has two *oriC*s, as there may be alternative explanations for multiple local minima in the skew. For example, **genome rearrangements** (which we will study in Chapter 6) move genes within a genome and often reposition them from the forward to the reverse half-strand and vice-versa, thus resulting in irregularities in the skew diagram. One example of a genome rearrangement is a **reversal**, which flips around a segment of chromosome and switches it to the opposite strand; Figure 1.16 shows what happens to the skew diagram after a reversal.

Another difficulty is presented by the fact that different species of bacteria may exchange genetic material in **horizontal gene transfer**. If a gene from the forward half-strand of one bacterium is transferred to the reverse half-strand of another (or vice-versa), then we will observe an irregularity in the skew diagram. As a result, the question about the number of *oriC*s of *Wigglesworthia glossinidia* remains unresolved.

However, if you could demonstrate that there exist two sets of identical *DnaA* boxes in the vicinity of two local minima in the skew diagram of *Wigglesworthia glossinidia*, then you would have the first solid evidence in favor of multiple bacterial *oriC*s. Maybe simply applying your solution for the Frequent Words with Mismatches and Reverse Complements Problem will reveal these *DnaA* boxes. Can you find other bacterial genomes where a single *oriC* is in doubt and check whether they indeed have multiple *oriC*s?

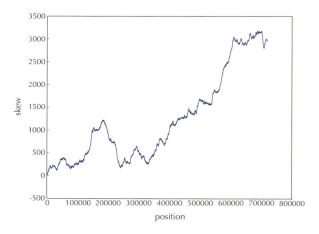

FIGURE 1.15 The skew diagram for *Wigglesworthia glossinidia*.

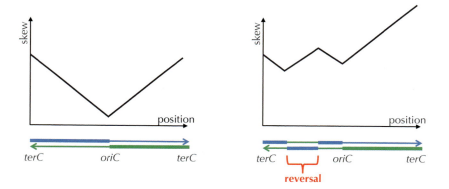

FIGURE 1.16 (Left) An "ideal" V-shaped skew diagram that achieves minimum skew at *oriC*. The skew diagram decreases along the reverse half-strand (shown by a thick line) and increases along the forward half-strand (shown by a thin line). We assume that a circular chromosome was cut at *terC*, resulting in a linear chromosome that starts and ends at *terC*. (Right) A skew diagram after a reversal that switches segments between the reverse and forward strands and alters the skew diagram. As before, the skew diagram still decreases along the segments of the genome shown by thick lines and increases along the segments shown by thin lines.

Finding replication origins in archaea

Archaea are unicellular organisms so distinct from other life forms that biologists have placed them into their own **domain of life** separate from bacteria and eukaryotes. Although archaea are visually similar to bacteria, they have some genomic features that are more closely related to eukaryotes. In particular, the replication machinery of archaea is more similar to eukaryotes than bacteria. Yet archaea use a much greater variety of energy sources than eukaryotes, feeding on ammonia, metals, or even hydrogen gas.

Figure 1.17 shows the skew diagram of *Sulfolobus solfataricus*, a species of archaea growing in acidic volcanic springs in temperatures over 80° C. In its skew diagram, you can see at least three local minima, represented by deep valleys, in addition to many more shallow valleys.

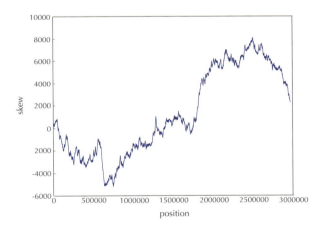

FIGURE 1.17 The skew diagram of *Sulfolobus solfataricus*.

Lundgren et al., 2004 demonstrated experimentally that *Sulfolobus solfataricus* indeed has three *oriC*s. Since then, multiple *oriC*s have been identified in many other archaea. However, no accurate computational approach has been developed to identify multiple *oriC*s in a newly sequenced archaea genome. For example, the methane-producing archaea *Methanococcus jannaschii* is considered the workhorse of archaea genomics, but its *oriC*(s) still remain unidentified! Its skew diagram (shown in Figure 1.18) suggests that it may have multiple *oriC*s: can you find them?

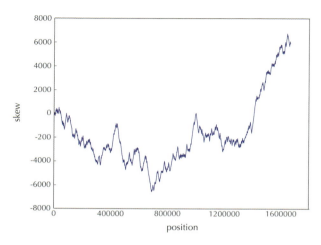

FIGURE 1.18 The skew diagram for *Methanococcus jannaschii*.

Finding replication origins in yeast

If you think that finding replication origins in bacteria is a complex problem, wait until you analyze replication origins in more complex organisms like yeast or humans, which have hundreds of replication origins. Among various yeast species, the yeast *Saccharomyces cerevisiae* has the best characterized replication origins. It has approximately 400 different *oriC*s, many of which may be used during the replication of any single yeast cell.

Having a large number of *oriC*s results in dozens of replication forks hurtling towards each other from different locations in the genome in ways that are not yet completely understood. However, researchers have discovered that the replication origins of *S. cerevisiae* share a (somewhat variable) pattern called the **ARS Consensus Sequence (ACS)**. The ACS is the binding site for the so-called **Origin Recognition Complex**, which initiates the loading of additional proteins required for origin firing. Many ACSs correspond to the following canonical thymine-rich pattern of length 11.

$$\textbf{TTTAT(G/A)TTT(T/A)(G/T)}$$

Here, the notation (X/Y) indicates that either nucleotide X or nucleotide Y may appear in that position.

However, various ACSs may differ from this canonical pattern, with lengths varying from 11 to 17 nucleotides. For example, the 11-nucleotide long pattern shown above is often part of a 17-nucleotide pattern:

$$(T/A)(T/A)(T/A)(T/A)\mathbf{TTTAT(G/A)TTT(T/A)(G/T)}(T/G)(T/C)$$

Recently, some progress has been made in characterizing the ACS in a few other yeast species. In some species like *S. bayanus*, the ACS is almost identical to that of *S. cerevisiae*, while in others such as *K. lactis*, it is very different. More alarmingly, at least for bioinformaticians, in some yeast species such as *S. pombe*, the Origin Recognition Complex binds to loosely defined AT-rich regions, which makes it next to impossible to find replication origins based on sequence analysis alone.

Despite recent efforts, finding *oriCs* in yeast remains an open problem, and no accurate software exists for predicting origins of replication from the sequence of yeast genomes. Can you explore this problem and devise an algorithm to predict replication origins in yeast?

Computing probabilities of patterns in a string

In the main text, we told you that the probability that a random DNA string of length 500 contains a 9-mer appearing three or more times is *approximately* 1/1300. In **DETOUR: Probabilities of Patterns in a String**, we describe a method to estimate this probability, but it is rather inaccurate. This open problem is aimed at finding better approximations or even deriving exact formulas for probabilities of patterns in strings.

PAGE 52

We start by asking a question: what is the probability that a specific k-mer *Pattern* will appear (at least once) as a substring of a random string of length N? This question proved to be not so simple and was first addressed by Solov'ev, 1966 (see also Sedgewick and Flajolet, 2013).

The first surprise is that different k-mers may have different probabilities of appearing in a random string. For example, the probability that *Pattern* = "01" appears in a random binary string of length 4 is 11/16, while the probability that *Pattern* = "11" appears in a random binary string of length 4 is 8/16. This phenomenon is called the **overlapping words paradox** because different occurrences of *Pattern* can overlap each other for some patterns (e.g., "11") but not others (e.g., "01"). See **DETOUR: The Overlapping Words Paradox**.

PAGE 62

We are interested in computing the following probabilities for a random N-letter string in an A-letter alphabet:

- $\Pr(N, A, Pattern, t)$, the probability that a string *Pattern* appears at least t times in a random string;

- $\Pr^*(N, A, Pattern, t)$, the probability that a string *Pattern* and its reverse complement $\overline{Pattern}$ appear at least t total times in a random string.

Note that the above two probabilities are relatively straightforward to compute. Several variants of these questions are open:

- $\text{Pr}_d(N, A, Pattern, t)$, the probability that a string *Pattern* approximately appears at least t times in a random string (with at most d mismatches);

- $\text{Pr}(N, A, k, t)$, the probability that there exists *any* k-mer appearing at least t times in a random string;

- $\text{Pr}_d(N, A, k, t)$, the probability that there exists *any* k-mer with at least t approximate occurrences in a random string (with at most d mismatches).

Charging Stations

The frequency array

To make **FREQUENTWORDS** faster, we will think about why this algorithm is slow in the first place. It slides a window of length k down *Text*, identifying a k-mer *Pattern* of *Text* at each step. For each such k-mer, it must slide a window down the entire length of *Text* in order to compute PATTERNCOUNT(*Text, Pattern*). Instead of doing all this sliding, we aspire to slide a window down *Text* only once. As we slide this window, we will keep track of the number of times that each k-mer *Pattern* has already appeared in *Text*, updating these numbers as we proceed.

To achieve this goal, we will first order all 4^k k-mers **lexicographically** (i.e., according to how they would appear in the dictionary) and then convert them into the 4^k different integers between 0 and $4^k - 1$. Given an integer k, we define the **frequency array** of a string *Text* as an array of length 4^k, where the i-th element of the array holds the number of times that the i-th k-mer (in the lexicographic order) appears in *Text* (Figure 1.19).

k-mer	AA	AC	AG	AT	CA	CC	CG	CT	GA	GC	GG	GT	TA	TC	TG	TT
index	0	1	2	3	4	5	6	7	8	9	10	11	12	13	14	15
frequency	3	0	2	0	1	0	0	0	0	1	3	1	0	0	1	0

FIGURE 1.19 The lexicographic order of DNA 2-mers (top), along with the index of each 2-mer in this order (middle), and the frequency array for AAGCAAAGGTGGG (bottom). For example, the frequency array at index 10 is equal to 3 because GG, the tenth DNA 2-mer according to lexicographic order, occurs three times in AAGCAAAGGTGGG.

To compute the frequency array, we need to determine how to transform a k-mer *Pattern* into an integer using a function PATTERNTONUMBER(*Pattern*). We also should know how to reverse this process, transforming an integer between 0 and $4^k - 1$ into a k-mer using a function NUMBERTOPATTERN(*index, k*). Figure 1.19 illustrates that PATTERNTONUMBER(GT) = 11 and NUMBERTOPATTERN(11, 2) = GT.

EXERCISE BREAK: Compute the following:

1. PATTERNTONUMBER(ATGCAA)

2. NUMBERTOPATTERN(5437, 7)

3. NUMBERTOPATTERN(5437, 8)

PAGE 41

CHARGING STATION (Converting Patterns Into Numbers and Vice-Versa): Check out this Charging Station to see how to implement PATTERNTONUMBER and NUMBERTOPATTERN.

The pseudocode below generates a frequency array by first initializing every element in the frequency array to zero (4^k operations) and then making a single pass down *Text* (approximately $|Text| \cdot k$ operations). For each *k*-mer *Pattern* that we encounter, we add 1 to the value of the frequency array corresponding to *Pattern*. As before, we refer to the *k*-mer beginning at position *i* of *Text* as *Text*(i, k).

COMPUTINGFREQUENCIES(*Text, k*)
    for $i \leftarrow 0$ to $4^k - 1$
        FREQUENCYARRAY(i) $\leftarrow 0$
    for $i \leftarrow 0$ to $|Text| - k$
        Pattern $\leftarrow$ *Text*(i, k)
        $j \leftarrow$ PATTERNTONUMBER(*Pattern*)
        FREQUENCYARRAY(j) $\leftarrow$ FREQUENCYARRAY(j) $+ 1$
    return FREQUENCYARRAY

We now have a faster algorithm for the Frequent Words Problem. After generating the frequency array, we can find all most frequent *k*-mers by simply finding all *k*-mers corresponding to the maximum element(s) in the frequency array.

FASTERFREQUENTWORDS(*Text , k*)
    FrequentPatterns $\leftarrow$ an empty set
    FREQUENCYARRAY $\leftarrow$ **COMPUTINGFREQUENCIES**(*Text, k*)
    maxCount $\leftarrow$ maximal value in FREQUENCYARRAY
    for $i \leftarrow 0$ to $4^k - 1$
        if FREQUENCYARRAY(i) $= maxCount$
            Pattern $\leftarrow$ NUMBERTOPATTERN(i, k)
            add *Pattern* to the set *FrequentPatterns*
    return *FrequentPatterns*

CHARGING STATION (Finding Frequent Words by Sorting): Although **FASTERFREQUENTWORDS** is fast for small k (i.e., you can use it to find *DnaA* boxes in an *oriC* region), it becomes impractical when k is large. If you are familiar with sorting algorithms and are interested in seeing a faster algorithm, check out this Charging Station.

PAGE 43

EXERCISE BREAK: Our claim that **FASTERFREQUENTWORDS** is faster than **FREQUENTWORDS** is only correct for certain values of $|Text|$ and k. Estimate the running time of **FASTERFREQUENTWORDS** and characterize the values of $|Text|$ and k when **FASTERFREQUENTWORDS** is indeed faster than **FREQUENTWORDS**.

Converting patterns to numbers and vice-versa

Our approach to computing PATTERNTONUMBER(*Pattern*) is based on a simple observation. If we remove the final symbol from all lexicographically ordered k-mers, the resulting list is still ordered lexicographically (think about removing the final letter from every word in a dictionary). In the case of DNA strings, every $(k-1)$-mer in the resulting list is repeated four times (Figure 1.20).

AAA	**AA**C	**AA**G	**AA**T	**AC**A	**AC**C	**AC**G	**AC**T
AGA	**AG**C	**AG**G	**AG**T	**AT**A	**AT**C	**AT**G	**AT**T
CAA	**CA**C	**CA**G	**CA**T	**CC**A	**CC**C	**CC**G	**CC**T
CGA	**CG**C	**CG**G	**CG**T	**CT**A	**CT**C	**CT**G	**CT**T
GAA	**GA**C	**GA**G	**GA**T	**GC**A	**GC**C	**GC**G	**GC**T
GGA	**GG**C	**GG**G	**GG**T	**GT**A	**GT**C	**GT**G	**GT**T
TAA	**TA**C	**TA**G	**TA**T	**TC**A	**TC**C	**TC**G	**TC**T
TGA	**TG**C	**TG**G	**TG**T	**TT**A	**TT**C	**TT**G	**TT**T

FIGURE 1.20 If we remove the final symbol from all lexicographically ordered DNA 3-mers, we obtain a lexicographic order of (red) 2-mers, where each 2-mer is repeated four times.

Thus, the number of 3-mers occurring before **AG**T is equal to four times the number of 2-mers occurring before **AG** plus the number of 1-mers occurring before T. Therefore,

$$\text{PATTERNTONUMBER}(\textbf{AG}\text{T}) = 4 \cdot \text{PATTERNTONUMBER}(\textbf{AG}) + \text{SYMBOLTONUMBER}(\text{T})$$
$$= 8 + 3 = 11,$$

where SYMBOLTONUMBER(*symbol*) is the function transforming symbols A, C, G, and T into the respective integers 0, 1, 2, and 3.

If we remove the final symbol of *Pattern*, denoted LASTSYMBOL(*Pattern*), then we will obtain a $(k-1)$-mer that we denote as PREFIX(*Pattern*). The preceding observation therefore generalizes to the formula

$$\text{PATTERNTONUMBER}(Pattern) = 4 \cdot \text{PATTERNTONUMBER}(\text{PREFIX}(Pattern)) +$$
$$\text{SYMBOLTONUMBER}(\text{LASTSYMBOL}(Pattern)). \quad (*)$$

This equation leads to the following **recursive algorithm**, i.e., a program that calls itself. If you want to learn more about recursive algorithms, see DETOUR: The Towers of Hanoi.

> **PATTERNTONUMBER**(*Pattern*)
>   **if** *Pattern* contains no symbols
>   **return** 0
>   *symbol* ← LASTSYMBOL(*Pattern*)
>   *Prefix* ← PREFIX(*Pattern*)
>   **return** 4 · **PATTERNTONUMBER**(*Prefix*) + SYMBOLTONUMBER(*symbol*)

In order to compute the inverse function NUMBERTOPATTERN(*index, k*), we return to (*) above, which implies that when we divide *index* = PATTERNTONUMBER(*Pattern*) by 4, the remainder will be equal to SYMBOLTONUMBER(*symbol*), and the quotient will be equal to PATTERNTONUMBER(PREFIX(*Pattern*)). Thus, we can use this fact to peel away symbols at the end of *Pattern* one at a time, as shown in Figure 1.21.

> **STOP and Think:** Once we have computed NUMBERTOPATTERN(9904, 7) in Figure 1.21, how would you compute NUMBERTOPATTERN(9904, 8)?

In the pseudocode below, we denote the quotient and the remainder when dividing integer n by integer m as QUOTIENT(*n, m*) and REMAINDER(*n, m*), respectively. For example, QUOTIENT(11, 4) = 2 and REMAINDER(11, 4) = 3. This pseudocode uses the function NUMBERTOSYMBOL(*index*), which is the inverse of SYMBOLTONUMBER and transforms the integers 0, 1, 2, and 3 into the respective symbols A, C, G, and T.

n	QUOTIENT$(n, 4)$	REMAINDER$(n, 4)$	NUMBERTOSYMBOL
9904	2476	0	A
2476	619	0	A
619	154	3	T
154	38	2	G
38	9	2	G
9	2	1	C
2	0	2	G

FIGURE 1.21 When computing *Pattern* = NUMBERTOPATTERN(9904, 7), we divide 9904 by 4 to obtain a quotient of 2476 and a remainder of 0. This remainder represents the final nucleotide of *Pattern*, or NUMBERTOSYMBOL(0) = A. We then iterate this process, dividing each subsequent quotient by 4, until we obtain a quotient of 0. The symbols in the nucleotide column, read upward from the bottom, yield *Pattern* = GCGGTAA.

```
NUMBERTOPATTERN(index , k)
    if k = 1
        return NUMBERTOSYMBOL(index)
    prefixIndex ← QUOTIENT(index, 4)
    r ← REMAINDER(index, 4)
    symbol ← NUMBERTOSYMBOL(r)
    PrefixPattern ← NUMBERTOPATTERN(prefixIndex, k − 1)
    return concatenation of PrefixPattern with symbol
```

Finding frequent words by sorting

To see how sorting can help us find frequent *k*-mers, we will consider a motivating example when *k* = 2. Given a string *Text* = AAGCAAAGGTGGG, list all its 2-mers in the order they appear in *Text*, and convert each 2-mer into an integer using PATTERNTONUMBER to produce an array INDEX, as shown below.

2-mer	AA	AG	GC	CA	AA	AA	AG	GG	GT	TG	GG	GG
INDEX	0	2	9	4	0	0	2	10	11	14	10	10

We will now sort INDEX to generate an array SORTEDINDEX, as shown in Figure 1.22.

STOP and Think: How can the sorted array in Figure 1.22 help us find frequent words?

2-mer	AA	AA	AA	AG	AG	CA	GC	GG	GG	GG	GT	TG
SORTEDINDEX	0	0	0	2	2	4	9	10	10	10	11	14
COUNT	1	2	3	1	2	1	1	1	2	3	1	1

FIGURE 1.22 Lexicographically sorted 2-mers in AAGCAAAGGTGG (top), along with arrays SORTEDINDEX (middle) and COUNT (bottom).

Since identical k-mers clump together in the sorted array (like $(0, 0, 0)$ for AA or $(10, 10, 10)$ for GG in Figure 1.22), frequent k-mers are the longest runs of identical integers in SORTEDINDEX. This insight leads to **FINDINGFREQUENTWORDSBYSORTING**, whose pseudocode is shown below. This algorithm uses an array COUNT for which COUNT(i) computes the number of times that the integer at position i in the array SORTEDINDEX appears in the first i elements of this array (Figure 1.22 (bottom)). In the pseudocode for **FINDINGFREQUENTWORDSBYSORTING**, we assume that you already know how to sort an array using an algorithm **SORT**.

FINDINGFREQUENTWORDSBYSORTING(*Text* , *k*)
    FrequentPatterns ← an empty set
    for i ← 0 to |*Text*| − *k*
        Pattern ← *Text*(i, k)
        INDEX(i) ← PATTERNTONUMBER(*Pattern*)
        COUNT(i) ← 1
    SORTEDINDEX ← **SORT**(INDEX)
    for i ← 1 to |*Text*| − *k*
        if SORTEDINDEX(i) = SORTEDINDEX($i − 1$)
            COUNT(i) = COUNT($i − 1$) + 1
    maxCount ← maximum value in the array COUNT
    for i ← 0 to |*Text*| − *k*
        if COUNT(i) = *maxCount*
            Pattern ← NUMBERTOPATTERN(SORTEDINDEX(i), k)
            add *Pattern* to the set *FrequentPatterns*
    return *FrequentPatterns*

Solving the Clump Finding Problem

Note: This Charging Station assumes that you have read **CHARGING STATION: The Frequency Array**.

The pseudocode below slides a window of length L down *Genome*. After computing the frequency array for the current window, it identifies (L, t)-clumps simply by finding which k-mers occur at least t times within the window. To keep track of these clumps, our algorithm uses an array CLUMP of length 4^k whose values are all initialized to zero. For each value of i between 0 and $4^k - 1$, we will set CLUMP(i) equal to 1 if NUMBERTOPATTERN(i, k) forms an (L, t)-clump in *Genome*.

```
CLUMPFINDING(Genome, k, t, L)
    FrequentPatterns ← an empty set
    for i ← 0 to 4^k − 1
        CLUMP(i) ← 0
    for i ← 0 to |Genome| − L
        Text ← the string of length L starting at position i in Genome
        FREQUENCYARRAY ← COMPUTINGFREQUENCIES(Text, k)
        for index ← 0 to 4^k − 1
            if FREQUENCYARRAY(index) ≥ t
                CLUMP(index) ← 1
    for i ← 0 to 4^k − 1
        if CLUMP(i) = 1
            Pattern ← NUMBERTOPATTERN(i, k)
            add Pattern to the set FrequentPatterns
    return FrequentPatterns
```

EXERCISE BREAK: Estimate the running time of **CLUMPFINDING**.

CLUMPFINDING makes $|Genome| - L + 1$ iterations, generating a frequency array for a string of length L at each iteration. Since this task takes roughly $4^k + L \cdot k$ time, the overall running time of **CLUMPFINDING** is $\mathcal{O}\left(|Genome| \cdot (4^k + L \cdot k)\right)$. As a result, when searching for *DnaA* boxes ($k = 9$) in a typical bacterial genome ($|Genome| > 1000000$), **CLUMPFINDING** becomes too slow.

STOP and Think: Can you speed up **CLUMPFINDING** by eliminating the need to generate a new frequency array at every iteration?

To improve **CLUMPFINDING**, we observe that when we slide our window of length L one symbol to the right, the frequency array does not change much, and so regenerating the frequency array from scratch is inefficient. For example, Figure 1.23 shows the frequency arrays ($k = 2$) for the 13-mers *Text* = **AA**GCAAAGGTGG**G** and *Text'* = **A**GCAAAGGTGG**GC** starting at positions 0 and 1 of the 14-mer **AA**GCAAAGGTGG**GC**. These two frequency arrays differ in only two elements corresponding to the first *k*-mer in *Text* (**AA**) and the last *k*-mer in *Text'* (**GC**). Specifically, the frequency array value corresponding to the **first** *k*-mer of *Text* is **reduced** by 1 in the frequency array of *Text'*, and the frequency array value corresponding to the **last** *k*-mer of *Text* is **increased** by 1 in the frequency array of *Text'*.

This observation helps us modify **CLUMPFINDING** as shown below. Note that we now only call **COMPUTINGFREQUENCIES** once, updating the frequency array as we go along.

BETTERCLUMPFINDING(*Genome, k, t, L*)
    FrequentPatterns ← an empty set
    for $i \leftarrow 0$ to $4^k - 1$
        CLUMP(i) ← 0
    Text ← *Genome*(0, *L*)
    FREQUENCYARRAY ← **COMPUTINGFREQUENCIES**(*Text, k*)
    for $i \leftarrow 0$ to $4^k - 1$
        if FREQUENCYARRAY(i) $\geq t$
            CLUMP(i) ← 1
    for $i \leftarrow 1$ to $|Genome| - L$
        FirstPattern ← *Genome*($i - 1, k$)
        index ← PATTERNTONUMBER(*FirstPattern*)
        FREQUENCYARRAY(*index*) ← FREQUENCYARRAY(*index*) − 1
        LastPattern ← *Genome*($i + L - k, k$)
        index ← PATTERNTONUMBER(*LastPattern*)
        FREQUENCYARRAY(*index*) ← FREQUENCYARRAY(*index*) + 1
        if FREQUENCYARRAY(*index*) $\geq t$
            CLUMP(*index*) ← 1
    for $i \leftarrow 0$ to $4^k - 1$
        if CLUMP(i) = 1
            Pattern ← NUMBERTOPATTERN(i, k)
            add *Pattern* to the set *FrequentPatterns*
    return *FrequentPatterns*

k-mer	AA	AC	AG	AT	CA	CC	CG	CT	GA	GC	GG	GT	TA	TC	TG	TT
INDEX	0	1	2	3	4	5	6	7	8	9	10	11	12	13	14	15
frequency	3	0	2	0	1	0	0	0	0	1	3	1	0	0	1	0
frequency'	2	0	2	0	1	0	0	0	0	2	3	1	0	0	1	0

FIGURE 1.23 The frequency arrays for two consecutive substrings of length 13 starting at positions 0 and 1 of **AA**GCAAAGGTGG**GC** are very similar to each other.

Solving the Frequent Words with Mismatches Problem

Note: This Charging Station uses some notation from **CHARGING STATION: The Frequency Array**.

PAGE 39

To prevent having to generate all 4^k k-mers in order to solve the Frequent Words with Mismatches Problem, our goal is to consider only those k-mers that are **close** to a k-mer in *Text*, i.e., those with Hamming distance at most d from this k-mer. Given a k-mer *Pattern*, we therefore define its ***d*-neighborhood** NEIGHBORS(*Pattern*, d) as the set of all k-mers that are close to *Pattern*. For example, NEIGHBORS(ACG, 1) consists of ten 3-mers:

ACG   **C**CG   **G**CG   **T**CG   A**A**G   A**G**G   A**T**G   AC**A**   AC**C**   AC**T**

EXERCISE BREAK: Estimate the size of NEIGHBORS(*Pattern*, d).

We will also use an array CLOSE of size 4^k whose values we initialize to zero. In the **FREQUENTWORDSWITHMISMATCHES** pseudocode below, we set CLOSE(i) = 1 whenever *Pattern* = NUMBERTOPATTERN(i, k) is close to some k-mer in *Text*. This allows us to apply **APPROXIMATEPATTERNCOUNT** only to close k-mers, a smarter approach than applying it to all k-mers.

CHARGING STATION (Generating the Neighborhood of a String): **FREQUENTWORDSWITHMISMATCHES** also calls **NEIGHBORS**(*Pattern*, d), a function that generates the d-neighborhood of a k-mer *Pattern*. Check out this Charging Station to learn how to implement this function.

PAGE 49

STOP and Think: Although **FREQUENTWORDSWITHMISMATCHES** is faster than the naive algorithm described in the main text for the typical parameters used in *oriC* searches, it is not necessarily faster for all parameter values. For which parameter values is **FREQUENTWORDSWITHMISMATCHES** slower than the naive algorithm?

FREQUENTWORDSWITHMISMATCHES(*Text*, *k*, *d*)
    FrequentPatterns ← an empty set
    for i ← 0 to $4^k - 1$
        CLOSE(i) ← 0
        FREQUENCYARRAY ← 0
    for i ← 0 to |*Text*| − k
        Neighborhood ← **NEIGHBORS**(*Text*(i, k), d)
        for each *Pattern* from *Neighborhood*
            index ← PATTERNTONUMBER(*Pattern*)
            CLOSE(*index*) ← 1
    for i ← 0 to $4^k - 1$
        if CLOSE(i) = 1
            Pattern ← NUMBERTOPATTERN(i, k)
            FREQUENCYARRAY(i) ← **APPROXIMATEPATTERNCOUNT**(*Text*, *Pattern*, d)
    maxCount ← maximal value in FREQUENCYARRAY
    for i ← 0 to $4^k - 1$
        if FREQUENCYARRAY(i) = *maxCount*
            Pattern ← NUMBERTOPATTERN(i, k)
            add *Pattern* to the set *FrequentPatterns*
    return *FrequentPatterns*

CHARGING STATION (Finding Frequent Words with Mismatches by Sorting): If you are familiar with sorting and are interested in seeing an even faster algorithm for the Frequent Words with Mismatches Problem, check out this Charging Station.

PAGE 51

Generating the neighborhood of a string

Our goal is to generate the d-neighborhood NEIGHBORS($Pattern, d$), the set of all k-mers whose Hamming distance from *Pattern* does not exceed d. We will first generate the 1-neigborhood of *Pattern* using the following pseudocode.

IMMEDIATENEIGHBORS(*Pattern*)
    Neighborhood ← the set consisting of the single string *Pattern*
    for $i = 1$ to $|Pattern|$
        symbol ← i-th nucleotide of *Pattern*
        for each nucleotide x different from *symbol*
            Neighbor ← *Pattern* with the i-th nucleotide substituted by x
            add *Neighbor* to *Neighborhood*
    return *Neighborhood*

Our idea for generating NEIGHBORS($Pattern, d$) is as follows. If we remove the first symbol of *Pattern* (denoted FIRSTSYMBOL(*Pattern*)), then we will obtain a $(k-1)$-mer that we denote by SUFFIX(*Pattern*).

STOP and Think: If we know NEIGHBORS(SUFFIX(*Pattern*), d), how does it help us construct NEIGHBORS(*Pattern*, d)?

Now, consider a $(k-1)$-mer *Pattern'* belonging to NEIGHBORS(SUFFIX(*Pattern*), d). By the definition of the d-neighborhood NEIGHBORS(SUFFIX(*Pattern*), d), we know that HAMMINGDISTANCE(*Pattern'*, SUFFIX(*Pattern*)) is either equal to d or less than d. In the first case, we can add FIRSTSYMBOL(*Pattern*) to the beginning of *Pattern'* in order to obtain a k-mer belonging to NEIGHBORS(*Pattern*, d). In the second case, we can add any symbol to the beginning of *Pattern'* and obtain a k-mer belonging to NEIGHBORS(*Pattern*, d).

In the following pseudocode for **NEIGHBORS**, we use the notation *symbol* • *Text* to denote the concatenation of a character *symbol* and a string *Text*, e.g., A • GCATG = AGCATG.

NEIGHBORS(*Pattern*, *d*)
    if *d* = 0
        return {*Pattern*}
    if |*Pattern*| = 1
        return {A, C, G, T}
    Neighborhood ← an empty set
    SuffixNeighbors ← NEIGHBORS(SUFFIX(*Pattern*), *d*)
    for each string *Text* from *SuffixNeighbors*
        if HAMMINGDISTANCE(SUFFIX(*Pattern*), *Text*) < *d*
            for each nucleotide *x*
                add *x* • *Text* to *Neighborhood*
        else
            add FIRSTSYMBOL(*Pattern*) • *Text* to *Neighborhood*
    return *Neighborhood*

STOP and Think: Consider the following questions.

1. What is the running time of **NEIGHBORS**?

2. **NEIGHBORS** generates all *k*-mers of Hamming distance at most *d* from *Pattern*. Modify **NEIGHBORS** to generate all *k*-mers of Hamming distance exactly *d* from *Pattern*.

If you are still learning how recursive algorithms (like **NEIGHBORS**) work, you may want to implement an iterative version of **NEIGHBORS** instead, shown below.

ITERATIVENEIGHBORS(*Pattern*, *d*)
    Neighborhood ← set consisting of single string *Pattern*
    for *j* = 1 to *d*
        for each string *Pattern'* in *Neighborhood*
            add **IMMEDIATENEIGHBORS**(*Pattern'*) to *Neighborhood*
            remove duplicates from *Neighborhood*
    return *Neighborhood*

Finding frequent words with mismatches by sorting

Note: This Charging Station uses some notation from **CHARGING STATION: Finding Frequent Words by Sorting**.

PAGE 43

The following pseudocode reduces the Frequent Words with Mismatches Problem to sorting.

```
FINDINGFREQUENTWORDSWITHMISMATCHESBYSORTING(Text, k, d)
    FrequentPatterns ← an empty set
    Neighborhoods ← an empty list
    for i ← 0 to |Text| − k
        add NEIGHBORS(Text(i, k), d) to Neighborhoods
    form an array NEIGHBORHOODARRAY holding all strings in Neighborhoods
    for i ← 0 to |Neighborhoods| − 1
        Pattern ← NEIGHBORHOODARRAY(i)
        INDEX(i) ← PATTERNTONUMBER(Pattern)
        COUNT(i) ← 1
    SORTEDINDEX ← SORT(INDEX)
    for i ← 0 to |Neighborhoods| − 1
        if SORTEDINDEX(i) = SORTEDINDEX(i + 1)
            COUNT(i + 1) ← COUNT(i) + 1
    maxCount ← maximum value in array COUNT
    for i ← 0 to |Neighborhoods| − 1
        if COUNT(i) = maxCount
            Pattern ← NUMBERTOPATTERN(SORTEDINDEX(i), k)
            add Pattern to FrequentPatterns
    return FrequentPatterns
```

Detours

Big-O notation

Computer scientists typically measure an algorithm's efficiency in terms of its **worst-case running time**, which is the largest amount of time an algorithm can take for the most difficult input of a given size. The advantage to considering the worst-case running time is that we are guaranteed that our algorithm will never behave worse than our worst-case estimate.

Big-O notation compactly describes the running time of an algorithm. For example, if your algorithm for sorting an array of n numbers takes roughly n^2 operations for the most difficult dataset, then we say that the running time of your algorithm is $\mathcal{O}(n^2)$. In reality, depending on your implementation, it may use any number of operations, such as $1.5n^2$, $n^2 + n + 2$, or $0.5n^2 + 1$; all these algorithms are $\mathcal{O}(n^2)$ because big-O notation only cares about the term that grows the fastest with respect to the size of the input. This is because as n grows very large, the difference in behavior between two $\mathcal{O}(n^2)$ functions, like $999 \cdot n^2$ and $n^2 + 3n + 9999999$, is negligible when compared to the behavior of functions from different classes, say $\mathcal{O}(n^2)$ and $\mathcal{O}(n^6)$. Of course, we would prefer an algorithm requiring $1/2 \cdot n^2$ steps to an algorithm requiring $1000 \cdot n^2$ steps.

When we write that the running time of an algorithm is $\mathcal{O}(n^2)$, we technically mean that it does not grow faster than a function with a leading term of $c \cdot n^2$, for some constant c. Formally, a function $f(n)$ is Big-O of function $g(n)$, or $\mathcal{O}(g(n))$, when $f(n) \leq c \cdot g(n)$ for some constant c and sufficiently large n.

Probabilities of patterns in a string

We mentioned that the probability that some 9-mer appears 3 or more times in a random DNA string of length 500 is approximately $1/1300$. We assure you that this calculation does not appear out of thin air. Specifically, we can generate a **random string** modeling a DNA strand by choosing each nucleotide for any position with probability $1/4$. The construction of random strings can be generalized to an arbitrary alphabet with A symbols, where each symbol is chosen with probability $1/A$.

EXERCISE BREAK: What is the probability that two randomly generated strings of length n in an A-letter alphabet are identical?

We now ask a simple question: what is the probability that a specific k-mer *Pattern* will appear (at least once) as a substring of a random string of length N? For example, say that we want to find the probability that "01" appears in a random **binary string** ($A = 2$) of length 4. Here are all possible such strings.

0000 00**01** 00**10** 00**11** **01**00 **01**0**1** **01**10 **01**11

1000 10**01** 10**10** 10**11** 1100 11**01** 1110 1111

Because "01" is a substring of 11 of these 4-mers, and because each 4-mer could be generated with probability 1/16, the probability that "01" appears in a random binary 4-mer is 11/16.

> **STOP and Think:** What is the probability that *Pattern* = "11" appears as a substring of a random binary 4-mer?

Surprisingly, changing *Pattern* from "01" to "11" changes the probability that it appears as a substring of a random binary string. Indeed, "**11**" appears in only 8 binary 4-mers:

0000 0001 0010 00**11** 0100 0101 0110 0**11**1

1000 1001 1010 10**11** **11**00 1**1**01 **11**10 **1111**

As a result, the probability of "11" appearing in a random binary string of length 4 is $8/16 = 1/2$.

> **STOP and Think:** Why do you think that "11" is less likely than "01" to appear as a substring of a random binary 4-mer?

Let $\Pr(N, A, Pattern, t)$ denote the probability that a string *Pattern* appears t or more times in a random string of length N formed from an alphabet of A letters. We saw that $\Pr(4, 2, "01", 1) = 11/16$ while $\Pr(4, 2, "11", 1) = 1/2$. Interestingly, when we make t greater than 1, we see that "01" is *less* likely to appear multiple times than "11". For example, the probability of finding "01" twice or more in a random binary 4-mer is given by $\Pr(4, 2, "01", 2) = 1/16$ because "0101" is the only binary 4-mer containing "01" twice, and yet $\Pr(4, 2, "11", 2) = 3/16$ because binary 4-mers "0111", "1110" and "1111" all have at least two occurrences of "11".

> **EXERCISE BREAK:** Compute $\Pr(100, 2, "01", 1)$.

We have seen that different k-mers have different probabilities of occurring multiple times as a substring of a random string. In general, this phenomenon is called the **overlapping words paradox** because different substring occurrences of *Pattern* can

PAGE 62 overlap each other for some choices of *Pattern* but not others (see **DETOUR: The Overlapping Words Paradox**).

For example, there are two overlapping occurrences of "11" in "1110", and three overlapping occurrences of "11" in "1111"; yet occurrences of "01" can never overlap with each other, and so "01" can never occur more than twice in a binary 4-mer. The overlapping words paradox makes computing $\Pr(N, A, Pattern, t)$ a rather complex problem because this probability depends heavily on the particular choice of *Pattern*. In light of the complications presented by the overlapping words paradox, we will try to *approximate* $\Pr(A, N, Pattern, t)$ rather than compute it exactly.

To approximate $\Pr(N, A, Pattern, t)$, we will assume that the *k*-mer *Pattern* is not overlapping. As a toy example, say we we wish to count the number of **ternary strings** ($A = 3$) of length 7 that contain "01" at least twice. Apart from the two occurrences of "01", we have three remaining symbols in the string. Let's assume that these symbols are all "2". The two occurrences of "**01**" can be inserted into "222" in ten different ways to form a 7-mer, as shown below.

$$\begin{array}{ccccc} 0101222 & 0120122 & 0122012 & 0122201 & 2010122 \\ 2012012 & 2012201 & 2201012 & 2201201 & 2220101 \end{array}$$

We inserted these two occurrences of "01" into "222", but we could have inserted them into any other ternary 3-mer. Because there are $3^3 = 27$ ternary 3-mers, we obtain an approximation of $10 \cdot 27 = 270$ for the number of ternary 7-mers that contain two or more instances of "01". Because there are $3^7 = 2187$ ternary 7-mers, we estimate the probability $\Pr(7, 3, "01", 2)$ as $270/2187$.

STOP and Think: Is $270/2187$ a good approximation for $\Pr(7, 3, "01", 2)$? Is the true probability $\Pr(7, 3, "01", 2)$ larger or smaller than $270/2187$?

To generalize the above method to approximate $\Pr(N, A, Pattern, t)$ for arbitrary parameter values, consider a string *Text* of length N having at least t occurrences of a *k*-mer *Pattern*. If we select exactly t of these occurrences, then we can think about *Text* as a sequence of $n = N - t \cdot k$ symbols interrupted by t insertions of the *k*-mer *Pattern*. If we fix these n symbols, then we wish to count the number of different strings *Text* that can be formed by inserting t occurrences of *Pattern* into a string formed by these n symbols.

For example, consider again the problem of embedding two occurrences of "01" into "222" ($n = 3$), and note that we have added five copies of a capital "X" below each 7-mer.

0101222	0120122	0122012	0122201	2010122
X X XXX	X XX XX	X XXX X	X XXXX	XX X XX

2012012	2012201	2201012	2201201	2220101
XX XX X	XX XXX	XXX X X	XXX XX	XXXX X

What do the "X" mean? Instead of counting the number of ways to insert two occurrences of "01" into "222", we can count the number of ways to select two of the five "X" to color blue.

XXXXX XXXXX XXXXX XXXXX XXXXX

XXXXX XXXXX XXXXX XXXXX XXXXX

In other words, we are counting the number of ways to choose 2 out of 5 objects, which can be counted by the **binomial coefficient** $\binom{5}{2} = 10$. More generally, the binomial coefficient $\binom{m}{k}$ represents the number of ways to choose k out of m objects and is equal to $m!/k!(m-k)!$

STOP and Think: How many ways are there to implant t instances of a (nonoverlapping) k-mer into a string of length n to produce a string of length $n + t \cdot k$?

To approximate $\Pr(N, A, Pattern, t)$, we want to count the number of ways to insert t instances of a k-mer $Pattern$ into a fixed string of length $n = N - t \cdot k$. We will therefore have $n + t$ occurrences of "X", from which we must select t for the placements of $Pattern$, giving a total of $\binom{n+t}{t}$. We then need to multiply $\binom{n+t}{t}$ by the number of strings of length n into which we can insert t instances of $Pattern$ to have an approximate total of $\binom{n+t}{t} \cdot A^n$ (the actual number will be smaller because of over-counting). Dividing by the number of strings of length N, we have our desired approximation,

$$\Pr(N, A, Pattern, t) \approx \frac{\binom{n+t}{t} \cdot A^n}{A^N} = \frac{\binom{N-t\cdot(k-1)}{t}}{A^{t\cdot k}}.$$

We will now compute the probability that the specific 5-mer ACTAT occurs at least $t = 3$ times in a random DNA string ($A = 4$) of length $N = 30$. Since $n = N - t \cdot k = 15$, our estimated probability is

$$\Pr(30, 4, \text{ACTAT}, 3) \approx \frac{\binom{30-3\cdot4}{3}}{4^{15}} = \frac{816}{1073741824} \approx 7.599 \cdot 10^{-7}.$$

The exact probability is closer to $7.572 \cdot 10^{-7}$, illustrating that our approximation is relatively accurate for non-overlapping patterns. However, it becomes inaccurate for overlapping patterns, e.g., $\Pr(30, 4, \text{AAAAA}, 3) \approx 1.148 \cdot 10^{-3}$.

We should not be surprised that the probability of finding ACTAT in a random DNA string of length 30 is so low. However, remember that our original goal was to approximate the probability that there exists *some* 5-mer appearing three or more times. In general, the probability that some k-mer appears t or more times in a random string of length N formed over an A-letter alphabet is written $\Pr(N, A, k, t)$.

We approximated $\Pr(N, A, Pattern, t)$ as

$$p = \frac{\binom{N - t \cdot (k-1)}{t}}{A^{t \cdot k}}.$$

Notice that the approximate probability that *Pattern* does *not* appear t or more times is therefore $1 - p$. Thus, the probability that *all* A^k patterns appear fewer than t times in a random string of length N can be approximated as

$$(1 - p)^{A^k}.$$

Moreover, the probability that there exists a k-mer appearing t or more times should be 1 minus this value, which gives us the following approximation:

$$\Pr(N, A, k, t) \approx 1 - (1 - p)^{A^k}.$$

Your calculator may have difficulty with this formula, which requires raising a number close to 1 to a very large power and can cause round-off errors. To avoid this, if we assume that p is about the same for any *Pattern*, then we can approximate $\Pr(N, A, k, t)$ by multiplying p by the total number of k-mers A^k,

$$\Pr(N, A, k, t) \approx p \cdot A^k = \frac{\binom{N - t \cdot (k-1)}{t}}{A^{t \cdot k}} \cdot A^k = \frac{\binom{N - t \cdot (k-1)}{t}}{A^{(t-1) \cdot k}}.$$

We acknowledge again that this approximation is a gross over-simplification, since the probability $\Pr(N, A, Pattern, t)$ varies across different choices of k-mers and because it assumes that occurrences of different k-mers are independent events. For example, in the main text, we wish to approximate $\Pr(500, 4, 9, 3)$, and the above formula results in the approximation

$$\Pr(500, 4, 9, 3) \approx \frac{\binom{500 - 3 \cdot 8}{3}}{4^{(3-1) \cdot 9}} = \frac{17861900}{68719476736} \approx \frac{1}{3847}.$$

Because of overlapping strings, this approximation deviates from the true value of $\Pr(500, 4, 9, 3)$, which is closer to $1/1300$.

The most beautiful experiment in biology

The Meselson-Stahl experiment, conducted in 1958 by Matthew Meselson and Franklin Stahl, is sometimes called "the most beautiful experiment in biology". In the late 1950s, biologists debated three conflicting models of DNA replication, illustrated in Figure 1.24. The **semiconservative hypothesis** (recall Figure 1.1 from page 3), suggested that each parent strand acts as a template for the synthesis of a daughter strand. As a result, each of the two daughter molecules contains one parent strand and one newly synthesized strand. The **conservative hypothesis** proposed that the entire double-stranded parent DNA molecule serves as a template for the synthesis of a new daughter molecule, resulting in one molecule with two parent strands and another with two newly synthesized strands. The **dispersive hypothesis** proposed that some mechanism breaks the DNA backbone into pieces and splices intervals of synthesized DNA, so that each of the daughter molecules is a patchwork of old and new double-stranded DNA.

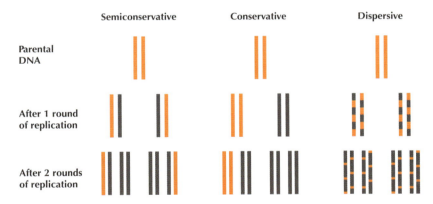

FIGURE 1.24 Semiconservative, conservative, and dispersive models of DNA replication make different predictions about the distribution of DNA strands after replication. Yellow strands indicate ^{15}N (heavy) segments of DNA, and black strands indicate ^{14}N (light) segments. The Meselson-Stahl experiment began with DNA consisting of 100% ^{15}N.

Meselson and Stahl's insight was that one isotope of nitrogen, **Nitrogen-14** (^{14}N), is lighter and more abundant than **Nitrogen-15** (^{15}N). Knowing that DNA naturally contains ^{14}N , Meselson and Stahl grew *E. coli* for many rounds of replication in a ^{15}N medium, which caused the bacteria to gain weight as they absorbed the heavier isotope into their DNA. When they were confident that the bacterial DNA was saturated with ^{15}N, they transferred the heavy *E. coli* cells to a less dense ^{14}N medium.

STOP and Think: What do you think happened when the "heavy" *E. coli* replicated in the "light" ^{14}N medium?

The brilliance of the Meselson-Stahl experiment is that all newly synthesized DNA would contain exclusively ^{14}N, and the three existing hypotheses for DNA replication predicted different outcomes for how this ^{14}N isotope would be incorporated into DNA. Specifically, after one round of replication, the conservative model predicted that half the *E. coli* DNA would still have only ^{15}N and therefore be heavier whereas the other half would have only ^{14}N and be lighter. Yet when they attempted to separate the *E. coli* DNA according to weight by using a centrifuge after one round of replication, all of the DNA had the same density! Just like that, they had refuted the conservative hypothesis once and for all.

Unfortunately, this experiment was not able to eliminate either of the other two models, as both the dispersive and semiconservative hypotheses predicted that all of the DNA after one round of replication would have the same density.

STOP and Think: What would the dispersive and semiconservative models predict about the density of *E. coli* DNA after two rounds of replication?

Let's first consider the dispersive model, which says that each daughter strand of DNA is formed by half mashed up pieces of the parent strand, and half new DNA. If this hypothesis were true, then after two replication cycles, any daughter strand of DNA should contain about 25% ^{15}N and about 75% ^{14}N. In other words, all the DNA should still have the same density. And yet when Meselson and Stahl spun the centrifuge after two rounds of *E. coli* replication, this is not what they observed!

Instead, they found that the DNA divided into two different densities. This is exactly what the semiconservative model predicted: after one cycle, every cell should possess one ^{14}N strand and one ^{15}N strand; after two cycles, half of the DNA molecules should have one ^{14}N strand and one ^{15}N strand, while the other half should have two ^{14}N strands, producing the two different densities they noticed.

STOP and Think: What does the semi-conservative model predict about the density of *E. coli* DNA after three rounds of replication?

Meselson and Stahl had rejected the conservative and dispersive hypotheses of replication, and yet they wanted to make sure that the semiconservative hypothesis was confirmed by further *E. coli* replication. This model predicted that after three rounds of replication, one-quarter of the DNA molecules should still have a ^{15}N strand, causing 25% of the DNA to have an intermediate density, whereas the remaining 75% should be lighter, having only ^{14}N. This is indeed what Meselson and Stahl witnessed in the lab, and the semiconservative hypothesis has stood strong to this day.

Directionality of DNA strands

The sugar component of a nucleotide has a ring of five carbon atoms, which are labeled as 1′, 2′, 3′, 4′, and 5′ in Figure 1.25 (left). The 5′ atom is joined onto the phosphate group in the nucleotide and eventually to the 3′ end of the neighboring nucleotide. The 3′ atom is joined onto another neighboring nucleotide in the nucleic acid chain. As a result, we call the two ends of the nucleotide the **5′-end** and the **3′-end** (pronounced "five prime end" and "three prime end", respectively).

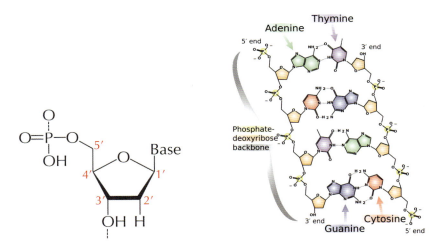

FIGURE 1.25 A nucleotide with sugar ring carbon atoms labeled 1′, 2′, 3′, 4′, and 5′.

When we zoom out to the level of the double helix, we can see in Figure 1.25 (right) that any DNA fragment is oriented with a 3′ atom on one end and a 5′ atom on the other end. As a standard, a DNA strand is always read in the 5′ → 3′ direction. Note that the orientations run opposite to each other in complementary strands.

The Towers of Hanoi

The **Towers of Hanoi** puzzle consists of three vertical pegs and a number of disks of different sizes, each with a hole in its center so that it fits on the pegs. The disks are initially stacked on the left peg (peg 1) so that disks increase in size from the top down (Figure 1.26). The puzzle is played by moving one disk at a time between pegs, with the goal of moving all disks from the left peg (peg 1) to the right peg (peg 3). However, you are not allowed to place a disk on top of a smaller disk.

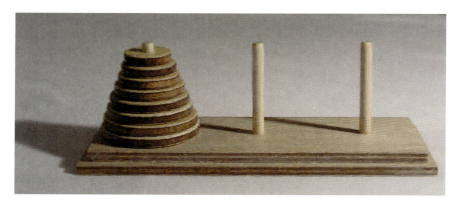

FIGURE 1.26 The Towers of Hanoi puzzle.

Towers of Hanoi Problem:

Solve the Towers of Hanoi puzzle.

> **Input**: An integer n.
> **Output**: A sequence of moves that will solve the Towers of Hanoi puzzle with n disks.

STOP and Think: What is the minimum number of steps needed to solve the Towers of Hanoi Problem for three disks?

Let's see how many steps are required to solve the Towers of Hanoi Problem for four disks. The first important observation is that sooner or later you will have to move the largest disk to the right peg. However, in order to move the largest disk, we first have to move all three smallest disks off the first peg. Furthermore, these three smallest disks must all be on the same peg because the largest disk cannot be placed on top of another disk. Thus, we first have to move the top three disks to the middle peg (7 moves), then move the largest disk to the right peg (1 move), then again move the three smallest disks from the middle peg to the top of the largest disk on the right peg (another 7 moves), for a total of 15 moves.

More generally, let $T(n)$ denote the minimum number of steps required to solve the Towers of Hanoi puzzle with n disks. To move n disks from the left peg to the right peg, you first need to move the $n-1$ smallest disks from the left peg to the middle peg ($T(n-1)$ steps), then move the largest disk to the right peg (1 step), and finally move the $n-1$ smallest disks from the middle peg to the right peg ($T(n-1)$ steps). This yields the recurrence relation

$$T(n) = 2T(n-1) + 1\,.$$

STOP and Think: Using the above recurrence relation, can you find a formula for $T(n)$ that does not require recursion?

We now have a recursive algorithm to move n disks from the left peg to the right peg. We will use three variables (each taking a different value from 1, 2, and 3) to denote the three pegs: *startPeg*, *destinationPeg*, and *transitPeg*. These three variables always represent different pegs, and so *startPeg* + *destinationPeg* + *transitPeg* is always equal to $1+2+3 = 6$. **HANOITOWERS**(n, *startPeg*, *destinationPeg*) moves n disks from *startPeg* to *destinationPeg* (using *transitPeg* as a temporary destination).

HANOITOWERS(*n*, *startPeg*, *destinationPeg*)
    if *n* = 1
        Move top disk from *startPeg* to *destinationPeg*
        return
    transitPeg = 6 − *startPeg* − *destinationPeg*
    HANOITOWERS(*n* − 1, *startPeg*, *transitPeg*)
    Move top disk from *startPeg* to *destinationPeg*
    HANOITOWERS(*n* − 1, *transitPeg*, *destinationPeg*)
    return

Even though this algorithm may seem straightforward, moving a 100-disk tower would require more steps than the number of atoms in the universe! The fast growth of the number of moves required by **HANOITOWERS** is explained by the fact that every time

HANOITOWERS is called for n disks, it calls itself twice for $n - 1$, which in turn triggers four calls for $n - 2$, and so on. For example, a call to HANOITOWERS$(4, 1, 3)$ results in calls HANOITOWERS$(3, 1, 2)$ and HANOITOWERS$(3, 2, 3)$; these calls, in turn, call HANOITOWERS$(2, 1, 3)$, HANOITOWERS$(2, 3, 2)$, HANOITOWERS$(2, 2, 1)$, and HANOITOWERS$(2, 1, 3)$.

The overlapping words paradox

We illustrate the overlapping words paradox with a two-player game called "Best Bet for Simpletons". Player 1 selects a binary k-mer A, and Player 2, knowing what A is, selects a different binary k-mer B. The two players then flip a coin multiple times, with coin flips represented by strings of "1" ("heads") and "0" ("tails"); the game ends when A or B appears as a block of k consecutive coin flips.

STOP and Think: Do the two players always have the same chance of winning?

At first glance, you might guess that every k-mer has an equal chance of winning. Yet suppose that Player 1 chooses "00" and Player 2 chooses "10". After two flips, either Player 1 wins ("00"), Player 2 wins ("10"), or the game continues ("01" or "11"). If the game continues, then Player 1 should surrender, since Player 2 will win as soon as "tails" ("0") is next flipped. Player 2 is therefore three times more likely to win!

It may seem that Player 1 should have the advantage by simply selecting the "strongest" k-mer. However, an intriguing feature of Best Bet for Simpletons is that if $k > 2$, then Player 2 can always choose a k-mer B that beats A, *regardless* of Player 1's choice of A. Another surprise is that Best Bet for Simpletons is a **non-transitive game**: if A defeats B, and B defeats C, then we cannot automatically conclude that A defeats C (c.f. rock-paper-scissors).

The analysis of Best Bet for Simpletons is based on the notion of a **correlation polynomial**. We say that B **i-overlaps** with A if the last i digits of A coincide with the first i digits of B. For example, "110110" 1-overlaps, 2-overlaps, and 5-overlaps with "011011", as shown in Figure 1.27.

Given two k-mers A and B, the **correlation** of A and B, denoted $\text{CORR}(A, B) = (c_0, \ldots, c_{k-1})$, is a k-letter binary word such that $c_i = 1$ if B $(k - i)$-overlaps with A, and 0 otherwise. The correlation polynomial of A and B is defined as

$$K_{A,B}(t) = c_0 + c_1 \cdot t + c_2 \cdot t^2 + \cdots + c_{k-1} \cdot t^{k-1}.$$

$$\text{CORR}(A, B)$$

B = 110110		0
B = 110110		1
B = 110110		0
B = 110110		0
B = 110110		1
B = 110110		1
A = 011011		

FIGURE 1.27 The correlation of k-mers A = "011011" and B = "110110" is the string "**010011**".

For the strings A and B in Figure 1.27, their correlation is "010011" and their correlation polynomial is $K_{A,B}(t) = t + t^4 + t^5$.

Next, we write $K_{A,B}$ as shorthand for $K_{A,B}(1/2)$. For the example in Figure 1.27, $K_{A,B} = \frac{1}{2} + \frac{1}{16} + \frac{1}{32} = \frac{19}{32}$. John Conway suggested the following deceivingly simple formula to compute the odds that B will defeat A:

$$\frac{K_{A,A} - K_{A,B}}{K_{B,B} - K_{B,A}}$$

Conway never published a proof of this formula, and Martin Gardner, a leading popular mathematics writer, said the following about the formula:

> *I have no idea why it works. It just cranks out the answer as if by magic, like so many of Conway's other algorithms.*

Bibliography Notes

Using the skew to find replication origins was first proposed by Lobry, 1996 and also described in Grigoriev, 1998. Grigoriev, 2011 provides an excellent introduction to the skew approach, and Sernova and Gelfand, 2008 gave a review of algorithms and software tools for finding replication origins in bacteria. Lundgren et al., 2004 demonstrated that archaea may have multiple *oriC*s. Wang et al., 2011 inserted an artificial *oriC* into the *E. coli* genome and showed that it triggers replication. Xia, 2012 was the first to conjecture that bacteria may have multiple replication origins. Gao and Zhang, 2008 developed the Ori-Finder software program for finding bacterial replication origins.

Liachko et al., 2013 provided the most comprehensive description of the replication origins of yeast. Solov'ev, 1966 was the first to derive accurate formulas for approximating the probabilities of patterns in a string. Gardner, 1974 wrote an excellent introductory article about the Best Bet for Simpletons paradox. Guibas and Odlyzko, 1981 provided an excellent coverage of the overlapping words paradox that illustrates the complexity of computing the probabilities of patterns in a random text. They also derived a rather complicated proof of Conway's formula for Best Bet for Simpletons. Sedgewick and Flajolet, 2013 gave an overview of various approaches for computing the probabilities of patterns in a string.

Do We Have a "Clock" Gene?

The daily schedules of animals, plants, and even bacteria are controlled by an internal timekeeper called the **circadian clock**. Anyone who has experienced the misery of jet lag knows that this clock never stops ticking. Rats and research volunteers alike, when placed in a bunker, naturally maintain a roughly 24-hour cycle of activity and rest in total darkness. And, like any timepiece, the circadian clock can malfunction, resulting in a genetic disease known as **delayed sleep-phase syndrome** (**DSPS**).

The circadian clock must have some basis on the molecular level, which presents many questions. How do *individual cells* in animals and plants (let alone bacteria) know when they should slow down or increase the production of certain proteins? Is there a "clock gene"? Can we explain why heart attacks occur more often in the morning, while asthma attacks are more common at night? And can we identify genes that are responsible for "breaking" the circadian clock to cause DSPS?

In the early 1970s, Ron Konopka and Seymour Benzer identified mutant flies with abnormal circadian patterns and traced the flies' mutations to a single gene. Biologists needed two more decades to discover a similar clock gene in mammals, which was just the first piece of the puzzle. Today, many more circadian genes have been discovered; these genes, having names like *timeless*, *clock*, and *cycle*, orchestrate the behavior of hundreds of other genes and display a high degree of evolutionary conservation across species.

We will first focus on plants, since maintaining the circadian clock in plants is a matter of life and death. Consider how many plant genes should pay attention to the time when the sun rises and sets; indeed, biologists estimate that over a thousand plant genes are circadian, including the genes related to photosynthesis, photo reception, and flowering. These genes must somehow know what time it is in order to change their gene transcript production, or **gene expression**, throughout the day (see DETOUR: PAGE 108 Gene Expression).

It turns out that every plant cell keeps track of day and night independently of other cells, and that just three plant genes, called LCY, CCA1, and TOC1, are the clock's master timekeepers. Such regulatory genes, and the **regulatory proteins** that they encode, are often controlled by external factors (e.g., nutrient availability or sunlight) in order to allow organisms to adjust their gene expression.

For example, regulatory proteins controlling the circadian clock in plants coordinate circadian activity as follows. TOC1 promotes the expression of LCY and CCA1, whereas LCY and CCA1 repress the expression of TOC1, resulting in a **negative feedback loop**. In the morning, sunlight activates the transcription of LCY and CCA1, triggering the repression of TOC1 transcription. As light diminishes, so does the production of LCY and CCA1, which in turn do not repress TOC1 any more. Transcription of TOC1 peaks at night and starts promoting the transcription of LCY and CCA1, which in turn repress the transcription of TOC1, and the cycle begins again.

LCY, CCA1, and TOC1 are able to control the transcription of other genes because the regulatory proteins that they encode are **transcription factors**, or master regulatory proteins that turn other genes on and off. A transcription factor regulates a gene by binding to a specific short DNA interval called a **regulatory motif**, or **transcription factor binding site**, in the gene's **upstream region**, a 600-1000 nucleotide-long region preceding the start of the gene. For example, CCA1 binds to AAAAAATCT in the upstream region of many genes regulated by CCA1.

The life of a bioinformatician would be easy if regulatory motifs were completely conserved, but the reality is more complex, as regulatory motifs may vary at some positions, e.g., CCA1 may instead bind to AA**GAAC**TCT. But how can we locate these regulatory motifs without knowing what they look like in advance? We need to develop algorithms for **motif finding**, the problem of discovering a "hidden message" shared by a collection of strings.

Motif Finding Is More Difficult Than You Think

Identifying the evening element

 PAGE 108 In 2000, Steve Kay used **DNA arrays** (see DETOUR: DNA Arrays) to determine which genes in the plant *Arabidopsis thaliana* are activated at different times of the day. He then extracted the upstream regions of nearly 500 genes that exhibited circadian behavior and looked for frequently appearing patterns in their upstream regions. If you concatenated these upstream regions into a single string, you would find that AAAATATCT is a surprisingly frequent word, appearing 46 times.

 EXERCISE BREAK: What is the expected number of occurrences of a 9-mer in 500 random DNA strings, each of length 1000?

Kay named AAAATATCT the **evening element** and performed a simple experiment to prove that it is indeed the regulatory motif responsible for circadian gene expression in *Arabidopsis thaliana*. After he mutated the evening element in the upstream region of one gene, the gene no longer exhibited circadian behavior.

Whereas the evening element in plants is very conserved, and thus easy to find, motifs having many mutations are more elusive. For example, if you infect a fly with a bacterium, the fly will switch on its **immunity genes** to fight the infection. Thus, some of the genes with elevated expression levels after the infection are likely to be immunity genes. Indeed, some of these genes have 12-mers similar to TCGGGGATTTCC in their upstream regions, the binding site of a transcription factor called **NF-κB** that activates various immunity genes in flies. However, NF-κB binding sites are nowhere near as conserved as the evening element. Figure 2.1 shows ten NF-κB binding sites from the *Drosophila melanogaster* genome; the most popular nucleotides in every column are shown by upper case colored letters.

```
 1    T C G G G G g T T T t t
 2    c C G G t G A c T T a C
 3    a C G G G G A T T T t C
 4    T t G G G G A c T T t t
 5    a a G G G G A c T T C C
 6    T t G G G G A c T T C C
 7    T C G G G G A T T c a t
 8    T C G G G G A T T c C t
 9    T a G G G G A a c T a C
10    T C G G G t A T a a C C
```

FIGURE 2.1 The ten candidate NF-κB binding sites appearing in the *Drosophila melanogaster* genome. The upper case colored letters indicate the most frequent nucleotide in each column.

Hide and seek with motifs

Our aim is to turn the biological challenge of finding regulatory motifs into a computational problem. Below, we have implanted a 15-mer hidden message at a randomly selected position in each of ten randomly generated DNA strings. This example mimics a transcription factor binding site hiding in the upstream regions of ten genes.

```
 1   atgaccgggatactgataaaaaaaagggggggggcgtacacattagataaacgtatgaagtacgttagactcggcgccgccg
 2   acccctattttttgagcagatttagtgacctggaaaaaaaatttgagtacaaaacttttccgaataaaaaaaaaggggggga
 3   tgagtatccctgggatgacttaaaaaaaagggggggtgctctcccgatttttgaatatgtaggatcattcgccagggtccga
 4   gctgagaattggatgaaaaaaaaggggggggtccacgcaatcgcgaaccaacgcggacccaaaggcaagaccgataaaggaga
 5   tcccttttgcggtaatgtgccgggaggctggttacgtagggaagccctaacggacttaataaaaaaaaggggggggcttatag
 6   gtcaatcatgttcttgtgaatggatttaaaaaaaaggggggggaccgcttggcgcacccaaattcagtgtgggcgagcgcaa
 7   cggttttggcccttgttagaggcccccgtaaaaaaaagggggggcaattatgagagagctaatctatcgcgtgcgtgttcat
 8   aacttgagttaaaaaaaaggggggggctggggcacatacaagaggagtcttccttatcagttaatgctgtatgacactatgta
 9   ttggcccattggctaaaagcccaacttgacaaatggaagatagaatccttgcataaaaaaaagggggggaccgaaagggaag
10   ctggtgagcaacgacagattcttacgtgcattagctcgcttccggggatctaatagcacgaagcttaaaaaaaaggggggga
```

This is a simple problem: applying an algorithm for the Frequent Words Problem to the concatenation of these strings will immediately reveal the most frequent 15-mer shown below as the implanted pattern. Since these short strings were randomly generated, it is unlikely that they contain other frequent 15-mers.

```
 1  atgaccgggatactgatAAAAAAAAGGGGGGGggcgtacacattagataaacgtatgaagtacgttagactcggcgccgccg
 2  acccctattttttgagcagatttagtgacctggaaaaaaaatttgagtacaaaacttttccgaataAAAAAAAAGGGGGGGa
 3  tgagtatccctgggatgactttAAAAAAAAGGGGGGGtgctctcccgatttttgaatatgtaggatcattcgccagggtccga
 4  gctgagaattggatgAAAAAAAAGGGGGGGtccacgcaatcgcgaaccaacgcggacccaaaggcaagaccgataaaggaga
 5  tcccttttgcggtaatgtgccgggaggctggttacgtagggaagccctaacggacttaatAAAAAAAAGGGGGGGcttatag
 6  gtcaatcatgttcttgtgaatggatttAAAAAAAAGGGGGGGgaccgcttggcgcacccaaattcagtgtgggcgagcgcaa
 7  cggttttggcccttgttagaggcccccgtAAAAAAAAGGGGGGGcaattatgagagagctaatctatcgcgtgcgtgttcat
 8  aacttgagttAAAAAAAAGGGGGGGctggggcacatacaagaggagtcttccttatcagttaatgctgtatgacactatgta
 9  ttggcccattggctaaaagcccaacttgacaaatggaagatagaatccttgcatAAAAAAAAGGGGGGGaccgaaagggaag
10  ctggtgagcaacgacagattcttacgtgcattagctcgcttccggggatctaatagcacgaagcttAAAAAAAAGGGGGGGa
```

Now imagine that instead of implanting exactly the same pattern into all sequences, we mutate the pattern before inserting it into each sequence by randomly changing the nucleotides at four randomly selected positions within each implanted 15-mer, as shown below.

```
 1  atgaccgggatactgatAgAAgAAAGGttGGGggcgtacacattagataaacgtatgaagtacgttagactcggcgccgccg
 2  acccctattttttgagcagatttagtgacctggaaaaaaaatttgagtacaaaacttttccgaatacAAtAAAAcGGcGGGa
 3  tgagtatccctgggatgactttAAAAtAAtGGaGtGGtgctctcccgatttttgaatatgtaggatcattcgccagggtccga
 4  gctgagaattggatgcAAAAAAAGGGattGtccacgcaatcgcgaaccaacgcggacccaaaggcaagaccgataaaggaga
 5  tcccttttgcggtaatgtgccgggaggctggttacgtagggaagcccaacggacttaatAtAAtAAAGGaaGGGcttatag
 6  gtcaatcatgttcttgtgaatggatttAAcAAtAAGGGctGGgaccgcttggcgcacccaaattcagtgtgggcgagcgcaa
 7  cggttttggcccttgttagaggcccccgtAtAAAcAAGGaGGGccaattatgagagagctaatctatcgcgtgcgtgttcat
 8  aacttgagttAAAAAAtAGGGaGccctggggcacatacaagaggagtcttccttatcagttaatgctgtatgacactatgta
 9  ttggcccattggctaaaagcccaacttgacaaatggaagatagaatccttgcatActAAAAAGGAGcGGaccgaaagggaag
10  ctggtgagcaacgacagattcttacgtgcattagctcgcttccggggatctaatagcacgaagcttActAAAAAGGaGcGGa
```

The Frequent Words Problem is not going to help us, since **AAAAAAAAGGGGGGG** does not even appear in the sequences above. Perhaps, then, we could apply our solution to the Frequent Words with Mismatches Problem. However, in Chapter 1, we implemented an algorithm for the Frequent Words with Mismatches Problem aimed at finding hidden messages with a small number of mismatches and a small k-mer size (e.g., one or two mismatches for *DnaA* boxes of length 9). This algorithm will become too slow when searching for the implanted motif above, which is longer and has more mutations.

Furthermore, concatenating all the sequences into a single string is inadequate because it does not correctly model the biological problem of motif finding. A *DnaA* box is a pattern that clumps, or appears frequently, within a relatively short interval of the genome. In contrast, a regulatory motif is a pattern that appears at least once (perhaps with variation) in each of many different regions that are scattered throughout the genome.

A brute force algorithm for motif finding

Given a collection of strings *Dna* and an integer *d*, a *k*-mer is a **(*k*, *d*)-motif** if it appears in every string from *Dna* with at most *d* mismatches. For example, the implanted 15-mer in the strings above represents a (15, 4)-motif.

Implanted Motif Problem:
Find all (k, d)-motifs in a collection of strings.

> **Input**: A collection of strings *Dna*, and integers *k* and *d*.
> **Output**: All (*k*, *d*)-motifs in *Dna*.

Brute force search (also known as **exhaustive search**) is a general problem-solving technique that explores all possible candidate solutions and checks whether each candidate solves the problem. Such algorithms require little effort to design and are guaranteed to produce a correct solution, but they may take an enormous amount of time, and the number of candidates may be too large to check.

A brute force approach for solving the Implanted Motif Problem is based on the observation that any (*k*, *d*)-motif must be at most *d* mismatches apart from some *k*-mer appearing in one of the strings of *Dna*. Therefore, we can generate all such *k*-mers and then check which of them are (*k*, *d*)-motifs. If you have forgotten how to generate these *k*-mers, recall **CHARGING STATION: Generating the Neighborhood of a String**.

PAGE 49

    MOTIFENUMERATION(Dna, k, d)
        Patterns ← an empty set
        for each k-mer Pattern in Dna
            for each k-mer Pattern' differing from Pattern by at most d mismatches
                if Pattern' appears in each string from Dna with at most d mismatches
                    add Pattern' to Patterns
        remove duplicates from Patterns
        return Patterns

MOTIFENUMERATION is unfortunately rather slow for large values of *k* and *d*, and so we will try a different approach instead. Maybe we can detect an implanted pattern simply by identifying the two most similar *k*-mers between each pair of strings in *Dna*? However, consider the implanted 15-mers **AgAAgAAAGGttGGG** and **cAAtAAAAcGGGGcG**, each of which differs from **AAAAAAAAGGGGGGG** by four mismatches. Although these

15-mers look similar to the correct motif **AAAAAAAAGGGGGGG**, they are not so similar when compared to each other, having eight mismatches:

Ag**A**A**g**A**A**A**GG**tt**GGG**
 | | | | | || |
c**AA**t**AAAA**c**GGGG**c**G**

Since these two implanted patterns are so different, we should be concerned whether we will be able to find them by searching for the most similar *k*-mers among pairs of strings in *Dna*.

In the rest of the chapter, we will benchmark our motif finding algorithms by using a particularly challenging instance of the Implanted Motif Problem. The **Subtle Motif Problem** refers to implanting a 15-mer with four random mutations in ten randomly generated 600 nucleotide-long strings (the typical length of many upstream regulatory regions). The instance of the Subtle Motif Problem that we will use has the implanted 15-mer **AAAAAAAAGGGGGGG**.

It turns out that thousands of pairs of randomly occurring 15-mers in our dataset for the Subtle Motif Problem are fewer than 8 nucleotides apart from each other, preventing us from identifying the true implanted motifs by pairwise comparisons.

Scoring Motifs

From motifs to profile matrices and consensus strings

Although the Implanted Motif Problem offers a useful abstraction of the biological problem of motif finding, it has some limitations. For example, when Steve Kay used a DNA array to infer the set of circadian genes in plants, he did not expect that *all* genes in the resulting set would have the evening element (or its variants) in their upstream regions. Similarly, biologists do not expect that all genes with an elevated expression level in infected flies must be regulated by NF-$\varkappa$B. DNA array experiments are inherently noisy, and some genes identified by these experiments have nothing to do with the circadian clock in plants or immunity genes in flies. For such noisy datasets, any algorithm for the Implanted Motif Problem would fail, because as long as a single sequence does not contain the transcription factor binding site, a (k, d)-motif does not exist!

A more appropriate problem formulation would score individual instances of motifs depending on how similar they are to an "ideal" motif (i.e., a transcription factor binding site that binds the best to the transcription factor). However, since the ideal motif is unknown, we attempt to select a k-mer from each string and score these k-mers depending on how similar they are *to each other*.

To define scoring, consider t DNA strings, each of length n, and select a k-mer from each string to form a collection *Motifs*, which we represent as a $t \times k$ **motif matrix**. In Figure 2.2, which shows the motif matrix for the NF-$\varkappa$B binding sites from Figure 2.1, we indicate the most frequent nucleotide in each column of the motif matrix by upper case letters. If there are multiple most popular nucleotides in a column, then we arbitrarily select one of them to break the tie. Note that positions 2 and 3 are the most conserved (nucleotide **G** is completely conserved in these positions), whereas position 10 is the least conserved.

By varying the choice of k-mers in each string, we can construct a large number of different motif matrices from a given sample of DNA strings. Our goal is to select k-mers resulting in the most "conserved" motif matrix, meaning the matrix with the most upper case letters (and thus the fewest number of lower case letters). Leaving aside the question of how we select such k-mers, we will first focus on how to score the resulting motif matrices, defining SCORE(*Motifs*) as the number of unpopular (lower case) letters in the motif matrix *Motifs*. Our goal is to find a collection of k-mers that *minimizes* this score.

EXERCISE BREAK: The minimum possible value of SCORE(*Motifs*) is 0 (if all rows in the $t \times k$ matrix *Motifs* are the same). What is the maximum possible value of SCORE(*Motifs*) in terms of t and k?

We can construct the $4 \times k$ **count matrix** COUNT(*Motifs*) counting the number of occurrences of each nucleotide in each column of the motif matrix; the (i, j)-th element of COUNT(*Motifs*) stores the number of times that nucleotide i appears in column j of *Motifs*. We will further divide all of the elements in the count matrix by t, the number of rows in *Motifs*. This results in a **profile matrix** $P = $ PROFILE(*Motifs*) for which $P_{i,j}$ is the *frequency* of the i-th nucleotide in the j-th column of the motif matrix. Note that the elements of any column of the profile matrix sum to 1.

Finally, we form a **consensus string**, denoted CONSENSUS(*Motifs*), from the most popular nucleotides in each column of the motif matrix (ties are broken arbitrarily). If we select *Motifs* correctly from the collection of upstream regions, then CONSENSUS(*Motifs*) provides an ideal candidate regulatory motif for these regions. For example, the consensus string for the NF-$\varkappa$B binding sites in Figure 2.2 is **TCGGGGATTTCC**.

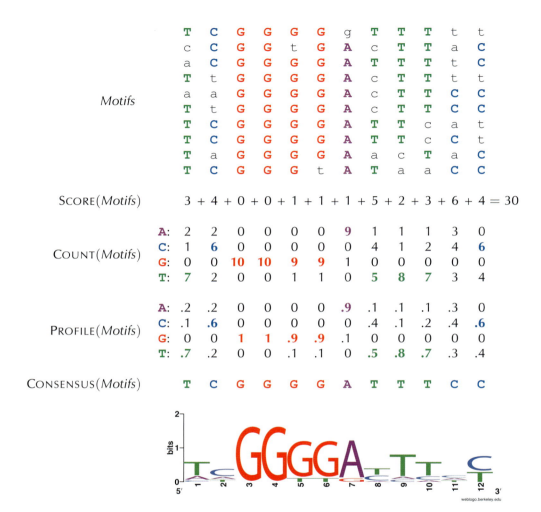

		T	C	G	G	G	G	g	T	T	T	t	t
		c	C	G	G	t	G	A	c	T	T	a	C
		a	C	G	G	G	G	A	T	T	T	t	C
		T	t	G	G	G	G	A	c	T	T	t	t
Motifs		a	a	G	G	G	G	A	c	T	T	C	C
		T	t	G	G	G	G	A	c	T	T	C	C
		T	C	G	G	G	G	A	T	T	c	a	t
		T	C	G	G	G	G	A	T	T	c	C	t
		T	a	G	G	G	G	A	a	c	T	a	C
		T	C	G	G	G	t	A	T	a	a	C	C

SCORE(*Motifs*) $\quad 3 + 4 + 0 + 0 + 1 + 1 + 1 + 5 + 2 + 3 + 6 + 4 = 30$

	A:	2	2	0	0	0	0	9	1	1	1	3	0
COUNT(*Motifs*)	**C:**	1	6	0	0	0	0	0	4	1	2	4	6
	G:	0	0	10	10	9	9	1	0	0	0	0	0
	T:	7	2	0	0	1	1	0	5	8	7	3	4

	A:	.2	.2	0	0	0	0	.9	.1	.1	.1	.3	0
PROFILE(*Motifs*)	**C:**	.1	.6	0	0	0	0	0	.4	.1	.2	.4	.6
	G:	0	0	1	1	.9	.9	.1	0	0	0	0	0
	T:	.7	.2	0	0	.1	.1	0	.5	.8	.7	.3	.4

CONSENSUS(*Motifs*) T C G G G G A T T T C C

FIGURE 2.2 From motif matrix to count matrix to profile matrix to consensus string to motif logo. The NF-*x*B binding sites form a 10 × 12 motif matrix, with the most frequent nucleotide in each column shown in upper case letters and all other nucleotides shown in lower case letters. SCORE(*Motifs*) counts the total number of unpopular (lower case) symbols in the motif matrix. The motif matrix results in a 4 × 12 count matrix holding the nucleotide counts in every column of the motif matrix; a profile matrix holding the frequencies of nucleotides in every column of the motif matrix; and a consensus string formed by the most frequent nucleotide in each column of the count matrix. Finally, the motif logo is a common way to visualize the conservation of various positions within a motif. The total height of the letters depicts the information content of the position.

Towards a more adequate motif scoring function

Consider the second column (containing 6 C, 2 A, and 2 T) and the final column (containing 6 C and 4 T) in the motif matrix from Figure 2.2. Both of these columns contribute 4 to SCORE(*Motifs*).

> **STOP and Think:** Does scoring these two columns equally make sense biologically?

For many biological motifs, certain positions feature two nucleotides with roughly the same ability to bind to a transcription factor. For example, the sixteen nucleotide-long CSRE transcription factor binding site in the yeast *S. cerevisiae* consists of five strongly conserved positions in addition to eleven weakly conserved positions, each of which features two nucleotides with similar frequencies (Figure 2.3).

1	2	3	4	5	6	7	8	9	10	11	12	13	14	15	16
C	G/C	G/T	T/A	C/T	G/C	C/G	A	T	G/T	C/G	A	T	C/T	C/T	G/T

FIGURE 2.3 The CSRE transcription factor binding site in *S. cerevisiae* is 16 nucleotides long, but only five of these positions (1, 8, 9, 12, 13) are strongly conserved. The remaining 11 positions can take one of two different nucleotides.

Following this example, a more appropriate representation of the consensus string **TCGGGGATTTCC** for the NF-*κ*B binding sites should include viable alternatives to the most popular nucleotides in each column (see Figure 2.4). In this sense, the last column (6 C, 4 T) in the motif matrix from Figure 2.2 is "more conserved" than the second column (6 C, 2 A, 2 T) and should receive a lower score.

1	2	3	4	5	6	7	8	9	10	11	12
T	C	G	G	G	G	A	T/C	T	T	C	C/T

FIGURE 2.4 Taking nucleotides in each column of the NF-*κ*B binding site motif matrix from Figure 2.2 with frequency at least 0.4 yields a representation of the NF-*κ*B binding sites with ten strongly conserved positions and two weakly conserved positions (8 and 12).

Entropy and the motif logo

Every column of PROFILE(*Motifs*) corresponds to a **probability distribution**, or a collection of nonnegative numbers that sum to 1. For example, the second column in Figure 2.2 corresponds to the probabilities 0.2, 0.6, 0.0, and 0.2 for A, C, G, and T, respectively.

   Entropy is a measure of the uncertainty of a probability distribution $(p_1, \ldots, p_N)$, and is defined as

$$H(p_1, \ldots, p_N) = -\sum_{i=1}^{N} p_i \cdot \log_2 (p_i).$$

For example, the entropy of the probability distribution (0.2, 0.6, 0.0, 0.2) corresponding to the second column of the profile matrix in Figure 2.2 is

$$-(0.2 \log_2 0.2 + 0.6 \log_2 0.6 + 0.0 \log_2 0.0 + 0.2 \log_2 0.2) \approx 1.371,$$

whereas the entropy of the more conserved final column $(0.0, 0.6, 0.0, 0.4)$ is

$$-(0.0 \log_2 0.0 + 0.6 \log_2 0.6 + 0.0 \log_2 0.0 + 0.4 \log_2 0.4) \approx 0.971,$$

and the entropy of the very conserved 5th column $(0.0, 0.0, 0.9, 0.1)$ is

$$-(0.0 \log_2 0.0 + 0.0 \log_2 0.0 + 0.9 \log_2 0.9 + 0.1 \log_2 0.1) \approx 0.467.$$

Note that technically, $\log_2 0$ is not defined, but in the computation of entropy, we assume that $0 \cdot \log_2 0$ is equal to 0.

STOP and Think: What are the maximum and minimum possible values for the entropy of a probability distribution containing four values?

The entropy of the completely conserved third column of the profile matrix in Figure 2.2 is 0, which is the minimum possible entropy. On the other hand, a column with equally-likely nucleotides (all probabilities equal to $1/4$) has maximum possible entropy $-4 \cdot 1/4 \cdot \log_2 (1/4) = 2$. In general, the more conserved the column, the smaller its entropy. Thus, entropy offers an improved method of scoring motif matrices: the entropy of a motif matrix is defined as the sum of the entropies of its columns. In this book, we will continue to use SCORE(*Motifs*) for simplicity, but the entropy score is used more often in practice.

EXERCISE BREAK: Compute the entropy of the NF-*x*B motif matrix from Figure 2.2.

Another application of entropy is the **motif logo**, a diagram for visualizing motif conservation that consists of a stack of letters at each position (see the bottom of Figure 2.2). The relative sizes of letters indicate their frequency in the column. The total height of the letters in each column is based on the **information content** of the column, which is defined as $2 - H(p_1, \ldots, p_N)$. The lower the entropy, the higher the information content, meaning that tall columns in the motif logo are highly conserved.

From Motif Finding to Finding a Median String

The Motif Finding Problem

Now that we have a good grasp of scoring a collection of *k*-mers, we are ready to formulate the Motif Finding Problem.

Motif Finding Problem:
Given a collection of strings, find a set of k-mers, one from each string, that minimizes the score of the resulting motif.

> **Input**: A collection of strings *Dna* and an integer *k*.
> **Output**: A collection *Motifs* of *k*-mers, one from each string in *Dna*, minimizing SCORE(*Motifs*) among all possible choices of *k*-mers.

A brute force algorithm for the Motif Finding Problem, **BRUTEFORCEMOTIFSEARCH**, considers every possible choice of *k*-mers *Motifs* from *Dna* (one *k*-mer from each string of *n* nucleotides) and returns the collection *Motifs* having minimum score. Because there are $n - k + 1$ choices of *k*-mers in each of *t* sequences, there are $(n - k + 1)^t$ different ways to form *Motifs*. For each choice of *Motifs*, the algorithm calculates SCORE(*Motifs*), which requires $k \cdot t$ steps. Thus, assuming that *k* is much smaller than *n*, the overall running time of the algorithm is $\mathcal{O}(n^t \cdot k \cdot t)$. We need to come up with a faster algorithm!

Reformulating the Motif Finding Problem

Because **BRUTEFORCEMOTIFSEARCH** is inefficient, we will think about motif finding in a different way. Instead of exploring all *Motifs* in *Dna* and deriving the consensus string from *Motifs* afterwards,

$$Motifs \rightarrow \text{CONSENSUS}(Motifs),$$

we will explore all potential *k*-mer consensus strings first and then find the best possible collection *Motifs* for each consensus string,

$$\text{CONSENSUS}(Motifs) \rightarrow Motifs.$$

To reformulate the Motif Finding Problem, we need to devise an alternative way of computing SCORE(*Motifs*). Until now, we have computed SCORE(*Motifs*), the number of lower case letters in the motif matrix, column-by-column. For example, in Figure 2.2, we computed SCORE(*Motifs*) for the NF-*κ*B motif matrix as

$$3 + 4 + 0 + 0 + 1 + 1 + 1 + 5 + 2 + 3 + 6 + 4 = 30.$$

Figure 2.5 illustrates that SCORE(*Motifs*) can just as easily be computed row-by-row as

$$3 + 4 + 2 + 4 + 3 + 2 + 3 + 2 + 4 + 3 = 30.$$

Note that each element in the latter sum represents the number of mismatches between the consensus string **TCGGGGATTTCC** and a motif in the corresponding row of the motif matrix, i.e., the Hamming distance between these strings. For the first row of the motif matrix in Figure 2.5, $d(\mathbf{TCGGGGATTTCC}, \mathbf{TCGGGG}g\mathbf{TTT}tt) = 3$.

Given a collection of *k*-mers $Motifs = \{Motif_1, ..., Motif_t\}$ and a *k*-mer *Pattern*, we now define $d(Pattern, Motifs)$ as the sum of Hamming distances between *Pattern* and each $Motif_i$,

$$d(Pattern, Motifs) = \sum_{i=1}^{t} \text{HAMMINGDISTANCE}(Pattern, Motif_i).$$

Because SCORE(*Motifs*) corresponds to counting the lower case elements of *Motifs* column-by-column and $d(\text{CONSENSUS}(Motifs), Motifs)$ corresponds to counting these elements row-by-row, we obtain that

$$\text{SCORE}(Motifs) = d(\text{CONSENSUS}(Motifs), Motifs).$$

T	**C**	**G**	**G**	**G**	**G**	g	**T**	**T**	**T**	t	t	3
c	**C**	**G**	**G**	t	**G**	**A**	c	**T**	**T**	a	**C**	4
a	**C**	**G**	**G**	**G**	**G**	**A**	**T**	**T**	**T**	t	**C**	2
T	t	**G**	**G**	**G**	**G**	**A**	c	**T**	**T**	t	t	4
a	a	**G**	**G**	**G**	**G**	**A**	c	**T**	**T**	**C**	**C**	3
T	t	**G**	**G**	**G**	**G**	**A**	c	**T**	**T**	**C**	**C**	2
T	**C**	**G**	**G**	**G**	**G**	**A**	**T**	**T**	c	a	t	3
T	**C**	**G**	**G**	**G**	**G**	**A**	**T**	**T**	c	**C**	t	2
T	a	**G**	**G**	**G**	**G**	**A**	a	c	**T**	a	**C**	4
T	**C**	**G**	**G**	**G**	t	**A**	**T**	a	a	**C**	**C**	+ 3

Motifs (label at left)

SCORE(*Motifs*)   3 + 4 + 0 + 0 + 1 + 1 + 1 + 5 + 2 + 3 + 6 + 4 = **30**

CONSENSUS(*Motifs*)   **T   C   G   G   G   G   A   T   T   T   C   C**

FIGURE 2.5 The motif and score matrices in addition to the consensus string for the NF-xB binding sites, reproduced from Figure 2.2. Rather than count the non-consensus elements (i.e., lower case nucleotides) column-by-column, we can count them row-by-row, as highlighted on the right of the motifs matrix. Each value at the end of a row corresponds to the Hamming distance between that row and the consensus string.

This equation gives us an idea. Instead of searching for a collection of k-mers *Motifs* minimizing SCORE(*Motifs*), let's instead search for a potential consensus string *Pattern* minimizing $d(Pattern, Motifs)$ among all possible k-mers *Pattern* and all possible choices of k-mers *Motifs* in *Dna*. This problem is equivalent to the Motif Finding Problem.

Equivalent Motif Finding Problem:

Given a collection of strings, find a pattern and a collection of k-mers (one from each string) that minimizes the distance between all possible patterns and all possible collections of k-mers.

Input: A collection of strings *Dna* and an integer k.
Output: A k-mer *Pattern* and a collection of k-mers *Motifs*, one from each string in *Dna*, minimizing $d(Pattern, Motifs)$ among all possible choices of *Pattern* and *Motifs*.

The Median String Problem

But wait a second — have we not just made our task more difficult? Instead of having to search for all *Motifs*, we now have to search all *Motifs* as well as all *k*-mers *Pattern*. The key observation for solving the Equivalent Motif Finding Problem is that, given *Pattern*, we don't need to explore all possible collections *Motifs* in order to minimize $d(Pattern, Motifs)$.

To explain how this can be done, we define MOTIFS(*Pattern, Dna*) as a collection of *k*-mers that minimizes $d(Pattern, Motifs)$ for a given *Pattern* and all possible sets of *k*-mers *Motifs* in *Dna*. For example, for the strings *Dna* shown below, the five colored 3-mers represent MOTIFS(**AAA**, *Dna*).

$$
Dna \quad
\begin{array}{l}
\texttt{ttacctt}\textbf{AAC} \\
\texttt{g}\textbf{ATA}\texttt{tctgtc} \\
\textbf{ACG}\texttt{gcgttcg} \\
\texttt{ccct}\textbf{AAA}\texttt{gag} \\
\texttt{cgtc}\textbf{AGA}\texttt{ggt}
\end{array}
$$

STOP and Think: Given a collection of strings *Dna* and a *k*-mer *Pattern*, design a fast algorithm for generating MOTIFS(*Pattern, Dna*).

The reason why we don't need to consider all possible collections *Motifs* in *Dna* = $\{Dna_1, ..., Dna_t\}$ is that we can generate the *k*-mers in MOTIFS(*Pattern, Dna*) one at a time; that is, we can select a *k*-mer in Dna_i independently of selecting *k*-mers in all other strings in *Dna*. Given a *k*-mer *Pattern* and a longer string *Text*, we use $d(Pattern, Text)$ to denote the minimum Hamming distance between *Pattern* and any *k*-mer in *Text*,

$$
d(Pattern, Text) = \min_{\text{all } k\text{-mers } Pattern' \text{ in } Text} \text{HAMMINGDISTANCE}(Pattern, Pattern').
$$

For example,

$$
d(\textbf{GATTCTCA}, \texttt{gcaaa}\textbf{GACGCTGA}\texttt{ccaa}) = \textbf{3}.
$$

A *k*-mer in *Text* that achieves the minimum Hamming distance with *Pattern* is denoted MOTIF(*Pattern, Text*). For the above example,

$$
\text{MOTIF}(\textbf{GATTCTCA}, \texttt{gcaaa}\textbf{GACGCTGA}\texttt{ccaa}) = \textbf{GACGCTGA}.
$$

We note that the notation MOTIF(*Pattern*, *Text*) is ambiguous because there may be multiple *k*-mers in *Text* that achieve the minimum Hamming distance with *Pattern*. For example, MOTIF(**AAG**, gc**AAT**cct**CAG**c) could be either **AAT** or **CAG**. However, this ambiguity does not affect the following analysis.

Given a *k*-mer *Pattern* and a set of strings *Dna* = {*Dna₁*, ..., *Dnaₜ*}, we define *d*(*Pattern*, *Dna*) as the sum of distances between *Pattern* and all strings in *Dna*,

$$d(Pattern, Dna) = \sum_{i=1}^{t} d(Pattern, Dna_i).$$

For example, for the strings *Dna* shown below, $d(\textbf{AAA}, Dna) = \textbf{1} + \textbf{1} + \textbf{2} + \textbf{0} + \textbf{1} = \textbf{5}$.

	ttacctt**AAC**	**1**
	g**ATA**tctgtc	**1**
Dna	**ACG**gcgttcg	**2**
	ccct**AAA**gag	**0**
	cgtc**AGA**ggt	**1**

Our goal is to find a *k*-mer *Pattern* that minimizes *d*(*Pattern*, *Dna*) over all *k*-mers *Pattern*, the same task that the Equivalent Motif Finding Problem is trying to achieve. We call such a *k*-mer a **median string** for *Dna*.

Median String Problem:

Find a median string.

> **Input**: A collection of strings *Dna* and an integer *k*.
> **Output**: A *k*-mer *Pattern* minimizing *d*(*Pattern*, *Dna*) among all *k*-mers *Pattern*.

2B

Notice that finding a median string requires solving a double minimization problem. We must find a *k*-mer *Pattern* that minimizes *d*(*Pattern*, *Dna*), where this function is itself computed by taking a minimum over all choices of *k*-mers from each string in *Dna*. The pseudocode for a brute-force algorithm, **MEDIANSTRING**, is given below.

MEDIANSTRING(*Dna*, *k*)
    distance ← ∞
    for each *k*-mer *Pattern* from AA...AA to TT...TT
        if *distance* > *d*(*Pattern*, *Dna*)
            distance ← *d*(*Pattern*, *Dna*)
            Median ← *Pattern*
    return *Median*

PAGE 107

CHARGING STATION (Solving the Median String Problem): Although this pseudocode is short, it is not without potential pitfalls. Check out this Charging Station if you fall into one of them.

STOP and Think: Instead of making a time-consuming search through all possible *k*-mers in **MEDIANSTRING**, can you only search through all *k*-mers that appear in *Dna*?

Why have we reformulated the Motif Finding Problem?

To see why we reformulated the Motif Finding Problem as the equivalent Median String Problem, consider the runtimes of **MEDIANSTRING** and **BRUTEFORCEMOTIFS**. The former algorithm computes *d*(*Pattern*, *Dna*) for each of the 4^k *k*-mers *Pattern*. Each computation of *d*(*Pattern*, *Dna*) requires a single pass over each string in *Dna*, which requires approximately $k \cdot n \cdot t$ operations for *t* strings of length *n* in *Dna*. Therefore, **MEDIANSTRING** has a running time of $\mathcal{O}\left(4^k \cdot n \cdot k \cdot t\right)$, which in practice compares favorably with the $\mathcal{O}\left(n^t \cdot k \cdot t\right)$ running time of **BRUTEFORCEMOTIFSEARCH** because the length of a motif (*k*) typically does not exceed 20 nucleotides, whereas *t* is measured in the thousands.

The Median String Problem teaches an important lesson, which is that sometimes rethinking how a problem is formulated can lead to dramatic improvements in the runtime required to solve it. In this case, our simple observation that SCORE(*Motifs*) could just as easily be computed row-by-row as column-by-column produced the faster **MEDIANSTRING** algorithm.

Of course, the ultimate test of a bioinformatics algorithm is how it performs in practice. Unfortunately, since **MEDIANSTRING** has to consider 4^k *k*-mers, it becomes too slow for the Subtle Motif Problem, for which *k* = 15. We will run **MEDIANSTRING** with $k = 13$ in the hope that it will capture a substring of the correct 15-mer motif. The algorithm still requires half a day to run on our computer and returns the median string **AAAAAtAGaGGGG** (with distance 29). This 13-mer is not a substring of the implanted pattern **AAAAAAAAGGGGGGG**, but it does come close.

> **STOP and Think:** How can a slightly incorrect median string of length 13 help us find the correct median string of length 15?

We have thus far assumed that the value of k is known in advance, which is not the case in practice. As a result, we are forced to run our motif finding algorithms for different values of k and then try to deduce the correct motif length. Since some regulatory motifs are rather long — later in the chapter, we will search for a biologically important motif of length 20 — **MEDIANSTRING** may be too slow to find them.

Greedy Motif Search

Using the profile matrix to roll dice

Many algorithms are iterative procedures that must choose among many alternatives at each iteration. Some of these alternatives may lead to correct solutions, whereas others may not. **Greedy algorithms** select the "most attractive" alternative at each iteration. For example, a greedy algorithm in chess might attempt to capture an opponent's most valuable piece at every move. Yet anyone who has played chess knows that this strategy of looking only one move ahead will likely produce disastrous results. In general, most greedy algorithms typically fail to find an exact solution of the problem; instead, they are often fast **heuristics** that trade accuracy for speed in order to find an *approximate* solution. Nevertheless, for many biological problems that we will study in this book, greedy algorithms will prove quite useful.

In this section, we will explore a greedy approach to motif finding. Again, let *Motifs* be a collection of k-mers taken from t strings *Dna*. Recall from our discussion of entropy that we can view each column of PROFILE(*Motifs*) as a four-sided biased die. Thus, a profile matrix with k columns can be viewed as a collection of k dice, which we will roll to randomly generate a k-mer. For example, if the first column of the profile matrix is $(0.2, 0.1, 0.0, 0.7)$, then we generate **A** as the first nucleotide with probability 0.2, **C** with probability 0.1, **G** with probability 0.0, and **T** with probability 0.7.

In Figure 2.6, we reproduce the profile matrix for the NF-$\varkappa$B binding sites from Figure 2.2, where the lone colored entry in the i-th column corresponds to the i-th nucleotide in **ACGGGGATTACC**. The probability Pr(**ACGGGGATTACC**|*Profile*) that *Profile* generates **ACGGGGATTACC** is computed by simply multiplying the highlighted entries in the profile matrix.

Profile

A:	.2	.2	.0	.0	.0	.0	**.9**	.1	.1	**.1**	.3	.0
C:	.1	**.6**	.0	.0	.0	.0	.0	.4	.1	**.2**	**.4**	**.6**
G:	.0	.0	**1**	**1**	**.9**	**.9**	.1	.0	.0	.0	.0	.0
T:	.7	.2	.0	.0	.1	.1	.0	**.5**	**.8**	.7	.3	.4

Pr(**ACGGGGATTACC**|*Profile*) $= .2 \cdot .6 \cdot 1 \cdot 1 \cdot .9 \cdot .9 \cdot .9 \cdot .5 \cdot .8 \cdot .1 \cdot .4 \cdot .6 = 0.000839808$

FIGURE 2.6 We can generate a random string based on a profile matrix by selecting the *i*-th nucleotide in the string with the probability corresponding to that nucleotide in the *i*-th column of the profile matrix. The probability that a profile matrix will produce a given string is given by the product of individual nucleotide probabilities.

A *k*-mer tends to have a higher probability when it is more similar to the consensus string of a profile. For example, for the NF-*κ*B profile matrix shown in Figure 2.6 and its consensus string **TCGGGGATTTCC**,

$$Pr(\textbf{TCGGGGATTTCC}|Profile) = 0.7 \cdot 0.6 \cdot 1.0 \cdot 1.0 \cdot 0.9 \cdot 0.9 \cdot 0.9 \cdot 0.5 \cdot 0.8 \cdot 0.7 \cdot 0.4 \cdot 0.6$$
$$= 0.0205753,$$

which is larger than the value of Pr(**ACGGGGATTACC**|*Profile*) $= 0.000839808$ that we computed in Figure 2.6.

EXERCISE BREAK: Compute Pr(**TCGTGGATTTCC**|*Profile*), where *Profile* is the matrix shown in Figure 2.6.

Given a profile matrix *Profile*, we can evaluate the probability of every *k*-mer in a string *Text* and find a ***Profile*-most probable** *k*-mer in *Text*, i.e., a *k*-mer that was most likely to have been generated by *Profile* among all *k*-mers in *Text*. For the NF-*κ*B profile matrix, **ACGGGGATTACC** is the *Profile*-most probable 12-mer in ggt**ACGGGGATTACC**t. Indeed, every other 12-mer in this string has probability 0. In general, if there are multiple *Profile*-most probable *k*-mers in *Text*, then we select the first such *k*-mer occurring in *Text*.

***Profile*-most Probable *k*-mer Problem**:

Find a Profile-most probable k-mer in a string.

> **Input**: A string *Text*, an integer *k*, and a 4 × *k* matrix *Profile*.
> **Output**: A *Profile*-most probable *k*-mer in *Text*.

Our proposed greedy motif search algorithm, **GREEDYMOTIFSEARCH**, tries each of the *k*-mers in Dna_1 as the first motif. For a given choice of *k*-mer $Motif_1$ in Dna_1, it then builds a profile matrix *Profile* for this lone *k*-mer, and sets $Motif_2$ equal to the *Profile*-most probable *k*-mer in Dna_2. It then iterates by updating *Profile* as the profile matrix formed from $Motif_1$ and $Motif_2$, and sets $Motif_2$ equal to the *Profile*-most probable *k*-mer in Dna_3. In general, after finding $i-1$ *k*-mers *Motifs* in the first $i-1$ strings of *Dna*, **GREEDYMOTIFSEARCH** constructs *Profile(Motifs)* and selects the *Profile*-most probable *k*-mer from Dna_i based on this profile matrix. After obtaining a *k*-mer from each string to generate a collection *Motifs*, **GREEDYMOTIFSEARCH** tests to see whether *Motifs* outscores the current best scoring collection of motifs and then moves $Motif_1$ one symbol over in Dna_1, beginning the entire process of generating *Motifs* again.

GREEDYMOTIFSEARCH(*Dna*, *k*, *t*)
    BestMotifs ← motif matrix formed by first *k*-mers in each string from *Dna*
    for each *k*-mer *Motif* in the first string from *Dna*
        $Motif_1$ ← *Motif*
        for i = 2 to *t*
            form *Profile* from motifs $Motif_1$, ..., $Motif_{i-1}$
            $Motif_i$ ← *Profile*-most probable *k*-mer in the *i*-th string in *Dna*
        Motifs ← ($Motif_1$, ..., $Motif_t$)
        if SCORE(*Motifs*) < SCORE(*BestMotifs*)
            BestMotifs ← *Motifs*
    return *BestMotifs*

If you are not satisfied with the performance of **GREEDYMOTIFSEARCH** — even if you implemented it correctly — then wait until we discuss this algorithm in the next section.

Analyzing greedy motif finding

In contrast to **MEDIANSTRING**, **GREEDYMOTIFSEARCH** is fast and can be run with $k = 15$ to solve the Subtle Motif Problem (recall that we settled for $k = 13$ in the case of **MedianString**). However, it trades speed for accuracy and returns the 15-mer **gtAAAtAgaGatGtG** (total distance: 58), which is very different from the true implanted motif **AAAAAAAAGGGGGGG**.

STOP and Think: Why does **GreedyMotifSearch** perform so poorly?

At first glance, **GreedyMotifSearch** may seem like a reasonable algorithm, but it is not! Let's see whether **GreedyMotifSearch** will find the (4, 1)-motif **ACGT** implanted in the following strings *Dna*:

$$tt\textbf{ACCT}taac$$
$$g\textbf{ATGT}ctgtc$$
$$acg\textbf{GCGT}tag$$
$$ccta\textbf{ACGA}g$$
$$cgtcag\textbf{AGGT}$$

We will assume that the algorithm has already correctly chosen the implanted 4-mer **ACCT** from the first string in *Dna* and constructed the corresponding *Profile*:

A:	**1**	0	0	0
C:	0	**1**	**1**	0
G:	0	0	0	0
T:	0	0	0	**1**

The algorithm is now ready to search for a *Profile*-most probable 4-mer in the second sequence. The issue, however, is that there are so many zeros in the profile matrix that the probability of every 4-mer but **ACCT** is zero! Thus, unless **ACCT** is present in every string in *Dna*, there is little chance that **GreedyMotifSearch** will find the implanted motif. Zeroes in the profile matrix are not just a minor annoyance but rather a persistent problem that we must address.

Motif Finding Meets Oliver Cromwell

What is the probability that the sun will not rise tomorrow?

In 1650, after the Scots proclaimed Charles II as king during the English Civil War, Oliver Cromwell made a famous appeal to the Church of Scotland. Urging them to see the error of their royal alliance, he pleaded,

I beseech you, in the bowels of Christ, think it possible that you may be mistaken.

The Scots rejected the appeal, and Cromwell invaded Scotland in response. His quotation later inspired the statistical maxim called **Cromwell's rule**, which states that we should not use probabilities of 0 or 1 unless we are talking about logical statements that can only be true or false. In other words, we should allow a small probability for extremely unlikely events, such as "this book was written by aliens" or "the sun will not rise tomorrow". We cannot speak to the likelihood of the former event, but in the 18th Century, the French mathematician Pierre-Simon Laplace actually estimated the probability that the sun will not rise tomorrow (1/1826251), given that it has risen every day for the past 5000 years. Although this estimate was ridiculed by his contemporaries, Laplace's approach to this question now plays an important role in statistics.

In any observed data set, there is the possibility, especially with low-probability events or small data sets, that an event with nonzero probability does not occur. Its observed frequency is therefore zero; however, setting the empirical probability of the event equal to zero represents an inaccurate oversimplification that may cause problems. By artificially adjusting the probability of rare events, these problems can be mitigated.

Laplace's Rule of Succession

Cromwell's rule is relevant to the calculation of the probability of a string based on a profile matrix. For example, consider the following *Profile*:

$$
\textit{Profile} \quad
\begin{array}{llllllllllll}
\textbf{A:} & .2 & .2 & .0 & .0 & .0 & .0 & .9 & .1 & .1 & .1 & .3 & .0 \\
\textbf{C:} & .1 & .6 & .0 & .0 & .0 & .0 & .0 & .4 & .1 & .2 & .4 & .6 \\
\textbf{G:} & .0 & .0 & 1 & 1 & .9 & .9 & .1 & .0 & .0 & .0 & .0 & .0 \\
\textbf{T:} & .7 & .2 & .0 & .0 & .1 & .1 & .0 & .5 & .8 & .7 & .3 & .4
\end{array}
$$

$$\Pr(\texttt{TCGTGGATTTCC}|\textit{Profile}) = .7 \cdot .6 \cdot 1 \cdot .0 \cdot .9 \cdot .9 \cdot .9 \cdot .5 \cdot .8 \cdot .7 \cdot .4 \cdot .6 = 0$$

The fourth symbol of **TCGTGGATTTCC** causes Pr(**TCGTGGATTTCC**|*Profile*) to equal zero. As a result, the entire string is assigned a zero probability, even though **TCGTGGATTTCC** differs from the consensus string at only one position. For that matter, **TCGTGGATTTCC** has the same low probability as **AAATCTTGGAA**, which is very different from the consensus string.

In order to improve this unfair scoring, bioinformaticians often substitute zeroes with small numbers called **pseudocounts**. The simplest approach to introducing pseudocounts, called **Laplace's Rule of Succession**, is similar to the principle that Laplace used to calculate the probability that the sun will not rise tomorrow. In the case of motifs, pseudocounts often amount to adding 1 (or some other small number) to each element of COUNT(*Motifs*). For example, say that we have the following motif, count, and profile matrices:

$$
Motifs \quad
\begin{matrix}
T & A & A & C \\
G & T & C & T \\
A & C & T & A \\
A & G & G & T \\
\end{matrix}
$$

$$
\text{COUNT}(Motifs) \quad
\begin{matrix}
\text{A:} & 2 & 1 & 1 & 1 \\
\text{C:} & 0 & 1 & 1 & 1 \\
\text{G:} & 1 & 1 & 1 & 0 \\
\text{T:} & 1 & 1 & 1 & 2 \\
\end{matrix}
\qquad
\text{PROFILE}(Motifs) \quad
\begin{matrix}
2/4 & 1/4 & 1/4 & 1/4 \\
0 & 1/4 & 1/4 & 1/4 \\
1/4 & 1/4 & 1/4 & 0 \\
1/4 & 1/4 & 1/4 & 2/4 \\
\end{matrix}
$$

Laplace's Rule of Succession adds 1 to each element of COUNT(*Motifs*), updating the two matrices to the following:

$$
\text{COUNT}(Motifs) \quad
\begin{matrix}
\text{A:} & 2{+}1 & 1{+}1 & 1{+}1 & 1{+}1 \\
\text{C:} & 0{+}1 & 1{+}1 & 1{+}1 & 1{+}1 \\
\text{G:} & 1{+}1 & 1{+}1 & 1{+}1 & 0{+}1 \\
\text{T:} & 1{+}1 & 1{+}1 & 1{+}1 & 2{+}1 \\
\end{matrix}
\qquad
\text{PROFILE}(Motifs) \quad
\begin{matrix}
3/8 & 2/8 & 2/8 & 2/8 \\
1/8 & 2/8 & 2/8 & 2/8 \\
2/8 & 2/8 & 2/8 & 1/8 \\
2/8 & 2/8 & 2/8 & 3/8 \\
\end{matrix}
$$

STOP and Think: How would you use Laplace's Rule of Succession to address the shortcomings of **GREEDYMOTIFSEARCH**?

An improved greedy motif search

The only change we need to introduce to **GREEDYMOTIFSEARCH** in order to eliminate zeroes from the profile matrices that it constructs is to replace line 6 of the pseudocode for **GREEDYMOTIFSEARCH**:

form *Profile* from motifs $Motif_1, \dots Motif_{i-1}$

with the following line:

apply Laplace's Rule of Succession to form *Profile* from motifs *Motif*$_1$, ... *Motif*$_{i-1}$

We now will apply Laplace's Rule of Succession to search for the $(4, 1)$-motif **ACGT** implanted in the following strings *Dna*:

$$
\begin{array}{l}
\text{tt}\textbf{ACCT}\text{taac} \\
\text{g}\textbf{ATGT}\text{ctgtc} \\
Dna \quad \text{acg}\textbf{GCGT}\text{tag} \\
\text{cccta}\textbf{ACGA}\text{g} \\
\text{cgtcag}\textbf{AGGT}
\end{array}
$$

Again, let's assume that the algorithm has already chosen the implanted 4-mer **ACCT** from the first sequence. We can construct the corresponding count and profile matrices using Laplace's Rule of Succession:

Motifs **ACCT**

$$
\text{COUNT}(Motifs) \quad
\begin{array}{l}
\text{A: } 1+1 \;\; 0+1 \;\; 0+1 \;\; 0+1 \\
\text{C: } 0+1 \;\; 1+1 \;\; 1+1 \;\; 0+1 \\
\text{G: } 0+1 \;\; 0+1 \;\; 0+1 \;\; 0+1 \\
\text{T: } 0+1 \;\; 0+1 \;\; 0+1 \;\; 1+1
\end{array}
\qquad
\text{PROFILE}(Motifs) \quad
\begin{array}{l}
2/5 \;\; 1/5 \;\; 1/5 \;\; 1/5 \\
1/5 \;\; 2/5 \;\; 2/5 \;\; 1/5 \\
1/5 \;\; 1/5 \;\; 1/5 \;\; 1/5 \\
1/5 \;\; 1/5 \;\; 1/5 \;\; 2/5
\end{array}
$$

We use this profile matrix to compute the probabilities of all 4-mers in the second string from *Dna*:

g**ATG**	**ATGT**	**TGT**c	**GT**ct	**T**ctg	ctgt	tgtc
$1/5^4$	$4/5^4$	$1/5^4$	$4/5^4$	$2/5^4$	$2/5^4$	$1/5^4$

There are two *Profile*-most probable 4-mers in the second sequence (**ATGT** and **GT**ct); let's assume that we get lucky again and choose the implanted 4-mer **ATGT**. We now have the following motif, count, and profile matrices:

$$
Motifs \quad
\begin{array}{l}
\textbf{ACCT} \\
\textbf{ATGT}
\end{array}
$$

$$
\text{COUNT}(Motifs) \quad
\begin{array}{l}
\text{A: } 2+1 \;\; 0+1 \;\; 0+1 \;\; 0+1 \\
\text{C: } 0+1 \;\; 1+1 \;\; 1+1 \;\; 0+1 \\
\text{G: } 0+1 \;\; 0+1 \;\; 1+1 \;\; 0+1 \\
\text{T: } 0+1 \;\; 1+1 \;\; 0+1 \;\; 2+1
\end{array}
\qquad
\text{PROFILE}(Motifs) \quad
\begin{array}{l}
3/6 \;\; 1/6 \;\; 1/6 \;\; 1/6 \\
1/6 \;\; 2/6 \;\; 2/6 \;\; 1/6 \\
1/6 \;\; 1/6 \;\; 2/6 \;\; 1/6 \\
1/6 \;\; 2/6 \;\; 1/6 \;\; 3/6
\end{array}
$$

We use this profile matrix to compute the probabilities of all 4-mers in the third string from *Dna*:

acg**G**	cg**GC**	g**GCG**	**GCGT**	**CGT**t	**GT**ta	**T**tag
$12/6^4$	$2/6^4$	$2/6^4$	$12/6^4$	$3/6^4$	$2/6^4$	$2/6^4$

Again, there are two *Profile*-most probable 4-mers in the second sequence (acg**G** and **GCGT**). This time, we will assume that acg**G** is selected instead of the implanted 4-mer **GCGT**. We now have the following motif, count, and profile matrices:

$$\begin{array}{c} \textbf{ACCT} \\ \textit{Motifs} \quad \textbf{ATGT} \\ \text{acg}\textbf{G} \end{array}$$

$$\text{COUNT}(\textit{Motifs}) \begin{array}{l} \text{A: } 3+1 \;\; 0+1 \;\; 0+1 \;\; 1+1 \\ \text{C: } 0+1 \;\; 2+1 \;\; 1+1 \;\; 0+1 \\ \text{G: } 0+1 \;\; 0+1 \;\; 2+1 \;\; 1+1 \\ \text{T: } 0+1 \;\; 1+1 \;\; 0+1 \;\; 2+1 \end{array} \qquad \text{PROFILE}(\textit{Motifs}) \begin{array}{l} 4/7 \;\; 1/7 \;\; 1/7 \;\; 1/7 \\ 1/7 \;\; 3/7 \;\; 2/7 \;\; 1/7 \\ 1/7 \;\; 1/7 \;\; 3/7 \;\; 2/7 \\ 1/7 \;\; 2/7 \;\; 1/7 \;\; 3/7 \end{array}$$

We use this profile matrix to compute probabilities of all 4-mers in the fourth string from *Dna*:

ccct	ccta	cta**A**	ta**AC**	a**ACG**	**ACGA**	**CGA**g
$18/7^4$	$3/7^4$	$2/7^4$	$1/7^4$	$16/7^4$	$36/7^4$	$2/7^4$

Despite the fact that we missed the implanted 4-mer in the third sequence, we have now found the implanted 4-mer in the fourth string in *Dna* as the *Profile*-most probable 4-mer **ACGA**. This provides us with the following motif, count, and profile matrices:

$$\begin{array}{c} \textbf{ACCT} \\ \textbf{ATGT} \\ \textit{Motifs} \quad \text{acg}\textbf{G} \\ \textbf{ACGA} \end{array}$$

$$\text{COUNT}(\textit{Motifs}) \begin{array}{l} \text{A: } 4+1 \;\; 0+1 \;\; 0+1 \;\; 0+1 \\ \text{C: } 0+1 \;\; 3+1 \;\; 1+1 \;\; 0+1 \\ \text{G: } 0+1 \;\; 0+1 \;\; 3+1 \;\; 1+1 \\ \text{T: } 0+1 \;\; 1+1 \;\; 0+1 \;\; 2+1 \end{array} \qquad \text{PROFILE}(\textit{Motifs}) \begin{array}{l} 5/8 \;\; 1/8 \;\; 1/8 \;\; 2/8 \\ 1/8 \;\; 4/8 \;\; 2/8 \;\; 1/8 \\ 1/8 \;\; 1/8 \;\; 4/8 \;\; 2/8 \\ 1/8 \;\; 2/8 \;\; 1/8 \;\; 3/8 \end{array}$$

We now use this profile to compute the probabilities of all 4-mers in the fifth string in *Dna*:

cgtc	gtca	tcag	cag**A**	ag**AG**	g**AGG**	**AGGT**
$1/8^4$	$8/8^4$	$8/8^4$	$8/8^4$	$10/8^4$	$8/8^4$	$60/8^4$

The *Profile*-most probable 4-mer of the fifth string in *Dna* is **AGGT**, the implanted 4-mer. As a result, **GREEDYMOTIFSEARCH** has produced the following motif matrix, which implies the correct consensus string **ACGT**:

$$
\begin{array}{rl}
& \text{\textbf{ACCT}} \\
& \text{\textbf{ATGT}} \\
\textit{Motifs} & \text{acg\textbf{G}} \\
& \text{\textbf{ACGA}} \\
& \text{\textbf{AGGT}} \\
\text{CONSENSUS}(\textit{Motifs}) & \text{\textbf{ACGT}}
\end{array}
$$

You have now seen the power of pseudocounts illustrated on a small example. Running **GREEDYMOTIFSEARCH** with pseudocounts to solve the Subtle Motif Problem returns a collection of 15-mers *Motifs* with SCORE(*Motifs*) = 41 and CONSENSUS(*Motifs*) = **AAAAAtAgaGGGGtt**. Thus, Laplace's Rule of Succession has provided a great improvement over the original **GREEDYMOTIFSEARCH**, which returned the consensus string **gTtAAAtAgaGatGtG** with SCORE(*Motifs*) = 58.

You may be satisfied with the performance of **GREEDYMOTIFSEARCH**, but you should know by now that your authors are never satisfied. Can we design an even more accurate motif finding algorithm?

Randomized Motif Search

Rolling dice to find motifs

We will now turn to **randomized algorithms** that flip coins and roll dice in order to search for motifs. Making random algorithmic decisions may sound like a disastrous idea — just imagine a chess game in which every move would be decided by rolling a die. However, an 18th Century French mathematician and naturalist, Comte de Buffon, first proved that randomized algorithms are useful by randomly dropping needles onto parallel strips of wood and using the results of this experiment to accurately approximate the constant π (see **DETOUR: Buffon's Needle**).

PAGE 109

Randomized algorithms may be nonintuitive because they lack the control of traditional algorithms. Some randomized algorithms are **Las Vegas algorithms**, which deliver solutions that are guaranteed to be exact, despite the fact that they rely on making random decisions. Yet most randomized algorithms, including the motif finding algorithms that we will consider in this chapter, are **Monte Carlo algorithms**. These algorithms are not guaranteed to return exact solutions, but they do quickly find *approximate* solutions. Because of their speed, they can be run many times, allowing us to choose the best approximation from thousands of runs.

We previously defined PROFILE(*Motifs*) as the profile matrix constructed from a collection of k-mers *Motifs* in *Dna*. Now, given a collection of strings *Dna* and an arbitrary $4 \times k$ matrix *Profile*, we define MOTIFS(*Profile*, *Dna*) as the collection of k-mers formed by the *Profile*-most probable k-mers in each sequence from *Dna*. For example, consider the following *Profile* and *Dna*:

$$
\textit{Profile} \quad
\begin{array}{llll}
\text{A:} & 4/5 & 0 & 0 & 1/5 \\
\text{C:} & 0 & 3/5 & 1/5 & 0 \\
\text{G:} & 1/5 & 1/5 & 4/5 & 0 \\
\text{T:} & 0 & 1/5 & 0 & 4/5
\end{array}
\qquad
\textit{Dna} \quad
\begin{array}{l}
\texttt{ttaccttaac} \\
\texttt{gatgtctgtc} \\
\texttt{acggcgttag} \\
\texttt{ccctaacgag} \\
\texttt{cgtcagaggt}
\end{array}
$$

Taking the *Profile*-most probable 4-mer from each row of *Dna* produces the following 4-mers (shown in red):

$$
\text{MOTIFS}(\textit{Profile}, \textit{Dna}) \quad
\begin{array}{l}
\texttt{tt}\textbf{acct}\texttt{taac} \\
\texttt{g}\textbf{atgt}\texttt{ctgtc} \\
\texttt{acg}\textbf{gcgt}\texttt{tag} \\
\texttt{cccta}\textbf{acga}\texttt{g} \\
\texttt{cgtcag}\textbf{aggt}
\end{array}
$$

In general, we can begin from a collection of randomly chosen k-mers *Motifs* in *Dna*, construct PROFILE(*Motifs*), and use this profile to generate a new collection of k-mers:

$$\text{MOTIFS}(\text{PROFILE}(\textit{Motifs}), \textit{Dna})$$

Why would we do this? Because our hope is that MOTIFS(PROFILE(*Motifs*), *Dna*) has a better score than the original collection of k-mers *Motifs*. We can then form the profile matrix of these k-mers,

$$\text{PROFILE}(\text{MOTIFS}(\text{PROFILE}(\textit{Motifs}), \textit{Dna})),$$

and use it to form the most probable k-mers,

$$\text{MOTIFS}(\text{PROFILE}(\text{MOTIFS}(\text{PROFILE}(Motifs), Dna)), Dna).$$

We can continue to iterate...

$$\dots \text{PROFILE}(\text{MOTIFS}(\text{PROFILE}(\text{MOTIFS}(\text{PROFILE}(Motifs), Dna)), Dna))\dots$$

for as long as the score of the constructed motifs keeps improving, which is exactly what **RANDOMIZEDMOTIFSEARCH** does. To implement this algorithm, you will need to randomly select the initial collection of k-mers that form the motif matrix *Motifs*. To do so, you will need a **random number generator** (denoted $\text{RANDOM}(N)$) that is equally likely to return any integer from 1 to N. You might like to think about this random number generator as an unbiased N-sided die.

RANDOMIZEDMOTIFSEARCH(*Dna, k, t*)
    randomly select k-mers *Motifs* $= (Motif_1, \dots, Motif_t)$ in each string from *Dna*
    BestMotifs $\leftarrow$ *Motifs*
    while forever
        Profile $\leftarrow$ PROFILE(*Motifs*)
        Motifs $\leftarrow$ MOTIFS(*Profile, Dna*)
        if SCORE(*Motifs*) < SCORE(*BestMotifs*)
            BestMotifs $\leftarrow$ *Motifs*
        else
            return *BestMotifs*

EXERCISE BREAK: Prove that **RANDOMIZEDMOTIFSEARCH** will eventually terminate.

Since a single run of **RANDOMIZEDMOTIFSEARCH** may generate a rather poor set of motifs, bioinformaticians usually run this algorithm thousands of times. On each run, they begin from a new randomly selected set of k-mers, selecting the best set of k-mers found in all these runs.

Why randomized motif search works

At first glance, **RANDOMIZEDMOTIFSEARCH** appears to be doomed. How can this algorithm, which starts from a random guess, possibly find anything useful? To explore **RANDOMIZEDMOTIFSEARCH**, let's run it on five short strings with the implanted $(4, 1)$-motif ACGT (shown in upper case letters below) and imagine that it chooses the following 4-mers *Motifs* (shown in red) at the first iteration. As expected, it misses the implanted motif in nearly every string.

$$
\begin{array}{ll}
& \texttt{ttACCTtaac} \\
& \texttt{gATGTctgtc} \\
Dna & \texttt{ccgGCGTtag} \\
& \texttt{cactaACGAg} \\
& \texttt{cgtcagAGGT}
\end{array}
$$

Below, we construct the profile matrix PROFILE(*Motifs*) of the chosen 4-mers.

Motifs				PROFILE(*Motifs*)				
t	a	a	c	A:	0.4	0.2	0.2	0.2
G	T	c	t	C:	0.2	0.4	0.2	0.2
c	c	g	G	G:	0.2	0.2	0.4	0.2
a	c	t	a	T:	0.2	0.2	0.2	0.4
A	G	G	T					

We can now compute the probabilities of every 4-mer in *Dna* based on this profile matrix. For example, the probability of the first 4-mer in the first string of *Dna* is PR(ttAC|*Profile*) = $0.2 \cdot 0.2 \cdot 0.2 \cdot 0.2 = 0.0016$. The maximum probabilities in every row are shown in red below.

ttAC	tACC	ACCT	CCTt	CTta	Ttaa	taac
.0016	.0016	**.0128**	.0064	.0016	.0016	.0016
gATG	ATGT	TGTc	GTct	Tctg	ctgt	tgtc
.0016	**.0128**	.0016	.0032	.0032	.0032	.0016
ccgG	cgGC	gGCG	GCGT	CGTt	GTta	Ttag
.0064	.0036	.0016	**.0128**	.0032	.0016	.0016
cact	acta	ctaA	taAC	aACG	ACGA	CGAg
.0032	.0064	.0016	.0016	.0032	**.0128**	.0016
cgtc	gtca	tcag	cagA	agAG	gAGG	AGGT
.0016	.0016	.0016	.0032	.0032	.0032	**.0128**

We select the most probable 4-mer in each row above as our new collection *Motifs* (shown below). Notice that this collection has captured all five implanted motifs in *Dna*!

Dna
```
ttACCTtaac
gATGTctgtc
ccgGCGTtag
cactaACGAg
cgtcagAGGT
```

STOP and Think: How is it possible that randomly chosen *k*-mers have led us to the correct implanted *k*-mer? If you think we manufactured this example, select your own initial 4-mers and see what happens.

For the Subtle Motif Problem with implanted 15-mer **AAAAAAAAGGGGGGG**, when we run **RANDOMIZEDMOTIFSEARCH** 100,000 times (each time with new randomly selected *k*-mers), it returns the 15-mers shown in Figure 2.7 as the lowest scoring collection *Motifs* across all iterations, resulting in the consensus string **AAAAAAAAacaGGGG** with score 43. These strings are only slightly less conserved than the collection of implanted (15, 4)-motifs with score 40 (or the motif returned by **GREEDYMOTIFSEARCH** with score 41), and it largely captures the implanted motif. Furthermore, unlike **GREEDYMOTIFSEARCH**, **RANDOMIZEDMOTIFSEARCH** can be run for a larger number of iterations to discover better and better motifs.

		Score
	AAAtAcAgACAGcGt	5
	AAAAAAtAgCAGGGt	3
	tAAAAtAAACAGcGG	3
	AcAgAAAAAaAGGGG	3
Motifs	AAAAtAAAACtGcGa	4
	AtAgAcgAACAcGGt	6
	cAAAAAgAgaAGGGG	4
	AtAgAAAAggAaGGG	5
	AAgAAAAAAgAGaGG	3
	cAtAAtgAACtGtGa	7
CONSENSUS(*Motifs*)	**AAAAAAAAACAGGGG**	**43**

FIGURE 2.7 The lowest scoring collection of strings *Motifs* produced by 100,000 runs of **RANDOMIZEDMOTIFSEARCH**, along with their consensus string and score for the Subtle Motif Problem.

STOP

STOP and Think: Does your run of RANDOMIZEDMOTIFSEARCH return a similar consensus string? How many times do you need to run RANDOMIZEDMOTIFSEARCH to obtain the implanted (15, 4)-motif with distance 40?

Although the motifs returned by RANDOMIZEDMOTIFSEARCH are slightly less conserved than the motifs returned by MEDIANSTRING, RANDOMIZEDMOTIFSEARCH has the advantage of being able to find longer motifs (since MEDIANSTRING becomes too slow for longer motifs). In the epilogue, we will see that this feature is important in practice.

How Can a Randomized Algorithm Perform So Well?

In the previous section, we began with a collection of implanted motifs (with consensus ACGT) that resulted in the following profile matrix.

	A:	**0.8**	0.0	0.0	0.2
	C:	0.0	**0.6**	0.2	0.0
	G:	0.2	0.2	**0.8**	0.0
	T:	0.0	0.2	0.0	**0.8**

If the strings in *Dna* were truly random, then we would expect that all nucleotides in the selected k-mers would be equally likely, resulting in an expected *Profile* in which every entry is approximately 0.25:

	A:	0.25	0.25	0.25	0.25
	C:	0.25	0.25	0.25	0.25
	G:	0.25	0.25	0.25	0.25
	T:	0.25	0.25	0.25	0.25

Such a **uniform profile** is essentially useless for motif finding because no string is more probable than any other according to this profile and because it does not provide any clues on what an implanted motif looks like.

At the opposite end of the spectrum, if we were incredibly lucky, we would choose the implanted k-mers *Motifs* from the very beginning, resulting in the first of the two profile matrices above. In practice, we are likely to obtain a profile somewhere in between these two extremes, such as the following:

A:	**0.4**	0.2	0.2	0.2
C:	0.2	**0.4**	0.2	0.2
G:	0.2	0.2	**0.4**	0.2
T:	0.2	0.2	0.2	**0.4**

This profile matrix has already started to point us toward the implanted motif ACGT, i.e., ACGT is the most likely 4-mer that can be generated by this profile. Fortunately, RANDOMIZEDMOTIFSEARCH is designed so that subsequent steps have a good chance of leading us toward this implanted motif (although it is not certain).

If you still doubt the efficacy of randomized algorithms, consider the following argument. We have already noticed that if the strings in *Dna* were random, then RANDOMIZEDMOTIFSEARCH would start from a nearly uniform profile, and there would be nothing to work with. However, the key observation is that the strings in *Dna* are not random because they include the implanted motif! These multiple occurrences of the same motif may create a bias in the profile matrix, directing it away from the uniform profile and toward the implanted motif. For example, consider again the original randomly selected *k*-mers *Motifs* (shown in red):

$$
\begin{array}{l}
\text{ttACCT}\mathbf{taac} \\
\text{gAT}\mathbf{GTct}\text{gtc} \\
\textit{Dna}\quad \mathbf{ccgG}\text{CGTtag} \\
\text{c}\mathbf{acta}\text{ACGAg} \\
\text{cgtcag}\mathbf{AGGT}
\end{array}
$$

You will see that the 4-mer **AGGT** in the last string happened to capture the implanted motif simply by chance. In fact, the profile formed from the remaining 4-mers (**taac**, **GTct**, **ccgG**, and **acta**) is uniform.

> **EXERCISE BREAK:** Compute the probability that ten randomly selected 15-mers from ten 600-nucleotide long strings (such as in the Subtle Motif Problem) capture at least one implanted 15-mer.

Although the probability that randomly selected *k*-mers match *all* implanted motifs is negligible, the probability that they capture *at least one* implanted motif is significant. Even in the case of difficult motif finding problems for which this probability is small, we can run RANDOMIZEDMOTIFSEARCH many times, so that it will almost certainly catch at least one implanted motif, thus creating a statistical bias pointing toward the correct motif.

Unfortunately, capturing a single implanted motif is often insufficient to steer RANDOMIZEDMOTIFSEARCH to an optimal solution. Therefore, since the number of starting positions of k-mers is huge, the strategy of randomly selecting motifs is often not as successful as in the simple example above. The chance that these randomly selected k-mers will be able to guide us to the optimal solution is relatively small.

EXERCISE BREAK: Compute the probability that ten randomly selected 15-mers from the ten 600-nucleotide long strings in the Subtle Motif Problem capture at least two implanted 15-mers.

Gibbs Sampling

Note that RANDOMIZEDMOTIFSEARCH may change all t strings in *Motifs* in a single iteration. This strategy may prove reckless, since some correct motifs (captured in *Motifs*) may potentially be discarded at the next iteration. GIBBSSAMPLER is a more cautious iterative algorithm that discards a single k-mer from the current set of motifs at each iteration and decides to either keep it or replace it with a new one. This algorithm thus moves with more caution in the space of all motifs, as illustrated below.

ttacctt**aac**	ttacctt**aac**	ttacctt**aac**	ttacctt**aac**
gat**a**tctgtc	gat**atc**tgtc	gat**a**tctgtc	gatatc**tgtc**
acggcgttcg →	acggcg**ttcg**	**acg**gcgttcg →	**acg**gcgttcg
ccct**aaa**gag	ccctaa**agag**	ccct**aaa**gag	ccct**aaa**gag
cgtc**aga**ggt	**cgt**cagaggt	cgtc**aga**ggt	cgtc**aga**ggt

RANDOMIZEDMOTIFSEARCH	**GIBBSSAMPLER**
(may change all k-mers in one step)	(changes one k-mer in one step)

Like RANDOMIZEDMOTIFSEARCH, GIBBSSAMPLER starts with randomly chosen k-mers in each of t DNA sequences, but it makes a random rather than a deterministic choice at each iteration. It uses randomly selected k-mers $Motifs = (Motif_1, \ldots, Motif_t)$ to come up with another (hopefully better scoring) set of k-mers. In contrast with RANDOMIZEDMOTIFSEARCH, which deterministically defines new motifs as

$$\text{MOTIFS}(\text{PROFILE}(Motifs), Dna),$$

GIBBSSAMPLER randomly selects an integer i between 1 and t and then randomly changes a single k-mer $Motif_i$.

To describe how **GIBBSSAMPLER** updates $Motifs$, we will need a slightly more advanced random number generator. Given a probability distribution $(p_1, \ldots, p_n)$, this random number generator, denoted $\text{RANDOM}(p_1, \ldots, p_n)$, models an n-sided biased die and returns integer i with probability p_i. For example, the standard six-sided fair die represents the random number generator

$$\text{RANDOM}(1/6, 1/6, 1/6, 1/6, 1/6, 1/6),$$

whereas a biased die might represent the random number generator

$$\text{RANDOM}(0.1, 0.2, 0.3, 0.05, 0.1, 0.25).$$

GIBBSSAMPLER further generalizes the random number generator by using the function $\text{RANDOM}(p_1, \ldots, p_n)$ defined for any set of non-negative numbers, i.e., not necessarily satisfying the condition $\sum_{i=1}^{n} p_i = 1$. Specifically, if $\sum_{i=1}^{n} p_i = C > 0$, then $\text{RANDOM}(p_1, \ldots, p_n)$ is defined as $\text{RANDOM}(p_1/C, \ldots, p_n/C)$, where $(p_1/C, \ldots, p_n/C)$ is a probability distribution. For example, given the values $(p_1, p_2, p_3) = (0.1, 0.2, 0.3)$ with $0.1 + 0.2 + 0.3 = 0.6$,

$$\text{RANDOM}(0.1, 0.2, 0.3) = \text{RANDOM}(0.1/0.6, 0.2/0.6, 0.3/0.6)$$
$$= \text{RANDOM}(1/6, 1/3, 1/2).$$

STOP and Think: Implement $\text{RANDOM}(p_1, \ldots, p_n)$ so that it uses $\text{RANDOM}(X)$ (for an appropriately chosen integer X) as a subroutine.

We have previously defined the notion of a *Profile*-most probable k-mer in a string. We now define a ***Profile*-randomly generated k-mer** in a string $Text$. For each k-mer $Pattern$ in $Text$, compute the probability $\text{Pr}(Pattern|Profile)$, resulting in $n = |Text| - k + 1$ probabilities $(p_1, \ldots, p_n)$. These probabilities do not necessarily sum to 1, but we can still form the random number generator $\text{RANDOM}(p_1, \ldots, p_n)$ based on them. **GIBBSSAMPLER** uses this random number generator to select a *Profile*-randomly generated k-mer at each step: if the die rolls the number i, then we define the *Profile*-randomly generated k-mer as the i-th k-mer in $Text$. While the pseudocode below repeats this procedure N times, in practice **GIBBSSAMPLER** depends on various stopping rules that are beyond the scope of this chapter.

GIBBSSAMPLER(*Dna, k, t, N*)
    randomly select *k*-mers *Motifs* = (*Motif*$_1$, ..., *Motif*$_t$) in each string from *Dna*
    BestMotifs ← *Motifs*
    for *j* ← 1 to *N*
        i ← RANDOM(*t*)
        Profile ← profile matrix formed from all strings in *Motifs* except for *Motif*$_i$
        Motif$_i$ ← *Profile*-randomly generated *k*-mer in the *i*-th sequence
        if SCORE(*Motifs*) < SCORE(*BestMotifs*)
            BestMotifs ← *Motifs*
    return *BestMotifs*

STOP and Think: Note that in contrast to **RANDOMIZEDMOTIFSEARCH**, which always moves from higher to lower scoring *Motifs*, **GIBBSSAMPLER** may move from lower to higher scoring *Motifs*. Why is this reasonable?

Gibbs Sampling in Action

We illustrate how **GIBBSSAMPLER** works on the same strings *Dna* that we considered before. Imagine that, at the initial step, the algorithm has chosen the following 4-mers (shown in red) and has randomly selected the third string for removal.

	ttACCT**taac**	ttACCT**taac**
	gATG**Tct**gtc	gATG**Tct**gtc
Dna	**ccgG**CGTtag ⟶	----------
	c**acta**ACGAg	c**acta**ACGAg
	cgtcag**AGGT**	cgtcag**AGGT**

This results in the following motif, count, and profile matrices.

$$
Motifs \quad \begin{matrix} t & a & a & c \\ G & T & c & t \\ a & c & t & a \\ A & G & G & T \end{matrix}
$$

COUNT(*Motifs*)
A: 2 1 1 1
C: 0 1 1 1
G: 1 1 1 0
T: 1 1 1 2

PROFILE(*Motifs*)
A: 2/4 1/4 1/4 1/4
C: 0   1/4 1/4 1/4
G: 1/4 1/4 1/4   0
T: 1/4 1/4 1/4 2/4

Note that the profile matrix is only slightly more conserved than the uniform profile, making us wonder whether we have any chance to be steered toward the implanted motif. We now use this profile matrix to compute the probabilities of all 4-mers in the deleted string ccgGCGTtag:

ccgG	cgGC	gGCG	GCGT	CGTt	GTta	Ttag
0	0	0	1/128	0	1/256	0

Note that all but two of these probabilities are zero. This situation is similar to the one we encountered with **GREEDYMOTIFSEARCH**, and as before, we need to augment zero probabilities with small pseudocounts to avoid disastrous results.

Application of Laplace's Rule of Succession to the count matrix above yields the following updated count and profile matrices:

$$\text{COUNT}(\textit{Motifs}) \quad \begin{array}{l} \text{A: } 3\ 2\ 2\ 2 \\ \text{C: } 1\ 2\ 2\ 2 \\ \text{G: } 2\ 2\ 2\ 1 \\ \text{T: } 2\ 2\ 2\ 3 \end{array} \qquad \text{PROFILE}(\textit{Motifs}) \quad \begin{array}{l} \text{A: } 3/8\ 2/8\ 2/8\ 2/8 \\ \text{C: } 1/8\ 2/8\ 2/8\ 2/8 \\ \text{G: } 2/8\ 2/8\ 2/8\ 1/8 \\ \text{T: } 2/8\ 2/8\ 2/8\ 3/8 \end{array}$$

After adding pseudocounts, the 4-mer probabilities in the deleted string ccgGCGTtag are recomputed as follows:

ccgG	cgGC	gGCG	GCGT	CGTt	GTta	Ttag
$4/8^4$	$8/8^4$	$8/8^4$	$24/8^4$	$12/8^4$	$16/8^4$	$8/8^4$

Since these probabilities sum to $C = 80/8^4$, our hypothetical seven-sided die is represented by the random number generator

$$\text{RANDOM} \left(\frac{4/8^4}{80/8^4}, \frac{8/8^4}{80/8^4}, \frac{8/8^4}{80/8^4}, \frac{24/8^4}{80/8^4}, \frac{12/8^4}{80/8^4}, \frac{16/8^4}{80/8^4}, \frac{8/8^4}{80/8^4} \right)$$
$$= \text{RANDOM} \left(\frac{4}{80}, \frac{8}{80}, \frac{8}{80}, \frac{24}{80}, \frac{12}{80}, \frac{16}{80}, \frac{8}{80} \right) .$$

Let's assume that after rolling this seven-sided die, we arrive at the *Profile*-randomly generated 4-mer GCGT (the fourth 4-mer in the deleted sequence). The deleted string ccgGCGTtag is now added back to the collection of motifs, and **GCGT** substitutes the previously chosen ccgG in the third string in *Dna*, as shown below. We then roll a fair five-sided die and randomly select the first string from *Dna* for removal.

```
      ttACCTtaac          ----------
      gATGTctgtc          gATGTctgtc
Dna   ccgGCGTtag   ⟶      ccgGCGTtag
      cactaACGAg          cactaACGAg
      cgtcagAGGT          cgtcagAGGT
```

After constructing the motif and profile matrices, we obtain the following:

$$
Motifs \quad
\begin{matrix}
G & T & c & t \\
G & C & G & T \\
a & c & t & a \\
A & G & G & T
\end{matrix}
\qquad
\text{PROFILE}(Motifs)
\quad
\begin{matrix}
\text{A:} & 2/4 & 0 & 0 & 1/4 \\
\text{C:} & 0 & 2/4 & 1/4 & 0 \\
\text{G:} & 2/4 & 1/4 & 2/4 & 0 \\
\text{T:} & 0 & 1/4 & 1/4 & 3/4
\end{matrix}
$$

Note that the profile matrix looks more biased toward the implanted motif than the previous profile matrix did. We update the count and profile matrices with pseudo-counts:

$$
\text{COUNT}(Motifs)
\quad
\begin{matrix}
\text{A:} & 3 & 1 & 1 & 2 \\
\text{C:} & 1 & 3 & 2 & 1 \\
\text{G:} & 3 & 2 & 3 & 1 \\
\text{T:} & 1 & 2 & 2 & 4
\end{matrix}
\qquad
\text{PROFILE}(Motifs)
\quad
\begin{matrix}
\text{A:} & 3/8 & 1/8 & 1/8 & 2/8 \\
\text{C:} & 1/8 & 3/8 & 2/8 & 1/8 \\
\text{G:} & 3/8 & 2/8 & 3/8 & 1/8 \\
\text{T:} & 1/8 & 2/8 & 2/8 & 4/8
\end{matrix}
$$

Then, we compute the probabilities of all 4-mers in the deleted string `ttACCTtaac`:

ttAC	tACC	ACCT	CCTt	CTta	Ttaa	taac
$2/8^4$	$2/8^4$	$72/8^4$	$24/8^4$	$8/8^4$	$4/8^4$	$1/8^4$

When we roll a seven-sided die, we arrive at the *Profile*-randomly generated k-mer **ACCT**, which we add to the collection *Motifs*. After rolling the five-sided die once again, we randomly select the fourth string for removal.

```
      ttACCTtaac          ttACCTtaac
      gATGTctgtc          gATGTctgtc
Dna   ccgGCGTtag   ⟶      ccgGCGTtag
      cactaACGAg          ----------
      cgtcagAGGT          cgtcagAGGT
```

We further add pseudocounts and construct the resulting count and profile matrices:

$$
\textit{Motifs} \quad
\begin{matrix}
A & C & C & T \\
G & T & c & t \\
G & C & G & T \\
A & G & G & T
\end{matrix}
$$

$$
\text{COUNT}(\textit{Motifs}) \quad
\begin{matrix}
\text{A:} & 3 & 1 & 1 & 1 \\
\text{C:} & 1 & 3 & 3 & 1 \\
\text{G:} & 3 & 2 & 3 & 1 \\
\text{T:} & 1 & 2 & 1 & 5
\end{matrix}
\qquad
\text{PROFILE}(\textit{Motifs}) \quad
\begin{matrix}
\text{A:} & 3/8 & 1/8 & 1/8 & 1/8 \\
\text{C:} & 1/8 & 3/8 & 3/8 & 1/8 \\
\text{G:} & 3/8 & 2/8 & 3/8 & 1/8 \\
\text{T:} & 1/8 & 2/8 & 1/8 & 5/8
\end{matrix}
$$

We now compute the probabilities of all 4-mers in the deleted string `cactaACGAg`:

cact	acta	ctaA	taAC	aACG	ACGA	CGAg
$15/8^4$	$9/8^4$	$2/8^4$	$1/8^4$	$9/8^4$	$27/8^4$	$2/8^4$

We need to roll a seven-sided die to produce a *Profile*-randomly generated 4-mer. Assuming the most probable scenario in which we select **ACGA**, we update the selected 4-mers as follows:

$$
\textit{Dna} \quad
\begin{matrix}
\texttt{tt}\textbf{ACCT}\texttt{taac} \\
\texttt{gAT}\textbf{GTct}\texttt{gtc} \\
\texttt{ccg}\textbf{GCGT}\texttt{tag} \\
\texttt{cacta}\textbf{ACGA}\texttt{g} \\
\texttt{cgtcag}\textbf{AGGT}
\end{matrix}
$$

You can see that the algorithm is beginning to converge. Rest assured that a subsequent iteration will produce all implanted motifs after we select the second string in *Dna* (when the incorrect 4-mer `GTct` will likely change into the implanted (4, 1)-motif `ATGT`).

STOP and Think: Run **GIBBSSAMPLER** on the Subtle Motif Problem. What do you find?

Although **GIBBSSAMPLER** performs well in many cases, it may converge to a suboptimal solution, particularly for difficult search problems with elusive motifs. A **local optimum** is a solution that is optimal within a small neighboring set of solutions, which is in contrast to a **global optimum**, or the optimal solution among all possible solutions. Since **GIBBSSAMPLER** explores just a small subset of solutions, it may "get stuck" in a local optimum. For this reason, similarly to **RANDOMIZEDMOTIFSEARCH**, it should be run many times with the hope that one of these runs will produce the best-scoring motifs. Yet convergence to a local optimum is just one of many issues we must consider in motif finding; see **DETOUR: Complications in Motif Finding** for some other challenges.

When we run GIBBSSAMPLER 2,000 times on the Subtle Motif Problem with implanted 15-mer **AAAAAAAAGGGGGGG** (each time with new randomly selected k-mers for $N = 200$ iterations), it returns a collection *Motifs* with consensus **AAAAAAgAGGGGGGt** and SCORE(*Motifs*) equal to 38. This score is even lower than the score of 40 expected from the implanted motifs!

Epilogue: How Does Tuberculosis Hibernate to Hide from Antibiotics?

Tuberculosis (TB) is an infectious disease that is caused by the *Mycobacterium tuberculosis* bacterium (MTB) and is responsible for over a million deaths each year. Although the spread of TB has been greatly reduced due to antibiotics, strains that resist all available treatments are now emerging. MTB is successful as a pathogen because it can persist in humans for decades without causing disease; in fact, one-third of the world population has **latent MTB infections**, in which MTB lies dormant within the host's body and may or may not reactivate at a later time. The widespread prevalence of latent infections makes it difficult to control TB epidemics. Biologists are therefore interested in finding out what makes the disease latent and how MTB activates itself within a host.

It remains unclear why MTB can stay latent for so long and how it survives during latency. The resistance of latent TB to antibiotics implies that MTB may have an ability to shut down expression of most genes and stay dormant, not unlike bears hibernating in the winter. Hibernation in bacteria is called **sporulation** because many bacteria form protective and metabolically dormant **spores** that can survive in tough conditions, allowing the bacteria to persist in the environment until conditions improve.

Hypoxia, or oxygen shortage, is often associated with latent forms of TB. Biologists have found that MTB becomes dormant in low-oxygen environments, presumably with the idea that the host's lungs will recover enough to potentially spread the disease in the future. Since MTB shows a remarkable ability to survive for years without oxygen, it is important to identify MTB genes responsible for the development of the latent state under hypoxic conditions. Biologists are interested in finding a **transcription factor** that "senses" the shortage of oxygen and starts a genetic program that affects the expression of many genes, allowing MTB to adapt to hypoxia.

In 2003, biologists found the **dormancy survival regulator** (**DosR**), a transcription factor that regulates many genes whose expression dramatically changes under hypoxic

PAGE 112

conditions. However, it remained unclear how DosR regulates these genes, and its transcription factor binding site remained unknown. In an attempt to resolve this puzzle, biologists performed a DNA array experiment and found 25 genes whose expression levels significantly changed in hypoxic conditions. Given the upstream regions of these genes, each of which is 250 nucleotides long, we would like to discover the "hidden message" that DosR uses to control the expression of these genes.

To simplify the problem a bit, we have selected just 10 of the 25 genes, resulting in the **DosR dataset**. We will try to identify motifs in this dataset using the arsenal of motif finding tools that we have developed. However, we will not give you a hint about the DosR motif.

What k-mer size should we choose in order to analyze the DosR dataset using **MEDIANSTRING** and **RANDOMIZEDMOTIFSEARCH**? Taking a wild guess and running these algorithms for k from 8 to 12 returns the consensus strings shown below.

	MEDIANSTRING			**RANDOMIZEDMOTIFSEARCH**	
k	**Consensus**	**Score**	**k**	**Consensus**	**Score**
8	CATCGGCC	11	8	CCGACGGG	13
9	GGCGGGGAC	16	9	CCATCGGCC	16
10	GGTGGCCACC	19	10	CCATCGGCCC	21
11	GGACTTCCGGC	20	11	ACCTTCGGCCC	25
12	GGACTTCCGGCC	23	12	GGACCAACGGCC	28

STOP and Think: Can you infer the DosR binding site from these median strings? What do you think is the length of the binding site?

Note that although the consensus strings returned by **RANDOMIZEDMOTIFSEARCH** generally deviate from the median strings, the consensus 12-mer (GGACCAACGGCC, with score 28) is very similar to the median string (GGACTTCCGGCC, with score 23).

While the motifs returned by **RANDOMIZEDMOTIFSEARCH** are slightly less conserved than the motifs returned by **MEDIANSTRING**, the former algorithm has the advantage of being able to find longer motifs (since **MEDIANSTRING** becomes too slow for longer motifs). The motif of length 20 returned by **RANDOMIZEDMOTIFSEARCH** is CGGGACCTACGTCCCTAGCC (with score 57). As shown below, the consensus strings of length 12 found by **RANDOMIZEDMOTIFSEARCH** and **MEDIANSTRING** are "embedded" with small variations in the longer motif of length 20:

GGACCAACGGCC
CGGGACCTACGTCCCTAGCC
GGACTTCCGGCC

Finally, in 2,000 runs with $N = 200$, GIBBSSAMPLER returned the same consensus string of length 20 for the DosR dataset as RANDOMIZEDMOTIFSEARCH but generated a different collection of motifs with a smaller score of 55.

As you have seen in this chapter, different motif finding algorithms generate somewhat different results, and it remains unclear how to identify the DosR motif in MTB. Try to answer this question and find all putative DosR motifs in MTB as well as all genes that they regulate. We will provide the upstream regions of all 25 genes identified in the DosR study to help you address the following problem.

CHALLENGE PROBLEM: Infer the profile of the DosR motif and find all its putative occurrences in *Mycobacterium tuberculosis*.

Charging Stations

Solving the Median String Problem

The first potential issue with implementing **MEDIANSTRING** is writing a function to compute $d(Pattern, Dna) = \sum_{i=1}^{t} d(Pattern, Dna_i)$, the sum of distances between *Pattern* and each string in $Dna = \{Dna_1, \ldots, Dna_t\}$. This task is achieved by the following pseudocode.

DISTANCEBETWEENPATTERNANDSTRINGS(*Pattern, Dna*)
    $k \leftarrow |Pattern|$
    $distance \leftarrow 0$
    for each string *Text* in *Dna*
        $HammingDistance \leftarrow \infty$
        for each *k*-mer *Pattern'* in *Text*
            if *HammingDistance* > HAMMINGDISTANCE(*Pattern, Pattern'*)
                $HammingDistance \leftarrow$ HAMMINGDISTANCE(*Pattern, Pattern'*)
        $distance \leftarrow distance + HammingDistance$
    return *distance*

To solve the Median String Problem, we need to iterate through all possible 4^k *k*-mers *Pattern* before computing $d(Pattern, Dna)$. The pseudocode below is a modification of **MEDIANSTRING** using the function NUMBERTOPATTERN (implemented in **CHARGING STATION: Converting Patterns Into Numbers and Vice-Versa**), which is applied to convert all integers from 0 to $4^k - 1$ into all possible *k*-mers.

PAGE
41

MEDIANSTRING(*Dna, k*)
    $distance \leftarrow \infty$
    for $i \leftarrow 0$ to $4^k - 1$
        $Pattern \leftarrow$ NUMBERTOPATTERN(i, k)
        if $distance >$ **DISTANCEBETWEENPATTERNANDSTRINGS**(*Pattern, Dna*)
            $distance \leftarrow$ **DISTANCEBETWEENPATTERNANDSTRINGS**(*Pattern, Dna*)
            $Median \leftarrow Pattern$
    return *Median*

Detours

Gene expression

Genes encode proteins, and proteins dictate cell function. To respond to changes in their environment, cells must therefore control their protein levels. The flow of information from DNA to RNA to protein means that the cell can adjust the amount of proteins that it produces during both transcription (DNA to RNA) and translation (RNA to protein).

Transcription begins when an RNA polymerase binds to a **promoter sequence** on the DNA molecule, which is often located just upstream from the starting point for transcription. The initiation of transcription is a convenient control point for the cell to regulate gene expression since it is at the very beginning of the protein production process. The genes transcribed in a cell are controlled by various transcription regulators that may increase or suppress transcription.

DNA arrays

A **DNA array** is a collection of DNA molecules attached to a solid surface. Each spot on the array is assigned a unique DNA sequence called a **probe** that measures the expression level of a specific gene, known as a **target**. In most arrays, probes are synthesized and then attached to a glass or silicon chip (Figure 2.8).

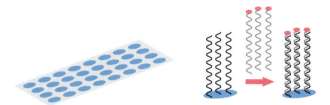

FIGURE 2.8 Fluorescently labeled DNA binds to a complementary probe on a DNA array.

Fluorescently labeled targets then bind to their corresponding probe (e.g., when their sequences are complementary), generating a fluorescent signal. The strength of this signal depends upon the amount of target sample that binds to the probe at a given spot. Thus, the higher the expression level of a gene, the higher the intensity of its fluorescent signal on the array. Since an array may contain millions of probes, biologists can measure the expression of many genes in a single array experiment. The DNA array experiment that identified the evening element in *Arabidopsis thaliana* measured the expression of 8,000 genes.

Buffon's needle

Comte de Buffon was a prolific 18th Century naturalist whose writings on natural history were popular at the time. However, his first paper was in mathematics; in 1733, he wrote an essay on a Medieval French game called "Le jeu de franc carreau". In this game, a single player flips a coin into the air, and the coin lands on a checkerboard. The player wins if the coin lands completely within one of the squares on the board, and loses otherwise (Figure 2.9 (left)). Buffon asked a natural question: what is the probability that the player wins?

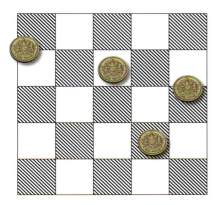
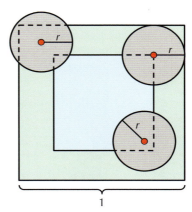

FIGURE 2.9 (Left) A game of "franc carreau" with four coins. Two of the coins have landed within one of the squares of the checkerboard and are considered winners, whereas the other two have landed on a boundary and are considered losers. (Right) Three coins shown on a single square of the checkerboard (the green outside square); one coin is a loser, another is a winner, and the third corresponds to a boundary case. You can see that if the coin has radius r, then the probability of winning the game corresponds to the probability that the center of the coin (shown as a red dot) lands within the blue square, which has side length $1 - 2r$. This probability is the ratio of the squares' areas, which is $(1 - 2r)^2$.

Let's assume that the checkerboard consists of just a single square with side length 1, that the coin has radius $r < 1/2$, and that the center of the coin always lands within the square. Then the player can only win if the center of the circle falls within an imaginary central square of side length $1 - 2r$ (Figure 2.9 (right)). Assuming that the coin lands anywhere on the larger square with uniform probability, then the probability that the coin falls completely within the smaller square is given by the ratio of the areas of the two squares, or $(1 - 2r)^2$.

Four decades later, Buffon published a paper describing a similar game in which the player uniformly drops a needle onto a floor covered by long wooden panels of equal width. In this game, which has become known as **Buffon's needle**, the player wins if the needle falls entirely within one of the panels. Note that computing the probability of a win is now complicated by the fact that the needle is described by an orientation in addition to its position. Nevertheless, the first game gives us an idea for how to solve this problem: once we fix a position for the center of the needle, its collection of different possible orientations sweep out a circle (Figure 2.10 (left)).

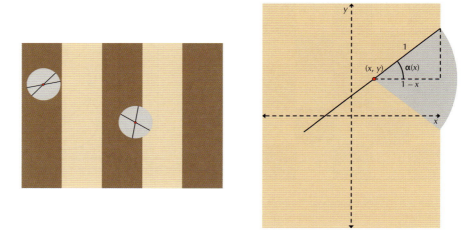

FIGURE 2.10 (Left) Once we fix a point for the center of the needle (shown as a red dot), its collection of possible orientations sweep out a circle. In the circle on the left, the needle will always lie within the dark brown panel, regardless of its orientation. In the circle on the right, one of the two needles lies within the dark brown panel, whereas another is shown crossing over into the adjacent panel. (Right) Once we fix a point (x, y) for the center of the needle, there is a critical angle $\alpha(x)$ such that all angles between $-\alpha(x)$ and $\alpha(x)$ will cause the needle to cross over into the next panel. In this figure, the length of the needle is equal to the width of the panel.

The probability that the player wins depends on the length of the needle with respect to the distance between wooden panels. We will assume that both of these lengths are equal to 2, and we will find the probability of a *loss* instead of a win. To this end, we first ask a simpler question: if the center of the needle were to land in the same place every time, then what is the likelihood that the needle crosses a panel?

To address this question, let's map the panel into which the needle falls onto a coordinate plane, with the y-axis dividing the panel into two smaller panels of width 1 (Figure 2.10 (right)). If the center of the needle lands at position (x, y) with $x > 0$, then its orientation can be described by an angle θ, where θ ranges from $-\pi/2$ to $\pi/2$ radians. If $\theta = 0$, then the needle will cross the line $y = 1$; if $\theta = \pi/2$, then the needle will not cross the line $y = 1$. Yet more importantly, since the needle's center position is fixed, there must be some critical angle $\alpha(x)$ such that the needle always touches this line if $-\alpha(x) \leq \theta \leq \alpha(x)$. If the needle is dropped randomly, then any value of θ is equally likely, and so we obtain that the probability of a loss given this position of the needle is equal to $2 \cdot \alpha(x)/\pi$.

Following the same reasoning, the needle can take any position x with equal probability. To find the probability of a loss, $\Pr(\text{loss})$, we must therefore compute an "average" of the values $2 \cdot \alpha(x)/\pi$ as x continuously ranges from -1 to 1. This average can be represented using an integral,

$$\Pr(\text{loss}) = \frac{\int_{-1}^{1} \frac{2 \cdot \alpha(x)}{\pi} \, dx}{1 - (-1)} = \int_{-1}^{1} \frac{\alpha(x)}{\pi} \, dx = 2 \int_{0}^{1} \frac{\alpha(x)}{\pi} \, dx.$$

Revisiting Figure 2.10 (right), applying some basic trigonometry tells us that $\cos \alpha(x)$ is equal to $1 - x$, so that $\alpha(x) = \arccos(1 - x)$. After making this substitution into the above equation — and consulting our dusty calculus textbook — $\Pr(\text{loss})$ must be equal to $2/\pi$. It is not difficult to see that this probability will be the same when the needle is dropped onto any number of wooden panels.

But what does Buffon's needle have to do with randomized algorithms? In 1812, none other than Laplace pointed out that Buffon's needle could be used to approximate π, and the world's first Monte Carlo algorithm was born. Specifically, we can approximate the probability P_e of a loss *empirically* by dully flipping a needle into the air thousands of times (or asking a computer to do it for us). Once we have computed this empirical probability, we can conclude that P_e is approximately equal to $2/\pi$, and thus

$$\pi \approx \frac{2}{P_e}.$$

STOP and Think: How does this approximation change in the following cases?

1. The needle is shorter than the width between panels.

2. The needle is longer than the width between panels.

Complications in motif finding

Motif finding becomes difficult if the **background nucleotide distribution** in the sample is skewed. In this case, searching for k-mers with the minimum score or entropy may lead to a biologically irrelevant motif composed from the most frequent nucleotides in the sample. For example, if A has frequency 85% and T, G, and C have frequencies of 5%, then k-mer AA...AA may represent a motif with minimum score, thus disguising biologically relevant motifs. For example, the relevant motif GCCG with score 5 in the example below loses out to the motif **aaaa** with score 1.

t**aaaa**GTCGa
acGCTG**aaaa**
Dna **aaaa**GCCTat
aCCCGa**ataa**
ag**aaaa**GGCG

To find biologically relevant motifs in samples with biased nucleotide frequencies, you may therefore want to use a generalization of entropy called "relative entropy" (see **DETOUR: Relative Entropy**).

PAGE 112

Another complication in motif finding is that many motifs are best represented in a different alphabet than the alphabet of 4 nucleotides. Let W denote either A or T, S denote either G or C, K denote either G or T, and Y denote either C or T. Now, consider the motif CSKWYWWATKWATYYK, which represents the CSRE motif in yeast (recall Figure 2.3 from page 75). This strong motif in a hybrid alphabet corresponds to 2^{11} different motifs in the standard 4-letter alphabet of nucleotides. However, each of these 2^{11} motifs is too weak to be found by the algorithms we have considered in this chapter.

Relative entropy

Given a collection of strings *Dna*, the **relative entropy** of a $4 \times k$ profile matrix $P = (p_{r,j})$ is defined as

$$\sum_{j=1}^{k} \sum_{r \in \{A,C,G,T\}} p_{r,j} \cdot \log_2(p_{r,j}/b_r) =$$

$$\sum_{j=1}^{k} \sum_{r \in \{A,C,G,T\}} p_{r,j} \cdot \log_2(p_{r,j}) - \sum_{j=1}^{k} \sum_{r \in \{A,C,G,T\}} p_{r,j} \cdot \log_2(b_r),$$

where b_r is the frequency of nucleotide r in *Dna*. Note that the sum in the expression for entropy is preceded by a negative sign ($-\sum_{j=1}^{k} \sum_{r \in \{A,C,G,T\}} p_{r,j} \cdot \log_2(p_{r,j})$), whereas the sum on the left side of the *relative* entropy equation does not have this negative sign. Therefore, although we minimized the entropy of a motif matrix, we will now attempt to maximize the relative entropy.

The term $-\sum_{j=1}^{k} \sum_{r \in \{A,C,G,T\}} p_{r,j} \cdot \log_2(b_r)$ is called the **cross-entropy** of the profile matrix P; note that the relative entropy of a profile matrix is simply the difference between the profile's cross-entropy and its entropy. For example, the relative entropy for the motif GCCG in the example from **DETOUR: Complications in Motif Finding** **PAGE 112** is equal to $9.85 - 3.53 = 6.32$, as shown below. In this example, $b_A = 0.5$, $b_C = 0.18$, $b_G = 0.2$, and $b_T = 0.12$.

		G	T	C	G
		G	C	T	G
Motifs		G	C	C	T
		C	C	C	G
		G	G	C	G

	A:	0.0	0.0	0.0	0.0
PROFILE(*Motifs*)	C:	0.2	0.6	0.8	0.0
	G:	0.8	0.2	0.0	0.8
	T:	0.0	0.2	0.2	0.2

Entropy	$0.72 + 1.37 + 0.72 + 0.72 =\ \ 3.53$
Cross-entropy	$2.35 + 2.56 + 2.47 + 2.47\ \ = 9.85$

For the more conserved but irrelevant motif aaaa, the relative entropy is equal to $4.18 - 0.72 = 3.46$, as shown below. Thus, GCCG loses to aaaa with respect to entropy but wins with respect to relative entropy.

	a	a	a	a
	a	a	a	a
Motifs	a	a	a	a
	a	t	a	a
	a	a	a	a

	A:	1.0	0.8	1.0	1.0
PROFILE(*Motifs*)	C:	0.0	0.0	0.0	0.0
	G:	0.0	0.0	0.0	0.0
	T:	0.0	0.2	0.0	0.0

Entropy $\quad 0.0 \;+ 0.72 + 0.0 \;+ 0.0 \;= 0.72$

Cross-entropy $\quad 0.94 + 1.36 + 0.94 + 0.94 = 4.18$

Bibliography Notes

Konopka and Benzer, 1971 bred flies with abnormally short (19 hours) and long (28 hours) circadian rhythms and then traced these abnormalities to a single gene. Harmer et al., 2000 discovered the evening transcription factor binding site that orchestrates the circadian clock in plants. Excellent coverage of this discovery is given by Cristianini and Hahn, 2006. Park et al., 2003 found a transcription factor that mediates the hypoxic response of *Mycobacterium tuberculosis*.

Hertz and Stormo, 1999 described the first greedy algorithm for motif finding. The general framework for Gibbs sampling was described by Geman and Geman, 1984 and was named Gibbs sampling in reference to its similarities with some approaches in statistical mechanics (Josiah Willard Gibbs was one of the founders of statistical mechanics). Lawrence et al., 1993 adapted Gibbs sampling for motif finding.

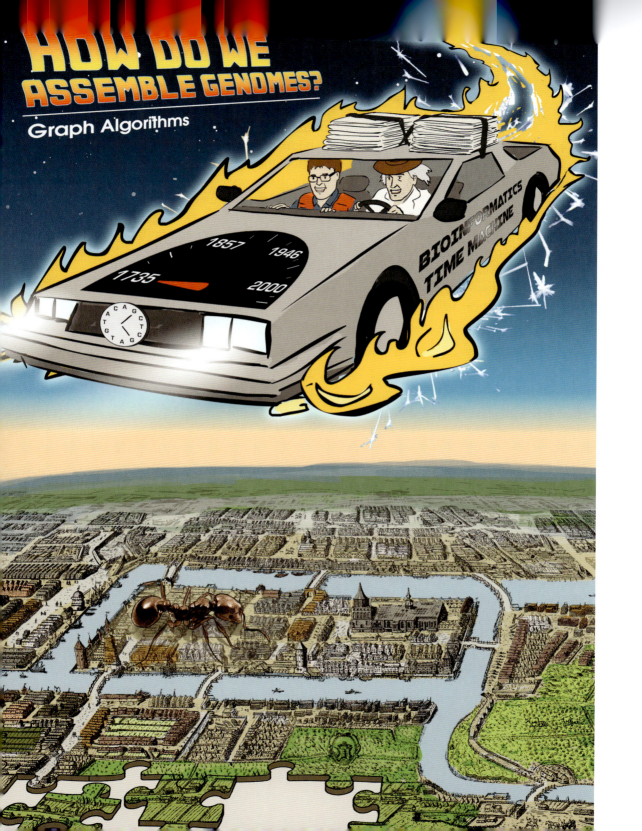

Exploding Newspapers

Imagine that we stack a hundred copies of the June 27, 2000 edition of the *New York Times* on a pile of dynamite, and then we light the fuse. We ask you to further suspend your disbelief and assume that the newspapers are not all incinerated but instead explode cartoonishly into smoldering pieces of confetti. How could we use the tiny snippets of newspaper to figure out what the news was on June 27, 2000? We will call this crazy conundrum the **Newspaper Problem** (see Figure 3.1).

FIGURE 3.1 Don't try this at home! Crazy as it may seem, the Newspaper Problem serves as an analogy for the computational framework of genome assembly.

The Newspaper Problem is even more difficult than it may seem. Because we had multiple copies of the same edition of the newspaper, and because we undoubtedly lost some information in the blast, we cannot simply glue together one of the newspaper copies in the same way that we would assemble a jigsaw puzzle. Instead, we need to use *overlapping* fragments from different copies of the newspaper to reconstruct the day's news, as shown in Figure 3.2.

Fine, you ask, *but what do exploding newspapers have to do with biology?* Determining the order of nucleotides in a genome, or **genome sequencing**, presents a fundamental task in bioinformatics. Genomes vary in length; your own genome is roughly 3 billion

atshirt, appr.

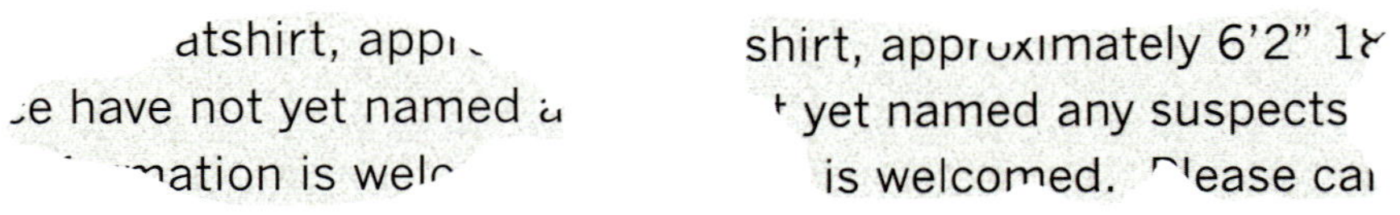

e have not yet named a

nation is welc

shirt, approximately 6'2" 1&

yet named any suspects

is welcomed. Please cal

FIGURE 3.2 In the Newspaper Problem, we need to use overlapping shreds of paper to figure out the news.

nucleotides long, whereas the genome of *Amoeba dubia*, an amorphous unicellular organism, is approximately 200 times longer! This unicellular organism competes with the rare Japanese flower *Paris japonica* for the title of species with the longest genome.

The first sequenced genome, belonging to a φX174 bacterial phage (i.e., a virus that preys on bacteria), had only 5,386 nucleotides and was completed in 1977 by Frederick Sanger. Four decades after this Nobel Prize-winning discovery, genome sequencing has raced to the forefront of bioinformatics research, as the cost of genome sequencing plummeted. Because of the decreasing cost of sequencing, we now have thousands of sequenced genomes, including those of many mammals (Figure 3.3).

To sequence a genome, we must clear some practical hurdles. The largest obstacle is the fact that biologists still lack the technology to read the nucleotides of a genome from beginning to end in the same way that you would read a book. The best they can do is sequence much shorter DNA fragments called **reads**. The reasons why researchers can sequence small pieces of DNA but not long genomes warrant their own discussion PAGE 170 in DETOUR: A Short History of DNA Sequencing Technologies. In this chapter, our aim is to turn an apparent handicap into a useful tool for assembling the genome back together.

The traditional method for sequencing genomes is described as follows. Researchers take a small tissue or blood sample containing millions of cells with identical DNA, use biochemical methods to break the DNA into fragments, and then sequence these fragments to produce reads (Figure 3.4). The difficulty is that researchers do not know where in the genome these reads came from, and so they must use overlapping reads to reconstruct the genome. Thus, putting a genome back together from its reads, or **genome assembly**, is just like the Newspaper Problem.

Even though researchers have sequenced many genomes, a giant genome like that of *Amoeba dubia* still remains beyond the reach of modern sequencing technologies. You might guess that the barrier to sequence such a genome would be experimental, but that is not true; biologists can easily generate enough reads to analyze a large genome, but assembling these reads still presents a major computational challenge.

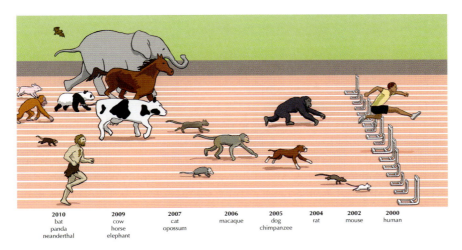

2010	2009	2007	2006	2005	2004	2002	2000
bat	cow	cat	macaque	dog	rat	mouse	human
panda	horse	opossum		chimpanzee			
neanderthal	elephant						

FIGURE 3.3 The first mammals with sequenced genomes.

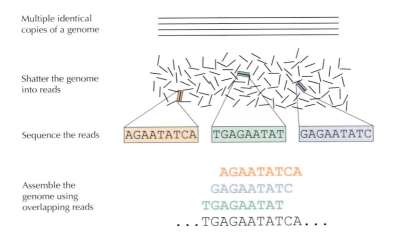

FIGURE 3.4 In DNA sequencing, many identical copies of a genome are broken in random locations to generate short reads, which are then sequenced and assembled into the nucleotide sequence of the genome.

The String Reconstruction Problem

Genome assembly is more difficult than you think

Before we introduce a computational problem modeling genome assembly, we will take a moment to discuss a few practical complications that make genome assembly more difficult than the Newspaper Problem.

First, DNA is double-stranded, and we have no way of knowing *a priori* which strand a given read derives from, meaning that we will not know whether to use a read or its reverse complement when assembling a particular strand of a genome. Second, modern sequencing machines are not perfect, and the reads that they generate often contain errors. Sequencing errors complicate genome assembly because they prevent us from identifying all overlapping reads. Third, some regions of the genome may not be covered by any reads, making it impossible to reconstruct the entire genome.

Since the reads generated by modern sequencers often have the same length, we may safely assume that reads are all *k*-mers for some value of *k*. The first part of this chapter will assume an ideal — and unrealistic — situation in which all reads come from the same strand, have no errors, and exhibit **perfect coverage**, so that every *k*-mer substring of the genome is generated as a read. Later, we will show how to relax these assumptions for more realistic datasets.

Reconstructing strings from k-mers

We are now ready to define a computational problem modeling genome assembly. Given a string *Text*, its **k-mer composition** COMPOSITION$_k$(*Text*) is the collection of all *k*-mer substrings of *Text* (including repeated *k*-mers). For example,

COMPOSITION$_3$(TATGGGGTGC) = {ATG, GGG, GGG, GGT, GTG, TAT, TGC, TGG}.

Note that we have listed *k*-mers in **lexicographic order** (i.e., how they would appear in a dictionary) rather than in the order of their appearance in TATGGGGTGC. We have done this because the correct ordering of reads is unknown when they are generated.

String Composition Problem:
Generate the k-mer composition of a string.

> **Input**: A string *Text* and an integer *k*.
> **Output**: COMPOSITION$_k$(*Text*), where the *k*-mers are arranged in lexicographic order.

HOW DO WE ASSEMBLE GENOMES?

Solving the String Composition Problem is a straightforward exercise, but in order to model genome assembly, we need to solve its inverse problem.

String Reconstruction Problem:

Reconstruct a string from its k-mer composition.

> **Input**: An integer k and a collection *Patterns* of k-mers.
> **Output**: A string *Text* with k-mer composition equal to *Patterns* (if such a string exists).

Before we ask you to solve the String Reconstruction Problem, let's consider the following example of a 3-mer composition:

AAT   ATG   GTT   TAA   TGT

The most natural way to solve the String Reconstruction Problem is to mimic the solution of the Newspaper Problem and "connect" a pair of k-mers if they overlap in $k - 1$ symbols. For the above example, it is easy to see that the string should start with TAA because there is no 3-mer ending in TA. This implies that the next 3-mer in the string should start with AA. There is only one 3-mer satisfying this condition, AAT:

TAA
AAT

In turn, AAT can only be extended by ATG, which can only be extended by TGT, and so on, leading us to reconstruct **TAATGTT**:

TAA
AA**T**
AT**G**
TG**T**
GT**T**
TAATGTT

It looks like we are finished with the String Reconstruction Problem and can let you move on to the next chapter. To be sure, let's consider another 3-mer composition:

AAT   ATG   ATG   ATG   CAT   CCA   GAT   GCC   GGA   GGG   GTT   TAA   TGC   TGG   TGT

If we start again with TAA, then the next 3-mer in the string should start with AA, and there is only one such 3-mer, AAT. In turn, AAT can only be extended by ATG:

$$
\begin{array}{l}
\text{\textbf{TAA}} \\
\text{AA\textbf{T}} \\
\text{AT\textbf{G}} \\
\text{\textbf{TAATG}}
\end{array}
$$

ATG can be extended either by TGC, or TGG, or TGT. Now we must decide which of these 3-mers to choose. Let's select TGT:

$$
\begin{array}{l}
\text{\textbf{TAA}} \\
\text{AA\textbf{T}} \\
\text{AT\textbf{G}} \\
\text{TG\textbf{T}} \\
\text{\textbf{TAATGT}}
\end{array}
$$

After TGT, our only choice is GTT:

$$
\begin{array}{l}
\text{\textbf{TAA}} \\
\text{AA\textbf{T}} \\
\text{AT\textbf{G}} \\
\text{TG\textbf{T}} \\
\text{GT\textbf{T}} \\
\text{\textbf{TAATGTT}}
\end{array}
$$

Unfortunately, now we are stuck at GTT because no 3-mers in the composition start with TT! We could try to extend TAA to the left, but no 3-mers in the composition end with TA.

You may have found this trap on your own and already discovered how to escape it. Like a good chess player, if you think a few steps ahead, then you would never extend ATG by TGT until reaching the end of the genome. With this thought in mind, let's take a step back, extending ATG by TGC instead:

$$
\begin{array}{l}
\text{\textbf{TAA}} \\
\text{AA\textbf{T}} \\
\text{AT\textbf{G}} \\
\text{TG\textbf{C}} \\
\text{\textbf{TAATGC}}
\end{array}
$$

Continuing the process, we obtain the following assembly:

```
TAA
 AAT
  ATG
   TGC
    GCC
     CCA
      CAT
       ATG
        TGG
         GGA
          GAT
           ATG
            TGT
             GTT
TAATGCCATGGATGTT
```

Yet this assembly is incorrect because we have only used fourteen of the fifteen 3-mers in the composition (we omitted GGG), making our reconstructed genome one nucleotide too short.

Repeats complicate genome assembly

The difficulty in assembling this genome arises because ATG is *repeated* three times in the 3-mer composition, which causes us to have the three choices TGG, TGC, and TGT by which to extend ATG. Repeated substrings in the genome are not a serious problem when we have just fifteen reads, but with millions of reads, repeats make it much more difficult to "look ahead" and construct the correct assembly.

If you followed **DETOUR: Probabilities of Patterns in a String** from Chapter 1, **PAGE 52** you know how unlikely it is to witness a long repeat in a randomly generated sequence of nucleotides. You also know that real genomes are anything but random. Indeed, approximately 50% of the human genome is made up of repeats, e.g., the approximately 300 nucleotide-long **Alu sequence** is repeated over a million times, with only a few nucleotides inserted/deleted/substituted each time (see **DETOUR: Repeats in the** **PAGE 172** **Human Genome**).

An analogy illustrating the difficulty of assembling a genome with many repeats is the Triazzle® jigsaw puzzle (Figure 3.5). People usually put together jigsaw puzzles by connecting matching pieces. However, every piece in the Triazzle matches more than one other piece; in Figure 3.5, each frog appears several times. If you proceed carelessly, then you will likely match most of the pieces but fail to fit the remaining ones. And yet the Triazzle has only 16 pieces, which should give us pause about assembling a genome from millions of reads.

FIGURE 3.5 Each Triazzle has only sixteen pieces but carries a warning: "It's Harder than it Looks!"

EXERCISE BREAK: Design a strategy for assembling the Triazzle puzzle.

String Reconstruction as a Walk in the Overlap Graph

From a string to a graph

Repeats in a genome necessitate some way of looking ahead to see the correct assembly in advance. Returning to our previous example, you may have already found that **TAATGCCATGGGATGTT** is a solution to the String Reconstruction Problem for the collection of fifteen 3-mers in the last section, as illustrated below. Note that we use a different color for each interval of the string between occurrences of **ATG**.

<pre>
TAA
 AAT
  ATG
   TGC
    GCC
     CCA
      CAT
       ATG
        TGG
         GGG
          GGA
           GAT
            ATG
             TGT
              GTT
TAATGCCATGGGATGTT
</pre>

STOP and Think: Is this the only solution to the String Reconstruction Problem for this collection of 3-mers?

In Figure 3.6, consecutive 3-mers in **TAATGCCATGGGATGTT** are linked together to form the **genome path**.

FIGURE 3.6 The fifteen color-coded 3-mers making up **TAATGCCATGGGATGTT** are joined into the genome path according to their order in the genome.

String Spelled by a Genome Path Problem:

Reconstruct a string from its genome path.

> **Input:** A sequence of k-mers $Pattern_1, \ldots, Pattern_n$ such that the last $k - 1$ symbols of $Pattern_i$ are equal to the first $k - 1$ symbols of $Pattern_{i+1}$ for $1 \leq n - 1$.
>
> **Output:** A string $Text$ of length $k + n - 1$ such that the i-th k-mer in $Text$ is equal to $Pattern_i$ (for $1 \leq i \leq n$).

Reconstructing a genome from its genome path is easy: as we proceed from left to right, the 3-mers "spell" out **TAATGCCATGGGATGTT**, adding one new symbol to the genome at each new 3-mer. Unfortunately, constructing this string's genome path requires us to know the genome in advance.

STOP and Think: Could you construct the genome path if you knew only the genome's 3-mer composition?

In this chapter, we will use the terms **prefix** and **suffix** to refer to the first $k - 1$ nucleotides and last $k - 1$ nucleotides of a k-mer, respectively. For example, PREFIX(**TAA**) = **TA** and SUFFIX(**TAA**) = **AA**. We note that the suffix of a 3-mer in the genome path is equal to the prefix of the following 3-mer in the path. For example, SUFFIX(**TAA**) = PREFIX(**AAT**) = **AA** in the genome path for **TAATGCCATGGGATGTT**.

This observation suggests a method of constructing a string's genome path from its k-mer composition: we will use an arrow to connect any k-mer *Pattern* to a k-mer *Pattern'* if the suffix of *Pattern'* is equal to the prefix of *Pattern'*.

STOP and Think: Apply this rule to the 3-mer composition of **TAATGCCATGGGATGTT**. Are you able to reconstruct the genome path of **TAATGCCATGGGATGTT**?

If we follow the rule of connecting two 3-mers with an arrow every time the suffix of one is equal to the prefix of the other, then we will connect all consecutive 3-mers in **TAATGCCATGGGATGTT** as in Figure 3.6. However, because we don't know this genome in advance, we wind up having to connect many other pairs of 3-mers as well. For example, each of the three occurrences of **ATG** should be connected to **TGC**, **TGG**, and **TGT**, as shown in Figure 3.7.

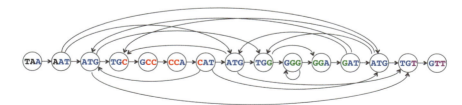

FIGURE 3.7 The graph showing all connections between nodes representing the 3-mer composition of **TAATGCCATGGGATGTT**. This graph has fifteen nodes and 25 edges. Note that the genome can still be spelled out by walking along the horizontal edges from **TAA** to **GTT**.

Figure 3.7 presents an example of a **graph**, or a network of **nodes** connected by **edges**. This particular graph is an example of a **directed graph**, whose edges have a direction and are represented by arrows (as opposed to **undirected graphs** whose edges do not have directions). If you are unfamiliar with graphs, see DETOUR: Graphs.

PAGE 173

The genome vanishes

The genome can still be traced out in the graph in Figure 3.7 by following the horizontal path from **TAA** to **GTT**. But in genome sequencing, we do not know in advance how to correctly order reads. Therefore we will arrange the 3-mers lexicographically, which produces the **overlap graph** shown in Figure 3.8. The genome path has disappeared!

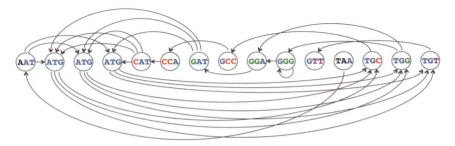

FIGURE 3.8 The same graph as the one in Figure 3.7 with 3-mers ordered lexicographically. The path through the graph representing the correct assembly is now harder to see.

The genome path may have disappeared to the naked eye, but it must still be there, since we have simply rearranged the nodes of the graph. Indeed, Figure 3.9 (top) highlights the genome path spelling out **TAATGCCATGGGATGTT**. However, if we had given you this graph to begin with, you would have needed to find a path through the graph visiting each node exactly once; such a path "explains" all the 3-mers in the 3-mer composition of the genome. Although finding such a path is currently just as difficult as trying to assemble the genome by hand, the graph nevertheless gives us a nice way of visualizing the overlap relationships between reads.

STOP and Think: Can any other strings be reconstructed by following a path visiting all the nodes in Figure 3.8?

To generalize the construction of the graph in Figure 3.8 to an arbitrary collection of *k*-mers *Patterns*, we form a node for each *k*-mer in *Patterns* and connect *k*-mers *Pattern* and *Pattern'* by a directed edge if SUFFIX(*Pattern*) = PREFIX(*Pattern'*). The resulting graph is called the **overlap graph** on these *k*-mers, denoted OVERLAP(*Patterns*).

Overlap Graph Problem:
Construct the overlap graph of a collection of k-mers.

> **Input**: A collection *Patterns* of *k*-mers.
> **Output**: The overlap graph OVERLAP(*Patterns*).

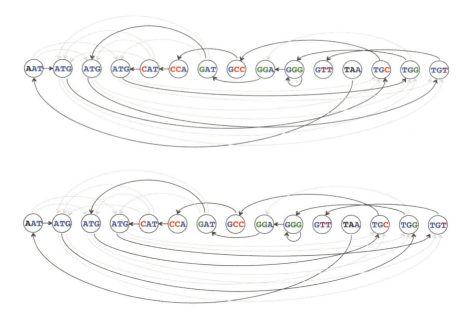

FIGURE 3.9 (Top) The genome path spelling out **TA**ATGCCATGGGATGTT, highlighted in the overlap graph. (Bottom) Another Hamiltonian path in the overlap graph spells the genome **TA**ATGGGATGCCATGTT. These two genomes differ by exchanging the positions of **CC** and **GG** but have the same 3-mer composition.

Two graph representations

If you have never worked with graphs before, you may be wondering how to represent graphs in your programs. To make a brief digression from our discussion of genome assembly, consider the graph in Figure 3.10 (top). We can move around this graph's nodes without changing the graph (e.g., the graphs in Figure 3.7 and Figure 3.8 are the same). As a result, when we are representing a graph computationally, the only information we need to store is the pair of nodes that each edge connects.

There are two standard ways of representing a graph. For a directed graph with n nodes, the $n \times n$ **adjacency matrix** ($A_{i,j}$) is defined by the following rule: $A_{i,j} = 1$ if a directed edge connects node i to node j, and $A_{i,j} = 0$ otherwise. Another (more memory-efficient) way of representing a graph is to use an **adjacency list**, for which we simply list all nodes connected to each node (see Figure 3.10).

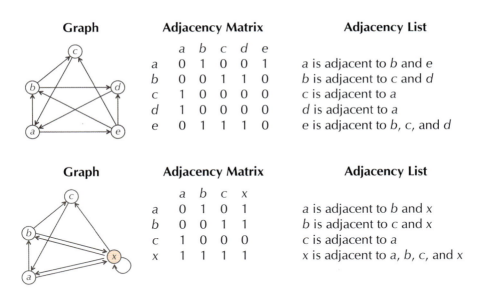

FIGURE 3.10 (Top) A graph with five nodes and nine edges, followed by its adjacency matrix and adjacency list. (Bottom) The graph produced by gluing nodes d and e into a single node x, along with the new graph's adjacency matrix and adjacency list.

Hamiltonian paths and universal strings

We now know that to solve the String Reconstruction Problem, we are looking for a path in the overlap graph that visits every node exactly once. A path in a graph visiting every node once is called a **Hamiltonian path**, in honor of the Irish mathematician

 William Hamilton (see DETOUR: The Icosian Game). As Figure 3.9 illustrates, a graph may have more than one Hamiltonian path.

Hamiltonian Path Problem:

Construct a Hamiltonian path in a graph.

> **Input**: A directed graph.
> **Output**: A path visiting every node in the graph exactly once (if such a path exists).

We do not ask you to solve the Hamiltonian Path Problem yet, since it is not clear how we could design an efficient algorithm for it. Instead, we want you to meet Nicolaas de Bruijn, a Dutch mathematician. In 1946, de Bruijn was interested in solving a purely theoretical problem, described as follows. A **binary string** is a string composed only of 0's and 1's; a binary string is *k*-**universal** if it contains every binary *k*-mer exactly once. For example, 0001110100 is a 3-universal string, as it contains each of the eight binary 3-mers (000, 001, 011, 111, 110, 101, 010, and 100) exactly once.

Finding a *k*-universal string is equivalent to solving the String Reconstruction Problem when the *k*-mer composition is the collection of all binary *k*-mers. Thus, finding a *k*-universal string is equivalent to finding a Hamiltonian path in the overlap graph formed on all binary *k*-mers (Figure 3.11). Although the Hamiltonian path in Figure 3.11 can easily be found by hand, de Bruijn was interested in constructing *k*-universal strings for arbitrary values of *k*. For example, to find a 20-universal string, you would have to consider a graph with over a million nodes. It is absolutely unclear how to find a Hamiltonian path in such a huge graph, or even whether such a path exists!

Instead of searching for Hamiltonian paths in huge graphs, de Bruijn developed a completely different (and somewhat non-intuitive) way of representing a *k*-mer composition using a graph. Later in this chapter, we will learn how he used this method to construct universal strings.

 EXERCISE BREAK: Construct a 4-universal string. How many different 4-universal strings can you construct?

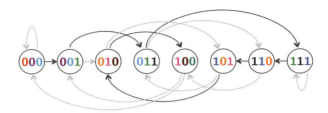

FIGURE 3.11 A Hamiltonian path highlighted in the overlap graph of all binary 3-mers. This path spells out the 3-universal binary string **0001110100**.

Another Graph for String Reconstruction

Gluing nodes and de Bruijn graphs

Let's again represent the genome **TAATGCCATGGGATGTT** as a sequence of its 3-mers:

TAA AAT ATG TGC GCC CCA CAT ATG TGG GGG GGA GAT ATG TGT GTT

This time, instead of assigning these 3-mers to *nodes*, we will assign them to *edges*, as shown in Figure 3.12. You can once again reconstruct the genome by following this path from left to right, adding one new nucleotide at each step. Since each pair of consecutive edges represent consecutive 3-mers that overlap in two nucleotides, we will label each node of this graph with a 2-mer representing the overlapping nucleotides shared by the edges on either side of the node. For example, the node with incoming edge **CAT** and outgoing edge **ATG** is labeled **AT**.

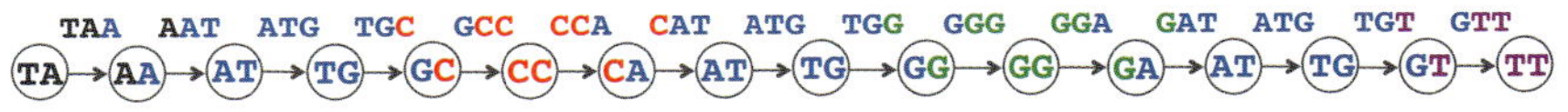

TAA   AAT   ATG   TGC   GCC   CCA   CAT   ATG   TGG   GGG   GGA   GAT   ATG   TGT   GTT
(TA)→(AA)→(AT)→(TG)→(GC)→(CC)→(CA)→(AT)→(TG)→(GG)→(GG)→(GA)→(AT)→(TG)→(GT)→(TT)

FIGURE 3.12 Genome **TAATGCCATGGGATGTT** represented as a path with edges (rather than nodes) labeled by 3-mers and nodes labeled by 2-mers.

Nothing seems new here until we start **gluing** identically labeled nodes. In Figure 3.13 (top panels), we bring the three **AT** nodes closer and closer to each other until they have been glued into a single node. Note that there are also three nodes labeled by **TG**, which we glue together in Figure 3.13 (middle panels). Finally, we glue together the two nodes labeled GG (**GG** and **GG**), as shown in Figure 3.13 (bottom panels), which produces a special type of edge called a **loop** connecting GG to itself.

The number of nodes in the resulting graph (Figure 3.13 (bottom right)) has reduced from 16 to 11, while the number of edges stayed the same. This graph is called the **de Bruijn graph** of **TAATGCCATGGGATGTT**, denoted DEBRUIJN₃(**TAATGCCATGGGATGTT**). Note that this de Bruijn graph has three different edges connecting **AT** to **TG**, representing three copies of the repeat **ATG**.

In general, given a genome *Text*, PATHGRAPH$_k$(*Text*) is the path consisting of $|Text| - k + 1$ edges, where the *i*-th edge of this path is labeled by the *i*-th *k*-mer in *Text* and the *i*-th node of the path is labeled by the *i*-th $(k-1)$-mer in *Text*. The de Bruijn graph DEBRUIJN$_k$(*Text*) is formed by gluing identically labeled nodes in PATHGRAPH$_k$(*Text*).

De Bruijn Graph from a String Problem:

Construct the de Bruijn graph of a string.

> **Input:** A string *Text* and an integer *k*.
> **Output:** DEBRUIJN$_k$(*Text*).

STOP and Think: Consider the following questions.

1. If we gave you the de Bruijn graph DEBRUIJN$_k$(*Text*) without giving you *Text*, could you reconstruct *Text*?

2. Construct the de Bruijn graphs DEBRUIJN₂(*Text*), DEBRUIJN₃(*Text*), and DEBRUIJN₄(*Text*) for *Text* = **TAATGCCATGGGATGTT**. What do you notice?

3. How does the graph DEBRUIJN₃(**TAATGCCATGGGATGTT**) compare to DEBRUIJN₃(**TAATGGGATGCCATGTT**)?

CHARGING STATION (The Effect of Gluing on the Adjacency Matrix): Figure 3.10 (bottom) shows how the gluing operation affects the adjacency matrix and adjacency list of a graph. Check out this Charging Station to see how gluing works for a de Bruijn graph.

PAGE 164

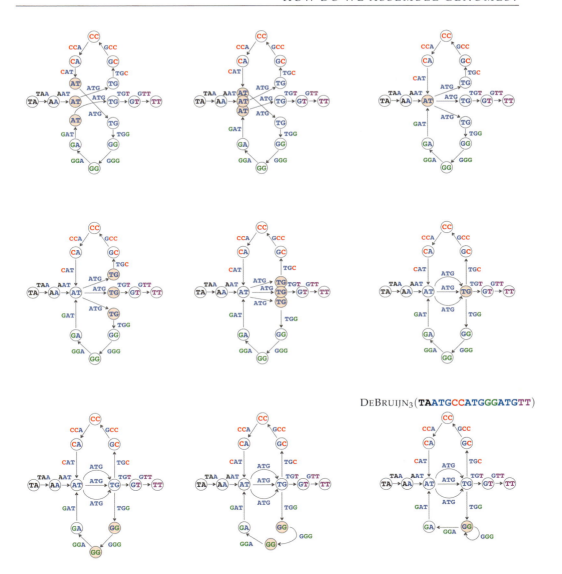

DeBruijn3(**TAATGCC**ATGGGATGTT)

FIGURE 3.13 (Top panels) Bringing the three nodes labeled **AT** in Figure 3.12 closer (left) and closer (middle) to each other to eventually glue them into a single node (right). (Middle panels) Bringing the three nodes labeled **TG** closer (left) and closer (middle) to each other to eventually glue them into a single node (right). (Bottom panels) Bringing the two nodes labeled GG closer (left) and closer (middle) to each other to eventually glue them into a single node (right). The path with 16 nodes from Figure 3.12 has been transformed into the graph DeBruijn3(**TAATGCC**ATGGGATGTT) with eleven nodes.

Walking in the de Bruijn Graph

Eulerian paths

Even though we have glued together nodes to form the de Bruijn graph, we have not changed its edges, and so the path from **TA** to **TT** reconstructing the genome is still hiding in DEBRUIJN₃(**TAATGCCATGGGATGTT**) (Figure 3.14), although this path has become "tangled" after gluing. Therefore, solving the String Reconstruction Problem reduces to finding a path in the de Bruijn graph that visits every *edge* exactly once. Such a path is called an **Eulerian Path** in honor of the great mathematician Leonhard Euler (pronounced "oiler").

Eulerian Path Problem:

Construct an Eulerian path in a graph.

> **Input**: A directed graph.
> **Output**: A path visiting every edge in the graph exactly once (if such a path exists).

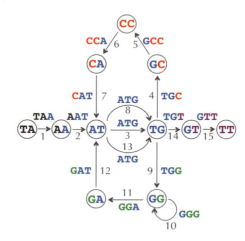

FIGURE 3.14 The path from **TA** to **TT** spelling out the genome **TAATGCCATGGGATGTT** has become "tangled" in the de Bruijn graph. The numbering of the fifteen edges of the path indicates an Eulerian path reconstructing the genome.

We now have an alternative way of solving the String Reconstruction Problem that amounts to finding an Eulerian path in the de Bruijn graph. But wait — to construct the de Bruijn graph of a genome, we glued together nodes of PATHGRAPH$_k$(*Text*). However, constructing this graph requires us to know the correct ordering of the k-mers in *Text*!

STOP and Think: Can you construct DEBRUIJN$_k$(*Text*) if you don't know *Text* but you do know its k-mer composition?

Another way to construct de Bruijn graphs

Figure 3.15 (top) represents the 3-mer composition of **TAATGCCATGGGATGTT** as a composition graph COMPOSITIONGRAPH$_3$(**TAATGCCATGGGATGTT**). As with the de Bruijn graph, each 3-mer is assigned to a directed edge, with its prefix labeling the first node of the edge and its suffix labeling the second node of the edge. However, the edges of this graph are **isolated**, meaning that no two edges share a node.

STOP and Think: Given *Text* = **TAATGCCATGGGATGTT**, glue identically labeled nodes in COMPOSITIONGRAPH$_3$(*Text*). How does the resulting graph differ from DEBRUIJN$_3$(*Text*) obtained by gluing the identically labeled nodes in PATHGRAPH$_3$(*Text*)?

Figure 3.15 shows how COMPOSITIONGRAPH$_3$(*Text*) changes after gluing nodes with the same label, for *Text* = **TAATGCCATGGGATGTT**. These operations glue the fifteen isolated edges in COMPOSITIONGRAPH$_3$(*Text*) into the path PATHGRAPH$_3$(*Text*). Follow-up gluing operations proceed in exactly the same way as when we glued nodes of PATHGRAPH$_3$(*Text*), which results in DEBRUIJN$_3$(*Text*). Thus, we can construct the de Bruijn graph from this genome's 3-mer composition without knowing the genome!

For an arbitrary string *Text*, we define COMPOSITIONGRAPH$_k$(*Text*) as the graph consisting of $|Text| - k + 1$ isolated edges, where edges are labeled by k-mers in *Text*; every edge labeled by a k-mer edge connects nodes labeled by the prefix and suffix of this k-mer. The graph COMPOSITIONGRAPH$_k$(*Text*) is just a collection of isolated edges representing the k-mers in the k-mer composition of *Text*, meaning that we can construct COMPOSITIONGRAPH$_k$(*Text*) from the k-mer composition of *Text*. Gluing nodes with the same label in COMPOSITIONGRAPH$_k$(*Text*) produces DEBRUIJN$_k$(*Text*).

Given an arbitrary collection of k-mers *Patterns* (where some k-mers may appear multiple times), we define COMPOSITIONGRAPH(*Patterns*) as a graph with $|Patterns|$ isolated edges. Every edge is labeled by a k-mer from *Patterns*, and the starting and

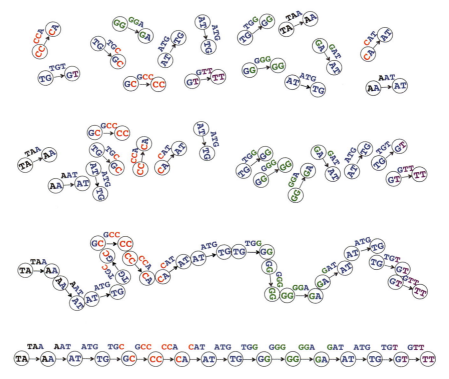

FIGURE 3.15 Gluing some identically labeled nodes transforms the graph COMPOSITIONGRAPH₃(**TAATGCCATGGGATGTT**) (top) into the graph PATHGRAPH₃(**TAATGCCATGGGATGTT**) (bottom). Gluing all identically labeled nodes produces DEBRUIJN₃(**TAATGCCATGGGATGTT**) from Figure 3.14.

ending nodes of an edge are labeled by the prefix and suffix of the *k*-mer labeling that edge. We then define DEBRUIJN(*Patterns*) by gluing identically labeled nodes in COMPOSITIONGRAPH(*Patterns*), which yields the following algorithm.

DEBRUIJN(*Patterns*)
    represent every *k*-mer in *Patterns* as an isolated edge between its prefix and suffix
    glue all nodes with identical labels, yielding the graph DEBRUIJN(*Patterns*)
    return DEBRUIJN(*Patterns*)

Constructing de Bruijn graphs from k-mer composition

Constructing the de Bruijn graph by gluing identically labeled nodes will help us later when we generalize the notion of de Bruijn graph for other applications. We will now describe another useful way to construct de Bruijn graphs without gluing.

Given a collection of k-mers *Patterns*, the nodes of $\text{DEBRUIJN}_k(Patterns)$ are simply all unique $(k-1)$-mers occurring as a prefix or suffix of 3-mers in *Patterns*. For example, say we are given the following collection of 3-mers:

AAT ATG ATG ATG CAT CCA GAT GCC GGA GGG GTT **TAA** TGC TGG TGT

Then the set of eleven *unique* 2-mers occurring as a prefix or suffix in this collection is as follows:

AA AT CA CC GA GC GG GT **TA** TG TT

For every k-mer in *Patterns*, we connect its prefix node to its suffix node by a directed edge in order to produce $\text{DEBRUIJN}(Patterns)$. You can verify that this process produces the same de Bruijn graph that we have been working with (Figure 3.16).

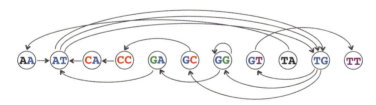

FIGURE 3.16 The de Bruijn graph above is the same as the graph in Figure 3.14, although it has been drawn differently.

De Bruijn Graph from k-mers Problem:

Construct the de Bruijn graph of a collection of k-mers.

    Input: A collection of k-mers *Patterns*.
    Output: The de Bruijn graph $\text{DEBRUIJN}(Patterns)$.

De Bruijn graphs versus overlap graphs

We now have two ways of solving the String Reconstruction Problem. We can either find a Hamiltonian path in the overlap graph or find an Eulerian path in the de Bruijn graph (Figure 3.17). Your inner voice may have already started complaining: *was it really worth my time to learn two slightly different ways of solving the same problem?* After all, we have only changed a single word in the statements of the Hamiltonian and Eulerian Path Problems, from finding a path visiting every *node* exactly once to finding a path visiting every *edge* exactly once.

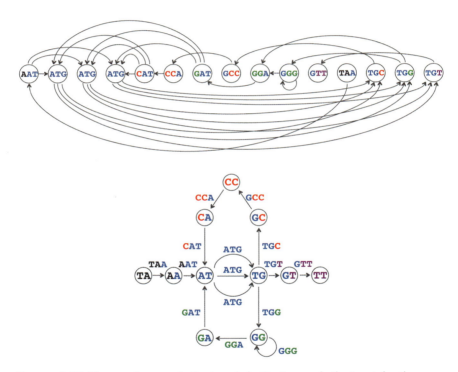

FIGURE 3.17 The overlap graph (top) and de Bruijn graph (bottom) for the same collection of 3-mers.

 STOP and Think: Which graph would you rather work with, the overlap graph or the de Bruijn graph?

Our guess is that you would probably prefer working with the de Bruijn graph, since it is smaller. However, this would be the wrong reason to choose one graph over the other. In the case of real assembly problems, both graphs will have millions of nodes, and so all that matters is finding an efficient algorithm for reconstructing the genome. If we can find an *efficient algorithm* for the Hamiltonian Path Problem, but not for the Eulerian path Problem, then you should select the overlap graph even though it looks more complex.

The choice between these two graphs is the pivotal decision of this chapter. To help you make this decision, we will ask you to hop onboard our bioinformatics time machine for a field trip to the 18th Century.

The Seven Bridges of Königsberg

Our destination is 1735 and the Prussian city of Königsberg. This city, which today is Kaliningrad, Russia, comprised both banks of the Pregel River as well as two river islands; seven bridges connected these four different parts of the city, as illustrated in Figure 3.18 (top). Königsberg's residents enjoyed taking walks, and they asked a simple question: *Is it possible to set out from my house, cross each bridge exactly once, and return home?* Their question became known as the **Bridges of Königsberg Problem**.

EXERCISE BREAK: Does the Bridges of Königsberg Problem have a solution?

In 1735, Leonhard Euler drew the graph in Figure 3.18 (bottom), which we call *Königsberg*; this graph's nodes represent the four sectors of the city, and its edges represent the seven bridges connecting different sectors. Note that the edges of *Königsberg* are **undirected**, meaning that they can be traversed in either direction.

STOP and Think: Redefine the Bridges of Königsberg Problem as a question about the graph *Königsberg*.

We have already defined an Eulerian path as a path in a graph traversing each edge of a graph exactly once. A cycle that traverses each edge of a graph exactly once is called an **Eulerian cycle**, and we say that a graph containing such a cycle is **Eulerian**. Note that an Eulerian cycle in *Königsberg* would immediately provide the residents of the city with the walk they had wanted. We now can redefine the Bridges of Königsberg Problem as an instance of the following more general problem.

Eulerian Cycle Problem:

Find an Eulerian cycle in a graph.

      Input: A graph.
      Output: An Eulerian cycle in this graph, if one exists.

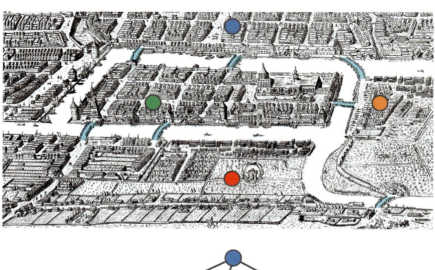

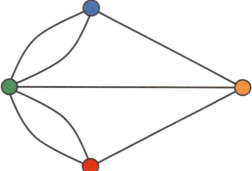

FIGURE 3.18 (Top) A map of Königsberg, adapted from Joachim Bering's 1613 illustration. The city was made up of four sectors represented by the blue, red, yellow, and green dots. The seven bridges connecting the different parts of the city have been highlighted to make them easier to see. (Bottom) The graph *Königsberg*.

Euler solved the Bridges of Königsberg Problem, showing that *no* walk can cross each bridge exactly once (i.e., the graph *Königsberg* is not Eulerian), which you may have already figured out for yourself. Yet his real contribution, and the reason why he is viewed as the founder of **graph theory**, a field of study that still flourishes today, is that he proved a theorem dictating when a graph will have an Eulerian cycle. His theorem immediately implies an efficient algorithm for constructing an Eulerian cycle in any Eulerian graph, even one having millions of edges. Furthermore, this algorithm can easily be extended into an algorithm constructing an Eulerian *path* (in a graph having such a path), which will allow us to solve the String Reconstruction Problem by using the de Bruijn graph.

On the other hand, it turns out that no one has ever been able to find an efficient algorithm solving the Hamiltonian Path Problem. The search for such an algorithm, or for a proof that an efficient algorithm does not exist for this problem, is at the heart of one of the most fundamental unanswered questions in computer science. Computer scientists classify an algorithm as **polynomial** if its running time can be bounded by a polynomial in the length of the input data. On the other hand, an algorithm is **exponential** if its runtime on some datasets is exponential in the length of the input data.

> **EXERCISE BREAK:** Classify the algorithms that we encountered in Chapter 1 as polynomial or exponential.

Although Euler's algorithm is polynomial, the Hamiltonian Path Problem belongs to a special class of problems for which all attempts to develop a polynomial algorithm have failed (see DETOUR: Tractable and Intractable Problems). Yet instead of trying to solve a problem that has stumped computer scientists for decades, we will set aside the overlap graph and instead focus on the de Bruijn graph approach to genome assembly.

PAGE 176

For the first two decades following the invention of DNA sequencing methods, biologists assembled genomes using overlap graphs, since they failed to realize that the Bridges of Königsberg held the key to DNA assembly (see DETOUR: From Euler to Hamilton to de Bruijn). Indeed, overlap graphs were used to assemble the human genome. It took bioinformaticians some time to figure out that the de Bruijn graph, first constructed to solve a completely theoretical problem, was relevant to genome assembly. Moreover, when the de Bruijn graph was brought to bioinformatics, it was considered an exotic mathematical concept with limited practical applications. Today, the de Bruijn graph has become the dominant approach for genome assembly.

PAGE 177

Euler's Theorem

We will now explore Euler's method for solving the Eulerian Cycle Problem. Euler worked with undirected graphs like *Königsberg*, but we will consider an analogue of his algorithm for directed graphs so that his method will apply to genome assembly.

Consider an ant, whom we will call Leo, walking along the edges of an Eulerian cycle. Every time Leo enters a node of this graph by an edge, he is able to leave this node by another, unused edge. Thus, in order for a graph to be Eulerian, the number of incoming edges at any node must be equal to the number of outgoing edges at that node. We define the **indegree** and **outdegree** of a node v (denoted $\text{IN}(v)$ and $\text{OUT}(v)$, respectively) as the number of edges leading into and out of v. A node v is **balanced** if $\text{IN}(v)=\text{OUT}(v)$, and a graph is **balanced** if all its nodes are balanced. Because Leo must always be able to leave a node by an unused edge, any Eulerian graph must be balanced. Figure 3.19 shows a balanced graph and an unbalanced graph.

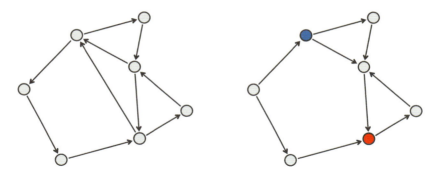

FIGURE 3.19 Balanced (left) and unbalanced (right) directed graphs. For the (unbalanced) blue node *v*, $\text{IN}(v) = 1$ and $\text{OUT}(v) = 2$, whereas for the (unbalanced) red node *w*, $\text{IN}(w) = 2$ and $\text{OUT}(w) = 1$.

STOP and Think: We now know that every Eulerian graph is balanced; is every balanced graph Eulerian?

The graph in Figure 3.20 is balanced but not Eulerian because it is **disconnected**, meaning that some nodes cannot be reached from other nodes. In any disconnected graph, it is impossible to find an Eulerian cycle. In contrast, we say that a directed graph is **strongly connected** if it is possible to reach any node from every other node.

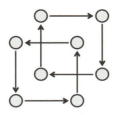

FIGURE 3.20 A balanced, disconnected graph.

We now know that an Eulerian graph must be both balanced and strongly connected. Euler's Theorem states that these two conditions are sufficient to guarantee that an arbitrary graph is Eulerian. As a result, it implies that we can determine whether a graph is Eulerian without ever having to draw any cycles.

Euler's Theorem: *Every balanced, strongly connected directed graph is Eulerian.*

Proof. Let *Graph* be an arbitrary balanced and strongly connected directed graph. To prove that *Graph* has an Eulerian cycle, place Leo at any node v_0 of *Graph* (the green node in Figure 3.21), and let him randomly walk through the graph under the condition that he cannot traverse the same edge twice.

FIGURE 3.21 Leo starts at the green node v_0 and walks through a balanced and strongly connected graph.

If Leo were incredibly lucky — or a genius — then he would traverse each edge exactly once and return back to v_0. However, odds are that he will "get stuck" somewhere before he can complete an Eulerian cycle, meaning that he reaches a node and finds no unused edges leaving that node.

STOP and Think: Where is Leo when he gets stuck? Can he get stuck in any node of the graph or only in certain nodes?

It turns out that the only node where Leo can get stuck is the starting node v_0! The reason why is that *Graph* is balanced: if Leo walks into any node other than v_0 (through an incoming edge), then he will always be able to escape via an unused outgoing edge. The only exception to this rule is the starting node v_0, since Leo used up one of the outgoing edges of v_0 on his first move. Now, because Leo has returned to v_0, the result of his walk was a cycle, which we call $Cycle_0$ (Figure 3.22 (left)).

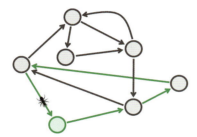 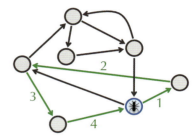

FIGURE 3.22 (Left) Leo produces a cycle $Cycle_0$ (formed by green edges) when he gets stuck at the green node v_0. In this case, he has not yet visited every edge in the graph. (Right) Starting at a new node v_1 (shown in blue), Leo first travels along $Cycle_0$, returning to v_1. Note that the blue node v_1, unlike the green node v_0, has unused outgoing and incoming edges.

STOP and Think: Is there a way to give Leo different instructions so that he selects a longer walk through the graph before he gets stuck?

As we mentioned, if $Cycle_0$ is Eulerian, then we are finished. Otherwise, because *Graph* is strongly connected, some node on $Cycle_0$ must have unused edges entering it and leaving it (why?). Naming this node v_1, we ask Leo to start at v_1 instead of v_0 and traverse $Cycle_0$ (thus returning to v_1), as shown in Figure 3.22 (right).

Leo is probably annoyed that we have asked him to travel along the exact same cycle, since as before, he will eventually return to v_1, the node where he started. However, now there are unused edges starting at this node, and so he can continue walking from v_1, using a new edge each time. The same argument as the one that we used before implies that Leo must eventually get stuck at v_1. The result of Leo's walk is a new cycle, $Cycle_1$ (Figure 3.23), which is larger than $Cycle_0$.

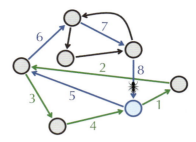

FIGURE 3.23 After traversing the previously constructed green cycle $Cycle_0$, Leo continues walking and eventually produces a larger cycle $Cycle_1$ formed of both the green and the blue cycles put together into a single cycle.

If $Cycle_1$ is an Eulerian cycle, then Leo has completed his job. Otherwise, we select a node v_2 in $Cycle_1$ that has unused edges entering it and leaving it (the red node in Figure 3.24 (left)). Starting at v_2, we ask Leo to traverse $Cycle_1$, returning to v_2, as shown in Figure 3.24 (left). Afterwards, he will randomly walk until he gets stuck at v_2, creating an even larger cycle that we name $Cycle_2$.

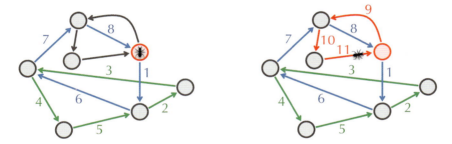

FIGURE 3.24 (Left) Starting at a new node v_2 (shown in red), Leo first travels along the previously constructed $Cycle_1$ (shown as green and blue edges). (Right) After completing the walk through $Cycle_1$, Leo continues randomly walking through the graph and finally produces an Eulerian cycle.

In Figure 3.24 (right), $Cycle_2$ happens to be Eulerian, although this is certainly not the case for an arbitrary graph. In general, Leo generates larger and larger cycles at each iteration, and so we are guaranteed that sooner or later some $Cycle_m$ will traverse all the edges in *Graph*. This cycle must be Eulerian, and so we (and Leo) are finished. $\square$

STOP and Think: Formulate and prove an analogue of Euler's Theorem for undirected graphs.

From Euler's Theorem to an Algorithm for Finding Eulerian Cycles

Constructing Eulerian cycles

The proof of Euler's Theorem offers an example of what mathematicians call a **constructive proof**, which not only proves the desired result, but also provides us with a method for constructing the object we need. In short, we track Leo's movements until he inevitably produces an Eulerian cycle in a balanced and strongly connected graph *Graph*, as summarized in the following pseudocode.

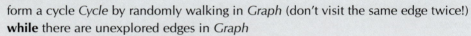

EULERIANCYCLE(*Graph*)
    form a cycle *Cycle* by randomly walking in *Graph* (don't visit the same edge twice!)
    while there are unexplored edges in *Graph*
        select a node *newStart* in *Cycle* with still unexplored edges
        form *Cycle'* by traversing *Cycle* (starting at *newStart*) and then randomly walking
        Cycle ← *Cycle'*
    return *Cycle*

It may not be obvious, but a good implementation of **EULERIANCYCLE** will work in linear time. To achieve this runtime speedup, you would need to use an efficient data structure in order to maintain the current cycle that Leo is building as well the list of unused edges incident to each node and the list of nodes on the current cycle that have unused edges.

From Eulerian cycles to Eulerian paths

We can now check if a directed graph has an Eulerian *cycle*, but what about an Eulerian *path*? Consider the de Bruijn graph in Figure 3.25 (left), which we already know has an Eulerian path, but which does not have an Eulerian cycle because nodes **TA** and **TT** are not balanced. However, we can transform this Eulerian path into an Eulerian cycle by adding a single edge connecting **TT** to **TA**, as shown in Figure 3.25 (right).

STOP and Think: How many unbalanced nodes does a graph with an Eulerian path have?

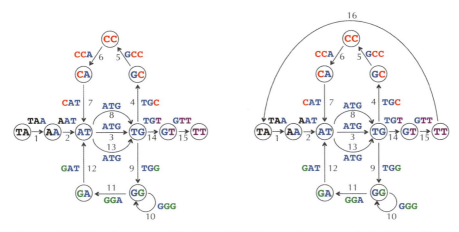

FIGURE 3.25 Transforming an Eulerian path (left) into an Eulerian cycle (right) by adding an edge.

More generally, consider a graph that does not have an Eulerian cycle but does have an Eulerian path. If an Eulerian path in this graph connects a node v to a different node w, then the graph is **nearly balanced**, meaning that all its nodes except v and w are balanced. In this case, adding an extra edge from w to v transforms the Eulerian path into an Eulerian cycle. Thus, a nearly balanced graph has an Eulerian path if and only if adding an edge between its unbalanced nodes makes the graph balanced and strongly connected.

You now have a method to assemble a genome, since the String Reconstruction Problem reduces to finding an Eulerian path in the de Bruijn graph generated from reads.

EXERCISE BREAK: Find an analogue of the nearly balanced condition that will determine when an *undirected* graph has an Eulerian path.

The analogue of Euler's theorem for undirected graphs immediately implies that there is no Eulerian path in 18th Century Königsberg, but the story is different in modern-day Kaliningrad (see DETOUR: The Seven Bridges of Kaliningrad).

 PAGE 178

Constructing universal strings

Now that you know how to use the de Bruijn graph to solve the String Reconstruction Problem, you can also construct a k-universal string for any value of k. We should note

147

that de Bruijn was interested in constructing *k*-universal *circular* strings. For example, **000**11101 is a 3-universal circular string, as it contains each of the eight binary 3-mers exactly once (Figure 3.26).

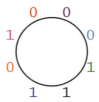

FIGURE 3.26 The circular 3-universal string **000**11101 contains each of the binary 3-mers (**000**, **001**, **011**, **111**, **110**, **101**, **010**, and **100**) exactly once.

---

k-Universal Circular String Problem:
Find a k-universal circular string.

> **Input**: An integer *k*.
> **Output**: A *k*-universal circular string.

Like its analogue for linear strings, the *k*-Universal Circular String Problem is just a specific case of a more general problem, which requires us to reconstruct a circular string given its *k*-mer composition. This problem models the assembly of a circular genome containing a single chromosome, like the genomes of most bacteria. We know that we can reconstruct a circular string from its *k*-mer composition by finding an Eulerian cycle in the de Bruijn graph constructed from these *k*-mers. Therefore, we can construct a *k*-universal circular binary string by finding an Eulerian cycle in the de Bruijn graph constructed from the collection of all binary *k*-mers (Figure 3.27).

EXERCISE BREAK: How many 3-universal circular strings are there?

Even though finding a 20-universal circular string amounts to finding an Eulerian cycle in a graph with over a million edges, we now have a fast algorithm for solving this problem. Let *BinaryStrings$_k$* be the set of all 2^k binary *k*-mers. The only thing we need to do is to solve the *k*-Universal Circular String Problem is to find an Eulerian cycle in DEBRUIJN(*BinaryStrings$_k$*). Note that the nodes of this graph represent all possible binary $(k-1)$-mers. A directed edge connects $(k-1)$-mer *Pattern* to $(k-1)$-mer *Pattern'* in this graph if there exists a k-mer whose prefix is *Pattern* and whose suffix is *Pattern'*.

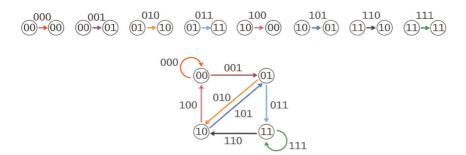

FIGURE 3.27 (Top) A graph consisting of eight isolated directed edges, one for each binary 3-mer. The nodes of each edge correspond to the 3-mer's prefix and suffix. (Bottom) Gluing identically labeled nodes in the graph on top results in a de Bruijn graph containing four nodes. An Eulerian cycle through the edges $000 \rightarrow 001 \rightarrow 011 \rightarrow 111 \rightarrow 110 \rightarrow 101 \rightarrow 010 \rightarrow 100 \rightarrow 000$ yields the 3-universal circular string 00011101.

STOP and Think: Figure 3.28 illustrates that DEBRUIJN($BinaryStrings_4$) is balanced and strongly connected and is thus Eulerian. Can you prove that for any k, DEBRUIJN($BinaryStrings_k$) is Eulerian?

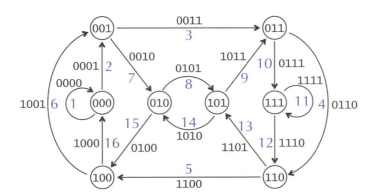

FIGURE 3.28 An Eulerian cycle spelling the cyclic 4-universal string 0000110010111101 in DEBRUIJN($BinaryStrings_4$).

Assembling Genomes from Read-Pairs

From reads to read-pairs

Previously, we described an idealized form of genome assembly in order to build up your intuition about de Bruijn graphs. In the rest of the chapter, we will discuss a number of practically motivated topics that will help you appreciate the advanced methods used by modern assemblers.

We have already mentioned that assembling reads sampled from a randomly generated text is a trivial problem, since random strings are not expected to have long repeats. Moreover, de Bruijn graphs become less and less tangled when read length increases (Figure 3.29). As soon as read length exceeds the length of all repeats in a genome (provided the reads have no errors), the de Bruijn graph turns into a path. However, despite many attempts, biologists have not yet figured out how to generate *long* and *accurate* reads. The most accurate sequencing technologies available today generate reads that are only about 300 nucleotides long, which is too short to span most repeats, even in short bacterial genomes.

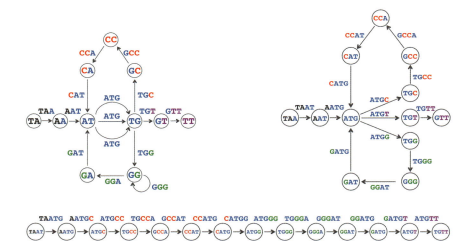

FIGURE 3.29 The graph DEBRUIJN₄(**TAATGCCATGGGATGTT**) (top right) is less tangled than the graph DEBRUIJN₃(**TAATGCCATGGGATGTT**) (top left). The graph DEBRUIJN₅(**TAATGCCATGGGATGTT**) (bottom) is a path.

We saw earlier that the string **TAATGCCATGGGATGTT** cannot be uniquely reconstructed from its 3-mer composition since another string (**TAATGGGATGCCATGTT**) has the same 3-mer composition.

Increasing read length would help identify the correct assembly, but since increasing read length presents a difficult experimental problem, biologists have suggested an indirect way of increasing read length by generating **read-pairs**, which are pairs of reads separated by a fixed distance d in the genome (Figure 3.30). You can think about a read-pair as a long "gapped" read of length $k + d + k$ whose first and last k-mers are known but whose middle segment of length d is unknown. Nevertheless, read-pairs contain more information than k-mers alone, and so we should be able to use them to improve our assemblies. If only you could infer the nucleotides in the middle segment of a read-pair, you would immediately increase the read length from k to $2 \cdot k + d$.

FIGURE 3.30 Read-pairs sampled from **TAATGCCATGGGATGTT** and formed by reads of length 3 separated by a gap of length 1. A simple but inefficient way to assemble these read-pairs is to construct the de Bruijn graph of individual reads (3-mers) within the read-pairs.

Transforming read-pairs into long virtual reads

Let *Reads* be the collection of all $2N$ k-mer reads taken from N read-pairs. Note that a read-pair formed by k-mer reads $Read_1$ and $Read_2$ corresponds to two edges in the de Bruijn graph DEBRUIJN$_k$(*Reads*). Since these reads are separated by distance d in the genome, there must be a path of length $k + d + 1$ in DEBRUIJN$_k$(*Reads*) connecting the node at the beginning of the edge corresponding to $Read_1$ with the node at the end of the edge corresponding to $Read_2$, as shown in Figure 3.31. If there is only one path of length $k + d + 1$ connecting these nodes, or if all such paths spell out the same string, then we can transform a read-pair formed by reads $Read_1$ and $Read_2$ into a virtual read of length $2 \cdot k + d$ that starts as $Read_1$, spells out this path, and ends with $Read_2$.

For example, consider the de Bruijn graph in Figure 3.31, which is generated from all reads present in the read-pairs in Figure 3.30. There is a unique string spelled by paths of length $k + d + 1 = 5$ between edges labeled **AAT** and **CCA** within a read-pair represented by the gapped read **AAT–CCA**. Thus, from two short reads of length k, we have generated a long virtual read of length $2 \cdot k + d$, achieving computationally what researchers still cannot achieve experimentally! After preprocessing the de Bruijn graph to produce long virtual reads, we can simply construct the de Bruijn graph from these long reads and use it for genome assembly.

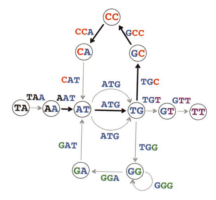

FIGURE 3.31 The highlighted path of length $k + d + 1 = 3 + 1 + 1 = 5$ between the edges labeled **AAT** and **CCA** spells out **AATGCCA**. (There are three such paths because there are three possible choices of edges labeled **ATG**.) Thus, the gapped read **AAT–CCA** can be transformed into a long virtual read **AATGCCA**.

Although the idea of transforming read-pairs into long virtual reads is used in many assembly programs, we have made an optimistic assumption: *"If there is only one path of length $k + d + 1$ connecting these nodes, or if all such paths spell out the same string ..."*. In practice, this assumption limits the application of the long virtual read approach to assembling read-pairs because highly repetitive genomic regions often contain multiple paths of the same length between two edges, and these paths often spell different strings (Figure 3.32). If this is the case, then we cannot reliably transform a read-pair into a long read. Instead, we will describe an alternative approach to analyzing read-pairs.

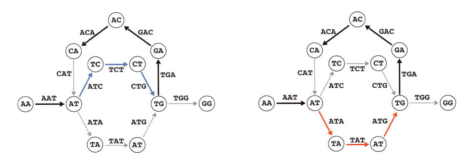

FIGURE 3.32 (Left) The highlighted path in DEBRUIJN₃(AATCTGACATATGG) spells out the long virtual read AATCTGACA, which is a substring of AATCTGACATATGG. (Right) The highlighted path in the same graph spells out the long virtual read AATATGACA, which does not occur in AATCTGACATATGG.

From composition to paired composition

Given a string *Text*, a (k, d)-mer is a pair of k-mers in *Text* separated by distance d. We use the notation $(Pattern_1 \mid Pattern_2)$ to refer to a (k, d)-mer whose k-mers are $Pattern_1$ and $Pattern_2$. For example, (**ATG** | **GGG**) is a $(3, 4)$-mer in **TAATGCCATGGGATGTT**. The (k, d)-mer composition of *Text*, denoted PAIREDCOMPOSITION$_{k, d}$(*Text*), is the collection of all (k, d)-mers in *Text* (including repeated (k, d)-mers). For example, here is PAIREDCOMPOSITION$_{3,1}$(**TAATGCCATGGGATGTT**):

$$
\begin{array}{ll}
\textbf{TAA} & \textbf{GCC} \\
\textbf{AAT} & \textbf{CCA} \\
\textbf{ATG} & \textbf{CAT} \\
\textbf{TGC} & \textbf{ATG} \\
\textbf{GCC} & \textbf{TGG} \\
\textbf{CCA} & \textbf{GGG} \\
\textbf{CAT} & \textbf{GGA} \\
\textbf{ATG} & \textbf{GAT} \\
\textbf{TGG} & \textbf{ATG} \\
\textbf{GGG} & \textbf{TGT} \\
\textbf{GGA} & \textbf{GTT} \\
\end{array}
$$

TAATGCCATGGGATGTT

EXERCISE BREAK: Generate the $(3, 2)$-mer composition of the string **TAATGCCATGGGATGTT**.

Since the order of $(3,1)$-mers in PAIREDCOMPOSITION(**TAATGCCATGGGATGTT**) is unknown, we list them according to the lexicographic order of the 6-mers formed by their concatenated 3-mers:

$$(\textbf{AAT} \mid \textbf{CCA}) \ (\textbf{ATG} \mid \textbf{CAT}) \ (\textbf{ATG} \mid \textbf{GAT}) \ (\textbf{CAT} \mid \textbf{GGA}) \ (\textbf{CCA} \mid \textbf{GGG}) \ (\textbf{GCC} \mid \textbf{TGG})$$
$$(\textbf{GGA} \mid \textbf{GTT}) \ (\textbf{GGG} \mid \textbf{TGT}) \ (\textbf{TAA} \mid \textbf{GCC}) \ (\textbf{TGC} \mid \textbf{ATG}) \ (\textbf{TGG} \mid \textbf{ATG})$$

Note that whereas there are repeated 3-mers in the 3-mer composition of this string, there are no repeated $(3,1)$-mers in its paired composition. Furthermore, although **TAATGCCATGGGATGTT** and **TAAATGCCATGGGATGTT** have the same 3-mer composition, they have different $(3,1)$-mer compositions. Thus, if we can generate the $(3,1)$-mer composition of these strings, then we will be able to distinguish between them. But how can we reconstruct a string from its (k,d)-mer composition? And can we adapt the de Bruijn graph approach for this purpose?

String Reconstruction from Read-Pairs Problem:

Reconstruct a string from its paired composition.

> **Input**: A collection of paired k-mers *PairedReads* and an integer d.
> **Output**: A string *Text* with (k,d)-mer composition equal to *PairedReads* (if such a string exists).

Paired de Bruijn graphs

Given a (k,d)-mer $(a_1 \ldots a_k \mid b_1, \ldots b_k)$, we define its **prefix** and **suffix** as the following $(k-1, d+1)$-mers:

$$\text{PREFIX}((a_1 \ldots a_k \mid b_1, \ldots b_k)) = (a_1 \ldots a_{k-1} \mid b_1 \ldots b_{k-1})$$
$$\text{SUFFIX}((a_1 \ldots a_k \mid b_1, \ldots b_k)) = (a_2 \ldots a_k \mid b_2 \ldots b_k)$$

For example, $\text{PREFIX}((\text{GAC} \mid \text{TCA})) = (\text{GA} \mid \text{TC})$ and $\text{SUFFIX}((\text{GAC} \mid \text{TCA})) = (\text{AC} \mid \text{CA})$.

Note that for consecutive (k,d)-mers appearing in *Text*, the suffix of the first (k,d)-mer is equal to the prefix of the second (k,d)-mer. For example, for the consecutive (k,d)-mers $(\textbf{TAA} \mid \textbf{GCC})$ and $(\textbf{AAT} \mid \textbf{CCA})$ in **TAATGCCATGGGATGTT**,

$$\text{SUFFIX}((\textbf{TAA} \mid \textbf{GCC})) = \text{PREFIX}((\textbf{AAT} \mid \textbf{CCA})) = (\textbf{AA} \mid \textbf{CC}) \, .$$

Given a string *Text*, we construct a graph PATHGRAPH$_{k,d}$(*Text*) that represents a path formed by $|Text| - (k + d + k) + 1$ edges corresponding to all (k, d)-mers in *Text*. We label edges in this path by (k, d)-mers and label the starting and ending nodes of an edge by its prefix and suffix, respectively (Figure 3.33).

FIGURE 3.33 PATHGRAPH$_{3,1}$(**TAA**TGCCATGGGATG**TT**). Each $(3, 1)$-mer has been displayed as a two-line expression to save space.

The **paired de Bruijn graph**, denoted DEBRUIJN$_{k,d}$(*Text*), is formed by gluing identically labeled nodes in PATHGRAPH$_{k,d}$(*Text*) (Figure 3.34). Note that the paired de Bruijn graph is less tangled than the de Bruijn graph constructed from individual reads.

STOP and Think: It is easy to construct a paired de Bruijn graph from a string *Text*. But how can we construct the paired de Bruijn graph from the (k, d)-mer composition of *Text*?

We define COMPOSITIONGRAPH$_{k,d}$(*Text*) as the graph consisting of $|Text| - (k + d + k) + 1$ isolated edges that are labeled by the (k, d)-mers in *Text*, and whose nodes are labeled by the prefixes and suffixes of these labels (see Figure 3.35). As you may have guessed, gluing identically labeled nodes in PAIREDCOMPOSITIONGRAPH$_{k,d}$(*Text*) results in exactly the same de Bruijn graph as gluing identically labeled nodes in PATHGRAPH$_{k,d}$(*Text*). Of course, in practice, we will not know *Text*; however, we can form COMPOSITIONGRAPH$_{k,d}$(*Text*) directly from the (k, d)-mer composition of *Text*, and the gluing step will result in the paired de Bruijn graph of this composition. The genome can be reconstructed by following an Eulerian path in this de Bruijn graph.

A pitfall of paired de Bruijn graphs

We saw earlier that every solution of the String Reconstruction Problem corresponds to an Eulerian path in the de Bruijn graph constructed from a *k*-mer composition. Likewise, every solution of the String Reconstruction from Read-Pairs Problem corresponds to an Eulerian path in the Paired de Bruijn graph constructed from a (k, d)-mer composition.

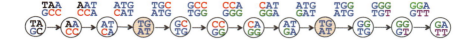

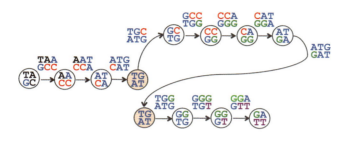

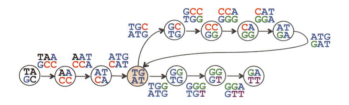

FIGURE 3.34 (Top) PATHGRAPH$_{3,1}$(**TA**ATGCCATGGGATGTT) is formed by eleven edges and twelve nodes. Only two of these nodes have the same label, (**TG** | **AT**). (Middle) Bringing the two identically labeled nodes closer to each other in preparation for gluing. (Bottom) The paired de Bruijn graph DEBRUIJN$_{3,1}$(**TA**ATGCCATGGGATGTT) is obtained from PATHGRAPH$_{3,1}$(**TA**ATGCCATGGGATGTT) by gluing the nodes sharing the label (**TG** | **AT**). This paired de Bruijn graph has a unique Eulerian path, which spells out **TA**ATGCCATGGGATGTT.

EXERCISE BREAK: In the paired de Bruijn graph shown in Figure 3.36, reconstruct the genome spelled by the following Eulerian path of $(2, 1)$-mers: (AG | AG) → (GC | GC) → (CA | CT) → (AG | TG) → (GC | GC) → (CT | CT) → (TG | TG) → (GC | GC) → (CT | CA).

We also saw that every Eulerian path in the de Bruijn graph constructed from a k-mer composition spells out a solution of the String Reconstruction Problem. But is this the case for the paired de Bruijn graph?

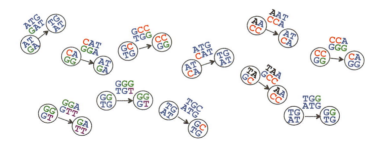

FIGURE 3.35 The graph COMPOSITIONGRAPH₃,₁(**TA**ATGCCATGGGATGTT) is a collection of isolated edges. Each edge is labeled by a (3, 1)-mer in **TA**ATGCCATGGGATGTT; the starting node of an edge is labeled by the prefix of the edge's (3, 1)-mer, and the ending node of an edge is labeled by the suffix of this (3, 1)-mer. Gluing identically labeled nodes yields the paired de Bruijn graph shown in Figure 3.34 (bottom).

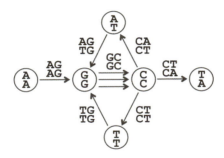

FIGURE 3.36 A paired de Bruijn graph constructed from a collection of nine (2, 1)-mers.

STOP and Think: The graph shown in Figure 3.36 has another Eulerian path: (AG|AG) → (GC|GC) → (CT|CT) → (TG|TG) → (GC|GC) → (CA|CT) → (AG|TG) → (GC|GC) → (CT|CA). Can you reconstruct a genome spelled by this path?

If you attempted the preceding question, then you know that not every Eulerian path in the paired de Bruijn graph constructed from a (k, d)-mer composition spells out a solution of the String Reconstruction from Read-Pairs Problem. You are now ready to solve this problem and become a genome assembly expert.

CHARGING STATION (Generating All Eulerian Cycles): You know how to construct a single Eulerian cycle in a graph, but it remains unclear how to find *all possible* Eulerian cycles, which will be helpful when solving the String Reconstruction from Read-Pairs Problem. Check out this Charging Station to see how to generate all Eulerian cycles in a graph.

PAGE 165

CHARGING STATION (Reconstructing a String Spelled by a Path in the Paired de Bruijn Graph): To solve the String Reconstruction from Read-Pairs Problem, you will need to reconstruct a string from its path in the paired de Bruijn graph. Check out this Charging Station to see an example of how this can be done.

PAGE 166

Epilogue: Genome Assembly Faces Real Sequencing Data

Our discussion of genome assembly has thus far relied upon various assumptions. Accordingly, applying de Bruijn graphs to real sequencing data is not a straightforward procedure. Below, we describe practical challenges introduced by quirks in modern sequencing technologies and some computational techniques that have been devised to address these challenges. In this discussion, we will first assume that reads are generated as k-mers instead of read-pairs for the sake of simplicity.

Breaking reads into k-mers

Given a k-mer substring of a genome, we define its **coverage** as the number of reads to which this k-mer belongs. We have taken for granted that a sequencing machine can generate all k-mers present in the genome, but this assumption of "perfect k-mer coverage" does not hold in practice. For example, the popular Illumina sequencing technology generates reads that are approximately 300 nucleotides long, but this technology still misses many 300-mers present in the genome (even if the average coverage is very high), and nearly all the reads that it does generate have sequencing errors.

STOP and Think: Given a set of reads having imperfect k-mer coverage, can you find a parameter $l < k$ so that the same reads have perfect l-mer coverage? What is the maximum value of this parameter?

Figure 3.37 (left) shows four 10-mer reads that capture some but not all of the 10-mers in an example genome. However, if we take the counterintuitive step of breaking these reads into *shorter* 5-mers (Figure 3.37, right), then these 5-mers exhibit perfect coverage. This **read breaking** approach, in which we break reads into shorter *k*-mers, is used by many modern assemblers.

```
ATGCCGTATGGACAACGACT          ATGCCGTATGGACAACGACT
ATGCCGTATG                    ATGCC
    GCCGTATGGA                 TGCCG
        GTATGGACAA             GCCGT
            GACAACGACT         CCGTA
                               CGTAT
                               GTATG
                               TATGG
                               ATGGA
                               TGGAC
                               GGACA
                               GACAA
                               ACAAC
                               CAACG
                               AACGA
                               ACGAC
                               CGACT
```

FIGURE 3.37 Breaking 10-mer reads (left) into 5-mers results in perfect coverage of a genome by 5-mers (right).

Read breaking must deal with a practical trade-off. On the one hand, the smaller the value of *k*, the larger the chance that the *k*-mer coverage is perfect. On the other hand, smaller values of *k* result in a more tangled de Bruijn graph, making it difficult to infer the genome from this graph.

Splitting the genome into contigs

Even after read breaking, most assemblies still have gaps in *k*-mer coverage, causing the de Bruijn graph to have missing edges, and so the search for an Eulerian path fails. In this case, biologists often settle on assembling **contigs** (long, contiguous segments of the genome) rather than entire chromosomes. For example, a typical bacterial sequencing project may result in about a hundred contigs, ranging in length from a few thousand to a few hundred thousand nucleotides. For most genomes, the order of these contigs along the genome remains unknown. Needless to say, biologists would prefer to have the entire genomic sequence, but the cost of ordering the contigs into a final assembly and closing the gaps using more expensive experimental methods is often prohibitive.

Fortunately, we can derive contigs from the de Bruijn graph. A path in a graph is called **non-branching** if $\text{IN}(v) = \text{OUT}(v) = 1$ for each intermediate node *v* of this path, i.e., for each node except possibly the starting and ending node of a path. A **maximal non-branching path** is a non-branching path that cannot be extended into a longer non-branching path. We are interested in these paths because the strings of nucleotides that they spell out must be present in any assembly with a given k-mer composition. For this reason, contigs correspond to strings spelled by maximal non-branching paths in the de Bruijn graph. For example, the de Bruijn graph in Figure 3.38, constructed for the 3-mer composition of **TAATGCCATGGGATGTT**, has nine maximal non-branching paths that spell out the contigs **TAAT**, **TGTT**, **TGCCAT**, **ATG**, **ATG**, **ATG**, **TGG**, **GGG**, and **GGAT**. In practice, biologists have no choice but to break genomes into contigs, even in the case of perfect coverage (like in Figure 3.38), since repeats prevent them from being able to infer a unique Eulerian path.

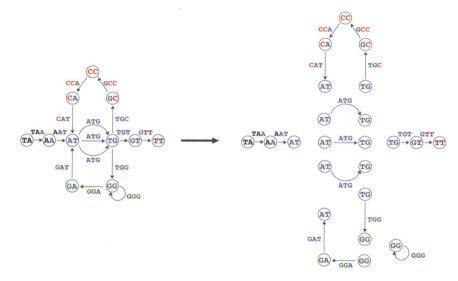

FIGURE 3.38 Breaking the graph DEBRUIJN₃ (**TAATGCCATGGGATGTT**) into nine maximal non-branching paths representing contigs **TAAT**, **TGTT**, **TGCCAT**, **ATG**, **ATG**, **ATG**, **TGG**, **GGG**, and **GGAT**.

Contig Generation Problem:

Generate the contigs from a collection of reads (with imperfect coverage).

> **Input**: A collection of k-mers *Patterns*.
> **Output**: All contigs in DEBRUIJN(*Patterns*).

CHARGING STATION (Maximal Non-Branching Paths in a Graph): If you have difficulties finding maximal non-branching paths in a graph, check out this Charging Station.

PAGE 169

Assembling error-prone reads

Error-prone reads represent yet another barrier to real sequencing projects. Adding the single erroneous read CGTA**C**GGACA (with a single error that misreads T as **C**) to the set of reads in Figure 3.37 results in erroneous 5-mers CGTA**C**, GTA**C**G, TA**C**GG, A**C**GGA, and **C**GGAC after read breaking. These 5-mers result in an erroneous path from node CGTA to node GGAC in the de Bruijn graph (Figure 3.39 (top)), meaning that if the correct read CGTATGGACA is generated as well, then we will have two paths connecting CGTA to GGAC in the de Bruijn graph. This structure is called a **bubble**, which we define as two short disjoint paths (e.g., shorter than some threshold length) connecting the same pair of nodes in the de Bruijn graph.

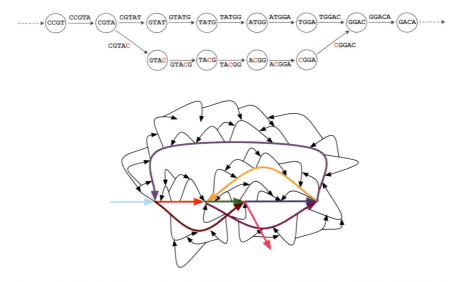

FIGURE 3.39 (Top) A correct path CGTA → GTAT → TATG → ATGG → TGGA → GGAC along with an incorrect path CGTA → GTA**C** → TA**C**G → A**C**GG → **C**GGA → GGAC form a bubble in a de Bruijn graph, making it difficult to identify which path is correct. (Bottom) An illustration of a de Bruijn graph with many bubbles. Bubble removal should leave only the colored paths remaining.

> **STOP and Think:** Design an algorithm for detecting bubbles in de Bruijn graphs. After a bubble is detected, you must decide which of two paths in the bubble to remove. How should you make this decision?

Existing assemblers remove bubbles from de Bruijn graphs. The practical challenge is that, since nearly all reads have errors, de Bruijn graphs have millions of bubbles (Figure 3.39 (bottom)). Bubble removal occasionally removes the correct path, thus introducing errors rather than fixing them. To make matters worse, in a genome having **inexact repeats**, where the repeated regions differ by a single nucleotide or some other small variation, reads from the two repeat copies will also generate bubbles in the de Bruijn graph because one of the copies may appear to be an erroneous version of the other. Applying bubble removal to these regions introduces assembly errors by making repeats appear more similar than they are. Thus, modern genome assemblers attempt to distinguish bubbles caused by sequencing errors (which should be removed) from bubbles caused by variations (which should be retained).

Inferring multiplicities of edges in de Bruijn graphs

Although the de Bruijn graph framework requires that we know the **multiplicity** of each k-mer in the genome (i.e., the number of times the k-mer appears), this information is not readily available from reads. However, the multiplicity of a k-mer in a genome can often be estimated using its coverage. Indeed, k-mers that appear t times in a genome are expected to have approximately t times higher coverage than k-mers that appear just once. Needless to say, coverage varies across the genome, and this condition is often violated. As a result, existing assemblers often assemble repetitive regions in genomes without knowing the exact number of times each k-mer from this region occurs in the genome.

You should now have a handle on the practical considerations involved in genome sequencing, but we will give you a challenge problem that does not encounter these issues. Why? Developing assembly algorithms for large genomes is a formidable challenge because even the seemingly simple problem of constructing the de Bruijn graph from a collection of all k-mers present in millions of reads is nontrivial. To make your life easier, we will give you a small bacterial genome for your first assembly dataset.

CHALLENGE PROBLEM: *Carsonella ruddii* is a bacterium that lives symbiotically inside some insects. Its sheltered life has allowed it to reduce its genome to only about 160,000 base pairs. With only about 200 genes, it lacks some genes necessary for survival, but these genes are supplied by its insect host. In fact, *Carsonella* has such a small genome that biologists have conjectured that it is losing its "bacterial" identity and turning into an **organelle**, which is part of the host's genome. This transition from bacterium to organelle has happened many times during evolutionary history; in fact, the mitochondrion responsible for energy production in human cells was once a free-roaming bacterium that we assimilated in the distant past.

Given a collection of simulated error-free read-pairs, use the paired de Bruijn graph to reconstruct the *Carsonella ruddii* genome. Compare this assembly to the assembly obtained from the classic de Bruijn graph (i.e., when all we know is the reads themselves and do not know the distance between paired reads) in order to better appreciate the benefits of read-pairs. For each k, what is the minimum value of d needed to enable reconstruction of the entire *Carsonella ruddii* genome from its (k, d)-mer composition?

EXERCISE BREAK: By the way, one more thing ... what was the headline of the June 27, 2000 edition of the *New York Times*?

Charging Stations

The effect of gluing on the adjacency matrix

Figure 3.40 uses *Text* = **TAATGCCATGGGATGTT** to illustrate how gluing converts the adjacency matrix of PATHGRAPH₃(*Text*) into the adjacency matrix of DEBRUIJN₃(*Text*).

	TA	AA	AT$_1$	TG$_1$	GC	CC	CA	AT$_2$	TG$_2$	GG$_1$	GG$_2$	GA	AT$_3$	TG$_3$	GT	TT
TA	0	1	0	0	0	0	0	0	0	0	0	0	0	0	0	0
AA	0	0	1	0	0	0	0	0	0	0	0	0	0	0	0	0
AT$_1$	0	0	0	1	0	0	0	0	0	0	0	0	0	0	0	0
TG$_1$	0	0	0	0	1	0	0	0	0	0	0	0	0	0	0	0
GC	0	0	0	0	0	1	0	0	0	0	0	0	0	0	0	0
CC	0	0	0	0	0	0	1	0	0	0	0	0	0	0	0	0
CA	0	0	0	0	0	0	0	1	0	0	0	0	0	0	0	0
AT$_2$	0	0	0	0	0	0	0	0	1	0	0	0	0	0	0	0
TG$_2$	0	0	0	0	0	0	0	0	0	1	0	0	0	0	0	0
GG$_1$	0	0	0	0	0	0	0	0	0	0	1	0	0	0	0	0
GG$_2$	0	0	0	0	0	0	0	0	0	0	0	1	0	0	0	0
GA	0	0	0	0	0	0	0	0	0	0	0	0	1	0	0	0
AT$_3$	0	0	0	0	0	0	0	0	0	0	0	0	0	1	0	0
TG$_3$	0	0	0	0	0	0	0	0	0	0	0	0	0	0	1	0
GT	0	0	0	0	0	0	0	0	0	0	0	0	0	0	0	1
TT	0	0	0	0	0	0	0	0	0	0	0	0	0	0	0	0

	TA	AA	AT	TG	GC	CC	CA	GG	GA	GT	TT
TA	0	1	0	0	0	0	0	0	0	0	0
AA	0	0	1	0	0	0	0	0	0	0	0
AT	0	0	0	3	0	0	0	0	0	0	0
TG	0	0	0	0	1	0	0	1	0	1	0
GC	0	0	0	0	0	1	0	0	0	0	0
CC	0	0	0	0	0	0	1	0	0	0	0
CA	0	0	1	0	0	0	0	0	0	0	0
GG	0	0	0	0	0	0	0	1	1	0	0
GA	0	0	1	0	0	0	0	0	0	0	0
GT	0	0	0	0	0	0	0	0	0	0	1
TT	0	0	0	0	0	0	0	0	0	0	0

FIGURE 3.40 Adjacency matrices. (Top) The 16×16 adjacency matrix of PATHGRAPH₃(**TAATGCCATGGGATGTT**). Note that we have used indexing to differentiate multiple occurrences of AT, TG, and GG in PATHGRAPH₃(**TAATGCCATGGGATGTT**). (Bottom) The 11×11 adjacency matrix of DEBRUIJN₃(**TAATGCCATGGGATGTT**), produced after gluing nodes labeled by identical 2-mers. Note that if there are m edges connecting nodes i and j, the (i, j)-th element of the adjacency matrix is m.

Generating all Eulerian cycles

The inherent difficulty in generating all Eulerian cycles in a graph is keeping track of potentially many different alternatives at any given node. On the opposite end of the spectrum, a **simple directed graph**, a connected graph in which each node has indegree and outdegree equal to 1, offers a trivial case, since there is only one Eulerian cycle.

Our idea, then, is to transform a single labeled directed graph *Graph* containing $n \geq 1$ Eulerian cycles to n different simple directed graphs, each containing a single Eulerian cycle. This transformation has the property that it is easily invertible, i.e., that given the unique Eulerian cycle in one of the simple directed graphs, we can easily reconstruct the original Eulerian cycle in *Graph*.

Given a node v in *Graph* (of indegree greater than 1) with incoming edge (u, v) and outgoing edge (v, w), we will construct a "simpler" **(u, v, w)-bypass graph** in which we remove the edges (u, v) and (v, w) from *Graph*, and add a new node x along with the edges (u, x) and (v, x) (Figure 3.41 (top)). The new edges (u, x) and (v, x) in the bypass graph inherit the labels of the removed edges (u, v) and (v, w), respectively. The critical property of this graph is revealed by the following exercise.

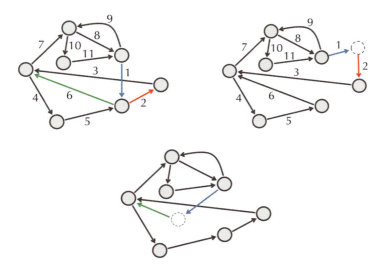

FIGURE 3.41 (Top) An Eulerian graph *Graph* (left) along with its (u, v, w)-bypass graph (right) constructed for the blue and red edges. (Bottom) The other bypass graph constructed for the blue and green edges.

> **EXERCISE BREAK:** Show that any Eulerian cycle in *Graph* passing through (u, v) and then (v, w) corresponds to an Eulerian cycle (with the same edge labels) in the (u, v, w)-bypass graph passing through (u, x) and then (x, w).

In general, given an incoming edge (u, v) into v along with k outgoing edges (v, w_1), ..., (v, w_k) from v, we can construct k different bypass graphs (Figure 3.41 (bottom)). Note that no two bypass graphs have the same Eulerian cycle.

Our idea, roughly stated, is to iteratively construct every possible bypass graph for *Graph* until we obtain a large family of simple directed graphs; each one of these graphs will correspond to a distinct Eulerian cycle in *Graph*. This idea is implemented by the pseudocode below.

ALLEULERIANCYCLES(*Graph*)
    AllGraphs ← the set consisting of a single graph *Graph*
    while there is a non-simple graph *G* in *AllGraphs*
        v ← a node with indegree larger than 1 in *G*
        for each incoming edge (u, v) into *v*
            for each outgoing edge (v, w) from *v*
                NewGraph ← (u, v, w)-bypass graph of *G*
                if *NewGraph* is connected
                    add *NewGraph* to *AllGraphs*
        remove *G* from *AllGraphs*
    for each graph *G* in *AllGraphs*
        output the (single) Eulerian cycle in *G*

There exists a more elegant approach to constructing all Eulerian cycles in an Eulerian graph that is based on a theorem that de Bruijn had a hand in proving. To learn about this theorem, see **DETOUR: The BEST Theorem**.

PAGE 179

Reconstructing a string spelled by a path in the paired de Bruijn graph

Consider the following Eulerian path formed by nine edges in the paired de Bruijn graph from Figure 3.36.

$$AG-AG \rightarrow GC-GC \rightarrow CA-CT \rightarrow AG-TG \rightarrow$$
$$GC-GC \rightarrow CT-CT \rightarrow TG-TG \rightarrow GC-GC \rightarrow CT-CA$$

We can arrange the $(2, 1)$-mers in this path into the nine rows shown below, revealing the string **AGCAGCTGCTGCA** spelled by this path:

AG–AG
GC–GC
CA–CT
AG–TG
GC–GC
CT–CT
TG–TG
GC–**G**C
CT–**CA**
AGCAGCTGCTGCA

Now, consider another Eulerian path in the paired de Bruijn graph from Figure 3.36:

AG–AG → GC–GC → CT–CT → TG–TG →
GC–GC → CA–CT → AG–TG → GC–GC → CT–CA

An attempt to assemble these $(2, 1)$-mers reveals that not every column has the same nucleotide (see the two columns shown in red below). This example illustrates that not all Eulerian paths in the paired de Bruijn graph spell solutions of the String Reconstruction from Read-Pairs Problem.

AG–**A**G
GC–GC
CT–**C**T
TG–**T**G
GC–GC
CA–CT
AG–TG
GC–GC
CT–**CA**
AGC**?**GC**?**GCTGCA

String Spelled by a Gapped Genome Path Problem:
Reconstruct a sequence of (k, d)-mers corresponding to a path in a paired de Bruijn graph.

Input: A sequence of (k, d)-mers $(a_1|b_1), \ldots, (a_n|b_n)$ such that $\text{SUFFIX}((a_i|b_i)) = \text{PREFIX}((a_{i+1}|b_{i+1}))$ for $1 \leq i \leq n - 1$.
Output: A string *Text* of length $k + d + k + n - 1$ such that the i-th (k, d)-mer of *Text* is equal to $(a_i|b_i)$ for $1 \leq i \leq n$ (if such a string exists).

Our approach to solving this problem will split the given (k, d)-mers $(a_1|b_1), \ldots, (a_n|b_n)$ into their initial k-mers, *FirstPatterns* $= (a_1, \ldots, a_n)$, and their terminal k-mers, *Second-Patterns* $= (b_1, \ldots, b_n)$. Assuming that we have implemented an algorithm solving the String Spelled by a Genome Path Problem (denoted **STRINGSPELLEDBYPATTERNS**), we can assemble *FirstPatterns* and *SecondPatterns* into strings *PrefixString* and *SuffixString*, respectively.

For the first example above, we have that *PrefixString* = AGCAGCTGCT and *SuffixString* = AGCTGCTGCA. These strings perfectly overlap starting at the fourth nucleotide of *PrefixString*:

$$
\begin{array}{rcl}
PrefixString & = & \text{AGCAGCTGCT} \\
SuffixString & = & \phantom{\text{AGC}}\text{AGCTGCTGCA} \\
Genome & = & \text{AGCAGCTGCTGCA}
\end{array}
$$

However, for the second example above, there is no perfect overlap:

$$
\begin{array}{rcl}
PrefixString & = & \text{AGC\textbf{T}GC\textbf{A}GCT} \\
SuffixString & = & \phantom{\text{AGC}}\text{\textbf{A}GC\textbf{T}GCTGCA} \\
Genome & = & \text{AGC\textbf{?}GC\textbf{?}GCTGCA}
\end{array}
$$

The following algorithm, **STRINGSPELLEDBYGAPPEDPATTERNS**, generalizes this approach to an arbitrary sequence *GappedPatterns* of (k, d)-mers. It constructs strings *PrefixString* and *SuffixString* as described above, and checks whether they have perfect overlap (i.e., form the prefix and suffix of a reconstructed string). It also assumes that the number of (k, d)-mers in *GappedPatterns* is at least d; otherwise, it is impossible to reconstruct a contiguous string.

STRINGSPELLEDBYGAPPEDPATTERNS(*GappedPatterns*, *k*, *d*)
    FirstPatterns ← the sequence of initial *k*-mers from *GappedPatterns*
    SecondPatterns ← the sequence of terminal *k*-mers from *GappedPatterns*
    PrefixString ← **STRINGSPELLEDBYPATTERNS**(*FirstPatterns*, *k*)
    SuffixString ← **STRINGSPELLEDBYPATTERNS**(*SecondPatterns*, *k*)
    for $i = k + d + 1$ to $|PrefixString|$
        if the *i*-th symbol in *PrefixString* ≠ the $(i - k - d)$-th symbol in *SuffixString*
            return "there is no string spelled by the gapped patterns"
    return *PrefixString* concatenated with the last $k + d$ symbols of *SuffixString*

Maximal non-branching paths in a graph

A node v in a directed graph *Graph* is called a **1-in-1-out node** if its indegree and outdegree are both equal to 1. We can rephrase the definition of a "maximal non-branching path" from the main text as a path whose internal nodes are 1-in-1-out nodes and whose initial and final nodes are not 1-in-1-out nodes. Also, note that the definition from the main text does not handle the case when *Graph* has a connected component that is an **isolated cycle**, in which all nodes are 1-in-1-out nodes (recall Figure 3.38).

    MAXIMALNONBRANCHINGPATHS, shown below, iterates through all nodes of the graph that are not 1-in-1-out nodes and generates all non-branching paths starting at each such node. In a final step, it finds all isolated cycles in the graph.

MAXIMALNONBRANCHINGPATHS(*Graph*)
    Paths ← empty list
    for each node *v* in *Graph*
        if *v* is not a 1-in-1-out node
            if OUT(*v*) > 0
                for each outgoing edge (v, w) from *v*
                    NonBranchingPath ← the path consisting of the single edge (v, w)
                    while *w* is a 1-in-1-out node
                        extend *NonBranchingPath* by the outgoing edge (w, u) from *w*
                        $w ← u$
                    add *NonBranchingPath* to the set *Paths*
    for each isolated cycle *Cycle* in *Graph*
        add *Cycle* to *Paths*
    return *Paths*

Detours

A short history of DNA sequencing technologies

In 1988, Radoje Drmanac, Andrey Mirzabekov, and Edwin Southern simultaneously and independently proposed the futuristic and at the time completely implausible method of **DNA arrays** for DNA sequencing. None of these three biologists knew of the work of Euler, Hamilton, and de Bruijn; none could have possibly imagined that the implications of his own experimental research would eventually bring him face-to-face with these mathematical giants.

A decade earlier, Frederick Sanger had sequenced the tiny 5,386 nucleotide-long genome of the φX174 virus. By the late 1980s, biologists were routinely sequencing viruses containing hundreds of thousands of nucleotides, but the idea of sequencing bacterial (let alone human) genomes remained preposterous, both experimentally and computationally. Indeed, generating a single read in the late 1980s cost more than a dollar, pricing mammalian genome sequences in the billions. DNA arrays were therefore invented with the goal of cheaply generating a genome's k-mer composition, albeit with a smaller read length k than the original DNA sequencing technology. For example, whereas Sanger's expensive sequencing technique generated 500 nucleotide-long reads in 1988, the DNA array inventors initially aimed at producing reads of length only 10.

DNA arrays work as follows. We first synthesize all 4^k possible DNA k-mers and attach them to a DNA array, which is a grid on which each k-mer is assigned a unique location. Next, we fluorescently label a single-stranded DNA fragment (with unknown sequence) and apply a solution containing this labeled DNA to the DNA array. The k-mers in a DNA fragment will hybridize (bind) to their reverse complementary k-mers on the array. All we need to do is use spectroscopy to analyze which sites on the array emit the fluorescence; the reverse complements of k-mers corresponding to these sites must therefore belong to the (unknown) DNA fragment. Thus, the set of fluorescent k-mers on the array reveals the composition of a DNA fragment (Figure 3.42).

At first, few believed that DNA arrays would work, because both the biochemical problem of synthesizing millions of short DNA fragments and the algorithmic problem of sequence reconstruction appeared too complicated. In 1988, *Science* magazine wrote that given the amount of work required to synthesize a DNA array, "using DNA arrays for sequencing would simply be substituting one horrendous task for another". It turned out that *Science* was only half right. In the mid-1990s, a number of companies perfected technologies for designing large DNA arrays, but DNA arrays ultimately failed to realize the dream that motivated their inventors because the fidelity of DNA hybridization with the array was too low and because the value of k was too small.

AAA	AGA	CAA	CGA	GAA	GGA	TAA	TGA
AAC	AGC	CAC	CGC	GAC	GGC	TAC	TGC
AAG	AGG	CAG	CGG	GAG	GGG	TAG	TGG
AAT	AGT	CAT	CGT	GAT	GGT	TAT	TGT
ACA	ATA	CCA	CTA	GCA	GTA	TCA	TTA
ACC	ATC	CCC	CTC	GCC	GTC	TCC	TTC
ACG	ATG	CCG	CTG	GCG	GTG	TCG	TTG
ACT	ATT	CCT	CTT	GCT	GTT	TCT	TTT

FIGURE 3.42 A toy DNA array containing all possible 3-mers. Taking the reverse complements of the fluorescently labeled 3-mers yields the collection {ACC, ACG, CAC, CCG, CGC, CGT, GCA, GTT, TAC, TTA}, which is the 3-mer composition of the twelve nucleotide-long string CGCACGTTACCG. Note that this DNA array provides no information regarding 3-mer multiplicities.

Yet the failure of DNA arrays was a spectacular one; while the original goal (DNA sequencing) dangled out of reach, two new unexpected applications of DNA arrays emerged. Today, arrays are used to measure gene expression as well as to analyze genetic variations. These unexpected applications transformed DNA arrays into a multi-billion dollar industry that included Hyseq, founded by Radoje Drmanac, one of the original inventors of DNA arrays.

After founding Hyseq, Drmanac did not abandon his dream of inventing an alternative DNA sequencing technology. In 2005, he founded Complete Genomics, one of the first Next Generation Sequencing (NGS) companies. Complete Genomics, Illumina, Life Technologies, and other NGS companies subsequently developed the technology to cheaply generate almost all k-mers from a genome, thus at last enabling the method of Eulerian assembly. While these technologies are quite different from the DNA array technology proposed in 1988, one can still recognize the intellectual legacy of DNA arrays in NGS approaches, a testament to the fact that good ideas never die, even if they fail at first.

Similarly to DNA arrays, NGS technologies initially generated millions of rather short error-prone reads (of length about 20 nucleotides) when the NGS revolution began in 2005. However, within a span of just a few years, NGS companies were able to increase read length and improve accuracy by an order of magnitude. Moreover, Pacific

Biosciences and Oxford Nanopore Technologies already generate error-ridden reads containing thousands of nucleotides. Perhaps your own start-up will find a way to generate a single read spanning the entire genome, thus making this chapter a footnote in the history of genome sequencing. Whatever the future brings, recent developments in NGS have already revolutionized genomics, and biologists are preparing to assemble the genomes of all mammalian species on Earth ... all while relying on a simple idea that Leonhard Euler conceived in 1735.

Repeats in the human genome

A **transposon** is a DNA fragment that can change its position within the genome, often resulting in a duplication (repeat). A transposon that inserts itself into a gene will most likely disable that gene. Diseases that are caused by transposons include hemophilia, porphyria, Duchenne muscular dystrophy, and many others. Transposons make up a large fraction of the human genome and are divided into two classes according to their mechanism of transposition, which can be described as either **retrotransposons** or **DNA transposons**.

Retrotransposons are copied in two stages: first they are transcribed from DNA to RNA, and the RNA produced is then **reverse transcribed** to DNA by a **reverse transcriptase**. This copied DNA fragment is then inserted at a new position into the genome. DNA transposons do not involve an RNA intermediate but instead are catalyzed by **transposases**. The transposase cuts out the DNA transposon, which is then inserted into a new site in the genome, resulting in a repeat.

The first transposons were discovered in maize by Barbara McClintock, for which she was awarded a Nobel Prize in 1983. About 85% of the maize genome and 50% of the human genome consist of transposons. The most common transposon in humans is the Alu sequence, which is approximately 300 bases long and accounts for approximately a million repeats (with mutations) in the human genome. The **Mariner sequence** is another transposon in the human genome that has about 14,000 repeats, making up 2.6 million base pairs. Mariner-like transposons exist in many species and can even be transmitted from one species to another. The Mariner transposon was used to develop the **Sleeping Beauty transposon system**, a synthetic DNA transposon constructed for the purposes of introducing new traits in animals and for gene therapy.

Graphs

The use of the word "graph" in this book is different from its use in high school mathematics; we do not mean a chart of data. You can think of a graph as a diagram showing cities connected by roads.

The first panel in Figure 3.43 shows a 4 × 4 chessboard with the four corner squares removed. A knight can move two steps in any of four directions (left, right, up, and down) followed by one step in a perpendicular direction. For example, a knight at square 1 can move to square 7 (two down and one left), square 9 (two down and one right), or square 6 (two right and one down).

 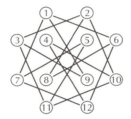 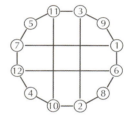

FIGURE 3.43 (Left) A hypothetical chessboard. (Middle) The Knight Graph represents each square by a node and connects two nodes with an edge if a knight can travel between the respective squares in a single move. (Right) An equivalent representation of the Knight Graph.

STOP and Think: Can a knight travel around this board, pass through each square exactly once, and return to the same square it started on?

The second panel in Figure 3.43 represents each of the chessboard's twelve squares as a node. Two nodes are connected by an edge if a knight can move between them in a single step. For example, node 1 is connected to nodes 6, 7, and 9. Connecting nodes in this manner produces a "Knight Graph" consisting of twelve nodes and sixteen edges.

We can describe a graph by its set of nodes and edges, where every edge is written as the pair of nodes that it connects. The graph in the second panel of Figure 3.43 is described by the node set

$$1, 2, 3, 4, 5, 6, 7, 8, 9, 10, 11, 12,$$

and the following edge set:

$$1—6 \quad 1—7 \quad 1—9 \quad 2—3 \quad 2—8 \quad 2—10 \quad 3—9 \quad 3—11$$
$$4—10 \quad 4—12 \quad 5—7 \quad 5—11 \quad 6—8 \quad 6—12 \quad 7—12 \quad 10—11$$

A **path** in a graph is a sequence of edges, where each successive edge begins at the node where the previous edge ends. For example, the path $8 \rightarrow 6 \rightarrow 1 \rightarrow 9$ in Figure 3.43 starts at node 8, ends at node 9, and consists of 3 edges. Paths that start and end at the same node are referred to as **cycles**. The cycle $3 \rightarrow 2 \rightarrow 10 \rightarrow 11 \rightarrow 3$ starts and ends at node 3 and consists of 4 edges.

The way a graph is drawn is irrelevant; two graphs with the same node and edge sets are equivalent, even if the particular pictures that represent the graph are different. The only thing that is important is which nodes are connected and which are not. Therefore, the graph in the second panel of Figure 3.43 is identical to the graph in the third panel. This graph reveals a cycle that visits every node in the Knight Graph once and describes a sequence of knight moves that visit every square exactly once.

EXERCISE BREAK: How many knight's tours exist for the chessboard in Figure 3.43?

The number of edges incident to a given node v is called the **degree** of v. For example, node 1 in the Knight Graph has degree 3, while node 5 has degree 2. The sum of degrees of all twelve nodes is, in this case, 32 (eight nodes have degree 3 and four nodes have degree 2), which is twice the number of edges in the graph.

STOP and Think: Can you connect seven phones in such a way that each is connected to exactly three others?

Many bioinformatics problems analyze **directed graphs**, in which every edge is directed from one node to another, as shown by the arrows in Figure 3.44. You can think of a directed graph as a diagram showing cities connected by one-way roads. Every node in a directed graph is characterized by indegree (the number of incoming edges) and outdegree (the number of outgoing edges).

STOP and Think: Prove that for every directed graph, the sum of indegrees of all nodes is equal to the sum of outdegrees of all nodes.

An undirected graph is **connected** if every two nodes have a path connecting them. Disconnected graphs can be partitioned into disjoint connected components.

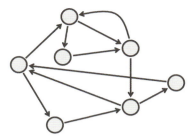

FIGURE 3.44 A directed graph.

The icosian game

We make an historical detour to Dublin, with the creation in 1857 of the **icosian game** by the Irish mathematician William Hamilton. This "game", which was a commercial flop, consisted of a wooden board with twenty pegholes and some lines connecting the holes, as well as twenty numbered pegs (Figure 3.45 (left)). The objective was to place the numbered pegs in the holes in such a way that peg 1 would be connected by a line on the board to peg 2, which would in turn be connected by a line to peg 3, and so on, until finally peg 20 would be connected by a line back to peg 1. In other words, if we follow the lines on the board from peg to peg in ascending order, we reach every peg exactly once and then arrive back at our starting peg.

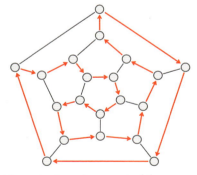

FIGURE 3.45 (Left) Hamilton's icosian game, with a winning placement of the pegs shown. (Right) The winning placement of the pegs can be represented as a Hamiltonian cycle in a graph. Each node in this graph represents a peghole on the board, and an edge connects two pegholes that are connected by a line segment on the board.

We can model the icosian game using a graph if we represent each peghole by a node and then transform lines that connect pegholes into edges that connect the corresponding nodes. This graph does have a Hamiltonian cycle solving the icosian game; one of them is shown in Figure 3.45 (right). Although a brute force approach to the Hamiltonian Cycle Problem works for these small graphs, it quickly becomes infeasible for large graphs.

Tractable and intractable problems

Inspired by Euler's Theorem, you probably are wondering whether there exists such a simple result leading to a fast algorithm for the Hamiltonian Cycle Problem. The key challenge is that while we are guided by Euler's Theorem in solving the Eulerian Cycle Problem, an analogous simple condition for the Hamiltonian Cycle Problem remains unknown. Of course, you could always explore all walks through the graph and report back if you find a Hamiltonian cycle. The problem with this brute force method is that for a graph on just a thousand nodes, there may be more walks through the graph than there are atoms in the universe!

For years, the Hamiltonian Cycle Problem eluded all attempts to solve it by some of the world's most brilliant researchers. After years of fruitless effort, computer scientists began to wonder whether this problem is **intractable**, i.e., that their failure to find a polynomial-time algorithm was not attributable to a lack of insight, but rather because such an algorithm for solving the Hamiltonian Cycle Problem simply does not exist. In the 1970s, computer scientists discovered thousands more algorithmic problems with the same fate as the Hamiltonian Cycle Problem. While these problems may appear to be simple, no one has been able to find fast algorithms for solving them. A large subset of these problems, including the Hamiltonian Cycle Problem, are now collectively known as *NP*-**complete**. A formal definition of *NP*-completeness is beyond the scope of this text.

All the *NP*-complete problems are *equivalent* to each other: an instance of any *NP*-complete problem can be transformed into an instance of any other *NP*-complete problem in polynomial time. Thus, if you find a fast algorithm for one *NP*-complete problem, you will automatically be able to use this algorithm to design a fast algorithm for any other *NP*-complete problem! The problem of efficiently solving *NP*-complete problems, or finally proving that they are intractable, is so fundamental that it was named one of seven "Millennium Problems" by the Clay Mathematics Institute in 2000. Find an efficient algorithm for any *NP*-complete problem, or show that one of these problems is intractable, and the Clay Institute will award you a prize of one million dollars.

Think twice before you embark on solving an *NP*-complete problem. So far, only one of the seven Millennium Problems has been solved; in 2003, Grigori Perelman proved the Poincaré Conjecture. A true mathematician, Perelman would later turn down the million-dollar prize, believing that the purity and beauty of mathematics is above all worldly compensation.

NP-complete problems fall within a larger class of difficult computational problems. A problem *A* is **NP-hard** if there is some *NP*-complete problem that can be reduced to *A* in polynomial time. Because *NP*-complete problems can be reduced to each other in polynomial time, all *NP*-complete problems are *NP*-hard. However, not every *NP*-hard problem is *NP*-complete (meaning that the former are "at least as difficult" to solve as the latter). One example of an *NP*-hard problem that is not *NP*-complete is the **Traveling Salesman Problem**, in which we are given a graph with weighted edges and we must produce a Hamiltonian cycle of minimum total weight.

From Euler to Hamilton to de Bruijn

Euler's presented his solution of the Bridges of Königsberg Problem to the Imperial Russian Academy of Sciences in St. Petersburg in 1735. Figure 3.46 shows Euler's drawing of the Seven Bridges of Königsberg.

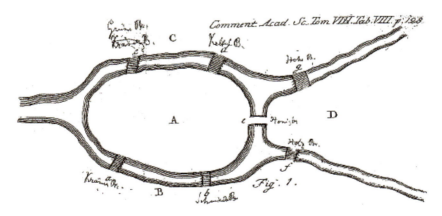

FIGURE 3.46 Euler's illustration of Königsberg, showing each of the four parts of the city labeled A, B, C, and D, along with the seven bridges crossing the different arms of the Pregel river.

Euler was the most prolific mathematician of all time; besides graph theory, he first introduced the notation *f(x)* to represent a function, *i* for the square root of -1, and π for the circular constant. Working very hard throughout his entire life, he became blind in his right eye in 1735. He kept working. In 1766, he lost the use of his left eye and commented: "Now I will have fewer distractions." He kept working. Even after going completely blind, he published hundreds of papers.

In this chapter, we have met three mathematicians of three different centuries, Euler, Hamilton, and de Bruijn, spread out across Europe (Figure 3.47). We might be inclined to feel a sense of adventure at their work and how it converged to this singular point in modern biology. Yet the first biologists who worked on DNA sequencing had no idea of how graph theory could be applied to this subject. What's more, the first paper applying the three mathematicians' ideas to genome assembly was published lifetimes after the deaths of Euler and Hamilton, when de Bruijn was in his seventies. So perhaps we might think of these three men not as adventurers, but instead as lonely wanderers. As is so often the mathematician's curse, each of the three passionately pursued abstract questions while having no idea where the answers might one day lead without him.

FIGURE 3.47 Leonhard Euler (left), William Hamilton (center), and Nicolaas de Bruijn (right).

The seven bridges of Kaliningrad

Königsberg was largely destroyed during World War II; its ruins were captured by the Soviet army. The city was renamed Kaliningrad in 1946 in honor of Soviet revolutionary Mikhail Kalinin.

Since the 18th Century, much has changed in the layout of Königsberg, and it just so happens that the bridge graph drawn today for the city of Kaliningrad still does not contain an Eulerian cycle. However, this graph does contain an Eulerian path, which means that Kaliningrad residents can walk crossing every bridge exactly once, but cannot do so and return to where they started. Thus, the citizens of Kaliningrad finally achieved at least a small part of the goal set by the citizens of Königsberg (although they have to take a taxi home). Yet strolling around Kaliningrad is not as pleasant as it would have been in 1735, since the beautiful old Königsberg was ravaged by the combination of Allied bombing in 1944 and dreadful Soviet architecture in the years following World War II.

The BEST Theorem

Given an adjacency matrix $A(G)$ of a directed Eulerian graph G, we define the matrix $A^*(G)$ by replacing the i-th diagonal entry of $-A(G)$ by INDEGREE(i) for each node i in G (Figure 3.48).

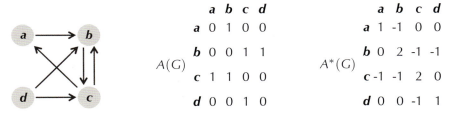

	a	b	c	d
a	0	1	0	0
b	0	0	1	1
c	1	1	0	0
d	0	0	1	0

$A(G)$

	a	b	c	d
a	1	-1	0	0
b	0	2	-1	-1
c	-1	-1	2	0
d	0	0	-1	1

$A^*(G)$

FIGURE 3.48 (Left) A graph G with two Eulerian cycles. (Middle) The adjacency matrix $A(G)$ of G. (Right) The matrix $A^*(G)$. Each i-cofactor of A^* is equal to 2. Thus, the BEST theorem computes the number of Eulerian cycles as $2 \cdot 0! \cdot 1! \cdot 1! \cdot 1! = 2$.

The *i-cofactor* of a matrix M is the determinant of the matrix obtained from M by deleting its i-th row and i-th column. It can be shown that for a given Eulerian graph G, all i-cofactors of $A^*(G)$ have the same value, which we denote as $c(G)$.

The following theorem provides a formula computing the number of Eulerian cycles in a graph. Its name is an acronym of its discoverers: de **B**ruijn, van Aardenne-**E**hrenfest, **S**mith, and **T**utte.

BEST Theorem: *The number of Eulerian cycles in an Eulerian graph is equal to*

$$c(G) \cdot \prod_{\text{all nodes } v \text{ in graph } G} (\text{INDEGREE}(v) - 1)!$$

The proof of the BEST Theorem, which is beyond the scope of this text, provides us with an alternative way to construct all Eulerian cycles in an Eulerian directed graph.

Bibliography Notes

After Euler's work on the Königsberg Bridge Problem (Euler, 1758), graph theory was forgotten for over a hundred years but was revived in the second half of the 19th Century. Graph theory flourished in the 20th Century, when it became an important area of mathematics with many practical applications. The de Bruijn graph was introduced independently by Nicolaas de Bruijn (de Bruijn, 1946) and I. J. Good (Good, 1946).

DNA sequencing methods were invented independently and simultaneously in 1977 by groups led by Frederick Sanger (Sanger, Nicklen, and Coulson, 1977) and Walter Gilbert (Maxam and Gilbert, 1977). DNA arrays were proposed simultaneously and independently in 1988 by Radoje Drmanac (Drmanac et al., 1989), Andrey Mirzabekov (Lysov et al., 1988) and Edwin Southern (Southern, 1988). The Eulerian approach to DNA arrays was described in 1989 (Pevzner, 1989).

The Eulerian approach to DNA sequencing was described by Idury and Waterman, 1995 and further developed by Pevzner, Tang, and Waterman, 2001. To address the challenge of assembly from short reads produced by next generation sequencing technologies, a number of assembly tools that are based on de Bruijn graphs have been developed (Zerbino and Birney, 2008, Butler et al., 2008). Paired de Bruijn graphs were introduced by Medvedev et al., 2011.

The Sleeping Beauty transposon system was developed by Ivics et al., 1997.

The Discovery of Antibiotics

In August 1928, before leaving for vacation, Scottish microbiologist Alexander Fleming stacked his cultures of infection-causing *Staphylococcus* bacteria on a laboratory bench. When he returned to work a few weeks later, Fleming noticed that one culture had been contaminated with *Penicillium* fungus, and that the colony of *Staphylococcus* surrounding it had been destroyed! Fleming named the bacteria-killing substance **penicillin**, and he suggested that it could be used to treat bacterial infections in humans.

When Fleming published his discovery in 1929, his article had little immediate impact. Subsequent experiments struggled to isolate the **antibiotic** agent (i.e., the compound that actually killed bacteria) from the fungus. As a result, Fleming eventually concluded that penicillin could not be practically applied to treat bacterial infections and abandoned his antibiotics research.

Searching for new drugs to treat wounded soldiers, the American and British governments intensified their search for antibiotics after the start of World War II; however, the challenge of mass-producing antibiotics remained. In March 1942, half of the total supply of penicillin owned by pharmaceutical giant Merck was used to treat a single infected patient.

Also in 1942, Russian biologists Georgy Gause and Maria Brazhnikova noticed that the *Bacillus brevis* bacterium killed the pathogenic bacterium *Staphylococcus aureus*. In contrast to Fleming's efforts with penicillin, they successfully isolated the antibiotic compound from *Bacillus brevis* and named it *Gramicidin Soviet*. Within a year, this antibiotic was distributed to Soviet military hospitals.

Meanwhile, American scientists were scouring various food markets for rotten groceries and finally found a moldy cantaloupe in Illinois with a high concentration of penicillin. This mundane discovery allowed the United States to produce 2 million doses of penicillin in time for the Allied invasion of Normandy in 1944, thus saving thousands of wounded soldiers' lives.

Gause continued his research into *Gramicidin Soviet* after World War II but failed to elucidate its chemical structure. Taking the torch from Gause, English biochemist Richard Synge studied *Gramicidin Soviet* and a wide array of other antibiotics produced by *Bacillus brevis*. A few years after World War II ended, he demonstrated that they represent short amino acid sequences (i.e., mini-proteins) called **peptides**. Gause received the Stalin Prize in 1946, and Synge won the Nobel Prize in 1952. The former award proved more valuable as it protected Gause from execution during the period of **Lysenkoism**, the Soviet campaign against "bourgeois" geneticists that intensified in the postwar era. See DETOUR: Gause and Lysenkoism.

PAGE 215

The mass-production of antibiotics initiated an arms race between pharmaceutical companies and pathogenic bacteria. The former worked to develop new antibiotic drugs, while the latter acquired resistance against these drugs. Although modern medicine won every battle for six decades, the last ten years have witnessed an alarming rise in antibiotic-resistant bacterial infections that cannot be treated even by the most powerful antibiotics. In particular, the *Staphylococcus aureus* bacterium that Gause had studied in 1942 mutated into a resistant strain known as **Methicillin-resistant** *Staphylococcus aureus* (**MRSA**). MRSA is now the leading cause of death from infections in hospitals; its death rate has even passed that of AIDS in the United States.

With the rise of MRSA at hand, developing new antibiotics represents a central challenge to modern medicine. A difficult problem in antibiotics research is that of **sequencing** newly discovered antibiotics, or determining the order of amino acids making up the antibiotic peptide.

How Do Bacteria Make Antibiotics?

How peptides are encoded by the genome

Let's begin by considering **Tyrocidine B1**, one of many antibiotics produced by *Bacillus brevis*. Tyrocidine B1 is defined by the 10 amino acid-long sequence shown below (using both the one-letter and three-letter notations for amino acids). Our goal in this section is to figure out how *Bacillus brevis* could have made this antibiotic.

Three-letter notation	Val-Lys-Leu-Phe-Pro-Trp-Phe-Asn-Gln-Tyr
One-letter notation	V K L F P W F N Q Y

The **Central Dogma of Molecular Biology** states that "DNA makes RNA makes protein." According to the Central Dogma, a gene from a genome is first **transcribed** into a strand of RNA composed of four **ribonucleotides**: adenine, cytosine, guanine, and uracil. A strand of RNA can be represented as an **RNA string**, formed over the four-letter alphabet $\{A, C, G, U\}$. You can think of the genome as a large cookbook, in which case the gene and its RNA transcript form a recipe in this cookbook. Then, the RNA transcript is **translated** into an amino acid sequence of a protein.

Much like replication, the chemical machinery underlying transcription and translation is fascinating, but from a computational perspective, both processes are straightforward. Transcription simply transforms a DNA string into an RNA string by replacing all occurrences of T with U. The resulting strand of RNA is translated into an amino acid sequence as follows. During translation, the RNA strand is partitioned into non-overlapping 3-mers called **codons**. Then, each codon is converted into one of 20 amino acids via the **genetic code**; the resulting sequence can be represented as an **amino acid string** over a 20-letter alphabet. As illustrated in Figure 4.1, each of the 64 RNA codons encodes its own amino acid (some codons encode the same amino acid), with the exception of three **stop codons** that do not translate into amino acids and serve to halt translation (see **DETOUR: Discovery of Codons**). For example, the DNA string **PAGE 216** **TATACGAAA** transcribes into the RNA string **UAUACGAAA**, which in turn translates into the amino acid string **YTK**.

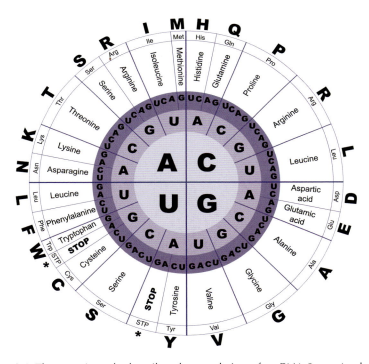

FIGURE 4.1 The genetic code describes the translation of an RNA 3-mer (codon) into one of 20 amino acids. The first three circles, moving from the inside out, represent the first, second, and third nucleotides of a codon. The fourth, fifth, and sixth circles define the translated amino acid in three ways: the amino acid's full name, its 3-letter abbreviation, and its single-letter abbreviation. Three of the 64 total RNA codons are stop codons, which halt translation.

We will represent the genetic code as an array GENETICCODE containing 64 elements, as shown in Figure 4.2. The following problem asks you to find the translation of an RNA string into an amino acid string.

Protein Translation Problem:

Translate an RNA string into an amino acid string.

> **Input**: An RNA string *Pattern* and the array GENETICCODE.
> **Output**: The translation of *Pattern* into an amino acid string *Peptide*.

EXERCISE BREAK: How many DNA strings of length 30 transcribe and translate into Tyrocidine B1?

0	AAA	K	16	CAA	Q	32	GAA	E	48	UAA	⋆
1	AAC	N	17	CAC	H	33	GAC	D	49	UAC	Y
2	AAG	K	18	CAG	Q	34	GAG	E	50	UAG	⋆
3	AAU	N	19	CAU	H	35	GAU	D	51	UAU	Y
4	ACA	T	20	CCA	P	36	GCA	A	52	UCA	S
5	ACC	T	21	CCC	P	37	GCC	A	53	UCC	S
6	ACG	T	22	CCG	P	38	GCG	A	54	UCG	S
7	ACU	T	23	CCU	P	39	GCU	A	55	UCU	S
8	AGA	R	24	CGA	R	40	GGA	G	56	UGA	⋆
9	AGC	S	25	CGC	R	41	GGC	G	57	UGC	C
10	AGG	R	26	CGG	R	42	GGG	G	58	UGG	W
11	AGU	S	27	CGU	R	43	GGU	G	59	UGU	C
12	AUA	I	28	CUA	L	44	GUA	V	60	UUA	L
13	AUC	I	29	CUC	L	45	GUC	V	61	UUC	F
14	AUG	M	30	CUG	L	46	GUG	V	62	UUG	L
15	AUU	I	31	CUU	L	47	GUU	V	63	UUU	F

FIGURE 4.2 The array GENETICCODE contains 64 elements, each of which is an amino acid or a stop codon (represented by ⋆).

Where is Tyrocidine encoded in the Bacillus brevis genome?

Thousands of different DNA 30-mers could code for Tyrocidine B1, and we would like to know which one appears in the *Bacillus brevis* genome. There are three different ways to divide a DNA string into codons for translation, one starting at each of the first three positions of the string. These different ways of dividing a DNA string into codons are called **reading frames**. Since DNA is double-stranded, a genome has six reading frames (three on each strand), as shown in Figure 4.3.

Translated peptides	GluThrPheSerLeuValSTPSerIle STPAsnPhePheLeuGlyLeuIleAsn **ValLysLeuPheProTrpPheAsnGlnTyr**
Transcribed RNA	GUGAAACUUUUUCCUUGGUUUAAUCAAUAU
DNA	5' GTGAAACTTTTTCCTTGGTTTAATCAATAT 3' 3' CACTTTGAAAAAGGAACCAAATTAGTTATA 5'
Transcribed RNA	CACUUUGAAAAAGGAACCAAAUUAGUUAUA
Translated peptides	HisPheLysLysArgProLysIleLeuIle SerValLysGluLysThrSTPAspIle PheSerLysGlyGlnAsnLeuSTPTyr

FIGURE 4.3 Six different reading frames give six different ways for the same fragment of DNA to be transcribed and translated (three from each strand). The top three amino acid strings are read from left to right, whereas the bottom three strings are read from right to left. The highlighted amino acid string spells out the sequence of Tyrocidine B1. Stop codons are represented by STP.

We say that a DNA string *Pattern* **encodes** an amino acid string *Peptide* if the RNA string transcribed from either *Pattern* or its reverse complement $\overline{Pattern}$ translates into *Peptide*. For example, the DNA string GAAACT is transcribed into GAAACU and translated into ET. The reverse complement of this DNA string, AGTTTC, is transcribed into AGUUUC and translated into SF. Thus, GAAACT encodes both ET and SF.

Peptide Encoding Problem:

Find substrings of a genome encoding a given amino acid sequence.

    Input: A DNA string *Text* and an amino acid string *Peptide*.
    Output: All substrings of *Text* encoding *Peptide* (if any such substrings exist).

STOP and Think: Solve the Peptide Encoding Problem for *Bacillus brevis* and Tyrocidine B1. Which starting positions in *Bacillus brevis* encode this peptide?

By solving the Peptide Encoding Problem for Tyrocidine B1, we should find a 30-mer in the *Bacillus brevis* genome encoding Tyrocidine B1, and yet no such 30-mer exists!

STOP and Think: How could a bacterium produce a peptide that is not encoded by the bacterium's genome?

From linear to cyclic peptides

Neither Gause nor Synge was aware of it, but tyrocidines and gramicidins are actually **cyclic peptides**. The cyclic representation for Tyrocidine B1 is shown in Figure 4.4 (left). Thus, Tyrocidine B1 has ten different linear representations, and we should run the Peptide Encoding Problem on every one of these sequences to find potential 30-mers coding for Tyrocidine B1. Yet when we solve the Peptide Encoding Problem for each of the ten strings in Figure 4.4 (right), we find no 30-mer in the *Bacillus brevis* genome encoding Tyrocidine B1!

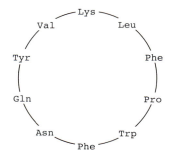

```
 1  Val-Lys-Leu-Phe-Pro-Trp-Phe-Asn-Gln-Tyr
 2  Lys-Leu-Phe-Pro-Trp-Phe-Asn-Gln-Tyr-Val
 3  Leu-Phe-Pro-Trp-Phe-Asn-Gln-Tyr-Val-Lys
 4  Phe-Pro-Trp-Phe-Asn-Gln-Tyr-Val-Lys-Leu
 5  Pro-Trp-Phe-Asn-Gln-Tyr-Val-Lys-Leu-Phe
 6  Trp-Phe-Asn-Gln-Tyr-Val-Lys-Leu-Phe-Pro
 7  Phe-Asn-Gln-Tyr-Val-Lys-Leu-Phe-Pro-Trp
 8  Asn-Gln-Tyr-Val-Lys-Leu-Phe-Pro-Trp-Phe
 9  Gln-Tyr-Val-Lys-Leu-Phe-Pro-Trp-Phe-Asn
10  Tyr-Val-Lys-Leu-Phe-Pro-Trp-Phe-Asn-Gln
```

FIGURE 4.4 Tyrocidine B1 is a cyclic peptide (left), and so it has ten different linear representations (right).

Dodging the Central Dogma of Molecular Biology

Hopefully, you are perplexed, because the Central Dogma of Molecular Biology implies that *all* peptides must be encoded by the genome. Nobel laureate Edward Tatum was just as confused, and in 1963, he devised an ingenious experiment. Protein translation is carried out by a molecular machine called a **ribosome**, and so Tatum reasoned that if he inhibited the ribosome, all protein production in *Bacillus brevis* should grind to a halt. To his amazement, all proteins did indeed shut down — except for tyrocidines and gramicidins! His experiment led Tatum to hypothesize that some yet unknown *non-ribosomal* mechanism must assemble these peptides.

In 1969, Fritz Lipmann (another Nobel laureate) demonstrated that tyrocidines and gramicidins are **non-ribosomal peptides** (**NRPs**), synthesized not by the ribosome, but by a giant protein called **NRP synthetase**. This enzyme pieces together antibiotic peptides without any reliance on RNA or the genetic code! We now know that every NRP synthetase assembles peptides by growing them one amino acid at a time, as shown in Figure 4.5.

The reason why many NRPs have pharmaceutical applications is that they have been optimized by eons of evolution as "molecular bullets" that bacteria and fungi use to kill their enemies. If these enemies happen to be pathogens, researchers are eager to borrow these bullets as antibacterial drugs. However, NRPs are not limited to antibiotics: many of them represent anti-tumor agents and immunosuppressors, while others are used by bacteria to communicate with other cells (see DETOUR: Quorum Sensing). PAGE 217

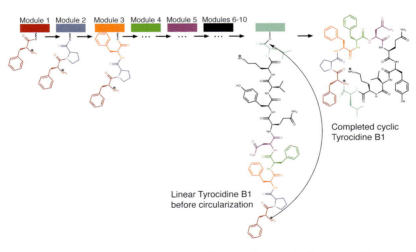

FIGURE 4.5 NRP synthetase is a giant multi-module protein that assembles a cyclic peptide one amino acid at a time. Each of ten different modules (shown by different colors) adds a single amino acid to the peptide, which in the figure is one of many tyrocidines produced by *Bacillus brevis*. In a final step, the peptide is circularized.

Sequencing Antibiotics by Shattering Them into Pieces

Introduction to mass spectrometry

Since NRPs do not adhere to the Central Dogma, we cannot infer them from the genome, which brings us back to where we started. What makes sequencing these peptides even more difficult is that many NRPs (including tyrocidines and gramicidins) are cyclic. Thus, the standard tools for sequencing linear peptides, which we will describe later, are not applicable to NRP analysis.

The workhorse of peptide sequencing is the **mass spectrometer**, an expensive molecular scale that shatters molecules into pieces and then weighs the resulting fragments. The mass spectrometer measures the mass of a molecule in **daltons** (**Da**); 1 Da is approximately equal to the mass of a single nuclear particle (i.e., a proton or neutron).

We will approximate the mass of a molecule by simply adding the number of protons and neutrons found in the molecule's constituent atoms, which yields the molecule's **integer mass**. For example, the amino acid glycine, which has chemical formula C_2H_3ON, has an integer mass of 57, since $2 \cdot 12 + 3 \cdot 1 + 1 \cdot 16 + 1 \cdot 14 = 57$. Yet 1 Da is not exactly equal to the mass of a proton/neutron, and we may need to account for different naturally occurring isotopes of each atom when weighing a molecule (see DETOUR: Molecular Mass). As a result, amino acids typically have non-integer masses (e.g., glycine has total integer mass equal to approximately 57.02 Da); for simplicity, however, we will work with the integer mass table given in Figure 4.6. Tyrocidine B1, which is represented by VKLFPWFNQY, has total mass 1322 Da (99 + 128 + 113 + 147 + 97 + 186 + 147 + 114 + 128 + 163 = 1322).

PAGE 217

```
G   A   S   P   V   T    C    I    L    N    D    K    Q    E    M    H    F    R    Y    W
57  71  87  97  99  101  103  113  113  114  115  128  128  129  131  137  147  156  163  186
```

FIGURE 4.6 Integer masses of amino acids. The integer mass of each amino acid is computed by adding the number of protons and neutrons in the amino acid molecule.

The mass spectrometer can break each molecule of Tyrocidine B1 into two linear fragments, and it analyzes samples that may contain billions of identical copies of the peptide, with each copy breaking in its own way. One copy may break into LFP and WFNQYVK (with respective masses 357 and 965), whereas another may break into PWFN and QYVKLF. Our goal is to use the masses of these and other fragments to sequence the peptide. The collection of all the fragment masses generated by the mass spectrometer is called an **experimental spectrum**.

STOP and Think: How can we use the experimental spectrum to sequence a peptide?

The Cyclopeptide Sequencing Problem

For now, we will assume for simplicity that the mass spectrometer breaks the copies of a cyclic peptide at every possible two bonds, so that the resulting experimental spectrum contains the masses of all possible linear fragments of the peptide, which are called **subpeptides**. For example, the cyclic peptide NQEL has 12 subpeptides: N, Q, E, L, NQ, QE, EL, LN, NQE, QEL, ELN, and LNQ. We will also assume that subpeptides may occur more than once if an amino acid occurs multiple times in the peptide; for example, ELEL also has 12 subpeptides: E, L, E, L, EL, LE, EL, LE, ELE, LEL, ELE, and LEL.

EXERCISE BREAK: How many subpeptides does a cyclic peptide of length n have?

The **theoretical spectrum** of a cyclic peptide *Peptide* is the collection of all of the masses of its subpeptides, in addition to the mass 0 and the mass of the entire peptide, with masses ordered from smallest to largest. We will denote the theoretical spectrum of *Peptide* by CYCLOSPECTRUM(*Peptide*) and assume that this theoretical spectrum can contain duplicate elements, as is the case for NQEL (shown below), where **NQ** and **EL** have the same mass.

	L	N	Q	E	LN	**NQ**	**EL**	QE	LNQ	ELN	QEL	NQE	NQEL
0	113	114	128	129	227	**242**	**242**	257	355	356	370	371	484

Generating Theoretical Spectrum Problem:
Generate the theoretical spectrum of a cyclic peptide.

> **Input**: An amino acid string *Peptide*.
> **Output**: CYCLOSPECTRUM(*Peptide*).

CHARGING STATION (Generating the Theoretical Spectrum of a Peptide):
One way to solve the Generating Theoretical Spectrum Problem is to construct a list containing all subpeptides of *Peptide*, then find the mass of each subpeptide by adding the integer masses of its constituent amino acids. This approach will work, but check out this Charging Station to see a more elegant algorithm.

Generating the theoretical spectrum of a known peptide is easy, but our aim is to solve the reverse problem of reconstructing an *unknown* peptide from its *experimental* spectrum. We will start by assuming that a biologist is lucky enough to generate an **ideal spectrum**, which is one coinciding with the peptide's theoretical spectrum.

STOP and Think: Consider the theoretical spectrum for Tyrocidine B1 shown in Figure 4.7. If an experiment produced this spectrum, how would you reconstruct the amino acid sequence of Tyrocidine B1?

0	97	99	113	114	128	128	147	147	163	186	227
241	242	244	260	261	262	283	291	333	340	357	388
389	390	390	405	430	430	447	485	487	503	504	518
543	544	552	575	577	584	631	632	650	651	671	672
690	691	738	745	747	770	778	779	804	818	819	835
837	875	892	892	917	932	932	933	934	965	982	989
1031	1039	1060	1061	1062	1078	1080	1081	1095	1136	1159	1175
1175	1194	1194	1208	1209	1223	1225	1322				

FIGURE 4.7 The theoretical spectrum for Tyrocidine B1 (VKLFPWFNQY), whose integer representation is 99-128-113-147-97-186-147-114-128-163.

Cyclopeptide Sequencing Problem:

Given an ideal spectrum, find a cyclic peptide whose theoretical spectrum matches the experimental spectrum.

   Input: A collection of (possibly repeated) integers *Spectrum* corresponding to an ideal spectrum.
   Output: An amino acid string *Peptide* such that CYCLOSPECTRUM(*Peptide*) = *Spectrum* (if such a string exists).

From now on, we will sometimes work directly with amino acid masses, taking the liberty to represent a peptide by a sequence of integers denoting the peptide's constituent amino acid masses. For example, we represent NQEL as 114-128-129-113 and Tyrocidine B1 (VKLFPWFNQY) as 99-128-113-147-97-186-147-114-128-163. We have therefore replaced an alphabet of 20 amino acids with an alphabet of only 18 integers because, recalling Figure 4.6, two amino acid pairs (I/L and K/Q) have the same integer mass.

   Note that in the general case that we are not restricted to the amino acid alphabet, the Cyclopeptide Sequencing Problem could have multiple solutions. For example, "peptides" 1-1-3-3 and 1-2-1-4 have the same theoretical spectrum $\{1, 1, 2, 3, 3, 4, 4, 5, 5, 6, 7, 7\}$.

STOP and Think: Can you find two peptides (in the alphabet of 18 amino acid masses) with identical theoretical spectra?

A Brute Force Algorithm for Cyclopeptide Sequencing

We first encountered brute force algorithms when looking for motifs in Chapter 2. In this chapter, we will discuss how to speed up brute force algorithms for peptide sequencing to make them practical.

Let's design a straightforward brute force algorithm for the Cyclopeptide Sequencing Problem. We denote the total mass of an amino acid string *Peptide* as MASS(*Peptide*). In mass spectrometry experiments, whereas the peptide that generated *Spectrum* is unknown, the peptide's mass is typically known and is denoted PARENTMASS(*Spectrum*).

For the sake of simplicity, we will also assume that for all experimental spectra, PARENTMASS(*Spectrum*) is equal to the largest mass in *Spectrum*. The following brute force cyclopeptide sequencing algorithm generates all possible peptides whose mass is equal to PARENTMASS(*Spectrum*) and then checks which of these peptides has theoretical spectra matching *Spectrum*.

BFCYCLOPEPTIDESEQUENCING(*Spectrum*)
    for every *Peptide* with MASS(*Peptide*) equal to PARENTMASS(*Spectrum*)
        if *Spectrum* = CYCLOSPECTRUM(*Peptide*)
            output *Peptide*

There should be no question that **BFCYCLOPEPTIDESEQUENCING** will solve the Cyclopeptide Sequencing Problem. However, we should be concerned about its running time: how many peptides are there having mass equal to PARENTMASS(*Spectrum*)?

Counting Peptides with Given Mass Problem:

Compute the number of peptides of given mass.

    Input: An integer m.
    Output: The number of linear peptides having integer mass m.

If you have difficulty solving this problem or getting the runtime down, please return to it after learning more about dynamic programming algorithms in Chapter 5. It turns out that there are *trillions* of peptides having the same integer mass (1322) as Tyrocidine B1 (Figure 4.8). Therefore, **BFCYCLOPEPTIDESEQUENCING** is completely impractical, and we will not even bother asking you to implement it.

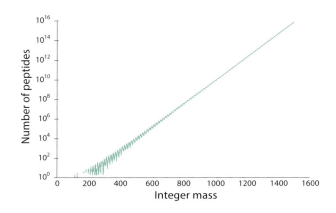

FIGURE 4.8 The number of peptides with given integer mass grows exponentially.

STOP and Think: Figure 4.8 suggests that for large m, the number of peptides with given integer mass m can be approximated as $k \cdot C^m$, where k and C are constants. Can you find these constants?

A Branch-and-Bound Algorithm for Cyclopeptide Sequencing

Just because the algorithm from the previous section failed miserably does not mean that all brute force approaches are doomed. Can we design a faster brute force algorithm based on a different idea?

Instead of checking all *cyclic* peptides with a given mass, our new approach to solving the Cyclopeptide Sequencing Problem will "grow" candidate *linear* peptides whose theoretical spectra are "consistent" with the experimental spectrum.

STOP and Think: What should it mean for a linear peptide to be consistent with an experimental spectrum? Would you classify VKF as consistent with the spectrum shown in Figure 4.7? What about VKY?

Given an experimental spectrum *Spectrum*, we will form a collection *Peptides* of candidate linear peptides initially consisting of the **empty peptide**, which is just an empty string (denoted `""`) having mass 0. At the next step, we will expand *Peptides* to contain all linear peptides of length 1. We continue this process, creating 18 new peptides of length $k + 1$ for each amino acid string *Peptide* of length k in *Peptides* by appending every possible amino acid mass to the end of *Peptide*.

To prevent the number of candidate peptides from increasing exponentially, every time we expand *Peptides*, we trim it by keeping only those linear peptides that remain consistent with the experimental spectrum. We then check if any of these new linear peptides has mass equal to MASS(*Spectrum*). If so, we circularize this peptide and check whether it provides a solution to the Cyclopeptide Sequencing Problem.

More generally, brute force algorithms that enumerate all candidate solutions but discard large subsets of hopeless candidates by using various consistency conditions are known as **branch-and-bound algorithms**. Each such algorithm consists of a **branching step** to increase the number of candidate solutions, followed by a **bounding step** to remove hopeless candidates. In our branch-and-bound algorithm for the Cyclopeptide Sequencing Problem, the branching step will extend each candidate peptide of length k into 18 peptides of length $k + 1$, and the bounding step will remove inconsistent peptides from consideration.

Note that the spectrum of a *linear* peptide does not contain as many masses as the spectrum of a *cyclic* peptide with the same amino acid sequence. For instance, the theoretical spectrum of the cyclic peptide NQEL contains 14 masses (corresponding to `""`, N, Q, E, L, LN, NQ, QW, EL, ELN, LNQ, NQE, QEL, and NQEL). However, the theoretical spectrum of the *linear* peptide NQEL, shown in Figure 4.9, does not contain masses corresponding to LN, LNQ, or ELN, since these subpeptides "wrap around" the end of the linear peptide.

0	113	114	128	129	242	242	257	370	371	484
`""`	L	N	Q	E	NQ	EL	QE	QEL	NQE	NQEL

FIGURE 4.9 The theoretical spectrum for the linear peptide NQEL.

EXERCISE BREAK: How many subpeptides does a linear peptide of length n have?

Given an experimental spectrum *Spectrum* of a cyclic peptide, a linear peptide is **consistent** with *Spectrum* if every mass in its theoretical spectrum is contained in *Spectrum*. If a mass appears more than once in the theoretical spectrum of the linear peptide, then it must appear *at least* that many times in *Spectrum* in order for the linear peptide to be consistent with *Spectrum*. For example, a linear peptide can still be consistent with the theoretical spectrum of NQEL if the peptide's spectrum contains 242 twice. But a peptide cannot be consistent with the theoretical spectrum of NQEL if its spectrum contains 113 twice.

The key to our new algorithm is that every linear subpeptide of a cyclic peptide *Peptide* is consistent with CYCLOSPECTRUM(*Peptide*). Thus, to solve the Cyclopeptide Sequencing Problem for *Spectrum*, we can safely ban all peptides that are *inconsistent* with *Spectrum* from the growing set *Peptides*, which powers the bounding step that we described above. For example, the linear peptide VKF (with spectrum $\{0, 99, 128, 147, 227, 275, 374\}$) will be banned because it is inconsistent with Tyrocidine B1's spectrum in Figure 4.7. But the linear peptide VKY will not be banned because every mass in its theoretical spectrum ($\{0, 99, 128, 163, 227, 291, 390\}$) is present in Figure 4.7.

What about the branching step? Given the current collection of linear peptides *Peptides*, define EXPAND(*Peptides*) as a new collection containing all possible extensions of peptides in *Peptides* by a single amino acid mass. We can now provide the pseudocode for the branch-and-bound algorithm, called **CYCLOPEPTIDESEQUENCING**.

CYCLOPEPTIDESEQUENCING(*Spectrum*)
    Peptides ← a set containing only the empty peptide
    while *Peptides* is nonempty
        Peptides ← EXPAND(*Peptides*)
        for each peptide *Peptide* in *Peptides*
            if MASS(*Peptide*) = PARENTMASS(*Spectrum*)
                if CYCLOSPECTRUM(*Peptide*) = *Spectrum*
                    output *Peptide*
                remove *Peptide* from *Peptides*
            else if *Peptide* is not consistent with *Spectrum*
                remove *Peptide* from *Peptides*

CHARGING STATION (How Fast is CYCLOPEPTIDESEQUENCING?): After the failure of **BFCYCLOPEPTIDESEQUENCING**, you may be hesitant to implement **CYCLOPEPTIDESEQUENCING**. The potential problem with this algorithm is that it may generate incorrect *k*-mers at intermediate stages (i.e., *k*-mers that are not subpeptides of a correct solution). In practice, however, this is not a concern. Check out this Charging Station to see an example.

It is hard to imagine a worst-case scenario in which **CYCLOPEPTIDESEQUENCING** takes a long time to run, but no one has been able to guarantee that this algorithm will not generate many incorrect k-mers at intermediate stages. **BFCYCLOPEPTIDESEQUENCING** is exponential, and although in practice, **CYCLOPEPTIDESEQUENCING** is much faster, this algorithm has not been proven to be polynomial. Thus, from the perspective of an introductory algorithms course focusing on theoretical computer science, the practical **CYCLOPEPTIDESEQUENCING** is just as inefficient as **BFCYCLOPEPTIDESEQUENCING**, since neither algorithm's running time can be bounded by a polynomial. See the Open Problems section to learn more about the algorithmic challenges related to this problem.

Mass Spectrometry Meets Golf

From theoretical to real spectra

Although **CYCLOPEPTIDESEQUENCING** successfully reconstructed Tyrocidine B1, this algorithm only works in the case of an ideal spectrum, i.e., when the experimental spectrum of a peptide coincides exactly with its theoretical spectrum. This inflexibility of **CYCLOPEPTIDESEQUENCING** presents a practical barrier, since mass spectrometers generate "noisy" spectra that are far from ideal — they are characterized by having both **false masses** and **missing masses**. A false mass is present in the experimental spectrum but absent from the theoretical spectrum; a missing mass is present in the theoretical spectrum but absent from the experimental spectrum (Figure 4.10).

Theoretical: 0   113 114 128 **129** 227 **242 242** 257   355 356 370 371 484

Experimental: 0 **99** 113 114 128   227   257 **299** 355 356 370 371 484

FIGURE 4.10 Theoretical and simulated experimental spectra for NQEL. Masses that are missing from the experimental spectrum are shown in blue, and false masses in the experimental spectrum are shown in green.

What is particularly worrisome about the example in Figure 4.10 is that the mass of the amino acid E (**129**) is missing, and the mass of the amino acid V (**99**) is false; as a result, the first step of **CYCLOPEPTIDESEQUENCING** would establish {V, L, N, Q} as the amino acid composition of our candidate peptides, which is incorrect. In fact, *any* false or missing mass will cause **CYCLOPEPTIDESEQUENCING** to throw out the correct peptide, because its theoretical spectrum differs from the experimental spectrum.

STOP and Think: How would you reformulate the Cyclopeptide Sequencing Problem to handle experimental spectra with errors?

Adapting cyclopeptide sequencing for spectra with errors

To generalize the Cyclopeptide Sequencing Problem to handle noisy spectra, we need to relax the requirement that a candidate peptide's theoretical spectrum must match the experimental spectrum *exactly*, and instead incorporate a **scoring function** that will select the peptide whose theoretical spectrum matches the given experimental spectrum *the most closely*. Given a cyclic peptide *Peptide* and a spectrum *Spectrum*, we define SCORE(*Peptide*, *Spectrum*) as the number of masses shared between CYCLOSPECTRUM(*Peptide*) and *Spectrum*. Recalling our example above, if

$$Spectrum = \{0, \mathbf{99}, 113, 114, 128, 227, 257, \mathbf{299}, 355, 356, 370, 371, 484\},$$

then SCORE(NQEL, *Spectrum*) = 11.

The scoring function should take into account the **multiplicities** of shared masses, i.e., how many times they occur in each spectrum. For example, suppose that *Spectrum* is the theoretical spectrum of NQEL (Figure 4.7); for this spectrum, mass 242 has multiplicity 2. If 242 has multiplicity 1 in the theoretical spectrum of *Peptide*, then 242 contributes 1 to SCORE(*Peptide*, *Spectrum*). If 242 has larger multiplicity in the theoretical spectrum of *Peptide*, then 242 contributes 2 to SCORE(*Peptide*, *Spectrum*).

Cyclopeptide Scoring Problem:

Compute the score of a cyclic peptide against a spectrum.

Input: An amino acid string *Peptide* and a collection of integers *Spectrum*.
Output: The score of *Peptide* against *Spectrum*, SCORE(*Peptide*, *Spectrum*).

We now can redefine the Cyclopeptide Sequencing Problem for noisy spectra.

Cyclopeptide Sequencing Problem (for spectra with errors):

Find a cyclic peptide having maximum score against an experimental spectrum.

Input: A collection of integers *Spectrum*.
Output: A cyclic peptide *Peptide* maximizing SCORE(*Peptide*, *Spectrum*) over all peptides *Peptide* with mass equal to PARENTMASS(*Spectrum*).

Our goal is to adapt the **CYCLOPEPTIDESEQUENCING** algorithm to find a peptide with maximum score. Remember that this algorithm had a stringent bounding step in which all candidate linear peptides having inconsistent spectra were thrown out. For example, we saw that the linear peptide VKF is inconsistent with the theoretical spectrum in Figure 4.7. However, we perhaps should not ban VKF in the case of experimental spectra, since they can have missing masses. Thus, we need to revise the bounding step to include more candidate linear peptides, while still ensuring that the number of peptides that we consider does not grow out of control.

> **STOP and Think:** How can we limit the growth of the list of candidate linear peptides in the case of experimental spectra?

To limit the number of candidate linear peptides under consideration, we will replace the list *Peptides* with the list *Leaderboard*, which holds the N highest scoring candidate peptides for further extension. At each step, we will expand all candidate peptides found in *Leaderboard*, then eliminate those peptides whose newly calculated scores are not high enough to keep them on the *Leaderboard*. This idea is similar to the notion of a "cut" in a golf tournament; after the cut, only the top N golfers are allowed to play in the next round, since they are the only players who have a reasonable chance of winning.

To be fair, a cut should include anyone who is tied with the Nth-place competitor. Thus, *Leaderboard* should be trimmed down to the "N highest-scoring linear peptides including ties", which may include more than N peptides. Given a list of peptides *Leaderboard*, a spectrum *Spectrum*, and an integer N, define TRIM(*Leaderboard*, *Spectrum*, N) as the collection of the top N highest-scoring linear peptides in *Leaderboard* (including ties) with respect to *Spectrum*.

> **STOP and Think:** Our peptide scoring function currently assumes that peptides are circular, but peptides should technically be scored as linear peptides until the final step. How would you score a linear peptide against a spectrum?

Note that SCORE(*Peptide*, *Spectrum*) currently only scores *Peptide* against *Spectrum* if *Peptide* is cyclic. However, to generalize this scoring function when *Peptide* is linear, we simply exclude those subpeptides of *Peptide* that wrap around the end of the string, resulting in a function LINEARSCORE(*Peptide*, *Spectrum*). For example, if *Spectrum* is the experimental spectrum of NQEL from Figure 4.10, then you can verify that LINEARSCORE(NQEL, *Spectrum*) = 8. This brings us to the pseudocode for **LEADERBOARDCYCLOPEPTIDESEQUENCING**.

> LEADERBOARDCYCLOPEPTIDESEQUENCING(*Spectrum*, *N*)
>   *Leaderboard* ← set containing only the empty peptide
>   *LeaderPeptide* ← empty peptide
>   **while** *Leaderboard* is non-empty
>   *Leaderboard* ← EXPAND(*Leaderboard*)
>   **for** each *Peptide* in *Leaderboard*
>   **if** MASS(*Peptide*) = PARENTMASS(*Spectrum*)
>   **if** SCORE(*Peptide*, *Spectrum*) > SCORE(*LeaderPeptide*, *Spectrum*)
>   *LeaderPeptide* ← *Peptide*
>   **else if** MASS(*Peptide*) > PARENTMASS(*Spectrum*)
>   remove *Peptide* from *Leaderboard*
>   *Leaderboard* ← TRIM(*Leaderboard*, *Spectrum*, *N*)
>   **output** *LeaderPeptide*

CHARGING STATION (Trimming the Peptide Leaderboard): The tricky aspect of implementing **LEADERBOARDCYCLOPEPTIDESEQUENCING** is making sure that the TRIM function is implemented correctly. Check out this Charging Station for some help with trimming *Leaderboard*.

We point out that because a linear peptide giving rise to the highest-scoring cyclic peptide may be trimmed early on, **LEADERBOARDCYCLOPEPTIDESEQUENCING** is a heuristic, not guaranteed to correctly solve the Cyclopeptide Sequencing Problem. When we develop a heuristic, we must ask: *how accurate is it?* Consider the simulated spectrum $Spectrum_{10}$ of Tyrocidine B1 shown in Figure 4.11 (top), with approximately 10% missing/false masses. Applying **LEADERBOARDCYCLOPEPTIDESEQUENCING** to this spectrum (with $N = 1000$) results in the correct cyclic peptide VKLFPWFNQY, which has a score of 86.

So far, **LEADERBOARDCYCLOPEPTIDESEQUENCING** has worked well, but as the number of errors increases, so does the likelihood that this algorithm will return an incorrect peptide. Let's see how this algorithm performs on a noisier simulated spectrum; in Figure 4.11 (bottom), we show $Spectrum_{25}$ for Tyrocidine B1, which has 25% missing/false masses.

When run on $Spectrum_{25}$, **LEADERBOARDCYCLOPEPTIDESEQUENCING** (with $N = 1000$) identifies VKLFP**AD**FNQY (score: 83) as a highest-scoring cyclic peptide instead of the correct peptide VKLFP**W**FNQY (score: 82). These two peptides are similar, owing to the fact that the combined mass of A (71) and D (115) is equal to the mass of W (186).

0	97	99	**113**	114	**128**	128	147	147	163	186	227
241	242	244	260	261	262	283	291	333	340	357	**385**
388	389	390	390	405	430	430	447	485	487	503	504
518	543	544	552	575	577	584	**631**	632	650	651	671
672	690	691	738	745	747	770	778	779	804	818	819
820	835	837	875	892	**892**	917	932	932	933	934	965
982	989	**1030**	**1031**	1039	1060	1061	1062	1078	1080	1081	1095
1136	1159	1175	1175	1194	1194	1208	1209	1223	1225	1322	

0	97	99	113	114	**115**	128	128	147	147	163	186
227	241	242	**244**	244	**256**	260	261	262	283	291	**309**
330	333	340	**347**	**357**	**385**	388	389	390	390	405	**430**
430	**435**	447	485	487	503	504	518	**543**	544	552	575
577	584	**599**	**608**	631	632	650	651	**653**	**671**	672	690
691	**717**	738	745	**747**	770	**778**	779	804	818	819	**827**
835	837	875	892	892	917	932	932	933	934	965	982
989	**1031**	1039	1060	**1061**	1062	1078	1080	1081	1095	1136	1159
1175	1175	1194	1194	1208	1209	1223	**1225**	1322			

FIGURE 4.11 (Top) A simulated experimental spectrum $Spectrum_{10}$ of Tyrocidine B1. This spectrum has approximately 10% missing (blue) and false (green) masses. Note that the blue masses are not actually in the spectrum, but we show them so that it is clear which masses are missing. (Bottom) A simulated experimental spectrum $Spectrum_{25}$ of Tyrocidine B1, with approximately 25% missing and false masses.

STOP and Think: How could we have eliminated the incorrect peptide VKLFP**AD**FNQY from consideration for $Spectrum_{25}$?

Notice that although the correct and incorrect peptides are similar, their amino acid compositions differ. If we could figure out the amino acid composition of Tyrocidine B1 from its spectrum alone and run **LEADERBOARDCYCLOPEPTIDESEQUENCING** on this smaller alphabet (rather than on the alphabet of all amino acids), then we could eliminate the incorrect peptide VKLFP**AD**FNQY from consideration.

From 20 to More than 100 Amino Acids

Until now, we have assumed that just 20 amino acids form the building blocks of proteins; these building blocks are called **proteinogenic amino acids**. There are actually two additional proteinogenic amino acids, called **selenocysteine** and **pyrrolysine**,

PAGE 218 which are incorporated into proteins by special biosynthetic mechanisms (see DETOUR: Selenocysteine and Pyrrolysine). Yet in addition to the 22 proteinogenic amino acids, NRPs contain **non-proteinogenic amino acids**, which expand the number of possible building blocks for antibiotic peptides from 20 to over 100.

Enlarging the amino acid alphabet spells trouble for our current approach to cyclopeptide sequencing. Indeed, the correct peptide now must "compete" with many more incorrect ones for a place on the leaderboard, increasing the chance that the correct peptide will be cut along the way.

For example, although Tyrocidine B1 contains only proteinogenic amino acids, its close relative, Tyrocidine B (Val-**Orn**-Leu-Phe-Pro-Trp-Phe-Asn-Gln-Tyr), contains a non-proteinogenic amino acid called **ornithine** (**Orn**). Because so many non-proteinogenic amino acids exist, bioinformaticians often assume that any integer between 57 and 200 may represent the mass of an amino acid; the "lightest" amino acid, Gly, has mass 57 Da, and most amino acids have masses smaller than 200 Da.

STOP and Think: Apply LEADERBOARDCYCLOPEPTIDESEQUENCING on the extended amino acid alphabet (containing the 144 integers between 57 and 200) to $Spectrum_{10}$, and identify the highest-scoring peptides.

When we apply LEADERBOARDCYCLOPEPTIDESEQUENCING for the extended alphabet to $Spectrum_{10}$, one of the highest-scoring peptides is VKLFPWFNQ**XZ**, where X has mass 98 and Z has mass 65. Apparently, non-standard amino acids successfully competed with standard amino acids for the limited number of positions on the leaderboard, resulting in VKLFPWFNQ**XZ** winning over the correct peptide VKLFPWFNQ**Y**. Since LEADERBOARDCYCLOPEPTIDESEQUENCING fails to identify the correct peptide even with only 10% false and missing masses, our stated aim from the previous section is now even more important. We must determine the amino acid composition of a peptide from its spectrum so that we may run LEADERBOARDCYCLOPEPTIDESEQUENCING on this smaller alphabet of amino acids.

STOP and Think: How can we determine which amino acids are present in an unknown peptide using only an experimental spectrum?

The Spectral Convolution Saves the Day

One way to determine the amino acid composition of a peptide from its experimental spectrum would be to take the smallest masses present in the spectrum (between 57 and 200 Da). However, even if only a single amino acid mass is missing, then this approach will fail to reconstruct the peptide's amino acid composition.

Let's take a different approach. Say that our experimental spectrum contains the masses of subpeptides NQ**E** and NQ. If we subtract these two masses, then we will obtain the mass **E** for free, even if it was not present in the experimental spectrum! If the underlying peptide is NQEL, then we can also find the mass of **E** by subtracting the masses of Q**E** and Q or NQ**E**L and LNQ.

Following this example, we define the **convolution** of a spectrum by taking all positive differences of masses in the spectrum. Figure 4.12 shows the convolutions of the theoretical (top) and simulated (bottom) spectra of NQEL from Figure 4.10.

As predicted, some of the values in Figure 4.12 appear more frequently than others. For example, **113** (the mass of **L**) has multiplicity 8. Six of the eight occurrences of **113** correspond to subpeptide pairs differing in an **L**: **L** and " "; **L**N and N; E**L** and E; **L**NQ and NQ; Q**E**L and QE; NQ**E**L and NQE. Interestingly, **129** (the mass of **E**) pops up three times in the convolution of the simulated spectrum, even though **129** was missing from the spectrum itself.

We now should feel confident about using the most frequently appearing integers in the convolution as a guess for the amino acid composition of an unknown peptide. In our simulated spectrum for NQEL, the most frequent elements of the convolution in the range from 57 to 200 are (multiplicities in parentheses):

$$\text{\textbf{113} (4), \textbf{114} (4), \textbf{128} (4), \textbf{99} (3), \textbf{129} (3)}.$$

Note that these most frequent elements capture all four amino acids in NQEL.

Spectral Convolution Problem:
Generate the convolution of a spectrum.

> **Input**: A collection of integers *Spectrum*.
> **Output**: The list of elements in the convolution of *Spectrum* in decreasing order of their multiplicities.

	""	L	N	Q	E	LN	NQ	EL	QE	LNQ	ELN	QEL	NQE
	0	113	114	128	129	227	242	242	257	355	356	370	371
0													
113	113												
114	114	1											
128	128	15	14										
129	129	16	15	1									
227	227	114	113	99	98								
242	242	129	128	114	113	15							
242	242	129	128	114	113	15							
257	257	144	143	129	128	30	15	15					
355	355	242	241	227	226	128	113	113	98				
356	356	243	242	228	227	129	114	114	99	1			
370	370	257	256	242	241	143	128	128	113	15	14		
371	371	258	257	243	242	144	129	129	114	16	15	1	
484	484	371	370	356	355	257	242	242	227	129	128	114	113

	""	false	L	N	Q	LN	QE	false	LNQ	ELN	QEL	NQE
	0	99	113	114	128	227	257	299	355	356	370	371
0												
99	99											
113	113	14										
114	114	15	1									
128	128	29	15	14								
227	227	128	114	113	99							
257	257	158	144	143	129	30						
299	299	200	186	185	171	72	42					
355	355	256	242	241	227	128	98	56				
356	356	257	243	242	228	129	99	57	1			
370	370	271	257	256	242	143	113	71	15	14		
371	371	272	258	257	243	144	114	72	16	15	1	
484	484	385	371	370	356	257	227	185	129	128	114	113

FIGURE 4.12 (Top) Spectral convolution for the theoretical spectrum of NQEL. The most frequent elements in the convolution between 57 and 200 are (multiplicities in parentheses): 113 (8), 114 (8), 128 (8), 129 (8). (Bottom) Spectral convolution for the simulated spectrum of NQEL. The most frequent elements in the convolution between 57 and 200 are (multiplicities in parentheses): 113 (4), 114 (4), 128 (4), 99 (3), 129 (3).

Recall that **LEADERBOARDCYCLOPEPTIDESEQUENCING** failed to reconstruct Tyrocidine B1 from $Spectrum_{10}$ when using the extended alphabet of amino acids. The ten most frequent elements of its spectral convolution in the range from 57 to 200 are (multiplicities in parentheses):

147 (35)	128 (31)	97 (28)	113 (28)	114 (26)
186 (23)	57 (21)	163 (21)	99 (18)	145 (18)

Every mass in this list except for 57 and 145 captures an amino acid in Tyrocidine B1!

We now have the outline for a new cyclopeptide sequencing algorithm. Given an experimental spectrum, we first compute the convolution of an experimental spectrum. We then select the M most frequent elements between 57 and 200 in the convolution to form an extended alphabet of amino acid masses. In order to be fair, we should include the top M elements of the convolution "with ties". Finally, we run **LEADERBOARDCYCLOPEPTIDESEQUENCING**, where amino acid masses are restricted to this alphabet. We call this algorithm **CONVOLUTIONCYCLOPEPTIDESEQUENCING**.

STOP and Think: Run **CONVOLUTIONCYCLOPEPTIDESEQUENCING** on the simulated spectra $Spectrum_{10}$ and $Spectrum_{25}$ with $N = 1000$ and $M = 20$. Identify the highest scoring peptides.

CONVOLUTIONCYCLOPEPTIDESEQUENCING (with $N = 1000$ and $M = 20$) now correctly reconstructs Tyrocidine B1 from $Spectrum_{10}$. The true test of this algorithm is whether it will work on a noisier spectrum. Recall that our previous algorithm failed on $Spectrum_{25}$; in contrast, **CONVOLUTIONCYCLOPEPTIDESEQUENCING** (with $N = 1000$ and $M = 20$) now correctly identifies Tyrocidine B1 from this spectrum!

Epilogue: From Simulated to Real Spectra

In this chapter, we have sheltered you from the gruesome realities of mass spectrometry by providing simulated spectra that are relatively easy to sequence (even those with false and missing masses). We committed a sin of omission by loosely describing the mass spectrometer as a "scale" and assuming that this complex machine simply weighs tiny peptide fragments one at a time. In truth, the mass spectrometer first converts subpeptides into ions (i.e., charged particles). Ionization of particles helps the mass spectrometer sort the ions by using an electromagnetic field; ions are separated not by their mass, but rather according to their **mass/charge ratio**. If fragment ion NQY (integer mass: $114 + 128 + 163 = 405$) has charge $+1$, then it contains one additional proton, resulting in a total integer mass of 406 and a mass/charge ratio of $406/1 = 406$. To be more precise, the *monoisotopic* mass of NQY is approximately $114.043 + 128.058 + 163.063 = 405.164$, and the mass of a proton is 1.007 Da, which makes the mass charge/ratio more closely equal to $(405.164 + 1.007)/1 = 406.171$ (see **DETOUR: Molecular Mass**).

PAGE 217

The mass spectrometer outputs a collection of **peaks**, which are shown in Figure 4.13 for a real Tyrocidine B1 spectrum. Each peak's x-coordinate represents an ion's mass/charge ratio, and its height represents the **intensity** (i.e., relative abundance) of ions having that mass/charge ratio. For example, in the experimental spectrum of Tyrocidine B1 shown in Figure 4.13, you will find a small (almost invisible) peak with a mass/charge ratio of 406.30, which corresponds to the fragment ion NQY having mass/charge ratio 406.171, with an error of approximately 0.13 Da.

As you can imagine, we must navigate a few practical barriers in order to analyze real spectra. First, the charge of each peak is unknown, often forcing researchers to try all possible charges from 1 to some parameter *maxCharge*, where the particular choice of *maxCharge* depends on the fragmentation technology used. This procedure generates *maxCharge* masses for each peak, so that the larger the value of *maxCharge*, the more false masses in the spectrum.

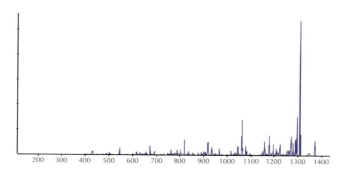

FIGURE 4.13 A real spectrum for Tyrocidine B1. A peak's x-coordinate represents its mass/charge ratio, and its height represents the intensity of ions having that mass/charge ratio.

Second, the spectrum in Figure 4.13 has nearly 1,000 peaks, most of which are **false peaks**, meaning that their mass/charge ratio does not correspond to any subpeptide's mass/charge ratio (for any charge value). Fortunately, false peaks typically have low intensities, necessitating a pre-processing step that removes low-intensity peaks before applying an algorithm. Figure 4.14 shows the list of the 95 mass/charge ratios for peaks that survived this preprocessing step for the Tyrocidine B1 spectrum in Figure 4.13. Their intensities may nevertheless vary by 2-3 orders of magnitude; for example, the intensity of the peak having mass/charge ratio 372.2 is 300 times smaller than the intensity of the peak with mass/charge ratio 1306.5.

372.2	397.2	402.0	**406.3**	415.1	**431.2**	**448.3**	449.3	452.2
471.3	**486.3**	**488.2**	500.5	**505.3**	516.1	536.1	**544.2**	**545.3**
562.5	571.3	599.2	614.4	615.4	616.4	618.2	**632.0**	655.5
656.3	**672.5**	**673.3**	677.3	**691.4**	**692.4**	712.1	722.3	**746.5**
760.4	761.6	762.5	**771.6**	788.4	802.3	803.3	818.5	**819.4**
831.4	**836.3**	853.3	875.5	**876.5**	901.5	915.9	916.5	917.8
918.4	**933.4**	**934.7**	**935.5**	949.4	**966.2**	995.4	1015.6	1027.5
1029.5	1031.5	1044.5	1046.5	**1061.5**	**1063.4**	**1079.2**	1083.7	
1088.4	1093.5	**1096.5**	1098.4	1158.5	1159.5	**1176.6**	1177.7	
1178.6	1192.7	**1195.4**	1207.5	**1210.4**	**1224.6**	1252.5	1270.5	
1271.5	1278.6	1279.6	1295.6	1305.6	1306.5	1307.5	1309.6	

FIGURE 4.14 The 95 mass/charge ratios having the highest intensity in Figure 4.13. The values shown in bold correspond to masses of subpeptides of Tyrocidine B1, if we allow a mass discrepancy of up to 0.3 Da (see Figure 4.15).

Mass	Subpeptide	Mass	Subpeptide	Mass	Subpeptide
406.2	NQY	431.2	FPW	448.2	WFN
486.2	KLFP	488.2	VKLF	505.2	NQYV
544.2	LFPW	545.2	PWFN	632.3	QYVKL
672.3	KLFPW	673.3	PWFNQ	691.3	LFPWF
692.3	FPWFN	746.3	NQYVKL	771.3	VKLFPW
819.4	KLFPWF	836.4	PWFNQY	876.4	QYVKLFP
918.4	VKLFPWF	933.4	LFPWFNQ	934.4	YVKLFPW
935.4	PWFNQYV	966.4	WFNQYVK	1061.5	KLFPWFNQ
1063.5	PWFNQYVK	1079.5	WFNQYVKL	1096.5	LFPWFNQY
1176.5	NQYVKLFPW	1195.6	LFPWFNQYV	1210.6	FPWFNQYVK
1224.6	KLFPWFNQY				

FIGURE 4.15 Values from Figure 4.14 corresponding to masses of subpeptides of Tyrocidine B1, with *maxCharge* = 1 and an allowable discrepancy of up to 0.3 Da. These 31 masses represent less than a third of the 95 subpeptides in the theoretical spectrum of Tyrocidine B1.

Only 31 of these 95 mass/charge ratios (shown in bold in Figure 4.14) can be matched to subpeptides of Tyrocidine B1, as illustrated in Figure 4.15.

You can now see that sequencing Tyrocidine B1 from a real spectrum, for which two-thirds of all masses are false, presents a much more difficult problem than sequencing this peptide from the simulated $Spectrum_{25}$. In the following challenge problem, you will need to further develop the methods we studied in this chapter to analyze a real spectrum.

CHALLENGE PROBLEM: Tyrocidine B1 is just one of many known NRPs produced by *Bacillus brevis*. A single bacterial species may produce dozens of different antibiotics, and even after 70 years of research, there are likely undiscovered antibiotics produced by *Bacillus brevis*. Try to sequence the tyrocidine corresponding to the real experimental spectrum below. Since the fragmentation technology used for generating this spectrum tends to produce ions with charge +1, you can safely assume that all charges are +1.

371.5	375.4	390.4	392.2	409.0	420.2	427.2	443.3	446.4	461.3
471.4	477.4	491.3	505.3	506.4	519.2	536.1	546.5	553.3	562.3
588.2	600.3	616.2	617.4	618.3	633.4	634.4	636.2	651.5	652.4
702.5	703.4	712.5	718.3	721.0	730.3	749.4	762.6	763.4	764.4
779.6	780.4	781.4	782.4	797.3	862.4	876.4	877.4	878.6	879.4
893.4	894.4	895.4	896.5	927.4	944.4	975.5	976.5	977.4	979.4
1005.5	1007.5	1022.5	1023.7	1024.5	1039.5	1040.3	1042.5	1043.4	1057.5
1119.6	1120.6	1137.6	1138.6	1139.5	1156.5	1157.6	1168.6	1171.6	1185.4
1220.6	1222.5	1223.6	1239.6	1240.6	1250.5	1256.5	1266.5	1267.5	1268.6

Hint: since the peptide from which this spectrum was generated is in the tyrocidine family, this peptide should be similar to Tyrocidine B1.

Open Problems

The Beltway and Turnpike Problems

In the case of the alphabet of arbitrary integers, the Cyclopeptide Sequencing Problem corresponds to a computer science problem known as the **Beltway Problem**. The Beltway Problem asks you to find a set of points on a circle such that the distances between all pairs of points (where distance is measured around the circle) match a given collection of integers.

The Beltway Problem's analogue in the case when the points lie along a line segment instead of on a circle is called the **Turnpike Problem**. The terms "beltway" and "turnpike" arise from an analogy with exits on circular and linear roads, respectively. In the case of n points on a circle and line, the inputs for the Beltway and Turnpike Problems consist of $n(n-1)+2$ and $\frac{n(n-1)}{2}+2$ distances, respectively (these formulas include the distance 0 as well as the length of the entire segment).

Various attempts to design polynomial algorithms for the Beltway and Turnpike Problems (or to prove that they are intractable) have failed. However, there is a **pseudo-polynomial algorithm** for the Turnpike Problem (see DETOUR: Pseudo-polynomial Algorithm for the Turnpike Problem). In contrast to a truly polynomial algorithm, which can be bounded by a polynomial in the length of the input, a pseudo-polynomial algorithm for the Turnpike Problem is polynomial in the total length of the line segment. For example, if n points are separated by huge distances, say on the order of 2^{100}, then a polynomial algorithm would still be fast, whereas a pseudo-polynomial algorithm would be prohibitively slow. Note that although the distances themselves will be huge, each distance can be stored using only about 100 bits, implying that the length of the input is small even for such large distances.

PAGE 219

Pseudo-polynomial algorithms are useful in practice because practical instances of the problems typically do not include huge distances. Interestingly, although a pseudo-polynomial algorithm exists for the Turnpike Problem, such an algorithm for the seemingly similar Beltway Problem remains undiscovered. Can you develop such an algorithm?

Sequencing cyclic peptides in primates

Bacteria and fungi do not have a monopoly on producing cyclic peptides; animals and plants make them too (albeit through a completely different mechanism). The first cyclic peptide found in animals (called θ-**defensin**) was discovered in 1999 in macaques. θ-defensin prevents viruses from entering cells and has strong anti-HIV activity. Yet the question of how primates make θ-defensin remains a mystery.

Needless to say, there is no 54-mer in the macaque genome encoding the 18 amino acid-long θ-defensin. Instead, this cyclic peptide is formed by concatenating two 9 amino acid-long peptides excised from two different proteins called RTD1a and RTD1b, as shown in Figure 4.16. It remains unclear which enzymes do this elaborate cutting and pasting.

Interestingly, macaques and baboons produce θ-defensin, whereas humans and chimpanzees do not. This discrepancy makes us wonder whether a mutation occurred

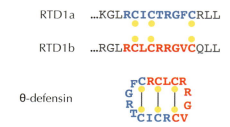

FIGURE 4.16 The 18 amino acid-long θ-defensin peptide is formed by cutting two 9 amino acid-long peptides **RCICTRGFC** and **RCLCRRGVC** from the RTD1a and RTD1b proteins, concatenating them, and then circularizing the resulting peptide (along with introducing three **disulfide bridges** that form bonds across the peptide).

in the human-chimpanzee ancestor that resulted in the loss of this very useful peptide. Interestingly, genes very similar to RTD1a and RTD1b do exist in humans, but a codon in one of these genes mutated into a stop codon, thus shortening the encoded protein. Since this stop codon is located before the 9 amino acid-long peptide contributing to θ-defensin, humans do not produce this peptide and thus cannot produce θ-defensin.

In a remarkable experiment, Alexander Cole demonstrated that humans could get θ-defensin back! Certain drugs can force the ribosome to ignore stop codons and continue translating RNA, even after encountering a stop codon. The researchers demonstrated that after treatment with such a drug, human cells began producing the human version of θ-defensin. The surprising conclusion of this experiment is that although humans and chimpanzees lost θ-defensin millions of years ago, we still possess the mysterious enzymes required to cut and paste its constituent peptides.

Some biologists believe that since the enzymes making θ-defensin still work in humans, they must be needed for something else. If these enzymes did not provide some selective advantage, then over time, mutations would cause their genes to become **pseudogenes**, or non-functional remnants of previously working genes. The most natural explanation for why these enzymes are still functional is that humans produce still undiscovered cyclic peptides, and that the enzymes needed for θ-defensin are also used to "cut-and-paste" other (still undiscovered) cyclic peptides. The hypothesis that we may possess undiscovered cyclic peptides is not as improbable as you might think because biologists still lack robust algorithms for cyclopeptide discovery from the billions of spectra generated in hundreds of labs analyzing the human proteome.

By default, researchers assume that all spectra ever acquired in human proteome studies originated from linear peptides. Could they be wrong? Can you devise a fast cyclopeptide sequencing algorithm that can analyze all these spectra and hopefully discover human cyclopeptides?

Charging Stations

Generating the theoretical spectrum of a peptide

Given an amino acid string *Peptide*, we will begin by assuming that it represents a *linear* peptide. Our approach to generating its theoretical spectrum is based on the assumption that the mass of any subpeptide is equal to the difference between the masses of two prefixes of *Peptide*. We can compute an array PREFIXMASS storing the masses of each prefix of *Peptide* in increasing order, e.g., for *Peptide* = NQEL, PREFIXMASS = $(0, 114, 242, 371, 484)$. Then, the mass of the subpeptide of *Peptide* beginning at position $i + 1$ and ending at position j can be computed as $\text{PREFIXMASS}(j) - \text{PREFIXMASS}(i)$. For example, when *Peptide* = NQEL,

$$\text{MASS}(\text{QE}) = \text{PREFIXMASS}(3) - \text{PREFIXMASS}(1) = 371 - 114 = 257\,.$$

The following pseudocode implements this idea. It also represents the alphabet of 20 amino acids and their integer masses as a pair of 20-element arrays AMINOACID and AMINOACIDMASS, corresponding to the top and bottom rows of Figure 4.6, respectively.

LINEARSPECTRUM(*Peptide*, AMINOACID, AMINOACIDMASS)
   PREFIXMASS$(0) \leftarrow 0$
   for $i \leftarrow 1$ to $|Peptide|$
      for $j \leftarrow 1$ to 20
         if AMINOACID$(j) = i$-th amino acid in *Peptide*
            PREFIXMASS$(i) \leftarrow$ PREFIXMASS$(i - 1) +$ AMINOACIDMASS(j)
   LinearSpectrum $\leftarrow$ a list consisting of the single integer 0
   for $i \leftarrow 0$ to $|Peptide| - 1$
      for $j \leftarrow i + 1$ to $|Peptide|$
         add PREFIXMASS$(j) -$ PREFIXMASS(i) to *LinearSpectrum*
   return the sorted list *LinearSpectrum*

If the amino acid string *Peptide* represents a cyclic peptide instead, then the masses in its theoretical spectrum can be divided into those found by **LINEARSPECTRUM** and those corresponding to subpeptides wrapping around the end of the linearized version of *Peptide*. Furthermore, each such subpeptide has mass equal to the difference between MASS(*Peptide*) and a subpeptide mass identified by **LINEARSPECTRUM**. For example, when *Peptide* = **NQEL**,

$$\text{MASS}(\textbf{LN}) = \text{MASS}(\textbf{NQEL}) - \text{MASS}(\textbf{QE}) = 484 - 257 = 227\,.$$

Thus, we can generate a cyclic spectrum by making only a small modification to the pseudocode of **LINEARSPECTRUM**.

CYCLICSPECTRUM(*Peptide*, AMINOACID, AMINOACIDMASS)
    PREFIXMASS(0) ← 0
    for i ← 1 to *Peptide*
        for j ← 1 to 20
            if AMINOACID(j) = i-th amino acid in *Peptide*
                PREFIXMASS(i) ← PREFIXMASS($i - 1$) + AMINOACIDMASS(j)
    peptideMass ← PREFIXMASS(|*Peptide*|)
    CyclicSpectrum ← a list consisting of the single integer 0
    for i ← 0 to |*Peptide*| − 1
        for j ← $i + 1$ to |*Peptide*|
            add PREFIXMASS(j) − PREFIXMASS(i) to *CyclicSpectrum*
            if $i > 0$ and $j <$ |*Peptide*|
                add *peptideMass* - (PREFIXMASS(j) − PREFIXMASS(i)) to *CyclicSpectrum*
    return sorted list *CyclicSpectrum*

How fast is **CYCLOPEPTIDESEQUENCING**?

Let's run **CYCLOPEPTIDESEQUENCING** on the following *Spectrum*:

0	97	97	99	101	103	196	198	198	200	202
295	297	299	299	301	394	396	398	400	400	497

CYCLOPEPTIDESEQUENCING first expands the set *Peptides* into the set of all 1-mers consistent with *Spectrum*:

97	99	101	103
P	V	T	C

The algorithm next appends each of the 18 amino acid masses to each of the 1-mers above. The resulting set *Peptides* containing $4 \cdot 18 = 72$ peptides of length 2 is then trimmed to keep only the 10 peptides that are consistent with *Spectrum*:

97-99	97-101	97-103	99-97	99-101
PV	PT	PC	VP	VT
99-103	101-97	101-99	103-97	103-99
VC	TP	TV	CP	CV

After expansion and trimming in the next iteration, the set *Peptides* contains 15 consistent 3-mers:

97-99-103	**97-99-101**	97-101-97	**97-101-99**	97-103-99
PVC	**PVT**	PTP	**PTV**	PCV
99-97-103	99-97-101	**99-101-97**	99-103-97	101-97-99
VPC	VPT	**VTP**	VCP	TPV
101-97-103	**101-99-97**	103-97-101	**103-97-99**	103-99-97
TPC	**TVP**	CPT	**CPV**	CVP

With one more iteration, the set *Peptides* contains ten consistent 4-mers. Observe that the six 3-mers highlighted in red above failed to expand into any 4-mers below, and so we now know that CYCLOPEPTIDESEQUENCING may generate some incorrect k-mers at intermediate iterations.

97-99-103-97	97-101-97-99	97-101-97-103	97-103-99-97
PVCP	PTPV	PTPC	PCVP
99-97-101-97	99-103-97-101	101-97-99-103	101-97-103-99
VPTP	VCPT	TPVC	TPCV
	103-97-101-97	103-99-97-101	
	CPTP	CVPT	

In the final iteration, we generate ten consistent 5-mers:

97-99-103-97-101	97-101-97-99-103	97-101-97-103-99
PVCPT	PTPVC	PTPCV
97-103-99-97-101	99-97-101-97-103	99-103-97-101-97
PCVPT	VPTPC	VCPTP
101-97-99-103-97	101-97-103-99-97	103-97-101-97-99
TPVCP	TPCVP	CPTPV
	103-99-97-101-97	
	CVPTP	

All these linear peptides correspond to the same cyclic peptide PVCPT, thus solving the Cyclopeptide Sequencing Problem. You can verify that **CYCLOPEPTIDESEQUENCING** also quickly reconstructs Tyrocidine B1 from the spectrum in Figure 4.7.

Trimming the peptide leaderboard

Note: This Charging Station uses some notation from **CHARGING STATION: Generating the Theoretical Spectrum of a Peptide**.

To implement the TRIM function in **LEADERBOARDCYCLOPEPTIDESEQUENCING**, we first will generate the theoretical spectra of all linear peptides from *Leaderboard*. Then, we will compute the scores of each theoretical spectrum against an experimental spectrum *Spectrum*. This requires implementing LINEARSCORE(*Peptide, Spectrum*).

Figure 4.17 shows a leaderboard of ten linear peptides represented as a list *Leaderboard* along with a ten-element array LINEARSCORES containing their scores.

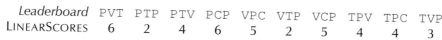

Leaderboard	PVT	PTP	PTV	PCP	VPC	VTP	VCP	TPV	TPC	TVP
LINEARSCORES	6	2	4	6	5	2	5	4	4	3

FIGURE 4.17 A collection of peptides *Leaderboard* (top) along with an array LINEARSCORES (bottom) holding the score of each peptide.

The **TRIM** algorithm, shown below, sorts all peptides in *Leaderboard* according to their scores, resulting in a sorted *Leaderboard* (Figure 4.18). **TRIM** then retains the top *N* scoring peptides including ties (e.g., for *N* = 5, the seven top-scoring peptides shown in blue will be retained), and removes all other peptides from *Leaderboard*.

TRIM(*Leaderboard*, *Spectrum*, *N*, AMINOACID, AMINOACIDMASS)
    for $j \leftarrow 1$ to $|Leaderboard|$
        Peptide $\leftarrow$ *j*-th peptide in *Leaderboard*
        LINEARSCORES$(j) \leftarrow$ LINEARSCORE(*Peptide*, *Spectrum*)
    sort *Leaderboard* according to the decreasing order of scores in LINEARSCORES
    sort LINEARSCORES in decreasing order
    for $j \leftarrow N + 1$ to $|Leaderboard|$
        if LINEARSCORES$(j) <$ LINEARSCORES(N)
            remove all peptides starting from the *j*-th peptide from *Leaderboard*
        return *Leaderboard*
    return *Leaderboard*

Leaderboard	PVT	PCP	VPC	VCP	PTV	TPV	TPC	TVP	PTP	VTP
LINEARSCORES	6	6	5	5	4	4	4	3	2	2

FIGURE 4.18 Arrays *Leaderboard* and LINEARSCORES from Figure 4.17 sorted according to score. The seven highest-scoring peptides, which will be retained after applying **TRIM** with $N = 5$, are shown in blue; remaining peptides are shown in red and will be removed from the leaderboard.

Detours

Gause and Lysenkoism

The term **Lysenkoism** refers to the politicization of genetics in the Soviet Union that began in the late 1920s and lasted for three decades until the death of Stalin. Lysenkoism was built on theories of inheritance by acquired characteristics, which ran counter to Mendelian laws.

In 1928, Trofim Lysenko, the son of Ukrainian peasants, claimed to have found a way to vastly increase the crop yield of wheat. During Stalin's rule, Soviet propaganda focused on inspirational stories of working class citizens, and it portrayed Lysenko as a genius, even though he had manufactured his experimental data. Empowered by his sudden hero status, Lysenko denounced genetics and started promoting his own "scientific" views. He called geneticists "fly lovers and people haters" and claimed that they were trying to undermine the onward march of Soviet agriculture.

Gause found himself among the few Soviet biologists who were not afraid of publicly denouncing Lysenko. By 1935, Lysenko announced that by opposing his theories, geneticists were directly opposing the teachings of Marxism. Stalin, who was in the audience, was the first to applaud, calling out, "Bravo, Comrade Lysenko!" This event gave Lysenko free reign to slander any geneticists who spoke out against him; many of Lysenkoism's opponents were imprisoned or even executed.

After World War II, Lysenko did not forget Gause's criticism: Lysenko's supporters demanded that Gause be expelled from the Russian Academy of Sciences. Lysenkoists made various attempts to invite Gause to denounce genetics and accept their pseudo-science. Gause was probably the only Soviet biologist at that time who could simply ignore such "invitations", the only other contemporary opponents of Lysenkoism being top Soviet nuclear physicists. However, Stalin left Gause and the physicists alone; in Stalin's mind, the development of antibiotics and the atomic bomb were too important. In 1949, when the director of the Russian secret police (Lavrentiy Beria) told Stalin of the dissident scientists, Stalin responded, "Make sure that our scientists have everything needed to do their job", adding, "there will always be time to execute them [later]".

Discovery of codons

In 1961, Sydney Brenner and Francis Crick established the rule of "one codon, one amino acid" during protein translation. They observed that deleting a single nucleotide or two consecutive nucleotides in a gene dramatically altered the protein product. Para-doxically, deleting *three* consecutive nucleotides resulted in only minor changes in the protein. For example, the phrase

THE · SLY · FOX · AND · THE · SHY · DOG

turns into gibberish after deleting one letter:

THE · SYF · OXA · NDT · HES · HYD · OG

or after deleting two letters:

THE · SFO · XAN · DTH · ESH · YDO · G

but it makes sense after deleting three letters:

THE · FOX · AND · THE · SHY · DOG

In 1964, Charles Yanofsky demonstrated that a gene and the protein that it produces are **collinear**, meaning that the first codon codes for the first amino acid in the protein, the second codon codes for the second amino acid, etc. For the next thirteen years, biologists believed that a protein was encoded by a long string of *contiguous* nucleotide triplets. However, the discovery of **split genes** in 1977 proved otherwise and necessitated the computational problem of predicting the locations of genes using only the genomic sequence (see DETOUR: Split Genes).

PAGE 220

Quorum sensing

The traditional view that bacteria act as loners and have few interactions with the rest of their colony has been challenged by the discovery of a communication method called **quorum sensing**. This finding has shown that bacteria are capable of coordinated activity when migrating to a better nutrient supply or adopting a **biofilm** formation for defense within hostile environments. The "language" used in quorum sensing is often based on the exchange of peptides (as well as other molecules) called **bacterial pheromones**. The nature of communications between bacteria can be amicable or adversarial.

When a single bacterium releases pheromones into its environment, their concentration is often too low to be detected; however, once the population density increases, pheromone concentrations reach a threshold level that allows the bacteria to activate certain genes in response.

For example, *Burkholderia cepacia* is a pathogen affecting individuals with **cystic fibrosis**. Most patients colonized with *B. cepacia* are coinfected with *Pseudomonas aeruginosa*. The correlation of the two strains in these patients led biologists to hypothesize that interspecies communication with *P. aeruginosa* may help *B. cepacia* enhance its own pathogenicity. Indeed, the addition of *P. aeruginosa* to clones of *B. cepacia* results in a significant increase in the synthesis of proteases (i.e., enzymes needed to break down proteins), suggesting the presence of quorum sensing — *B. cepacia* may profit from pheromones made by a different species in order to improve its own chances of survival.

Molecular mass

The **dalton** (abbreviated **Da**) is the unit used for measuring atomic masses on a molecular scale. One dalton is equivalent to one twelfth of the mass of carbon-12 and has a value of approximately $1.66 \cdot 10^{-27}$ kg. The **monoisotopic mass** of a molecule is equal to the sum of the masses of the atoms in that molecule, using the mass of the most abundant **isotope** for each element. Figure 4.19 provides the elemental composition and monoisotopic masses of all 20 standard amino acids.

Amino acid	3-letter code	Chemical formula	Mass (Da)
Alanine	Ala	C_3H_5NO	71.03711
Cysteine	Cys	C_3H_5NOS	103.00919
Aspartic acid	Asp	$C_4H_5NO_3$	115.02694
Glutamic acid	Glu	$C_5H_7NO_3$	129.04259
Phenylalanine	Phe	C_9H_9NO	147.06841
Glycine	Gly	C_2H_3NO	57.02146
Histidine	His	$C_6H_7N_3O$	137.05891
Isoleucine	Ile	$C_6H_{11}NO$	113.08406
Lysine	Lys	$C_6H_{12}N_2O$	128.09496
Leucine	Leu	$C_6H_{11}NO$	113.08406
Methionine	Met	C_5H_9NOS	131.04049
Asparagine	Asn	$C_4H_6N_2O_2$	114.04293
Proline	Pro	C_5H_7NO	97.05276
Glutamine	Gln	$C_5H_8N_2O_2$	128.05858
Arginine	Arg	$C_6H_{12}N_4O$	156.10111
Serine	Ser	$C_3H_5NO_2$	87.03203
Threonine	Thr	$C_4H_7NO_2$	101.04768
Valine	Val	C_5H_9NO	99.06841
Tryptophan	Trp	$C_{11}H_{10}N_2O$	186.07931
Tyrosine	Tyr	$C_9H_9NO_2$	163.06333

FIGURE 4.19 Elemental composition and monoisotopic masses of amino acids.

Selenocysteine and pyrrolysine

Selenocysteine is a proteinogenic amino acid that exists in all kingdoms of life as a building block of a special class of proteins called selenoproteins. Unlike other amino acids, selenocysteine is not directly encoded in the genetic code. Instead, it is encoded in a special way by a UGA codon, which is normally a stop codon, through a mechanism known as **translational recoding**.

   Pyrrolysine is a proteinogenic amino acid that exists in some archaea and methane-producing bacteria. In organisms incorporating pyrrolysine, this amino acid is encoded by UAG, which also normally acts as a stop codon.

Pseudo-polynomial algorithm for the Turnpike Problem

If $A = (a_1 = 0, a_2, \ldots, a_n)$ is a set of n points on a line segment in increasing order $(a_1 < a_2 < \cdots < a_n)$, then ΔA denotes the collection of all pairwise differences between points in A. For example, if $A = (0, 2, 4, 7)$, then

$$\Delta A = (-7, -5, -4, -3, -2, -2, 0, 0, 0, 0, 2, 2, 3, 4, 5, 7).$$

The turnpike problem asks us to reconstruct A from ΔA.

Turnpike Problem:

Given all pairwise distances between points on a line segment, reconstruct the positions of those points.

> **Input**: A collection of integers L.
> **Output**: A set of integers A such that $\Delta A = L$.

We will now outline an approach to solving the Turnpike Problem that is polynomial in the length of the line segment. Given a collection of integers $A = (a_1, \ldots, a_n)$, the **generating function** of A is the polynomial

$$A(x) = \sum_{i=1}^{n} x^{a_i}.$$

For example, if $A = (0, 2, 4, 7)$, then

$$A(x) = x^0 + x^2 + x^4 + x^7$$
$$\Delta A(x) = x^{-7} + x^{-5} + x^{-4} + x^{-3} + 2x^{-2} + 4x^0 + 2x^2 + x^3 + x^4 + x^5 + x^7$$

You can verify that the above generating function for $\Delta A(x)$ is equal to $A(x) \cdot A(x^{-1})$. Thus, the Turnpike Problem reduces to a problem about polynomial factorization. Just as an integer can be broken down into its prime factors, a polynomial with integer coefficients can be factored into "prime" polynomials having integer coefficients. If we can factor $\Delta A(x)$ and determine which prime factors contribute to $A(x)$ and which prime factors contribute to $A(x^{-1})$, then we will know $A(x)$ and therefore A. In 1982, Rosenblatt and Seymour described such a method to represent $\Delta A(x)$ as $A(x) \cdot A(x^{-1})$. Since a polynomial can be factored in time polynomial in its maximum exponent, $\Delta A(x)$ can be factored in time polynomial in the total length of the line segment, which yields the desired pseudo-polynomial algorithm for the Turnpike Problem.

STOP and Think: Can the generating function approach be modified to address the case when there are errors in the pairwise differences?

Split genes

In 1977, Phillip Sharp and Richard Roberts independently discovered **split genes**, which are genes formed by discontiguous intervals of DNA.

Sharp hybridized RNA encoding an adenovirus protein called hexon against a single-strand of adenovirus DNA. If the hexon gene were contiguous, then he expected to see a one-to-one hybridization of RNA bases with DNA bases.

Yet to Sharp's surprise, when he viewed the RNA-DNA hybridization under an electron microscope, he saw three loop structures, rather than the continuous duplex segment suggested by the contiguous gene model (Figure 4.20). This observation implied that the hexon mRNA must be built from four non-contiguous fragments of the adenovirus genome. These four segments, called **exons**, are separated by three fragments (the loops in Figure 4.20) called **introns**, to form a split gene. Split genes are analogous to a magazine article printed on pages 12, 17, 40, and 95, with many pages of advertising appearing in-between.

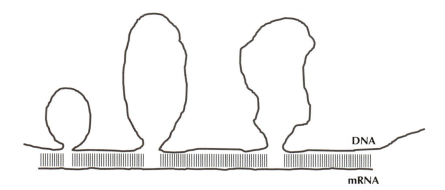

FIGURE 4.20 A rendering of Sharp's electron microscopy experiment that led to the discovery of split genes. When hexon RNA is hybridized against the DNA that generated it, three distinct loops are formed. Because the loops are present in the DNA and are not present in RNA, these loops (called introns) must be removed during the process of RNA formation.

The discovery of split genes caused an interesting quandary: *What happens to the introns?* In other words, the RNA that is transcribed from a split gene (called **precursor** mRNA or **pre-mRNA**) should be longer than the RNA that is used as a template for protein synthesis (called **messenger RNA** or **mRNA**). Some biological process must remove the introns in pre-mRNA and concatenate the exons into a single mRNA string. This process of converting pre-mRNA into mRNA is known as **splicing**, and it is carried out by a molecular machine called the **spliceosome**.

The discovery of split genes led to many new avenues of research. Biologists still debate what purpose introns serve; some introns are viewed as "junk DNA", while others contain important regulatory elements. Furthermore, the partition of a gene into exons often varies from species to species. For example, a gene in the chicken genome may have a different number of exons than the related gene in the human genome.

Bibliography Notes

The pseudo-polynomial algorithm for the Turnpike Problem was proposed by Rosenblatt and Seymour, 1982. The first cyclopeptide sequencing algorithm was proposed by Ng et al., 2009. Tang et al., 1999 discovered θ-defensin. Venkataraman et al., 2009 showed that humans cells can be tricked into producing θ-defensin.

Cracking the Non-Ribosomal Code

The RNA Tie Club

Following Watson & Crick's publication of DNA's double helix structure in 1953, physicist George Gamow founded the "RNA Tie Club" for renowned scientists. A necktie embroidered with a double helix signified membership in this club, which was restricted to twenty regular members (one for each amino acid) as well as four honorary members (one for each nucleotide). Gamow wanted the RNA Tie Club to serve more than a social function; by convening top scientific minds, he hoped to decode the message hidden within DNA by determining how RNA is converted into amino acids. Indeed, Sydney Brenner and Francis Crick struck first one year later by discovering that amino acids are translated from codons (i.e., triplets of nucleotides).

The RNA Tie Club would eventually boast eight Nobel laureates, but scientists from outside of the club would decipher the genetic code. In 1961, Marshall Nirenberg synthesized RNA strands consisting only of uracil (UUUUUUUUUUUU...), added ribosomes and amino acids, and produced a peptide consisting only of phenylalanine (PhePhePhePhe...). Nirenberg thus concluded that the RNA codon UUU codes for the amino acid phenylalanine. Following Nirenberg's success, Har Gobind Khorana synthesized the RNA strand UCUCUCUCUCUC... and demonstrated that it translates into SerLeuSerLeu... Following these insights, the rest of the *ribosomal* genetic code was rapidly elucidated.

Nearly four decades later, Mohamed Marahiel set out to solve the much more challenging puzzle of cracking the **non-ribosomal code**. You will recall from Chapter 4 that bacteria and fungi produce antibiotics and other non-ribosomal peptides (NRPs) without any reliance on the ribosome and the genetic code. Instead, these organisms manufacture NRPs by employing a giant protein called NRP synthetase:

$$DNA \longrightarrow RNA \longrightarrow NRP\ synthetase \longrightarrow NRP$$

The NRP synthetase that encodes the 10 amino acid-long antibiotic Tyrocidine B1 (which we worked with in Chapter 4) includes 10 segments called **adenylation domains (A-domains)**; each A-domain is about 500 amino acids long and is responsible for adding a single amino acid to Tyrocidine B1.

A generation earlier, the RNA Tie Club had asked, "How does RNA encode an amino acid?" Now Marahiel set out to answer the far more challenging question, "How does each A-domain encode an amino acid?"

From protein comparison to the non-ribosomal code

Fortunately, Marahiel already knew the amino acid sequences of some A-domains, along with the amino acids that they add to the growing peptide. Below are three of these A-domains (taken from three different bacteria), which code for aspartic acid (Asp), ornithine (Orn), and valine (Val), respectively. In the interest of space, we will show you only short fragments taken from the three A-domains.

```
YAFDLGYTCMFPVLLGGGELHIVQKETYTAPDEIAHYIKEHGITYIKLTPSLFHTIVNTASFAFDANFESLRLIVLGGEKIIPIDVIAFRKMYGHTEFINHYGPTEATIGA
AFDVSAGDFARALLTGGQLIVCPNEVKMDPASLYAIIKKYDITIFEATPALVIPLMEYIYEQKLDISQLQILIVGSDSCSMEDFKTLVSRFGSTIRIVNSYGVTEACIDS
IAFDASSWEIYAPLLNGGTVVCIDYYTTIDIKALEAVFKQHHIRGAMLPPALLKQCLVSAPTMISSLEILFAAGDRLSSQDAILARRAVGSGVYNAYGPTENTVLS
```

STOP and Think: You now have a portion of the data that Marahiel had in 1999 when he discovered the non-ribosomal code. What would you do to infer the non-ribosomal code?

Marahiel conjectured that since A-domains have similar function (i.e., adding an amino acid to the growing peptide), different A-domains should have similar parts. A-domains should also have differing parts to incorporate different amino acids. However, only three conserved columns (shown in red below) are common to the three sequences and have likely arisen by pure chance:

```
YAFDLGYTCMFPVLLGGGELHIVQKETYTAPDEIAHYIKEHGITYIKLTPSLFHTIVNTASFAFDANFESLRLIVLGGEKIIPIDVIAFRKMYGHTEFINHYGPTEATIGA
AFDVSAGDFARALLTGGQLIVCPNEVKMDPASLYAIIKKYDITIFEATPALVIPLMEYIYEQKLDISQLQILIVGSDSCSMEDFKTLVSRFGSTIRIVNSYGVTEACIDS
IAFDASSWEIYAPLLNGGTVVCIDYYTTIDIKALEAVFKQHHIRGAMLPPALLKQCLVSAPTMISSLEILFAAGDRLSSQDAILARRAVGSGVYNAYGPTENTVLS
```

STOP and Think: How else are the three sequences similar?

If we slide the second sequence only one amino acid to the right, adding a **space symbol** ("−") to the beginning of the sequence, then we find 11 conserved columns!

```
YAFDLGYTCMFPVLLGGGELHIVQKETYTAPDEIAHYIKEHGITYIKLTPSLFHTIVNTASFAFDANFESLRLIVLGGEKIIPIDVIAFRKMYGHTEFINHYGPTEATIGA
-AFDVSAGDFARALLTGGQLIVCPNEVKMDPASLYAIIKKYDITIFEATPALVIPLMEYIYEQKLDISQLQILIVGSDSCSMEDFKTLVSRFGSTIRIVNSYGVTEACIDS
IAFDASSWEIYAPLLNGGTVVCIDYYTTIDIKALEAVFKQHHIRGAMLPPALLKQCLVSAPTMISSLEILFAAGDRLSSQDAILARRAVGSGVYNAYGPTENTVLS
```

Adding a few more space symbols reveals 14 conserved columns:

```
YAFDLGYTCMFPVLLGGGELHIVQKETYTAPDEIAHYIKEHGITYIKLTPSLFHTIVNTASFAFDANFESLRLIVLGGEKIIPIDVIAFRKMYGHTEFINHYGPTEATIGA
-AFDVSAGDFARALLTGGQLIVCPNEVKMDPASLYAIIKKYDITIFEATPALVIPLMEYI-YEQKLDISQLQILIVGSDSCSMEDFKTLVSRFGSTIRIVNSYGVTEACIDS
IAFDASSWEIYAPLLNGGTVVCIDYYTTIDIKALEAVFKQHHIRGAMLPPALLKQCLVSA----PTMISSLEILFAAGDRLSSQDAILARRAVGSGVYNAYGPTENTVLS
```

and even more sliding reveals 19 conserved columns:

```
YAFDLGYTCMFPVLLGGGELHIVQKETYTAPDEIAHYIKEHGITYIKLTPSLFHTIVNTASFAFDANFESLRLIVLGGEKIIPIDVIAFRKMYGHTE-FINHYGPTEATIGA
-AFDVSAGDFARALLTGGQLIVCPNEVKMDPASLYAIIKYDITIFEATPALVIPLMEYI-YEQKLDISQLQILIVGSDSCSMEDFKTLVSRFGSTIRIVNSYGVTEACIDS
IAFDASSWEIYAPLLNGGTVVCIDYYTTIDIKALEAVFKQHHIRGAMLPPALLKQCLVSA----PTMISSLEILFAAGDRLSSQDAILARRAVGSGV-Y-NAYGPTENTVLS
```

It turns out that the red columns represent the **conserved core** shared by many A-domains. Now that Marahiel knew how to correctly *align* the A-domains, he hypothesized that some of the remaining variable columns should code for `Asp`, `Orn`, and `Val`. He discovered that the non-ribosomal code is defined by 8 amino acid-long non-ribosomal **signatures**, which are shown as purple columns below.

```
YAFDLGYTCMFPVLLGGGELHIVQKETYTAPDEIAHYIKEHGITYIKLTPSLFHTIVNTASFAFDANFESLRLIVLGGEKIIPIDVIAFRKMYGHTE-FINHYGPTEATIGA
-AFDVSAGDFARALLTGGQLIVCPNEVKMDPASLYAIIKKYDITIFEATPALVIPLMEYI-YEQKLDISQLQILIVGSDSCSMEDFKTLVSRFGSTIRIVNSYGVTEACIDS
IAFDASSWEIYAPLLNGGTVVCIDYYTTIDIKALEAVFKQHHIRGAMLPPALLKQCLVSA----PTMISSLEILFAAGDRLSSQDAILARRAVGSGV-Y-NAYGPTENTVLS
```

The purple columns define the signatures **LTKVLGHIG**, **VGEIVGSID**, and **AWMFAAAVL**, coding for `Asp`, `Orn`, and `Val`, respectively:

$$\begin{aligned} \textbf{LTKVGHIG} &\rightarrow \texttt{Asp} \\ \textbf{VGEIGSID} &\rightarrow \texttt{Orn} \\ \textbf{AWMFAAVL} &\rightarrow \texttt{Val} \end{aligned}$$

It is important to note that without first constructing the conserved core, Marahiel would not have been able to infer the non-ribosomal code, since the 24 amino acids in the signatures above do not line up in the original alignment:

```
YAFDLGYTCMFPVLLGGGELHIVQKETYTAPDEIAHYIKEHGITYIKLTPSLFHTIVNTASFAFDANFESLRLIVLGGEKIIPIDVIAFRKMYGHTEFINHYGPTEATIGA
AFDVSAGDFARALLTGGQLIVCPNEVKMDPASLYAIIKKYDITIFEATPALVIPLMEYIYEQKLDISQLQILIVGSDSCSMEDFKTLVSRFGSTIRIVNSYGVTEACIDS
IAFDASSWEIYAPLLNGGTVVCIDYYTTIDIKALEAVFKQHHIRGAMLPPALLKQCLVSAPTMISSLEILFAAGDRLSSQDAILARRAVGSGVYNAYGPTENTVLS
```

Even after identifying the conserved core, you may be wondering whether Marahiel had a crystal ball; why did he choose these particular 8 purple columns? Why should signatures have 8 amino acids and not 5, or better yet 3? See **DETOUR: Fireflies and the Non-Ribosomal Code** for a better appreciation of the complexities underlying Marahiel's work. Suffice it to say that fifteen years after Marahiel's initial discovery, the non-ribosomal code is still not fully understood. **PAGE 282**

What do oncogenes and growth factors have in common?

Marahiel's cracking of the non-ribosomal code is just one of many biological problems that have benefited from sequence comparison. Another striking example of the power of sequence comparison was established in 1983 when Russell Doolittle compared the newly sequenced **platelet derived growth factor (PDGF)** gene with all other genes known at the time. Doolittle stunned cancer biologists when he showed that PDGF was very similar to the sequence of a gene known as **v-sis**. The two genes' similarity was puzzling because their functions differ greatly; the PDGF gene encodes a protein stimulating cell growth, whereas v-sis is an **oncogene**, or a gene in viruses that causes a cancer-like transformation of infected human cells. Following Doolittle's discovery, scientists hypothesized that some forms of cancer might be caused by a good gene doing the right thing at the wrong time. The link between PDGF and v-sis established a new paradigm; searching all new sequences against sequence databases is now the first order of business in genomics.

However, the question remains: what is the best way to compare sequences algorithmically? Returning to the A-domain example, the insertion of spaces to reveal the conserved core probably looked like a magic trick to you. It is completely unclear what algorithm we have used to decide where to insert the space symbols, or how we should quantify the "best" alignment of the three sequences.

Introduction to Sequence Alignment

Sequence alignment as a game

To simplify matters, we will compare only two sequences at a time, returning to multiple sequence comparison at the end of the chapter. The Hamming distance, which counts mismatches in two strings, rigidly assumes that we align the i-th symbol of one sequence against the i-th symbol of the other. However, since biological sequences are subject to insertions and deletions, it is often the case that the i-th symbol of one sequence corresponds to a symbol at a completely different position in the other sequence. The goal, then, is to find the most appropriate correspondence of symbols.

For example, ATGCATGC and TGCATGCA have no matching positions, and so their Hamming distance is equal to 8:

ATGCATGC
TGCATGCA

Yet these strings have six matching positions if we align them differently:

ATGCATGC–
–TGCATGCA

Strings ATGCTTA and TGCATTAA have more subtle similarities:

ATGC–TTA–
–TGCATTAA

These examples lead us to postulate a notion of a good alignment as one that matches as many symbols as possible. You can think about maximizing the number of matched symbols in two strings as a single-person game (Figure 5.1). At each turn, you have two choices. You can remove the first symbol from each sequence, in which case you earn a point if the symbols match; alternatively, you can remove the first symbol from either of the two sequences, in which case you earn no points but may set yourself up to earn more points in later moves. Your goal is to maximize the number of points.

Sequence alignment and the longest common subsequence

We now define an **alignment** of sequences v and w as a two-row matrix such that the first row contains the symbols of v (in order), the second row contains the symbols of w (in order), and space symbols may be interspersed throughout both strings, as long as two space symbols are not aligned against each other. Here is the alignment of ATGTTATA and ATCGTCC from Figure 5.1.

$$\texttt{A T - G T T A T A}$$
$$\texttt{A T C G T - C - C}$$

An alignment presents one possible scenario by which v could have evolved into w. Columns containing the same letter in both rows are called **matches** and represent conserved nucleotides, whereas columns containing different letters are called **mismatches** and represent single-nucleotide substitutions. Columns containing a space symbol are called **indels**: a column containing a space symbol in the top row of the alignment is called an **insertion**, as it implies the insertion of a symbol when transforming v into w; a column containing a space symbol in the bottom row of the alignment is called a **deletion**, as it indicates the deletion of a symbol when transforming v into w. The alignment above has four matches, two mismatches, one insertion, and two deletions.

The matches in an alignment of two strings define a **common subsequence** of the two strings, or a sequence of symbols appearing in the same order (although not necessarily consecutively) in both strings. For example, the alignment in Figure 5.1 indicates that **ATGT** is a common subsequence of **ATGT**TATA and **ATCGT**CC. An alignment of two strings maximizing the number of matches therefore corresponds to a **longest common subsequence** of these strings. Note that two strings may have more than one longest common subsequence.

Growing alignment	Remaining symbols	Score
	A T G T T A T A A T C G T C C	
A A	T G T T A T A T C G T C C	+1
A T A T	G T T A T A C G T C C	+1
A T – A T C	G T T A T A G T C C	
A T – G A T C G	T T A T A T C C	+1
A T – G T A T C G T	T A T A C C	+1
A T – G T T A T C G T –	A T A C C	
A T – G T T A A T C G T – C	T A C	
A T – G T T A T A T C G T – C –	A C	
A T – G T T A T A A T C G T – C – C		

FIGURE 5.1 One way of playing the alignment game for the strings ATGTTATA and ATCGTCC, with score 4. At each step, we choose to remove either one or both symbols from the left of the two sequences in the "remaining symbols" column. If we remove both symbols, then we align them in the "growing alignment". If we remove only one symbol, then we align this symbol with a space symbol in the growing alignment. Matched symbols are shown in red (and receive score 1). Mismatched symbols are shown in purple; symbols aligned against space symbols are shown in blue or green depending on which sequence they were removed from.

Longest Common Subsequence Problem:

Find a longest common subsequence of two strings.

> **Input**: Two strings.
>
> **Output**: A longest common subsequence of these strings.

If we limit our attention to the two A-domains coding for `Asp` and `Orn` from the introduction, then in addition to the 19 matches that we have already found, we can find 10 more matches (shown in blue below), yielding a common subsequence of length 29.

```
YAFDLGYTCMFPVLLGGGELHIVQKETYTAPDEIAHYIKEHGITYIKLTPSLFHTIVNTASFAFDANFESLRLIVLGGEKIIPIDVIAFRKMYGHTE-FINHYGPTEATIGA
-AFDVSAGDFARALLTGGQLIVCPNEVKMDPASLYAIIKKYDITIFEATPALVIPLMEYI-YEQKLDISQLQILIVGSDSCSMEDFKTLVSRFGSTIRIVNSYGVTEACIDS
```

STOP and Think: What is the longest common subsequence of these strings?

None of the algorithmic approaches we have studied thus far will help us solve the Longest Common Subsequence Problem, and so before asking you to solve this problem, we will change course to describe a different problem that may seem completely unrelated to sequence alignment.

The Manhattan Tourist Problem

What is the best sightseeing strategy?

Imagine you are a tourist in Midtown Manhattan, and you want to see as many sights as possible on your way from the corner of 59th Street and 8th Avenue to the corner of 42nd Street and 3rd Avenue (Figure 5.2 (left)). However, you are short on time, and at each intersection, you can only move south ($\downarrow$) or east ($\rightarrow$). You can choose from many different paths through the map, but no path will visit all the sights. The challenge of finding a legal path through the city that visits the most sights is called the **Manhattan Tourist Problem**.

We will represent the map of Manhattan as a directed graph *ManhattanGraph* in which we model each intersection as a node and each city block between two intersections as a directed edge indicating the legal direction of travel ($\downarrow$ or $\rightarrow$), as shown in Figure 5.2 (right). We then assign each directed edge a **weight** equal to the number of attractions along the corresponding block. The starting (blue) node is called the **source node**, and the ending (red) node is called the **sink node**. Adding the weights along

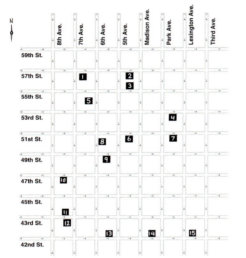

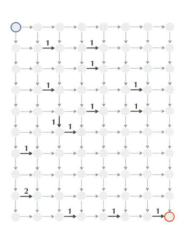

FIGURE 5.2 (Left) A simplification of Midtown Manhattan. You start at the intersection of 59th Street and 8th Avenue in the northwest corner and end at the intersection of 42nd Street and 3rd Avenue in the southeast corner, traveling only south (↓) or east (→) between intersections. The attractions shown are: Carnegie Hall (1), Tiffany & Co. (2), the Sony Building (3), the Museum of Modern Art (4), the Four Seasons Hotel (5), St. Patrick's Cathedral (6), the General Electric Building (7), Radio City Music Hall (8), Rockefeller Center (9), the Paramount Building (10), the New York Times Building (11), Times Square (12), the General Society of Mechanics and Tradesmen (13), Grand Central Terminal (14), and the Chrysler Building (15). (Right) The directed graph *ManhattanGraph* in which every edge is weighted by the number of attractions along that city block (edge weights equal to 0 are not shown).

a path from the source to the sink yields the number of attractions along that path. Therefore, to solve the Manhattan Tourist Problem, we need to find a **maximum-weight path** connecting the source to the sink (also called a **longest path**) in *ManhattanGraph*.

We can model any rectangular grid of streets using a similar directed graph; Figure 5.3 (left) shows the graph for a hypothetical city with even more attractions. In contrast to the Cartesian plane, we orient the axes of this grid down and to the right. Therefore, the blue source node is assigned the coordinates $(0,0)$, and the red sink node is assigned the coordinates (n,m). This implies the following generalization of our original problem.

Manhattan Tourist Problem:

Find a longest path in a rectangular city.

> **Input**: A weighted $n \times m$ rectangular grid with $n + 1$ rows and $m + 1$ columns.
>
> **Output**: A longest path from source $(0,0)$ to sink (n,m) in the grid.

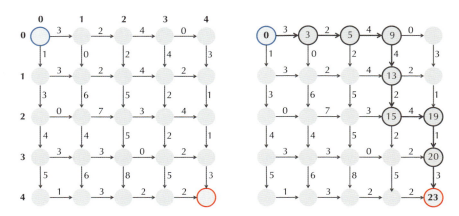

FIGURE 5.3 (Left) An $n \times m$ city grid represented as a graph with weighted edges for $n = m = 4$. The bottom left node is indexed as (4, 0), and the upper right node is indexed as (0, 4). (Right) A path through the graph found by the greedy algorithm is not the longest path.

EXERCISE BREAK: How many different paths are there from source to sink in an $n \times m$ rectangular grid?

Applying a brute force approach to the Manhattan Tourist Problem is impractical because the number of paths is huge. A sensible greedy approach would choose between the two possible directions at each node ($\rightarrow$ or $\downarrow$) according to how many attractions you would see if you moved only one block south versus moving one block east. For example, in Figure 5.3 (right), we start off by moving east from $(0, 0)$ rather than south because the horizontal edge has three attractions, while the vertical edge has only one. Unfortunately, this greedy strategy may miss the longest path in the long run. Figure 5.3 (right).

STOP and Think: Find a longer path than the one in Figure 5.3 (right).

Sightseeing in an arbitrary directed graph

In reality, the streets in Midtown Manhattan do not form a perfect rectangular grid because Broadway Avenue cuts diagonally across the grid, but the network of streets can still be represented by a directed graph. In fact, the Manhattan Tourist Problem is just a special case of the more general problem of finding the longest path in an arbitrary directed graph, such as the ones in Figure 5.4.

Longest Path in a Directed Graph Problem:
Find a longest path between two nodes in an edge-weighted directed graph.

    Input: An edge-weighted directed graph with source and sink nodes.
    Output: A longest path from source to sink in the directed graph.

STOP and Think: What is the length of a longest path between the source and sink in the directed graph shown in Figure 5.4 (right)?

If a directed graph contained a directed cycle (e.g., the four central edges of weight 1 in Figure 5.4 (right)), then a tourist could traverse this cycle indefinitely, revisiting the same attractions over and over again and creating a path of huge length. For this reason, the graphs that we will consider in this chapter do not contain directed cycles; such graphs are called **directed acyclic graphs (DAGs)**.

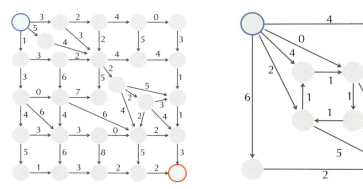

FIGURE 5.4 Directed graphs corresponding to hypothetical irregular city grids.

Longest Path in a DAG Problem:

Find a longest path between two nodes in an edge-weighted DAG.

> **Input**: An edge-weighted DAG with source and sink nodes.
> **Output**: A longest path from source to sink in the DAG.

STOP and Think: Do you see any similarities between the Longest Path in a DAG Problem and the Longest Common Subsequence Problem?

Sequence Alignment is the Manhattan Tourist Problem in Disguise

In Figure 5.5, we add two arrays of integers to an alignment of ATGTTATA and ATCGTCC. The array [0 1 2 2 3 4 5 6 7 8] holds the number of symbols of ATGTTATA used up to a given column in the alignment. Similarly, the array [0 1 2 3 4 5 5 6 6 7] holds the number of symbols of ATCGTCC used up to a given column. In Figure 5.5, we have added a third array, [↘ ↘ → ↘ ↘ ↓ ↘ ↓ ↘], recording whether each column represents a **match**/**mismatch** (↘/↘), an **insertion** (→), or a **deletion** (↓).

This third array corresponds to a path from source to sink in an 8×7 rectangular grid, shown in Figure 5.6 (left). The *i*-th node of this path is made up of the *i*-th element of [0 1 2 2 3 4 5 6 7 8] and the *i*-th element of [0 1 2 3 4 5 5 6 6 7]:

$$(0,0) \searrow (1,1) \searrow (2,2) \rightarrow (2,3) \searrow (3,4) \searrow (4,5) \downarrow (5,5) \searrow (6,6) \downarrow (7,6) \searrow (8,7)$$

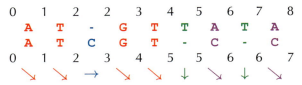

FIGURE 5.5 An alignment of `ATGTTATA` and `ATCGTCC`. The array in the first row counts the number of symbols of `ATGTTATA` used up to a given position. The array in the fourth row counts the number of symbols of `ATCGTCC` used up to a given position. And the array in the last row records whether each column of the alignment represents a **match**/**mismatch** ($\searrow$/$\searrow$), **insertion** ($\rightarrow$), or **deletion** ($\downarrow$).

Note that in addition to horizontal and vertical edges, we have added diagonal edges connecting (i, j) to $(i + 1, j + 1)$ in Figure 5.6.

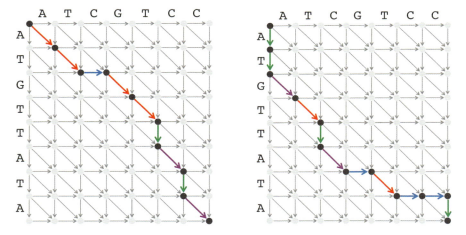

FIGURE 5.6 Every alignment corresponds to a path in the alignment graph from source to sink, and vice-versa. (Left) The path $(0, 0)$ $\searrow$ $(1, 1)$ $\searrow$ $(2, 2)$ $\rightarrow$ $(2, 3)$ $\searrow$ $(3, 4)$ $\searrow$ $(4, 5)$ $\downarrow$ $(5, 5)$ $\searrow$ $(6, 6)$ $\downarrow$ $(7, 6)$ $\searrow$ $(8, 7)$ is highlighted above and corresponds to the alignment of `ATGTTATA` and `ATCGTCC` in Figure 5.5. (Right) Another path in the alignment graph.

We call the DAG in Figure 5.6 the **alignment graph** of strings v and w, denoted AlignmentGraph(v, w), and we call a path from source to sink in this DAG an **alignment path**. Every alignment of v and w can be viewed as a set of instructions to construct a unique alignment path in AlignmentGraph(v, w), where each **match**/**mismatch**, **insertion**, and **deletion** corresponds to an edge $\searrow$/$\searrow$, $\rightarrow$, and $\downarrow$, respectively. Furthermore, this process is reversible, as we can convert each alignment path into a unique alignment.

EXERCISE BREAK: Construct the alignment of `ATGTTATA` and `ATCGTCC` corresponding to the alignment path in Figure 5.6 (right).

STOP and Think: Can you use the alignment graph to find a longest common subsequence of two strings?

Recall that finding a longest common subsequence of two strings is equivalent to finding an alignment of these strings maximizing the number of matches. In Figure 5.7, we highlight all diagonal edges of ALIGNMENTGRAPH(`ATGTTATA`, `ATCGTCC`) corresponding to matches. If we assign a weight of 1 to all these edges and 0 to all other edges, then the Longest Common Subsequence Problem is equivalent to finding a longest path in this weighted DAG!

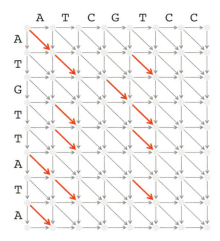

FIGURE 5.7 ALIGNMENTGRAPH(`ATGTTATA`, `ATCGTCC`) with all edges of weight 1 colored red (all other edges have weight 0). These edges correspond to potential matched symbols in an alignment of the two strings.

Thus, we need to design an algorithm for the Longest Path in a DAG Problem, but to do so, we need to know more about **dynamic programming**, a powerful algorithmic paradigm that is used for solving thousands of problems from various scientific fields.

If you are already familiar with dynamic programming, then you may want to skip the next section.

An Introduction to Dynamic Programming: The Change Problem

Changing money greedily

Imagine that you bought this textbook in a bookstore for $69.24, which you paid for with $70 in cash. You are due 76 cents in change, and the cashier now must make a decision whether to give you a fistful of 76 1-cent coins or just four coins ($25 + 25 + 25 + 1 = 76$). Making change in this example is easy, but it casts light on a more general problem: how can a cashier make change using the fewest number of coins?

Different currencies have different possible coin values, or **denominations**. In the United States, the coin denominations are $(100, 50, 25, 10, 5, 1)$; in the Roman Republic, they were $(120, 40, 30, 24, 20, 10, 5, 4, 1)$. The heuristic used by cashiers all over the world to make change, which we call **GreedyChange**, iteratively selects the largest coin denomination possible.

GreedyChange(*money*)
    Change ← empty collection of coins
    while *money* > 0
        coin ← largest denomination that is less than or equal to *money*
        add a coin with denomination *coin* to the collection of coins *Change*
        money ← *money* − *coin*
    return *Change*

STOP and Think: Does **GreedyChange** always return the minimum possible number of coins?

Say we want to change 48 units of currency (denarii) in ancient Rome. **GreedyChange** returns five coins ($48 = 40 + 5 + 1 + 1 + 1$), and yet we can make change using only two coins ($48 = 24 + 24$). Thus, **GreedyChange** is suboptimal for some denominations!

STOP and Think: During the reign of Augustus, Roman coin denominations were changed to $(1600, 800, 400, 200, 100, 50, 25, 2, 1)$. Why did these denominations make Roman cashiers' lives easier? More generally, find a condition on coin denominations that dictates when **GreedyChange** will make change with the fewest number of coins.

Since **GREEDYCHANGE** is incorrect, we need to come up with a different approach. We can represent coins from d arbitrary denominations by an array of integers

$$\text{COINS} = (coin_1, \ldots, coin_d) \, ,$$

where the values $coin_i$ are given in decreasing order. We say that an array of d positive integers $(change_1, \ldots, change_d)$ with the **number of coins** $change_1 + \cdots + change_d$ **changes** an integer $money$ (for the denominations COINS) if

$$coin_1 \cdot change_1 + \cdots + coin_d \cdot change_d = money \, .$$

For example, for the Roman denominations $\text{COINS} = (120, 40, 30, 24, 20, 10, 5, 4, 1)$, both $(0, 1, 0, 0, 0, 0, 0, 1, 0, 3)$ and $(0, 0, 0, 2, 0, 0, 0, 0, 0)$ change $money = 48$.

We will consider the problem of finding the minimum number of coins needed to make change, instead of actually producing these coins. Let $\text{MINNUMCOINS}(money)$ denote the minimum number of coins needed to change $money$ for a given collection of denominations (e.g., for the Roman denominations, $\text{MINNUMCOINS}(48) = 2$).

Change Problem:

Find the minimum number of coins needed to make change.

> **Input**: An integer $money$ and an array COINS of d positive integers.
> **Output**: The minimum number of coins with denominations COINS that changes $money$.

Changing money recursively

Since the greedy solution used by Roman cashiers to solve the Change Problem is incorrect, we will consider a different approach. Suppose you need to change 76 denarii, and you only have coins of the three smallest denominations: $\text{COINS} = (5, 4, 1)$. A minimal collection of coins totaling 76 denarii must be one of the following:

- a minimal collection of coins totaling 75 denarii, plus a 1-denarius coin;

- a minimal collection of coins totaling 72 denarii, plus a 4-denarius coin;

- a minimal collection of coins totaling 71 denarii, plus a 5-denarius coin.

For the general denominations COINS = $(coin_1, \ldots, coin_d)$, MINNUMCOINS($money$) is equal to the minimum of d numbers:

$$\text{MINNUMCOINS}(money) = \min \begin{cases} \text{MINNUMCOINS}(money - coin_1) + 1 \\ \quad \vdots \\ \text{MINNUMCOINS}(money - coin_d) + 1 \end{cases}$$

We have just produced a **recurrence relation**, or an equation for MINNUMCOINS($money$) in terms of MINNUMCOINS(m) for smaller values m. The above recurrence relation motivates the following recursive algorithm, which solves the Change Problem by computing MINNUMCOINS(m) for smaller and smaller values of m. In this algorithm, |COINS| refers to the number of denominations in COINS. See **DETOUR: The Towers of Hanoi** if you did not encounter recursive algorithms in Chapter 1.

PAGE 60

RECURSIVECHANGE(*money*, COINS)
    if *money* = 0
        return 0
    minNumCoins ← ∞
    for *i* ← 1 to |COINS|
        if *money* ≥ *coin$_i$*
            numCoins ← **RECURSIVECHANGE**(*money* − *coin$_i$*, COINS)
            if *numCoins* + 1 < *minNumCoins*
                minNumCoins ← *numCoins* + 1
    return *minNumCoins*

STOP and Think: Implement **RECURSIVECHANGE** and run it on *money* = 76 with COINS = (5, 4, 1). What happens?

RECURSIVECHANGE may appear efficient, but it is completely impractical because it recalculates the optimal coin combination for a given value of *money* over and over again. For example, when *money* = 76 and COINS = (5, 4, 1), MINNUMCOINS(70) gets computed six times, five of which are shown in Figure 5.8. This may not seem like a problem, but MINNUMCOINS(30) will be computed billions of times!

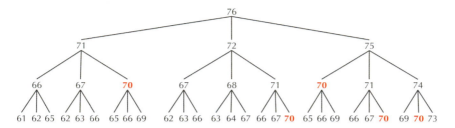

FIGURE 5.8 A tree illustrating the computation of MINNUMCOINS(76) for the denominations COINS = (5, 4, 1). The edges of this tree represent recursive calls of **RECURSIVECHANGE** for different input values, with five of the six computations of MINNUMCOINS(70) highlighted in red. When MINNUMCOINS(70) is computed for the sixth time (corresponding to the path 76 → 75 → 74 → 73 → 72 → 71 → 70), **RECURSIVECHANGE** has already been called hundreds of times.

Changing money using dynamic programming

To avoid the many recursive calls needed to compute MINNUMCOINS(*money*), we will use a dynamic programming strategy. Wouldn't it be nice to know all the values of MINNUMCOINS(*money* − *coin$_i$*) by the time we compute MINNUMCOINS(*money*)? Instead of making time-consuming calls to **RECURSIVECHANGE**(*money* − *coin$_i$*, COINS), we could simply look up the values of MINNUMCOINS(*money* − *coin$_i$*) in an array and thus compute MINNUMCOINS(*money*) using just |COINS| comparisons.

The key to dynamic programming is to take a step that may seem counterintuitive. Instead of computing MINNUMCOINS(*m*) for every value of *m* from 76 *downward* toward *m* = 1 via recursive calls, we will invert our thinking and compute MINNUMCOINS(*m*) from *m* = 1 *upward* toward 76, storing all these values in an array so that we only need to compute MINNUMCOINS(*m*) once for each value of *m*. MINNUMCOINS(*m*) is still computed via the same recurrence relation:

$$\text{MINNUMCOINS}(m) = \min \begin{cases} \text{MINNUMCOINS}(m-5)+1 \\ \text{MINNUMCOINS}(m-4)+1 \\ \text{MINNUMCOINS}(m-1)+1 \end{cases}$$

For example, assuming that we have already computed MINNUMCOINS(*m*) for *m* < 6,

$$\text{MinNumCoins}(6) = \min \begin{cases} \text{MinNumCoins}(1) + 1 = 2 \\ \text{MinNumCoins}(2) + 1 = 3 \\ \text{MinNumCoins}(5) + 1 = 2 \end{cases}$$

$$= 2\,.$$

Following the same reasoning,

$$\text{MinNumCoins}(7) = \min \begin{cases} \text{MinNumCoins}(2) + 1 = 3 \\ \text{MinNumCoins}(3) + 1 = 4 \\ \text{MinNumCoins}(6) + 1 = 3 \end{cases}$$

$$= 3\,.$$

Continuing these calculations results in Figure 5.9.

m	0	1	2	3	4	5	6	7	8	9	10	11	12
MinNumCoins(m)	0	1	2	3	1	1	2	3	2	2	2	3	3

FIGURE 5.9 MinNumCoins(m) for values of m between 1 and 12.

EXERCISE BREAK: Use dynamic programming to fill in the next ten values of MinNumCoins(m) in Figure 5.9.

Notice that MinNumCoins(2) is used in the computation of both MinNumCoins(6) and MinNumCoins(7), but instead of draining computational resources by having to compute this value both times, we simply consult the pre-computed value in the array. The following dynamic programming algorithm calculates MinNumCoins(*money*) with runtime $\mathcal{O}(money \cdot |\text{Coins}|)$.

```
DPChange(money, Coins)
    MinNumCoins(0) ← 0
    for m ← 1 to money
        MinNumCoins(m) ← ∞
        for i ← 1 to |Coins|
            if m ≥ coinᵢ
                if MinNumCoins(m − coinᵢ) + 1 < MinNumCoins(m)
                    MinNumCoins(m) ← MinNumCoins(m − coinᵢ) + 1
    return MinNumCoins(money)
```

STOP and Think: If *money* $= 10^9$, **DPCHANGE** requires a huge array of size 10^9. Modify the **DPCHANGE** algorithm so that the array size required does not exceed the value of the largest coin denomination.

STOP and Think: Recall that our original goal was to make change, not just compute MINNUMCOINS(*money*). Modify **DPCHANGE** so that it not only computes the minimum number of coins but also returns these coins.

The Manhattan Tourist Problem Revisited

You should now be ready to implement an algorithm solving the Manhattan Tourist Problem. The following pseudocode computes the length of the longest path to node (i, j) in a rectangular grid and is based on the observation that the only way to reach node (i, j) in the Manhattan Tourist Problem is either by moving south ($\downarrow$) from $(i - 1, j)$ or east ($\rightarrow$) from $(i, j - 1)$.

```
SOUTHOREAST(i, j)
    if i = 0 and j = 0
        return 0
    x ← −∞, y ← −∞
    if i > 0
        x ← SOUTHOREAST(i − 1, j)+ weight of vertical edge into (i, j)
    if j > 0
        y ← SOUTHOREAST(i, j − 1)+ weight of horizontal edge into (i, j)
    return max{x, y}
```

STOP and Think: How many times is **SOUTHOREAST**$(3, 2)$ called in the computation of **SOUTHOREAST**$(9, 7)$?

Similarly to **RECURSIVECHANGE**, **SOUTHOREAST** suffers from a huge number of recursive calls, and we need to reframe this algorithm using dynamic programming. Remember how **DPCHANGE** worked from small instances *upward*? To find the length of a longest path from source $(0, 0)$ to sink (n, m), we will first find the lengths of longest paths from the source to *all* nodes (i, j) in the grid, expanding slowly *outward* from the source.

At first glance, you may think that we have created additional work for ourselves by solving $n \times m$ different problems instead of a single problem. Yet **SouthOrEast** also solves all these smaller problems, just as **RecursiveChange** and **DPChange** both computed MinNumCoins(m) for all values of $m < money$. The trick behind dynamic programming is to solve each of the smaller problems once rather than billions of times.

We will henceforth denote the length of a longest path from $(0,0)$ to (i,j) as $s_{i,j}$. Computing $s_{0,j}$ (for $0 \le j \le m$) is easy, since we can only reach $(0,j)$ by moving right ($\rightarrow$) and do not have any flexibility in our choice of path. Thus, $s_{0,j}$ is the sum of the weights of the first j horizontal edges leading out from the source. Similarly, $s_{i,0}$ is the sum of the weights of the first i vertical edges from the source (Figure 5.10).

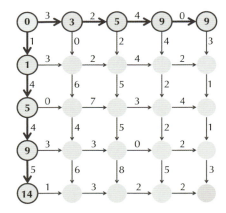

FIGURE 5.10 Computing $s_{i,0}$ and $s_{0,j}$ is easy because there is only one path from the source to $(i,0)$ and only one path from the source to $(0,j)$.

For $i > 0$ and $j > 0$, the only way to reach node (i,j) is by moving down from node $(i-1,j)$ or by moving right from node $(i,j-1)$. Thus, $s_{i,j}$ can be computed as the maximum of two values:

$$s_{i,j} = \max \begin{cases} s_{i-1,j} + \text{ weight of vertical edge from } (i-1,j) \text{ to } (i,j) \\ s_{i,j-1} + \text{ weight of horizontal edge from } (i,j-1) \text{ to } (i,j) \end{cases}$$

Now that we have computed $s_{0,1}$ and $s_{1,0}$, we can compute $s_{1,1}$. You can arrive at $(1,1)$ by traveling down from $(0,1)$ or right from $(1,0)$. Therefore, $s_{1,1}$ is the maximum of two values:

$$s_{1,1} = \max \begin{cases} s_{0,1} + \text{ weight of vertical edge from } (0,1) \text{ to } (1,1) & = 3+0=3 \\ s_{1,0} + \text{ weight of horizontal edge from } (1,0) \text{ to } (1,1) = 1+3=4 \end{cases}$$

Since our goal is to find the longest path from $(0,0)$ to $(1,1)$, we conclude that $s_{1,1} = 4$. Because we chose the horizontal edge from $(1,0)$ to $(1,1)$, the longest path through $(1,1)$ must use this edge, which we highlight in Figure 5.11 (top left). Similar logic allows us to compute the rest of the values in column 1; for each $s_{i,1}$, we highlight the edge that we chose leading into $(i,1)$, as shown in Figure 5.11 (top right).

Continuing column-by-column (Figure 5.11 (bottom left)), we can compute every score $s_{i,j}$ in a single sweep of the graph, eventually calculating $s_{4,4} = 34$.

For each node (i,j), we will highlight the edge leading into (i,j) that we used to compute $s_{i,j}$. However, note that we have a tie when we compute $s_{3,3}$:

$$s_{3,3} = \max \begin{cases} s_{2,3} + \text{ weight of vertical edge from } (2,3) \text{ to } (3,3) & = 20+2=22 \\ s_{3,2} + \text{ weight of horizontal edge from } (3,2) \text{ to } (3,3) = 22+0=22 \end{cases}$$

To reach $(3,3)$, we could have used *either* the horizontal or vertical incoming edge, and so we highlight both of these edges in the completed graph in Figure 5.11 (bottom left).

STOP and Think: Thus far, we have only discussed how to find the length of a longest path. How could you use the highlighted edges in Figure 5.11 (bottom left) to reconstruct a longest path?

We now have the outline of a dynamic programming algorithm for finding the length of a longest path in the Manhattan Tourist Problem, called **MANHATTANTOURIST**. In the pseudocode below, $down_{i,j}$ and $right_{i,j}$ are the respective weights of the vertical and horizontal edges entering node (i,j). We denote the matrices holding $(down_{i,j})$ and $(right_{i,j})$ as *Down* and *Right*, respectively.

EXERCISE BREAK: Modify **MANHATTANTOURIST** in order to find the length of the longest path from source to sink in the graph shown in Figure 5.11 (bottom right).

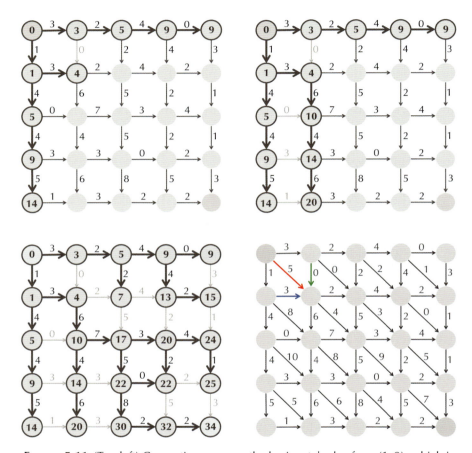

FIGURE 5.11 (Top left) Computing $s_{1,1}$ uses the horizontal edge from (1, 0), which is highlighted. (Top right) Computing all values $s_{i,1}$ in column 1. (Bottom left) The graph displaying all scores $s_{i,j}$. (Bottom right) A graph with diagonal edges constructed for an imaginary city. Node (1, 1) has three predecessors ((0, 0), (0, 1), and (1, 0)) that are used in the computation of $s_{1,1}$.

$\textsc{ManhattanTourist}(n, m, Down, Right)$
    $s_{0,0} \leftarrow 0$
    for $i \leftarrow 1$ **to** n
        $s_{i,0} \leftarrow s_{i-1,0} + down_{i,0}$
    for $j \leftarrow 1$ **to** m
        $s_{0,j} \leftarrow s_{0,j-1} + right_{0,j}$
    for $i \leftarrow 1$ **to** n
        for $j \leftarrow 1$ **to** m
            $s_{i,j} \leftarrow \max\{s_{i-1,j} + down_{i,j},\ s_{i,j-1} + right_{i,j}\}$
    return $s_{n,m}$

From Manhattan to an Arbitrary Directed Acyclic Graph

Sequence alignment as building a Manhattan-like graph

After seeing how dynamic programming solved the Manhattan Tourist Problem, you should be prepared to adapt $\textsc{ManhattanTourist}$ for alignment graphs with diagonal edges. Recall Figure 5.7, in which we modeled the Longest Common Subsequence Problem as finding the longest path in an alignment graph "city" whose "attractions'" (matches) all lie on diagonal edges with weight 1.

You can probably work out the recurrence relation for the alignment graph on your own, but imagine for a second that you have not already learned that an LCS can be represented by a longest path in the alignment graph. As **DETOUR: Finding a Longest Common Subsequence without Building a City** explains, we don't need to build a **PAGE 283** Manhattan-like city to compute the length of an LCS. However, the arguments required to do so are tedious. More importantly, various alignment applications are much more complex than the Longest Common Subsequence Problem and require building a DAG with appropriately chosen edge weights in order to model the specifics of a biological problem. Rather than treating each subsequent alignment application as a frightening new challenge, we would like to equip you with a generic dynamic programming algorithm that will find a longest path in any DAG. Moreover, many bioinformatics problems have nothing to do with alignment, yet they can also be solved as applications of the Longest Path in a DAG Problem.

Dynamic programming in an arbitrary DAG

Given a node b in a DAG, let s_b denote the length of a longest path from the source to b. We call node a a **predecessor** of node b if there is an edge connecting a to b in the DAG; note that the indegree of a node is equal to the number of its predecessors. The **score** s_b of node b with indegree k is computed as a maximum of k terms:

$$s_b = \max_{\text{all predecessors } a \text{ of node } b} \{s_a + \text{weight of edge from } a \text{ to } b\}.$$

For example, in the graph shown in Figure 5.11 (bottom right), node $(1,1)$ has three predecessors. You can arrive at $(1,1)$ by traveling right from $(1,0)$, down from $(0,1)$, or diagonally from $(0,0)$, Assuming that we have already computed $s_{0,0}$, $s_{0,1}$, and $s_{1,0}$, we can therefore compute $s_{1,1}$ as the maximum of three values:

$$s_{1,1} = \max \begin{cases} s_{0,1} + \text{weight of edge } \downarrow \text{ connecting } (0,1) \text{ to } (1,1) = 3 + 0 = 3 \\ s_{1,0} + \text{weight of edge } \rightarrow \text{ connecting } (1,0) \text{ to } (1,1) = 1 + 3 = 4 \\ s_{0,0} + \text{weight of edge } \searrow \text{ connecting } (0,0) \text{ to } (1,1) = 0 + 5 = 5 \end{cases}$$

To compute scores for any node (i,j) of this graph, we use the following recurrence:

$$s_{i,j} = \max \begin{cases} s_{i-1,j} \; + \text{weight of edge } \downarrow \text{ between } (i-1,j) \text{ and } (i,j) \\ s_{i,j-1} \; + \text{weight of edge } \rightarrow \text{ between } (i,j-1) \text{ and } (i,j) \\ s_{i-1,j-1} + \text{weight of edge } \searrow \text{ between } (i-1,j-1) \text{ and } (i,j) \end{cases}$$

An analogous argument can be applied to the alignment graph to compute the length of an LCS between sequences v and w. Since in this case all edges have weight 0 except for diagonal edges of weight 1 that represent matches ($v_i = w_j$), we obtain the following recurrence for computing the length of an LCS:

$$s_{i,j} = \max \begin{cases} s_{i-1,j} & + 0 \\ s_{i,j-1} & + 0 \\ s_{i-1,j-1} & + 1, \text{ if } v_i = w_j \end{cases}$$

STOP and Think: The above recurrence does not incorporate mismatch edges. Why is this not a problem?

A similar approach can be developed to find the longest path in any DAG, as suggested by the next exercise.

EXERCISE BREAK: What is the length of a longest path between the blue and red nodes in the DAG shown in Figure 5.12?

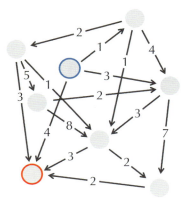

FIGURE 5.12 A weighted DAG without the obvious order inherent in the graphs previously encountered in this chapter.

Topological orderings

Do not worry if you struggled to solve the last exercise. The hitch to using dynamic programming in order to find the length of a longest path in a DAG is that we must decide on the *order* in which to visit nodes when computing the values s_b according to the recurrence

$$s_b = \max_{\text{all predecessors } a \text{ of node } b} \{s_a + \text{weight of edge from } a \text{ to } b\}.$$

This ordering of nodes is important, since by the time we reach node b, the values s_a for all its predecessors must have already been computed. We have managed to hide this issue for rectangular grids because the order in which we have computed the $s_{i,j}$ ensured that we would never consider a node before visiting all of its predecessors.

To illustrate the importance of visiting nodes in the correct order, consider the DAG in Figure 5.13, which corresponds to a "Dressing Challenge Problem". How would you order the nodes of this graph so that you don't put on your boots before your tights?

FIGURE 5.13 The DAG associated with the Dressing Challenge Problem. If a directed edge connects two items of clothing, then the first item must be put on before the second item.

To solve the Dressing Challenge Problem, we need to arrange the nodes in the DAG in Figure 5.13 along a line so that every directed edge connects a node to a node on its right (Figure 5.14). To get dressed without any mishaps, you can simply visit nodes from left to right.

To find a longest path in an arbitrary DAG, we first need to order the nodes of the DAG so that every node falls after all its predecessors. Formally, an ordering of nodes $(a_1, \ldots, a_k)$ in a DAG is called a **topological ordering** if every edge (a_i, a_j) of the DAG connects a node with a smaller index to a node with a larger index, i.e., $i < j$.

EXERCISE BREAK: Construct a topological ordering of the DAG in Figure 5.12.

EXERCISE BREAK: How many topological orderings does the Dressing Challenge DAG have?

The reason why **MANHATTANTOURIST** is able to find a longest path in a rectangular grid is that its pseudocode implicitly orders nodes according to the "column-by-column" topological ordering shown in Figure 5.15 (left). The "row-by-row" ordering (Figure 5.15 (right)) gives another topological ordering of a rectangular grid.

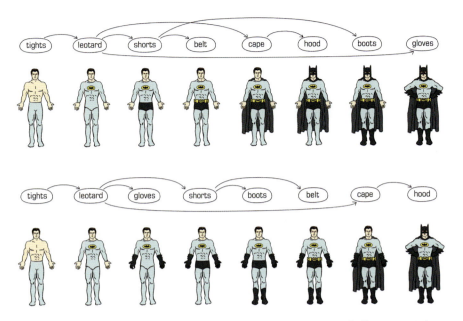

FIGURE 5.14 Two different topological orderings of the Dressing Challenge DAG from Figure 5.13.

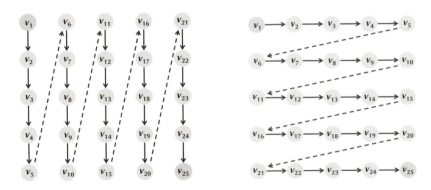

FIGURE 5.15 The column-by-column (left) and row-by-row (right) topological orderings of a rectangular grid.

STOP and Think: Rewrite the **MANHATTANTOURIST** pseudocode based on the topological ordering shown in Figure 5.16.

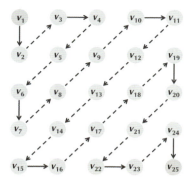

FIGURE 5.16 Another topological ordering of the rectangular grid from Figure 5.15.

It can be proven that any DAG has a topological ordering, and that this topological ordering can be constructed in time proportional to the number of edges in the graph **PAGE 284** (see **DETOUR: Constructing a Topological Ordering**). Once we have a topological ordering, we can compute the length of the longest path from source to sink by visiting the nodes of the DAG in the order dictated by the topological ordering, which is achieved by the following algorithm. For simplicity, we assume that the source node is the only node with indegree 0 in *Graph*.

LONGESTPATH(*Graph, source, sink*)
    for each node *b* in *Graph*
        $s_b \leftarrow -\infty$
    $s_{source} \leftarrow 0$
    topologically order *Graph*
    for each node *b* in *Graph* (following the topological order)
        $s_b \leftarrow \max_{\text{all predecessors } a \text{ of node } b}\{s_a + \text{weight of edge from } a \text{ to } b\}$
    return s_{sink}

Since every edge participates in only a single recurrence, the runtime of **LONGESTPATH** is proportional to the number of edges in the DAG *Graph*.

We can now efficiently compute the *length* of a longest path in an arbitrary DAG, but we do not yet know how to convert **LONGESTPATH** into an algorithm that will *construct* this longest path. In the next section, we will use the Longest Common Subsequence Problem to explain how to construct a longest path in a DAG.

Backtracking in the Alignment Graph

In Figure 5.11 (bottom left), we highlighted each edge selected by **MANHATTANTOURIST**. To form a longest path, we simply need to find a path from source to sink formed by highlighted edges (more than one such path may exist). However, if we were to walk from source to sink along the highlighted edges, we might reach a dead end, such as the node $(1, 2)$. In contrast, every path from the sink will bring us back to the source if we **backtrack** in the direction opposite to each highlighted edge (Figure 5.17).

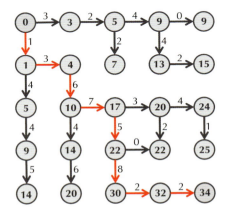

FIGURE 5.17 Following edges from the sink backwards to the source produces the red path in the DAG above, which highlights a longest path from the source to sink.

We can use this backtracking idea to construct an LCS of strings v and w. We know that if we assign a weight of 1 to the edges in ALIGNMENTGRAPH(v, w) corresponding to matches and assign a weight of 0 to all other edges, then $s_{|v|, |w|}$ gives the length of an LCS. The following algorithm maintains a record of which edge in ALIGNMENTGRAPH(v, w) was used to compute each value $s_{i, j}$ by utilizing **backtracking pointers**, which take one of the three values $\downarrow$, $\rightarrow$, or $\searrow$. Backtracking pointers are stored in a matrix *Backtrack*.

STOP and Think: How does changing the order of the three "if" statements in the **LCSBACKTRACK** pseudocode affect the computation of *Backtrack*?

LCSBacktrack(*v*, *w*)
    for *i* ← 0 **to** |*v*|
        $s_{i,0}$ ← 0
    for *j* ← 0 **to** |*w*|
        $s_{0,j}$ ← 0
    for *i* ← 1 **to** |*v*|
        for *j* ← 1 **to** |*w*|

$$s_{i,j} \leftarrow \max \begin{cases} s_{i-1,j} \\ s_{i,j-1} \\ s_{i-1,j-1} + 1, \ \text{if } v_i = w_j \end{cases}$$

        if $s_{i,j} = s_{i-1,j}$
            $Backtrack_{i,j}$ ← "↓"
        else if $s_{i,j} = s_{i,j-1}$
            $Backtrack_{i,j}$ ← "→"
        else if $s_{i,j} = s_{i-1,j-1} + 1$ **and** $v_i = w_j$
            $Backtrack_{i,j}$ ← "↘"
    return *Backtrack*

We now need to find a path from the source to the sink formed by the highlighted edges. The algorithm below solves the Longest Common Subsequence Problem by using the information in *Backtrack*. **OutputLCS**(*Backtrack*, *v*, *i*, *j*) outputs an LCS between the *i*-prefix of *v* and the *j*-prefix of *w*. The initial invocation that outputs an LCS of *v* and *w* is **OutputLCS**(*Backtrack*, *v*, |*v*|, |*w*|).

OutputLCS(*Backtrack*, *v*, *i*, *j*)
    if *i* = 0 **or** *j* = 0
        return
    if $Backtrack_{i,j}$ = ↓
        OutputLCS(*Backtrack*, *v*, *i* − 1, *j*)
    else if $Backtrack_{i,j}$ = →
        OutputLCS(*Backtrack*, *v*, *i*, *j* − 1)
    else
        OutputLCS(*Backtrack*, *v*, *i* − 1, *j* − 1)
        output v_i

STOP and Think: **OutputLCS** is a recursive algorithm, but it is efficient. What makes it different from the inefficient recursive algorithms for making change and finding a longest path in a DAG?

The backtracking method can be generalized to construct a longest path in any DAG. Whenever we compute s_b as

$$s_b = \max_{\text{all predecessors } a \text{ of node } b} \{s_a + \text{weight of edge from } a \text{ to } b\},$$

we simply need to store a predecessor of b that was used in the computation of s_b so that we can backtrack later on. You are now ready to use backtracking to find the longest path in an arbitrary DAG.

EXERCISE BREAK: Currently, **OutputLCS** finds a single LCS of two strings. Modify **OutputLCS** (and **LCSBacktrack**) to find every LCS of two strings.

Scoring Alignments

What is wrong with the LCS scoring model?

Recall Marahiel's alignment of the A-domains coding for `Asp` and `Orn`, which had **19** + **10** matches:

```
YAFDLGYTCMFPVLLGGGELHIVQKETYTAPDEIAHYIKEHGITYIKLTPSLFHTIVNTASFAFDANFESLRLIVLGGEKIIPIDVIAFRKMYGHTE-FINHYGPTEATIGA
-AFDVSAGDFARALLTGGQLIVCPNEVKMDPASLYAIIKKYDITIFEATPALVIPLMEYI-YEQKLDISQLQILIVGSDSCSMEDFKTLVSRFGSTIRIVNSYGVTEACIDS
```

It is not difficult to construct an alignment having even more matches at the expense of introducing more indels. Yet the more indels we add, the less biologically relevant the alignment becomes, as it diverges further and further from the biologically correct alignment found by Marahiel. Below is the alignment with the maximum number of matches, representing an LCS of length **19** + **8** + **19** = 46. This alignment is so long that we cannot fit it on a single line.

```
YAFDL--G-YTCMFP--VLL-GGGELHIV---Q-K-E--T-YTAPDEIAHYIK--EHGITYI---KLTPSL-FHT
-AFDVSAGD----FARA-LLTGG-QL-IVCPNEVKMDPASLY-A---I---IKKYD--IT-IFEA--TPALV---

IVNTASFAFDANFE-----S-LR-LIVLGG-----EKIIPIDVIAFRK-M---YGHTEFI---NHYGPTEATIGA
IPLMEYIY-----EQKLDISQLQILIV-GSDSCSME-----D---F-KTLVSRFGST--IRIVNSYGVTEACIDS
```

STOP and Think: If Marahiel had constructed this alignment, would he have been able to infer the eight amino acid-long signatures of the non-ribosomal code?

Below, we highlight the purple amino acids representing the non-ribosomal signatures. Although these signatures are grouped in eight conserved columns in Marahiel's alignment from the beginning of the chapter, only five of these columns have "survived" in the LCS alignment above, making it impossible to infer the non-ribosomal signatures:

```
YAFDL--G-YTCMFP--VLL-GGGELHIV---Q-K-E--T-YTAPDEIAHYIK--EHGITYI---KLTPSL-FHT
-AFDVSAGD----FARA-LLTGG-QL-IVCPNEVKMDPASLY-A---I---IKKYD--IT-IFEA--TPALV---

IVNTASFAFDANFE-----S-LR-LIVLGG-----EKIIPIDVIAFRK-M---YGHTEFI---NHYGPTEATIGA
IPLMEYIY-----EQKLDISQLQILIV-GSDSCSME-----D---F-KTLVSRFGST--IRIVNSYGVTEACIDS
```

The frivolous matches hiding the real evolutionary scenario have appeared because nothing stopped us from introducing an excessive number of indels when building an LCS. Recalling our original alignment game in which we rewarded matched symbols, we need some way of *penalizing* indels and mismatches. First, let's handle indels. Say that in addition to assigning matches a premium of +1, we assess each indel a penalty of -4. The top-scoring alignment of the A-domains gets closer to the biologically correct alignment, with six of the columns corresponding to correctly aligned signatures.

```
YAFDLGYTCMFP-VLL-GGGELHIV-QKETYTAPDEI-AHYIKEHGITYI-KLTPSLFHTIVNTASFAFDANFE
-AFDVS-AGDFARALLTGG-QL-IVCPNEVKMDPASLYA-IIKKYDIT-IFEATPAL--VIPLME-YIYEQKLD

-S-LR-LIVLGGEKIIPIDVIAFRKM---YGHTE-FINHYGPTEATIGA
ISQLQILIV-GSDSC-SME--DFKTLVSRFGSTIRIVNSYGVTEACIDS
```

Scoring matrices

To generalize the alignment scoring model, we still award +1 for matches, but we also penalize mismatches by some positive constant μ (the **mismatch penalty**) and indels by some positive constant σ (the **indel penalty**). As a result, the **score** of an alignment is equal to

$$\text{\# matches} - \mu \cdot \text{\# mismatches} - \sigma \cdot \text{\# indels}.$$

For example, with the parameters $\mu = 1$ and $\sigma = 2$, the alignment below will be assigned a score of -4:

```
A   T   -   G   T   T   A   T   A
A   T   C   G   T   -   C   -   C
+1  +1  -2  +1  +1  -2  -1  -2  -1
```

Biologists have further refined this cost function to allow for the fact that some mutations may be more likely than others, which calls for mismatches and indel penalties that differ depending on the specific symbols involved. We will extend the k-letter alphabet to include the space symbol and then construct a $(k+1) \times (k+1)$ **scoring matrix** *Score* holding the score of aligning every pair of symbols. The scoring matrix for comparing DNA sequences ($k = 4$) when all mismatches are penalized by μ and all indels are penalized by σ is shown below.

	A	C	G	T	–
A	+1	$-\mu$	$-\mu$	$-\mu$	$-\sigma$
C	$-\mu$	+1	$-\mu$	$-\mu$	$-\sigma$
G	$-\mu$	$-\mu$	+1	$-\mu$	$-\sigma$
T	$-\mu$	$-\mu$	$-\mu$	+1	$-\sigma$
–	$-\sigma$	$-\sigma$	$-\sigma$	$-\sigma$	

Although scoring matrices for DNA sequence comparison are usually defined only by the parameters μ and σ, scoring matrices for protein sequence comparison weight different mutations differently and become quite involved (see **DETOUR: PAM Scoring Matrices**). **PAGE 285**

From Global to Local Alignment

Global alignment

You should now be ready to modify the alignment graph to solve a generalized form of the alignment problem that takes a scoring matrix as input.

Global Alignment Problem:
Find a highest-scoring alignment of two strings as defined by a scoring matrix.

> **Input**: Two strings and a scoring matrix *Score*.
> **Output**: An alignment of the strings whose alignment score (as defined by *Score*) is maximized among all possible alignments of the strings.

5E

To solve the Global Alignment Problem, we still must find a longest path in the alignment graph after updating the edge weights to reflect the values in the scoring matrix

(Figure 5.18). Recalling that deletions correspond to vertical edges ($\downarrow$), insertions correspond to horizontal edges ($\rightarrow$), and matches/mismatches correspond to diagonal edges ($\searrow$/$\searrow$), we obtain the following recurrence for $s_{i,j}$, the length of a longest path from $(0,0)$ to (i,j):

$$s_{i,j} = \max \begin{cases} s_{i-1,j} & + \, Score(v_i, -) \\ s_{i,j-1} & + \, Score(-, w_j) \\ s_{i-1,j-1} & + \, Score(v_i, w_j). \end{cases}$$

When the match reward is +1, the mismatch penalty is μ, and the indel penalty is σ, the alignment recurrence can be written as follows:

$$s_{i,j} = \max \begin{cases} s_{i-1,j} & - \, \sigma \\ s_{i,j-1} & - \, \sigma \\ s_{i-1,j-1} + 1, & \text{if } v_i = w_j \\ s_{i-1,j-1} - \mu, & \text{if } v_i \neq w_j. \end{cases}$$

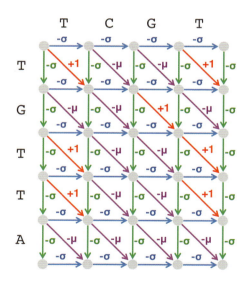

FIGURE 5.18 ALIGNMENTGRAPH(TGTTA, TCGT), with each edge colored according to whether it represents a match, mismatch, insertion, or deletion.

Limitations of global alignment

Analysis of **homeobox genes** offers an example of a problem for which global alignment may fail to reveal biologically relevant similarities. These genes regulate embryonic development and are present in a large variety of species, from flies to humans. Homeobox genes are long, and they differ greatly between species, but an approximately 60 amino acid-long region in each gene, called the **homeodomain**, is highly conserved. For instance, consider the mouse and human homeodomains below.

Mouse

...**AR**RSR**T**H**F**TK**F**QTD**I**LIE**AFE**KN**RFP**GIV**TREKLA**QQ**TG**I**P**ESRI**HI**WFQ**NRR**ARHPDPG...
...**AR**QKQ**T**F**I**TW**T**QKN**RL**VQ**AFE**RN**FP**DTA**TRKKLA**EQ**TG**L**Q**ESRI**QM**WFQ**KQ**RS**LYLKKS...

Human

The immediate question is how to find this conserved segment within the much longer genes and ignore the flanking areas, which exhibit little similarity. Global alignment seeks similarities between two strings across their entire length; however, when searching for homeodomains, we are looking for smaller, *local* regions of similarity and do not need to align the entire strings. For example, the global alignment below has 22 matches, 18 indels, and 2 mismatches, resulting in the score $22 - 18 - 2 = 2$ (if $\sigma = \mu = 1$):

GCC-**C**-A**GTC**-**TATGT**-**CAG**GGGG**CACG**--**A**-**G**CATGCACA-
GCCGCC-**GTC**G**T**-**T**-**T**TCAG----**CA**-**G**TTATGT-**T**-**CA**GAT

However, these sequences can be aligned differently (with 17 matches and 32 indels) based on a highly conserved interval represented by the substrings CAGTCTATGTCAG and CAGTTATGTTCAG:

---**G**----**C**-----**C**--**CAGT**C**TATG**-**TCAG**GGGG**C**ACGAGCA**T**GCACA
GCCG**CCGT**C**GTTTT**CAG**CAGT**-**TATG**T**TCAG**-----**A**------**T**-----

This alignment has fewer matches and a lower score of $17 - 32 = -15$, even though the conserved region of the alignment contributes a score of $12 - 2 = 10$, which is hardly an accident.

Figure 5.19 shows the two alignment paths corresponding to these two different alignments. The upper path, corresponding to the second alignment above, loses out because it contains many heavily penalized indels on either side of the diagonal corresponding to the conserved interval. As a result, global alignment outputs the biologically irrelevant lower path.

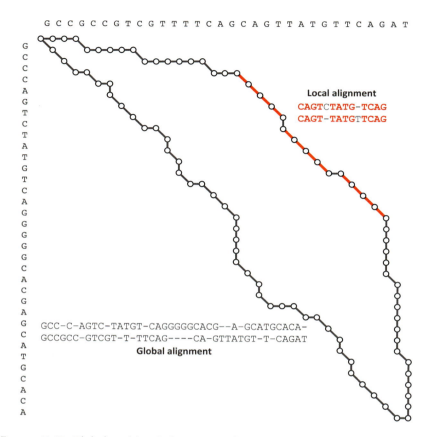

FIGURE 5.19 Global and local alignments of two DNA strings that share a highly conserved interval. The relevant alignment that captures this interval (upper path) loses to an irrelevant alignment (lower path), since the former incurs heavy indel penalties.

When biologically significant similarities are present in some parts of sequences v and w and absent from others, biologists attempt to ignore global alignment and instead align *substrings* of v and w, which yields a **local alignment** of the two strings. The problem of finding substrings that maximize the global alignment score over all substrings of v and w is called the **Local Alignment Problem**.

Local Alignment Problem:

Find the highest-scoring local alignment between two strings.

      Input: Strings v and w as well as a scoring matrix *Score*.
      Output: Substrings of v and w whose global alignment score (as defined by
      Score) is maximized among all substrings of v and w.

The straightforward way to solve the Local Alignment Problem is to find the longest path connecting every pair of nodes in the alignment graph (rather than just those connecting the source and sink, as in the Global Alignment Problem), and then to select the path having maximum weight over all these longest paths.

STOP and Think: What is the runtime of this approach?

Free taxi rides in the alignment graph

For a faster local alignment approach, imagine a "free taxi ride" from the source $(0,0)$ to the node representing the start node of the conserved (red) interval in Figure 5.19. Imagine also a free taxi ride from the end node of the conserved interval to the sink. If such rides were available (Figure 5.20), then you could reach the starting node of the conserved interval for free, instead of incurring heavy penalties as in global alignment. Then, you could travel along the conserved interval to its end node, accumulating positive match scores. Finally, you could take another free ride from the end node of the conserved interval to the sink. The resulting score of this ride is equal to the alignment score of only the conserved intervals, as desired.

    Connecting the source $(0,0)$ to every other node by adding a zero-weight edge and connecting every node to the sink (n, m) by a zero-weight edge will result in a DAG perfectly suited for solving the Local Alignment Problem (Figure 5.21). Because of free taxi rides, we no longer need to construct a longest path between every pair of nodes in the graph — the longest path from source to sink yields an optimal local alignment!

    The total number of edges in the graph in Figure 5.21 is $\mathcal{O}(|v| \cdot |w|)$, which is still small. Since the runtime of finding a longest path in a DAG is defined by the number of edges in the graph, the resulting local alignment algorithm will be fast. As for computing the values $s_{i,j}$, adding zero-weight edges from $(0,0)$ to every node has made the source node $(0,0)$ a predecessor of every node (i, j). Therefore, there are now four edges entering (i, j), which adds only one new term to the longest path recurrence relation:

$$s_{i,j} = \max \begin{cases} 0 \\ s_{i-1,j} & + Score(v_i, -) \\ s_{i,j-1} & + Score(-, w_j) \\ s_{i-1,j-1} + Score(v_i, w_j) \end{cases}$$

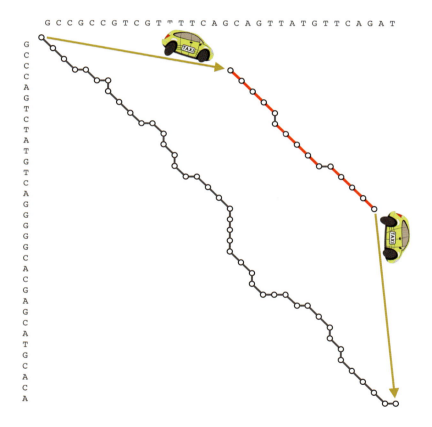

FIGURE 5.20 Modifying Figure 5.19 by adding "free taxi ride" edges (having weight 0) connecting the source to the start node of the conserved interval and connecting the end node of the conserved interval to the sink. These new edges allow us to score only the local alignment containing the conserved interval.

Also, because node (n, m) now has every other node as a predecessor, $s_{n,m}$ will be equal to the largest value of $s_{i,j}$ over the entire alignment graph.

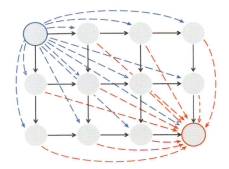

FIGURE 5.21 The local alignment algorithm introduces zero-weight edges (shown by blue dashed lines) connecting the source $(0, 0)$ to every other node in the alignment graph, as well as zero-weight edges (shown by red dashed lines) connecting every node to the sink node.

You might still be wondering why we are allowed to free taxi rides through the alignment graph. The point is that you are in charge of designing whatever Manhattan-like DAG you like, as long as it adequately models the specific alignment problem at hand. Transformations like free taxi rides will become a common theme in this chapter. Various alignment problems can be solved by constructing an appropriate DAG with as few edges as possible (to minimize runtime), assigning edge weights to model the requirements of the problem, and then finding a longest path in this DAG.

The Changing Faces of Sequence Alignment

In this section, we will describe three sequence comparison problems and let you apply what you have already learned to solve them. Hint: the idea is to frame each problem as an instance of the Longest Path in a DAG Problem.

Edit distance

In 1966, Vladimir Levenshtein introduced the notion of the **edit distance** between two strings as the minimum number of **edit operations** needed to transform one string into another. Here, an edit operation is the insertion, deletion, or substitution of a single symbol. For example, TGCATAT can be transformed into ATCCGAT with five edit operations, implying that the edit distance between these strings is at most 5.

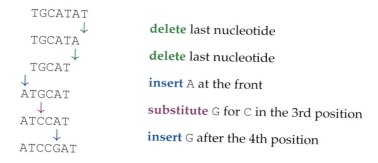

STOP

STOP and Think: Can you transform TGCATAT into ATCCGAT using a smaller number of operations?

In fact, the edit distance between TGCATAT and ATCCGAT is 4:

```
          TGCATAT
          ↓                insert A at the front
          ATGCATAT
          ↓                delete the 6th nucleotide
          ATGCAAT
          ↓                substitute A for G in the 5th position
          ATGCGAT
          ↓                substitute G for C in the 3rd position
          ATCCGAT
```

Levenshtein introduced edit distance but did not describe an algorithm for computing it, which we leave to you.

Edit Distance Problem:

Find the edit distance between two strings.

> **Input:** Two strings.
> **Output:** The edit distance between these strings.

Fitting alignment

Say that we wish to compare the approximately 20,000 amino acid-long NRP synthetase from *Bacillus brevis* with the approximately 600 amino acid-long A-domain from *Streptomyces roseosporus*, the bacterium that produces the powerful antibiotic Daptomycin. We hope to find a region within the longer protein sequence *v* that has high similarity with all of the shorter sequence *w*. Global alignment will not work because it tries to align all of *v* to all of *w*; local alignment will not work because it tries to align substrings of both *v* and *w*. Thus, we have a distinct alignment application called the **Fitting Alignment Problem**.

"Fitting" *w* to *v* requires finding a substring *v'* of *v* that maximizes the global alignment score between *v'* and *w* among all substrings of *v*. For example, the best global, local, and fitting alignments of *v* = GTAGGCTTAAGGTTA and *w* = TAGATA are shown below (with mismatch and indel penalties equal to 1).

Global	Local	Fitting
GTAGGCTTAAGGTTA	GTAG**GCTTAAGGTTA**	G**TAGGCTTA**AGGTTA
-**TAG**----**A**---**T**-**A**	**TAGATA**	**TAGA**--**TA**

Note that the optimal local alignment (with score 3) is not a valid fitting alignment. On the other hand, the score of the optimal global alignment (**6** − **9** = −3) is smaller than that of the best fitting alignment (**5** − **1** − **2** = +2).

Fitting Alignment Problem:
Construct a highest-scoring fitting alignment between two strings.

> **Input**: Strings *v* and *w* as well as a scoring matrix *Score*.
> **Output**: A highest-scoring fitting alignment of *v* and *w* as defined by *Score*.

Overlap alignment

In Chapter 3, we discussed how to use overlapping reads to assemble a genome, a problem that was complicated by errors in reads. Aligning the ends of the hypothetical reads shown below offers a way to find overlaps between error-prone reads.

ATGCA**TGCCGG**

T-**CC**-**G**AAAC

An **overlap alignment** of strings $v = v_1 \ldots v_n$ and $w = w_1 \ldots w_m$ is a global alignment of a suffix of v with a prefix of w. An optimal overlap alignment of strings v and w maximizes the global alignment score between an i-suffix of v and a j-prefix of w (i.e., between $v_i \ldots v_n$ and $w_1 \ldots w_j$) among all possible i and j.

Overlap Alignment Problem:

Construct a highest-scoring overlap alignment between two strings.

Input: Two strings and a scoring matrix *Score*.

Output: A highest-scoring overlap alignment between the two strings as defined by *Score*.

Penalizing Insertions and Deletions in Sequence Alignment

Affine gap penalties

We have seen that introducing mismatch and indel penalties can produce more biologically adequate global alignments. However, even with this more robust scoring model, the A-domain alignment that we previously constructed (with indel penalty $\sigma = 4$) still reveals only six of the eight conserved purple columns corresponding to the non-ribosomal signatures:

```
YAFDLGYTCMFP-VLL-GGGELHIV-QKETYTAPDEI-AHYIKEHGITYI-KLTPSLFHTIVNTASFAFDANFE
-AFDVS-AGDFARALLTGG-QL-IVCPNEVKMDPASLYA-IIKKYDIT-IFEATPAL--VIPLME-YIYEQKLD

-S-LR-LIVLGGEKIIPIDVIAFRKM---YGHTE-FINHYGPTEATIGA
ISQLQILIV-GSDSC-SME--DFKTLVSRFGSTIRIVNSYGVTEACIDS
```

STOP and Think: Would increasing the indel penalty from $\sigma = 4$ to $\sigma = 10$ reveal the biologically correct alignment?

In our previously defined **linear scoring model**, if σ is the penalty for the insertion or deletion of a single symbol, then $\sigma \cdot k$ is the penalty for the insertion or deletion of an interval of k symbols. This cost model unfortunately results in inadequate scoring for biological sequences. Mutations are often caused by errors in DNA replication that insert or delete an entire interval of k nucleotides as a single event instead of as k independent insertions or deletions. Thus, penalizing such an indel by $\sigma \cdot k$ represents an excessive penalty. For example, the alignment on the right is more adequate than the alignment on the left, but they would currently receive the same score.

GATCCAG   GATCCAG

GA–C–AG   GA––CAG

A **gap** is a contiguous sequence of space symbols in a row of an alignment. One way to score gaps more appropriately is to define an **affine penalty** for a gap of length k as $\sigma + \epsilon \cdot (k - 1)$, where σ is the **gap opening penalty**, assessed to the first symbol in the gap, and ϵ is the **gap extension penalty**, assessed to each additional symbol in the gap. We typically select ϵ to be smaller than σ so that the affine penalty for a gap of length k is smaller than the penalty for k independent single-nucleotide indels ($\sigma \cdot k$). For example, if $\sigma = 5$ and $\epsilon = 1$, then the alignment on the left above is penalized by $2\sigma = 10$, whereas the alignment on the right above is only penalized by $\sigma + \epsilon = 6$.

Alignment with Affine Gap Penalties Problem:

Construct a highest-scoring global alignment of two strings (with affine gap penalties).

> **Input**: Two strings, a scoring matrix *Score*, and numbers σ and ϵ.
> **Output**: A highest scoring global alignment between these strings, as defined by *Score* and by the gap opening and extension penalties σ and ϵ.

STOP and Think: How would you modify the alignment graph to solve this problem?

Figure 5.22 illustrates how affine gap penalties can be modeled in the alignment graph by introducing a new "long" edge for each gap. Since we do not know in advance where gaps should be located, we need to add edges accounting for every possible gap. Thus, affine gap penalties can be accommodated by adding all possible vertical and horizontal edges in the alignment graph to represent all possible gaps. Specifically, we add edges connecting (i, j) to both $(i + k, j)$ and $(i, j + k)$ with weights $\sigma + \epsilon \cdot (k - 1)$ for all possible gap sizes k, as illustrated in Figure 5.23. For two sequences of length n, the number of edges in the resulting alignment graph modeling affine gap penalties increases from $\mathcal{O}(n^2)$ to $\mathcal{O}(n^3)$.

STOP and Think: Can you design a DAG with just $\mathcal{O}(n^2)$ edges to solve the Alignment with Affine Gap Penalties Problem?

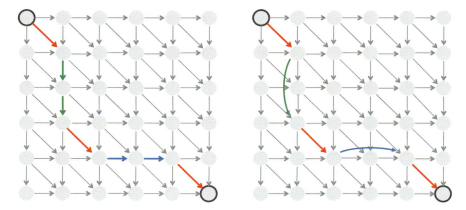

FIGURE 5.22 Representing gaps in the alignment graph on the left as "long" insertion and deletion edges in the alignment graph on the right. For a gap of length k, the weight of the corresponding long edge is equal to $\sigma + \varepsilon \cdot (k - 1)$.

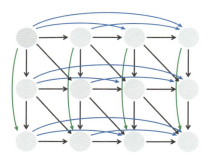

FIGURE 5.23 Adding edges corresponding to indels for all possible gap sizes adds a large number of edges to the alignment graph.

Building Manhattan on three levels

The trick to decreasing the number of edges in the DAG for the Alignment with Affine Gap Penalties Problem is to *increase* the number of nodes. To this end, we will build an alignment graph on three levels; for each node (i, j), we will construct three different nodes: $(i, j)_{\text{lower}}$, $(i, j)_{\text{middle}}$, and $(i, j)_{\text{upper}}$. The middle level will contain diagonal edges of weight $Score(v_i, w_j)$ representing matches and mismatches. The lower level will have only vertical edges with weight $-\epsilon$ to represent gap extensions in v, and the upper level will have only horizontal edges with weights $-\epsilon$ to represent gap extensions in w (Figure 5.24).

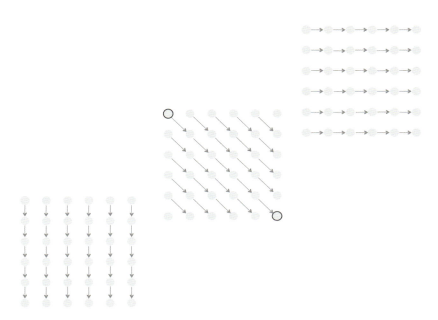

FIGURE 5.24 Building a three-level graph for alignment with affine gap penalties. The lower level corresponds to gap extensions in v, the middle level corresponds to matches and mismatches, and the upper level corresponds to gap extensions in w.

Life in such a three-level city would be difficult because there is currently no way to move between different levels. To address this issue, we add edges responsible for opening and closing a gap. To model gap opening, we connect each node $(i, j)_{\text{middle}}$ to both $(i + 1, j)_{\text{lower}}$ and $(i, j + 1)_{\text{upper}}$; we then weight these edges with $-\sigma$. Closing gaps does not carry a penalty, and so we introduce zero-weight edges connecting nodes $(i, j)_{\text{lower}}$ and $(i, j)_{\text{upper}}$ with the corresponding node $(i, j)_{\text{middle}}$. As a result, a gap of length k starts and ends at the middle level and is charged $-\sigma$ for the first symbol, $-\epsilon$ for each subsequent symbol, and 0 to close the gap, producing a total penalty of $\sigma + \epsilon \cdot (k - 1)$, as desired. Figure 5.25 illustrates how the path in Figure 5.22 traverses the three-level alignment graph.

The DAG in Figure 5.25 may be complicated, but it uses only $\mathcal{O}(n \cdot m)$ edges for sequences of length n and m, and a longest path in this graph still constructs an optimal alignment with affine gap penalties. The three-level alignment graph translates into the system of three recurrence relations shown below. Here, $lower_{i,j}$, $middle_{i,j}$, and $upper_{i,j}$ are the lengths of the longest paths from the source node to $(i,j)_{\text{lower}}$, $(i,j)_{\text{middle}}$, and $(i,j)_{\text{upper}}$, respectively.

$$lower_{i,j} = \max \begin{cases} lower_{i-1,j} & -\epsilon \\ middle_{i-1,j} & -\sigma \end{cases}$$

$$middle_{i,j} = \max \begin{cases} lower_{i,j} \\ middle_{i-1,j-1} + Score(v_i, w_j) \\ upper_{i,j} \end{cases}$$

$$upper_{i,j} = \max \begin{cases} upper_{i,j-1} & -\epsilon \\ middle_{i,j-1} & -\sigma \end{cases}$$

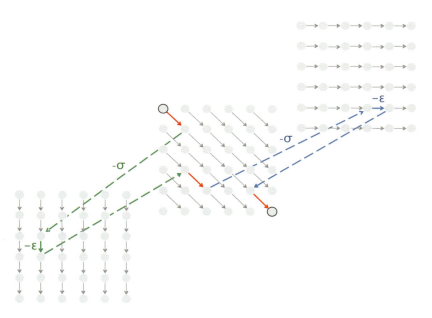

FIGURE 5.25 Every path from source to sink in the standard alignment graph shown in Figure 5.22 corresponds to a path from source to sink in the three-level graph of the same length (and vice-versa). Every node in the middle level has one outgoing (blue) edge to the upper level and one outgoing (green) edge to the lower level, both represented by dashed edges and having weight equal to the gap opening penalty. Every node in the middle level also has one incoming blue edge from the upper level and one incoming green edge from the lower level, both represented by dashed edges and having zero weight (these edges close a gap).

The variable $lower_{i,j}$ computes the score of an optimal alignment between the i-prefix of v and the j-prefix of w ending with a deletion (i.e., a gap in w), whereas the variable $upper_{i,j}$ computes the score of an optimal alignment of these prefixes ending with an insertion (i.e., a gap in v), and the variable $middle_{i,j}$ computes the score of an optimal alignment ending with a match or mismatch. The first term in the recurrences for $lower_{i,j}$ and $upper_{i,j}$ corresponds to extending the gap, whereas the second term corresponds to initiating the gap.

STOP and Think: Compute an optimal alignment with affine gap penalties for the A-domains considered in the beginning of this section. How does varying the gap opening and extension penalties affect the quality of the alignment?

Space-Efficient Sequence Alignment

Computing alignment score using linear memory

To introduce fitting alignments, we used the example of aligning a 20,000 amino acid-long NRP synthetase from *Bacillus brevis* against a 600 amino acid-long A-domain from *Streptomyces roseosporus*. However, you may not be able to construct this alignment on your computer because the memory required to store the dynamic programming matrix is substantial.

The runtime of the dynamic programming algorithm for aligning two strings of lengths n and m is proportional to the number of edges in their alignment graph, which is $\mathcal{O}(n \cdot m)$. The memory required by this algorithm is also $\mathcal{O}(n \cdot m)$, since we need to store the backtracking references. We will now demonstrate how to construct an alignment in just $\mathcal{O}(n)$ space at the expense of doubling the runtime, meaning that the runtime is still $\mathcal{O}(n \cdot m)$.

A **divide-and-conquer algorithm** often works when a solution to a large problem can be constructed from solutions of smaller problem instances. Such a strategy proceeds in two phases. The **divide** phase splits a problem instance into smaller instances and solves them; the **conquer** phase stitches the smaller solutions into a solution to the original problem (see **DETOUR: Divide-and-Conquer Algorithms**). **PAGE 287**

Before we proceed with the divide-and-conquer algorithm for linear-space alignment, note that if we only wish to compute the *score* of an alignment rather than the alignment itself, then the space required can easily be reduced to just twice the number of nodes in a single column of the alignment graph, or $\mathcal{O}(n)$. This reduction derives from the observation that the only values needed to compute the alignment scores in column j are the alignment scores in column $j - 1$. Therefore, the alignment scores in the columns before column $j - 1$ can be discarded when computing the alignment scores for column j, as illustrated in Figure 5.26. Unfortunately, finding the longest path requires us to store an entire matrix of backtracking pointers, which causes the quadratic space requirement. The idea of the space reduction technique is that we don't need to store any backtracking pointers if we are willing to spend a little more time.

STOP and Think: How could we construct an alignment without storing any backtracking pointers?

The Middle Node Problem

Given strings $v = v_1 \ldots v_n$ and $w = w_1 \ldots w_m$, define $middle = \lfloor m/2 \rfloor$. The **middle column** of ALIGNMENTGRAPH(v, w) is the column containing all nodes $(i, middle)$ for $0 \leq i \leq n$. A longest path from source to sink in the alignment graph must cross the middle column somewhere, and our first task is to figure out where using only $\mathcal{O}(n)$ memory. We refer to a node on this longest path belonging to the middle column as a **middle node**. (Note that different longest paths may have different middle nodes, and a given longest path may have more than one middle node.) In Figure 5.27 (top left), $middle = 3$, and the alignment path crosses the middle column at the (unique) middle node $(4, 3)$.

The key observation is that we can find a longest path's middle node without having to construct this path in the alignment graph. We will classify a path from the source to the sink as an *i-path* if it passes through the middle column at row i. For example, the highlighted path in Figure 5.27 is a 4-path. For each i between 0 and n, we would like to find the length of a longest i-path (denoted LENGTH(i)) because the largest value of LENGTH(i) over all i will reveal a middle node.

Let FROMSOURCE(i) denote the length of the longest path from the source ending at $(i, middle)$ and TOSINK(i) denote the length of the longest path from $(i, middle)$ to the sink. Certainly,

$$\text{LENGTH}(i) = \text{FROMSOURCE}(i) + \text{TOSINK}(i),$$

and so we need to compute FROMSOURCE(i) and TOSINK(i) for each i.

STOP and Think: Can you compute FROMSOURCE(i) and TOSINK(i) in linear space? How much time would it take?

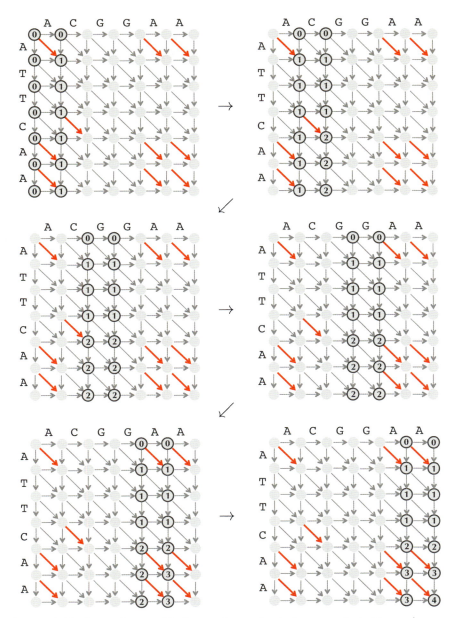

FIGURE 5.26 Computing an LCS alignment score by storing scores in just two columns of the alignment graph.

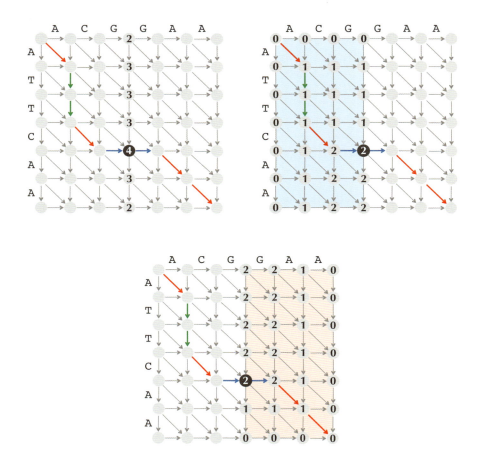

FIGURE 5.27 (Top left) The alignment graph of ATTCAA and ACGGAA, with the optimal LCS alignment path highlighted. The number inside each node (i, *middle*) in the middle column is equal to LENGTH(i). The node maximizing LENGTH(i) is a middle node (multiple middle nodes may exist); the middle node in this graph is colored black. (Top right) Computing FROMSOURCE(i) for all i can be done in $\mathcal{O}(n)$ space and $\mathcal{O}(n \cdot m/2)$ time. (Bottom) Computing TOSINK(i) for all i can also be done in $\mathcal{O}(n)$ space and $\mathcal{O}(n \cdot m/2)$ time; this requires reversing the direction of all edges and treating the sink as the source.

The value of FROMSOURCE(i) is simply $s_{i,middle}$, which we already know can be computed in linear space. Thus, the values of FROMSOURCE(i) for all i are stored as $s_{i,middle}$ in the middle column of the alignment graph, and computing them requires sweeping through half of the alignment graph from column 0 to the middle column. Since we need to explore roughly half the edges of the alignment graph to compute FROMSOURCE(i), we say that the runtime needed for computing all values FROMSOURCE(i) is proportional to half of the "area" of the alignment graph, or $n \cdot m/2$ (Figure 5.27 (top right)).

Computing TOSINK(i) is equivalent to finding the longest path from the sink to ($i, middle$) if all the edge directions are reversed. Instead of reversing the edges, we can reverse the *strings* $v = v_1 \ldots v_n$ and $w = w_1 \ldots w_m$ and find $s_{n-i, m-middle}$ in the alignment graph for $v_n \ldots v_1$ and $w_m \ldots w_1$. Computing TOSINK(i) is therefore similar to computing FROMSOURCE(i) and can also be done in $\mathcal{O}(n)$ space and runtime proportional to $n \cdot m/2$, or half of the area of the alignment graph (Figure 5.27 (bottom)). In total, we can compute all values LENGTH(i) = FROMSOURCE(i) + TOSINK(i) in linear space with runtime proportional to $n \cdot m/2 + n \cdot m/2 = n \cdot m$, which is the total area of the alignment graph.

It looks like we have wasted a lot of time just to find a single node on the alignment path! You may think that this approach is doomed to fail because we have already spent $\mathcal{O}(n \cdot m)$ time (the entire area of the alignment graph) to gain very little information.

A surprisingly fast and memory-efficient alignment algorithm

Once we have found a middle node, we automatically know two rectangles through which a longest path must travel on either side of this node. As shown in Figure 5.28, one of these rectangles consists of all nodes above and to the left of the middle node, whereas the other rectangle consists of all nodes below and to the right of the middle node. Thus, the area of the two highlighted rectangles is half the total area of the alignment graph.

We can now *divide* the problem of finding the longest path from $(0,0)$ to (n, m) into two subproblems: finding a longest path from $(0,0)$ to the middle node; and finding a longest path from the middle node to (n, m). The *conquer* step finds the two middle nodes within the smaller rectangles, which can be done in time proportional to the sum of the areas of these rectangles, or $n \cdot m/2$ (Figure 5.28 (right)). Note that we have now reconstructed three nodes of an optimal path. In the next iteration, we will divide and conquer to find four middle nodes in time equal to the sum of the areas of the even smaller blue rectangles, which have total area $n \cdot m/4$ (Figure 5.29). We have now reconstructed nearly all nodes of an optimal alignment path!

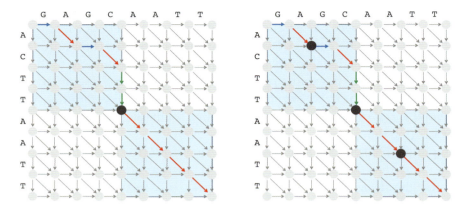

FIGURE 5.28 (Left) A middle node (shown in black) defines two highlighted rectangles and illustrates that an optimal path passing through this middle node must travel within these rectangles. We can therefore eliminate the remaining parts of the alignment graph from consideration for an optimal alignment path. (Right) Finding middle nodes (shown as two more black circles) within previously identified rectangles.

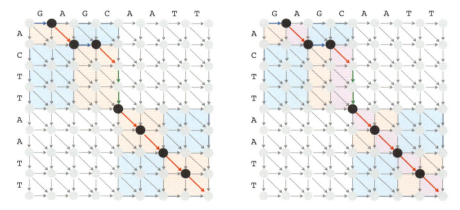

FIGURE 5.29 Finding middle nodes (highlighted as black circles) within previously identified blue rectangles.

STOP and Think: How much time would it take to find all nodes on an optimal alignment path?

In general, at each new step before the final step, we double the number of middle nodes found while halving the runtime required to find middle nodes. Proceeding in this way, we will find middle nodes of all rectangles (and thus construct the entire alignment!) in time equal to

$$n \cdot m + \frac{n \cdot m}{2} + \frac{n \cdot m}{4} + \cdots < 2 \cdot n \cdot m = \mathcal{O}(n \cdot m).$$

Thus, we have arrived at a linear-time alignment algorithm that requires only linear space.

The Middle Edge Problem

Instead of asking you to implement a divide-and-conquer algorithm based on finding a middle node, we will use a more elegant approach based on finding a **middle edge**, or an edge in an optimal alignment path starting at the middle node (more than one middle edge may exist for a given middle node). Once we find the middle edge, we again know two rectangles through which the longest path must travel on either side of the middle edge. But now these two rectangles take up even less than half of the area of the alignment graph (Figure 5.30), which is an advantage of selecting the middle edge instead of the middle node.

Middle Edge in Linear Space Problem:

Find a middle edge in the alignment graph in linear space.

Input: Two strings and a scoring matrix *Score*.
Output: A middle edge in the alignment graph of these strings (where the edge lengths are defined by *Score*).

The pseudocode below for **LINEARSPACEALIGNMENT** describes how to recursively find a longest path in the alignment graph constructed for a substring $v_{top+1} \cdots v_{bottom}$ of v and a substring $w_{left+1} \cdots w_{right}$ of w. **LINEARSPACEALIGNMENT** calls the function MIDDLENODE($top, bottom, left, right$), which returns the coordinate i of the middle node (i, j) defined by the substrings $v_{top+1} \cdots v_{bottom}$ and $w_{left+1} \cdots w_{right}$. The algorithm also calls MIDDLEEDGE($top, bottom, left, right$), which returns "→" , "↓", or "↘" depending on whether the middle edge is horizontal, vertical, or diagonal. The linear-space alignment of strings v and w is constructed by calling **LINEARSPACEALIGNMENT**$(0, n, 0, m)$. The case *left = right* describes the alignment of an empty string against the string $v_{top+1} \cdots v_{bottom}$, which is trivially computed as the score of a gap formed by *bottom − top* vertical edges.

LINEARSPACEALIGNMENT(*top, bottom, left, right*)
    if *left = right*
        return alignment formed by *bottom − top* vertical edges
    if *top = bottom*
        return alignment formed by *right − left* horizontal edges
    middle ← ⌊(*left + right*)/2⌋
    midNode ← MIDDLENODE(*top, bottom, left, right*)
    midEdge ← MIDDLEEDGE(*top, bottom, left, right*)
    LINEARSPACEALIGNMENT(*top, midNode, left, middle*)
    output *midEdge*
    if *midEdge* = "→" or *midEdge* = "↘"
        middle ← *middle* + 1
    if *midEdge* = "↓" or *midEdge* = "↘"
        midNode ← *midNode* + 1
    LINEARSPACEALIGNMENT(*midNode, bottom, middle, right*)

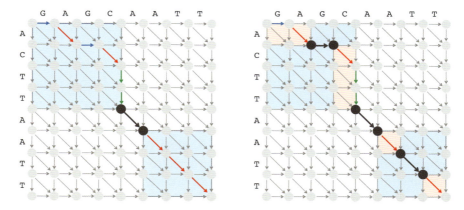

FIGURE 5.30 (Left) A middle edge (shown in bold) starts at the middle node (shown as a black circle). The optimal path travels inside the first highlighted rectangle, passes the middle edge, and travels inside the second highlighted rectangle afterwards. We can eliminate the remaining parts of the alignment graph, which takes up over half of the area formed by the graph, from further consideration. (Right) Finding middle edges (shown in bold) within previously identified rectangles.

Epilogue: Multiple Sequence Alignment

Building a three-dimensional Manhattan

Amino acid sequences of proteins performing the same function are likely to be somewhat similar, but these similarities may be elusive in the case of distant species. You now possess an arsenal of algorithms for aligning pairs of sequences, but if sequence similarity is weak, pairwise alignment may not identify biologically related sequences. However, simultaneous comparison of many sequences often allows us to find similarities that pairwise sequence comparison fails to reveal. Bioinformaticians sometimes say that while pairwise alignment whispers, multiple alignment shouts.

We are now ready to use pairwise sequence analysis to build up our intuition for comparison of multiple sequences. In our three-way alignment of A-domains from the introduction, we found 19 conserved columns:

```
YAFDLGYTCMFPVLLGGGELHIVQKETYTAPDEIAHYIKEHGITYIKLTPSLFHTIVNTA
-AFDVSAGDFARALLTGGQLIVCPNEVKMDPASLYAIIKKYDITIFEATPALVIPLMEYI
IAFDASSWEIYAPLLNGGTVVCIDYYTTIDIKALEAVFKQHHIRGAMLPPALLKQCLVSA

SFAFDANFESLRLIVLGGEKIIPIDVIAFRKMYGHTE-FINHYGPTEATIGA
-YEQKLDISQLQILIVGSDSCSMEDFKTLVSRFGSTIRIVNSYGVTEACIDS
----PTMISSLEILFAAGDRLSSQDAILARRAVGSGV-Y-NAYGPTENTVLS
```

However, similarities between A-domains are not limited to these 19 columns, as we can find $10 + 9 + 12 = 31$ semi-conservative columns, each of which has two matching amino acids:

```
YAFDLGYTCMFPVLLGGGELHIVQKETYTAPDEIAHYIKEHGITYIKLTPSLFHTIVNTA
-AFDVSAGDFARALLTGGQLIVCPNEVKMDPASLYAIIKKYDITIFEATPALVIPLMEYI
IAFDASSWEIYAPLLNGGTVVCIDYYTTIDIKALEAVFKQHHIRGAMLPPALLKQCLVSA

SFAFDANFESLRLIVLGGEKIIPIDVIAFRKMYGHTE-FINHYGPTEATIGA
-YEQKLDISQLQILIVGSDSCSMEDFKTLVSRFGSTIRIVNSYGVTEACIDS
----PTMISSLEILFAAGDRLSSQDAILARRAVGSGV-Y-NAYGPTENTVLS
```

A **multiple alignment** of t strings $v^1, \ldots, v^t$, also called a **t-way alignment**, is specified by a matrix having t rows, where the i-th row contains the symbols of v^i in order, interspersed with space symbols. We also assume that no column in a multiple alignment contains only space symbols. In the 3-way alignment below, we have highlighted the most popular symbol in each column using upper case letters:

A	T	–	G	T	T	a	T	A
A	g	C	G	a	T	C	–	A
A	T	C	G	T	–	C	T	c

0	1	2	2	3	4	5	6	7	8
0	1	2	3	4	5	6	7	7	8
0	1	2	3	4	5	5	6	7	8

The multiple alignment matrix is a generalization of the pairwise alignment matrix to more than two sequences. The three arrays shown below this alignment record the respective number of symbols in **ATGTTATA**, **AGCGATCA**, and **ATCGTCTC** encountered up to a given position. Together, these three arrays correspond to a path in a three-dimensional grid:

$$(0, 0, 0) \to (1, 1, 1) \to (2, 2, 2) \to (2, 3, 3) \to (3, 4, 4) \to (4, 5, 5) \to (5, 6, 5) \to$$
$$(6, 7, 6) \to (7, 7, 7) \to (8, 8, 8)$$

As the alignment graph for two sequences is a grid of squares, the alignment graph for three sequences is a grid of cubes. Every node in the 3-way alignment graph has up to seven incoming edges, as shown in Figure 5.31.

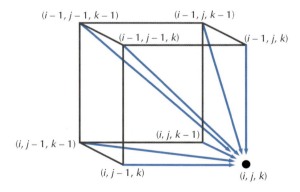

FIGURE 5.31 One cube making up the alignment graph for three sequences. Each node in the alignment graph for three sequences has up to seven incoming edges.

The score of a multiple alignment is defined as the sum of scores of the alignment columns (or, equivalently, weights of edges in the alignment path), with an optimal alignment being one that maximizes this score. In the case of an amino acid alphabet, we can use a very general scoring method that is defined by a t-dimensional matrix containing 21^t entries that describes the scores of all possible combinations of t symbols (representing 20 amino acids and the space symbol). See **DETOUR: Scoring Multiple** **PAGE 289** **Alignments**. Intuitively, we should reward more conserved columns with higher scores. For example, in the Multiple Longest Common Subsequence Problem, the score of a column is equal to 1 if all of the column's symbols are identical, and 0 if even one symbol disagrees.

Multiple Alignment Problem:

Find the highest-scoring alignment between multiple strings under a given scoring matrix.

> **Input**: A collection of t strings and a t-dimensional matrix *Score*.
> **Output**: A multiple alignment of these strings whose score (as defined by the matrix *Score*) is maximized among all possible alignments of these strings.

A straightforward dynamic programming algorithm applied to the t-dimensional alignment graph solves the Multiple Alignment Problem for t strings. For three sequences v, w, and u, we define $s_{i,j,k}$ as the length of the longest path from the source $(0,0,0)$ to node (i,j,k) in the alignment graph. The recurrence for $s_{i,j,k}$ in the three-dimensional case is similar to the recurrence for pairwise alignment:

$$s_{i,j,k} = \max \begin{cases} s_{i-1,j,k} & + \ Score(v_i,-,-) \\ s_{i,j-1,k} & + \ Score(-,w_j,-) \\ s_{i,j,k-1} & + \ Score(-,-,u_k) \\ s_{i-1,j-1,k} & + \ Score(v_i,w_j,-) \\ s_{i-1,j,k-1} & + \ Score(v_i,-,u_k) \\ s_{i,j-1,k-1} & + \ Score(-,w_j,u_k) \\ s_{i-1,j-1,k-1} & + \ Score(v_i,w_j,u_k) \end{cases}$$

In the case of t sequences of length n, the alignment graph consists of approximately n^t nodes, and each node has up to $2^t - 1$ incoming edges, yielding a total runtime of $\mathcal{O}(n^t \cdot 2^t)$. As t grows, the dynamic programming algorithm becomes impractical. Many heuristics for suboptimal multiple alignments have been proposed to address this runtime bottleneck.

A greedy multiple alignment algorithm

Note that the multiple alignment

AT—GTTaTA
AgCGaTC—A
ATCGT—CTc

induces three pairwise alignments:

AT—GTTaTA AT—GTTaTA C—AAgCGaT
AgCGaTC—A ATCGT—CTc ATCGT—CTc

But can we work in the opposite direction, combining optimal pairwise alignments into a multiple alignment?

STOP and Think:

1. Does an optimal multiple alignment induce optimal pairwise alignments?

2. Try combining the pairwise alignments below into a multiple alignment of the strings CCCCTTTT, TTTTGGGG, and GGGGCCCC.

CCCCTTTT———— ————CCCCTTTT TTTTGGGG————
————TTTTGGGG GGGGCCCC———— ————GGGGCCCC

Unfortunately, we cannot always combine optimal pairwise alignments into a multiple alignment because some pairwise alignments may be incompatible. Indeed, the first pairwise alignment in the above question implies that CCCC occurs before TTTT in the multiple alignment constructed from these three pairwise alignments. The third pairwise alignment implies that TTTT occurs before GGGG in the multiple alignment. But the second pairwise alignment implies that GGGG occurs before CCCC in the multiple alignment. Thus, CCCC must occur before TTTT, which must occur before GGGG, which must occur before CCCC, a contradiction.

To avoid incompatibility, some multiple alignment algorithms attempt to greedily construct a multiple alignment from pairwise alignments that are not necessarily optimal. The greedy heuristic starts by selecting the two strings having the highest scoring pairwise alignment (among all possible pairs of strings) and then uses this pairwise alignment as a building block for iteratively adding one string at a time to the growing multiple alignment. We align the two closest strings at the first step because they often provide the best chance of building a reliable multiple alignment. For the same reason, we then select the string having maximum score against the current alignment at each stage. But what does it mean to align a string against an alignment of other strings?

An alignment of nucleotide sequences with k columns can be represented as a $4 \times k$ profile matrix like the one in Figure 5.32, which holds the nucleotide frequencies from each column (amino acid alignments are represented by $20 \times k$ profile matrices). The greedy multiple alignment heuristic adds a string to the current alignment by constructing a pairwise alignment between the string and the profile of the current alignment. As a result, the problem of constructing a multiple alignment of t sequences is reduced to constructing $t - 1$ pairwise alignments.

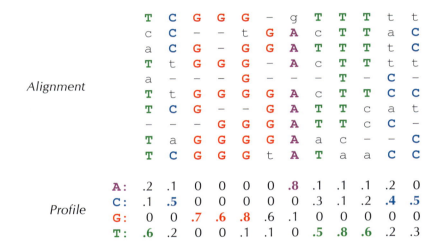

FIGURE 5.32 A profile matrix for a multiple alignment of ten sequences. Each column of the profile matrix sums to 1 minus the frequency of the space symbol. The most popular nucleotides in each column are shown as uppercase colored letters.

STOP and Think: Design an algorithm for aligning a string against a profile matrix. How would you score the columns in such an alignment?

Although greedy multiple alignment algorithms work well for similar sequences, their performance deteriorates for dissimilar sequences because greedy methods may be misled by a spurious pairwise alignment. If the first two sequences picked for building a multiple alignment are aligned in a way that is incompatible with the optimal multiple alignment, then the error in this initial pairwise alignment will propagate all the way through to the final multiple alignment.

After learning how to align multiple sequences, you are now ready to solve a challenge problem that is comparable to the task that Marahiel and his collaborators faced in 1999.

> **CHALLENGE PROBLEM:** In 1999, Marahiel derived the non-ribosomal code for only 14 of the 20 proteinogenic amino acids (`Ala, Asn, Asp, Cys, Gln, Glu, Ile, Leu, Phe, Pro, Ser, Thr, Tyr, Val`) because he lacked A-domain sequences for the remaining 6 amino acids. With the availability of many more A-domains, you now have the chance to fill in the gaps in Marahiel's original paper. Construct the multiple alignment of 397 A-domains, reveal the conservative columns in this alignment, and make your best guess about the signatures encoding all 20 proteinogenic amino acids based on Marahiel's alignment.

Detours

Fireflies and the non-ribosomal code

When Marahiel started his groundbreaking work on decoding the non-ribosomal code in the late 1990s, 160 A-domains had already been sequenced, and the amino acids that they encode had been experimentally identified. However, it was still not clear exactly how each A-domain encoded a specific amino acid.

We showed an alignment of three A-domain intervals in the main chapter, but Marahiel actually aligned all of the 160 identified A-domains in order to reveal the conservative core. Yet it still remained unclear which columns in this alignment defined the non-ribosomal signatures.

Help came from an unusual ally: *Photinus pyralis*, the most common species of firefly. Fireflies produce an enzyme called **luciferase** that helps them emit light to attract mates at night. Different species have different glow patterns, and females respond to males from the same species by identifying the color, duration, and intensity of their flash.

What do fireflies have to do with the non-ribosomal code? Firefly luciferase belongs to a class of enzymes called **adenylate-forming enzymes**, which share similarities with adenylation domains. For this reason, when Peter Brick published the three-dimensional structure of firefly luciferase in 1996, Marahiel was quick to take notice. In 1997, he and Brick joined forces and used firefly luciferase as a scaffold to reconstruct the first three-dimensional structure of an A-domain, which coded for phenylalanine (Phe); it is worth noting that this A-domain belonged to an NRP synthetase encoding *Gramicidin Soviet*, the first mass-produced antibiotic.

Marahiel and Brick actually constructed the three-dimensional structure of a larger complex containing both the A-domain and Phe. This three-dimensional structure provided information about amino acid residues in the A-domain located close to Phe, a hypothetical **active pocket** of the A-domain. Marahiel further demonstrated experimentally and computationally that amino acids in this active pocket define the non-ribosomal code, thus producing the 8 purple columns in the 3-way alignment that we showed at the beginning of the chapter.

Figure 5.33 shows the partial non-ribosomal code deduced by Marahiel. Although he was able to deduce some signatures, the non-ribosomal code is very **redundant**, meaning that multiple mutated variants of a signature all code for the same amino acid. For some amino acids, this redundancy is pronounced, e.g., Marahiel identified three very different signatures AWMFAAVL, AFWIGGTF, and FESTAAVY coding for Val.

Amino acid	Signature	Amino acid	Signature
Ala	LLFGIAVL	Leu	AFMLGMVF
Asn	LTKLGEVG	Orn	MENLGLIN
Asp	LTKVGHIG	Orn	VGEIGSID
Cys	HESDVGIT	Phe	AWTIAAVC
Cys	LYNLSLIW	Pro	VQLIAHVV
Gln	AQDLGVVD	Ser	VWHLSLID
Glu	AWHFGGVD	Thr	FWNIGMVH
Glu	AKDLGVVD	Tyr	GTITAEVA
Ile	GFFLGVVY	Tyr	ALVTGAVV
Ile	AFFYGITF	Tyr	ASTVAAVC
Leu	AWFLGNVV	Val	AFWIGGTF
Leu	AWLYGAVM	Val	FESTAAVY
Leu	GAYTGEVV	Val	AWMFAAVL

FIGURE 5.33 Marahiel's partial non-ribosomal code. Some proteinogenic amino acids are missing from this table because they were not present in Marahiel's dataset.

Finding a longest common subsequence without building a city

Define the **i-prefix** of a string as the substring formed by its first i letters and the **j-prefix** of a string as the substring formed by its final j letters. Also, given strings v and w, let $LCS_{i,j}$ denote an LCS between the i-prefix of v and the j-prefix of w, and let $s_{i,j}$ be the length of $LCS_{i,j}$. By definition, $s_{i,0} = s_{0,j} = 0$ for all values of i and j. Next, $LCS_{i,j}$ could contain both v_i and w_j, in which case these symbols match, and $LCS_{i,j}$ extends an LCS of the shorter prefixes $v_1 \ldots v_{i-1}$ and $w_1 \ldots w_{j-1}$. Otherwise, either v_i or w_j is not present in $LCS_{i,j}$. If v_i is not present in $LCS_{i,j}$, then this LCS is therefore also an LCS of $v_1 \ldots v_{i-1}$ and $w_1 \ldots w_j$. A similar argument applies to the case when w_j is not present in $LCS_{i,j}$. Therefore, $s_{i,j}$ satisfies the following recurrence, the same one we derived in the main text using a Manhattan-like grid:

$$s_{i,j} = \max \begin{cases} s_{i-1,j} \\ s_{i,j-1} \\ s_{i-1,j-1} + 1, \text{ if } v_i = w_j \end{cases}$$

Constructing a topological ordering

The first applications of topological ordering resulted from large management projects in an attempt to schedule a sequence of tasks based on their dependencies (such as the Dressing Challenge). In these projects, tasks are represented by nodes, and an edge connects node a to node b if task a must be completed before task b can be started.

STOP and Think: Prove that every DAG has a node with no incoming edges and a node with no outgoing edges.

The following algorithm for constructing a topological ordering is based on the observation that every DAG has at least one node with no incoming edges. We will label one of these nodes as v_1 and then remove this node from the graph along with all its outgoing edges. The resulting graph is also a DAG, which in turn must have a node with no incoming edges; we label this node v_2, and again remove it from the graph along with its outgoing edges. The resulting algorithm proceeds until all nodes have been removed, producing a topological order $v_1, \ldots, v_n$. This algorithm runs in time proportional to the number of edges in the input DAG.

TOPOLOGICALORDERING(*Graph*)
  List ← empty list
  Candidates ← set of all nodes in *Graph* with no incoming edges
  while *Candidates* is non-empty
    select an arbitrary node *a* from *Candidates*
    add *a* to the end of *List* and remove it from *Candidates*
    for each outgoing edge from *a* to another node *b*
      remove edge (a, b) from *Graph*
      if *b* has no incoming edges
        add *b* to *Candidates*
  if *Graph* has edges that have not been removed
    return "the input graph is not a DAG"
  else
    return *List*

PAM scoring matrices

Mutations of a gene's nucleotide sequence often change the amino acid sequence of the translated protein. Some of these mutations impair the protein's ability to function, making them rare events in molecular evolution. `Asn`, `Asp`, `Glu`, and `Ser` are the most "mutable" amino acids, whereas `Cys` and `Trp` are the least mutable. Knowledge of the likelihood of each possible mutation allows biologists to construct amino acid scoring matrices for biologically sound sequence alignments in which different substitutions are penalized differently. The (i, j)-th entry of the amino acid scoring matrix *Score* usually reflects how often the *i*-th amino acid substitutes the *j*-th amino acid in alignments of related protein sequences. As a result, optimal alignments of amino acid sequences may have very few matches but still represent biologically adequate alignments.

How do biologists know which mutations are more likely than others? If we know a large set of pairwise alignments of *related sequences* (e.g., sharing at least 90% of amino acids), then computing $Score(i, j)$ is based on counting how many times the corresponding amino acids are aligned. However, we need to know the scoring matrix in advance in order to build this set of starter alignments — a catch-22!

Fortunately, the correct alignment of very similar sequences is so obvious that it can be constructed even with a primitive scoring scheme that does not account for varying mutation propensities (such as +1 for matches and -1 for mismatches and indels), thus resolving the conundrum. After constructing these obvious alignments, we can use them to compute a new scoring matrix that we can use iteratively to form less and less obvious alignments.

This simplified description hides some details. For example, the probability of `Ser` mutating into `Phe` in species that diverged 1 million years ago is smaller than the probability of the same mutation in species that diverged 100 million years ago. This observation implies that scoring matrices for protein comparison should depend on the similarity of the organisms and the speed of evolution of the proteins of interest. In practice, the proteins that biologists use to create an initial alignment are extremely similar, having 99% of their amino acids conserved (e.g., most proteins shared by humans and chimpanzees). Sequences that are 99% similar are said to be 1 **PAM unit** diverged ("PAM" stands for "point accepted mutation"). You can think of a PAM unit as the amount of time in which an "average" protein mutates 1% of its amino acids.

The **PAM$_1$ scoring matrix** is defined as follows from many pairwise alignments of 99% similar proteins. Given a set of pairwise alignments, let $M(i, j)$ be the number of times that the i-th and j-th amino acids appear in the same column, divided by the total number of times that the i-th amino acid appears in all sequences. Let $f(j)$ be the frequency of the j-th amino acid in the sequences, or the number of times it appears across all sequences divided by the combined lengths of the two sequences. The (i, j)-th entry of the PAM$_1$ matrix is defined as

$$\log \left(\frac{M(i, j)}{f(j)} \right).$$

For a larger number of PAM units n, the PAM$_n$ matrix is computed based on the observation that the matrix M^n (the result of multiplying M by itself n times) holds the empirical probabilities that one amino acid mutates to another during n PAM units. The (i, j)-th entry of the PAM$_n$ scoring matrix is thus given by

$$\log \left(\frac{M^n(i, j)}{f(j)} \right).$$

The PAM$_{250}$ scoring matrix is shown in Figure 5.34.

This approach assumes that the frequencies of the amino acids $f(j)$ remain constant over time, and that the mutational processes in an interval of 1 PAM unit operate consistently over long periods. For large n, the resulting PAM matrices often allow us to find related proteins, even when the alignment has few matches.

	A	C	D	E	F	G	H	I	K	L	M	N	P	Q	R	S	T	V	W	Y	-
A	2	-2	0	0	-3	1	-1	-1	-1	-2	-1	0	1	0	-2	1	1	0	-6	-3	-8
C	-2	12	-5	-5	-4	-3	-3	-2	-5	-6	-5	-4	-3	-5	-4	0	-2	-2	-8	0	-8
D	0	-5	4	3	-6	1	1	-2	0	-4	-3	2	-1	2	-1	0	0	-2	-7	-4	-8
E	0	-5	3	4	-5	0	1	-2	0	-3	-2	1	-1	2	-1	0	0	-2	-7	-4	-8
F	-3	-4	-6	-5	9	-5	-2	1	-5	2	0	-3	-5	-5	-4	-3	-3	-1	0	7	-8
G	1	-3	1	0	-5	5	-2	-3	-2	-4	-3	0	0	-1	-3	1	0	-1	-7	-5	-8
H	-1	-3	1	1	-2	-2	6	-2	0	-2	-2	2	0	3	2	-1	-1	-2	-3	0	-8
I	-1	-2	-2	-2	1	-3	-2	5	-2	2	2	-2	-2	-2	-2	-1	0	4	-5	-1	-8
K	-1	-5	0	0	-5	-2	0	-2	5	-3	0	1	-1	1	3	0	0	-2	-3	-4	-8
L	-2	-6	-4	-3	2	-4	-2	2	-3	6	4	-3	-3	-2	-3	-3	-2	2	-2	-1	-8
M	-1	-5	-3	-2	0	-3	-2	2	0	4	6	-2	-2	-1	0	-2	-1	2	-4	-2	-8
N	0	-4	2	1	-3	0	2	-2	1	-3	-2	2	0	1	0	1	0	-2	-4	-2	-8
P	1	-3	-1	-1	-5	0	0	-2	-1	-3	-2	0	6	0	0	1	0	-1	-6	-5	-8
Q	0	-5	2	2	-5	-1	3	-2	1	-2	-1	1	0	4	1	-1	-1	-2	-5	-4	-8
R	-2	-4	-1	-1	-4	-3	2	-2	3	-3	0	0	0	1	6	0	-1	-2	2	-4	-8
S	1	0	0	0	-3	1	-1	-1	0	-3	-2	1	1	-1	0	2	1	-1	-2	-3	-8
T	1	-2	0	0	-3	0	-1	0	0	-2	-1	0	0	-1	-1	1	3	0	-5	-3	-8
V	0	-2	-2	-2	-1	-1	-2	4	-2	2	2	-2	-1	-2	-2	-1	0	4	-6	-2	-8
W	-6	-8	-7	-7	0	-7	-3	-5	-3	-2	-4	-4	-6	-5	2	-2	-5	-6	17	0	-8
Y	-3	0	-4	-4	7	-5	0	-1	-4	-1	-2	-2	-5	-4	-4	-3	-3	-2	0	10	-8
-	-8	-8	-8	-8	-8	-8	-8	-8	-8	-8	-8	-8	-8	-8	-8	-8	-8	-8	-8	-8	

FIGURE 5.34 The PAM$_{250}$ scoring matrix for protein alignment with indel penalty 8.

Divide-and-conquer algorithms

We will use the problem of sorting a list of integers as an example of a divide-and-conquer algorithm. We begin from the problem of **merging**, in which we want to combine two sorted lists $List_1$ and $List_2$ into a single sorted list (Figure 5.35). The **MERGE** algorithm combines two sorted lists into a single sorted list in $\mathcal{O}(|List_1| + |List_2|)$ time by iteratively choosing the smallest remaining element in $List_1$ and $List_2$ and moving it to the growing sorted list.

$List_1$	**2** 5 7 8	2 **5** 7 8	2 **5** 7 8	2 **5** 7 8	2 5 **7** 8	2 5 **7 8**
$List_2$	**3** 4 6	**3** 4 6	3 **4** 6	3 4 **6**	3 4 **6**	3 4 6
$SortedList$	2	3	4	5	6	**7 8**

FIGURE 5.35 Merging the sorted lists $(2, 5, 7, 8)$ and $(3, 4, 6)$ results in the sorted list $(2, 3, 4, 5, 6, 7, 8)$.

MERGE($List_1$, $List_2$)

    $SortedList \leftarrow$ empty list

    while both $List_1$ and $List_2$ are non-empty

        if the smallest element in $List_1$ is smaller than the smallest element in $List_2$

            move the smallest element from $List_1$ to the end of $SortedList$

        else

            move the smallest element from $List_2$ to the end of $SortedList$

    move any remaining elements from either $List_1$ or $List_2$ to the end of $SortedList$

    return $SortedList$

MERGE would be useful for sorting an arbitrary list if we knew how to divide an arbitrary (unsorted) list into two already sorted half-sized lists. However, it may seem that we are back to where we started, except now we have to sort two smaller lists instead of one big one. Yet sorting two smaller lists is a preferable computational problem. To see why, let's consider the **MERGESORT** algorithm, which **divides** an unsorted list into two parts and then recursively **conquers** each smaller sorting problem before merging the sorted lists.

MERGESORT($List$)

    if $List$ consists of a single element

        return $List$

    $FirstHalf \leftarrow$ first half of $List$

    $SecondHalf \leftarrow$ second half of $List$

    $SortedFirstHalf \leftarrow$ **MERGESORT**($FirstHalf$)

    $SortedSecondHalf \leftarrow$ **MERGESORT**($SecondHalf$)

    $SortedList \leftarrow$ **MERGE**($SortedFirstHalf$, $SortedSecondHalf$)

    return $SortedList$

STOP and Think: What is the runtime of **MERGESORT**?

Figure 5.36 shows the **recursion tree** of **MERGESORT**, consisting of $\log_2 n$ levels, where n is the size of the original unsorted list. At the bottom level, we must merge two sorted lists of approximately $n/2$ elements each, requiring $\mathcal{O}(n/2 + n/2) = \mathcal{O}(n)$ time. At the next highest level, we must merge four lists of $n/4$ elements, requiring $\mathcal{O}(n/4 + n/4 + n/4 + n/4) = \mathcal{O}(n)$ time. This pattern can be generalized: the i-th level contains 2^i lists, each having approximately $n/2^i$ elements, and requires $\mathcal{O}(n)$ time to merge. Since there are $\log_2 n$ levels in the recursion tree, **MERGESORT** therefore requires $\mathcal{O}(n \cdot \log_2 n)$ runtime overall, which offers a speedup over naive $\mathcal{O}(n^2)$ sorting algorithms.

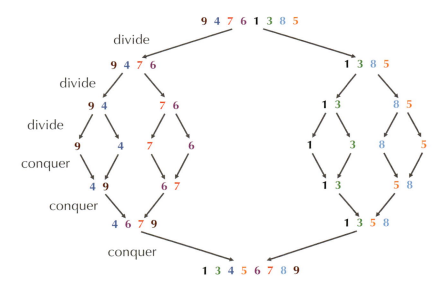

FIGURE 5.36 The recursion tree for sorting an 8-element list with **MERGESORT**. The *divide* (upper) steps consist of $\log_2 8 = 3$ levels, where the input list is split into smaller and smaller sublists. The *conquer* (lower) steps consist of the same number of levels, as the sorted sublists are merged back together.

Scoring multiple alignments

The choice of scoring function can drastically affect the quality of a multiple alignment. In the main chapter, we described a way to score t-way alignments by using a t-dimensional scoring matrix. Below, we describe more practical approaches to scoring alignments.

The columns of a *t*-way alignment describe a path in a *t*-dimensional alignment graph whose edge weights are defined by the scoring function. Using the statistically motivated entropy score, the score of a multiple alignment is defined as the sum of the entropies of its columns. Recall from Chapter 2 that the entropy of a column is equal to $-\sum p_x \cdot \log_2 p_x$, where the sum is taken over all symbols x present in the column, and p_x is the frequency of symbol x in the column.

In Chapter 2, we saw that more highly conserved columns will have lower entropy scores. Because we wish to maximize the alignment score, we use the negative of entropy in order to ensure that more highly conserved columns receive higher scores. Finding a longest path in the *t*-dimensional alignment graph therefore corresponds to finding a multiple alignment with minimal entropy.

Another popular scoring approach is the **Sum-of-Pairs score** (**SP-score**). A multiple alignment *Alignment* of t sequences induces a pairwise alignment between the *i*-th and *j*-th sequences, having score $s(Alignment, i, j)$. The SP-score for a multiple alignment simply adds the scores of each induced pairwise alignment:

$$\text{SP-Score}(Alignment) = \sum_{1 \leq i < j \leq t} s(Alignment, i, j).$$

EXERCISE BREAK: Compute the entropy score and SP-score of Marahiel's 3-way alignment, reproduced below.

```
YAFDLGYTCMFPVLLGGGELHIVQKETYTAPDEIAHYIKEHGITYIKLTPSLFHTIVNTA
-AFDVSAGDFARALLTGGQLIVCPNEVKMDPASLYAIIKKYDITIFEATPALVIPLMEYI
IAFDASSWEIYAPLLNGGTVVCIDYYTTIDIKALEAVFKQHHIRGAMLPPALLKQCLVSA

SFAFDANFESLRLIVLGGEKIIPIDVIAFRKMYGHTE-FINHYGPTEATIGA
-YEQKLDISQLQILIVGSDSCSMEDFKTLVSRFGSTIRIVNSYGVTEACIDS
----PTMISSLEILFAAGDRLSSQDAILARRAVGSGV-Y-NAYGPTENTVLS
```

Bibliography Notes

Edit distance was introduced by Levenshtein, 1966. The local alignment algorithm described in the text was proposed by Smith and Waterman, 1981. When Doolittle et al., 1983 revealed the similarities between oncogenes and PDGF, they did not know about the Smith-Waterman algorithm. The 3-D structures of firefly luciferase and the A-domain from *Bacilus brevis* were published by Conti, Franks, and Brick, 1996 as well as Conti et al., 1997. The non-ribosomal code was first presented by Stachelhaus, Mootz, and Marahiel, 1999.

Of Mice and Men

"I have further been told," said the cat, "that you can also transform yourself into the smallest of animals, for example, a rat or a mouse. But I can scarcely believe that. I must admit to you that I think it would be quite impossible."

"Impossible!" cried the ogre. "You shall see!"

He immediately changed himself into a mouse and began to run about the floor. As soon as the cat saw this, he fell upon him and ate him up.

How different are the human and mouse genomes?

When Charles Perrault described the transformation of an ogre into a mouse in "Puss in Boots", he could hardly have anticipated that three centuries later, research would show that the human and mouse genomes are surprisingly similar. Nearly every human gene has a mouse counterpart, although mice greatly outperform us when it comes to the olfactory genes responsible for smell. We are essentially mice without tails — we even have the genes needed to make a tail, but these genes have been "silenced" during our evolution.

We started with a fairy tale question: "How can an ogre transform into a mouse?" Since we share most of the same genes with mice, we now ask a question about mammalian evolution: "What evolutionary forces have transformed the genome of the human-mouse ancestor into the present-day human and mouse genomes?"

If a precocious child had grown out of reading fairy tales and wanted to learn about how the human and mouse genomes differ, then here is what we would tell her. You can cut the 23 human chromosomes into 280 pieces, shuffle these DNA fragments, and then glue the pieces together in a new order to form the 20 mouse chromosomes. The truth, however, is that evolution has not employed a single dramatic cut-and-paste operation; instead, it applies smaller changes known as **genome rearrangements**, which will be our focus in this chapter.

Unfortunately, our bioinformatics time machine won't take us more than a few centuries into the past. If it did, we could travel 75 million years back in time, watching humans slowly change into a small, furry animal that lived with dinosaurs. Then, we could travel back to the present, watching how this animal evolved into the mouse. In this chapter, we hope to understand the genome rearrangements that have separated the human and mouse genomes without having to revamp our time machine.

Synteny blocks

PAGE 340 To simplify genome comparison, we will first focus on the X chromosome, which is one of the two sex-determining chromosomes in mammals and has retained nearly all its genes throughout mammalian evolution (see **DETOUR: Why is the Gene Content of Mammalian X Chromosomes So Conserved?**). We can therefore view the X chromosome as a "mini-genome" when comparing mice to humans, since this chromosome's genes have not jumped around onto different chromosomes (and vice-versa).

It turns out not only that most human genes have mouse counterparts, but also that hundreds of similar genes often line up one after another in the same order in the two species genomes. Each of the eleven colored segments in Figure 6.1 represents such a procession of similar genes and is called a **synteny block**. Later, we will explain how to construct synteny blocks and what the left and right **directions** of the blocks signify.

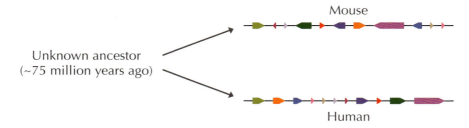

FIGURE 6.1 Mouse and human X chromosomes represented as eleven colored, directed segments (synteny blocks).

Synteny blocks simplify the comparison of the mouse and human X chromosomes from about 150 million base pairs to only eleven units. This simplification is analogous to comparing two similar photographs. If we compare the images one pixel at a time, we may be overwhelmed by the scale of the problem; instead, we need to zoom out in order to notice higher-level patterns. It is no accident that biologists use the term "resolution" to discuss the level at which genomes are analyzed.

Reversals

You have probably been wondering how the genome changes when it undergoes a genome rearrangement. Genome rearrangements were discovered 90 years ago when Alfred Sturtevant was studying fruit fly mutants with scarlet- and peach-colored eyes as well as abnormally shaped deltoid wings. Sturtevant analyzed the genes coding for these traits, called **scarlet**, **peach**, and **delta**, and he was amazed to find that the arrangement of these genes in *Drosophila melanogaster* (**scarlet**, **peach**, **delta**) differed from their arrangement in *Drosophila simulans* (**scarlet**, **delta**, **peach**). He immediately conjectured that the chromosomal segment containing **peach** and **delta** must have been flipped around (see **DETOUR: Discovery of Genome Rearrangements**). Sturtevant had witnessed the most common form of genome rearrangement, called a **reversal**, which flips around an interval of a chromosome and inverts the directions of any synteny blocks within the interval.

PAGE 340

Figure 6.2 shows a series of seven reversals transforming the mouse X chromosome into the human X chromosome. If this scenario is correct, then the X chromosome of the human-mouse ancestor must be represented by one of the intermediate synteny block orderings. Unfortunately, this series of seven reversals offers only one of 1,070 different seven-step scenarios transforming the mouse X chromosome into the human X chromosome. We have no clue which scenario is correct, or even whether the correct scenario had exactly seven reversals.

STOP and Think: Can you convert the mouse X chromosome into the human X chromosome using only six reversals?

Regardless of how many reversals separate the human and mouse X chromosomes, reversals must be rare genomic events. Indeed, genome rearrangements typically cause the death or sterility of the mutated organism, thus preventing it from passing the rearrangement on to the next generation. However, a tiny fraction of genome rearrangements may have a positive effect on survival and propagate through a species as the result of natural selection. When a population becomes isolated from the rest of its species for long enough, rearrangements can even create a new species.

Rearrangement hotspots

Geology provides a thought-provoking analogy for thinking about genome evolution. You might like to think of genome rearrangements as "genomic earthquakes" that dramatically change the chromosomal architecture of an organism. Genome rearrangements contrast with much more frequent point mutations, which work slowly and are analogous to "genomic erosion".

You can visualize a reversal as breaking the genome on both sides of a chromosomal interval, flipping the interval, and then gluing the resulting segments in a new order. Keeping in mind that earthquakes occur more frequently along fault lines, we wonder

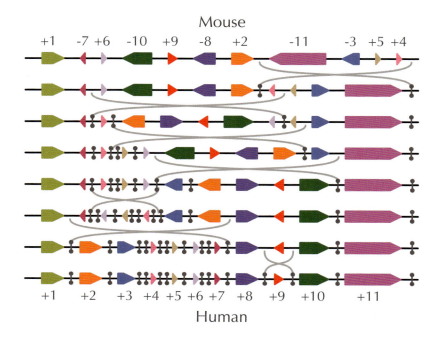

FIGURE 6.2 Transforming the mouse X chromosome into the human X chromosome with seven reversals. Each synteny block is uniquely colored and labeled with an integer between 1 and 11; the positive or negative sign of each integer indicates the synteny block's direction (pointing right or left, respectively). Two short vertical segments delineate the endpoints of the inverted interval in each reversal. Suppose that this evolutionary scenario is correct and that, say, the fifth synteny block arrangement from the top presents the true ancestral arrangement. Then the first four reversals happened on the evolutionary path from mice to the human-mouse common ancestor (traveling backward in time), and the final three reversals happened on the evolutionary path from the common ancestor to humans (traveling forward in time). In this chapter, we are not trying to reconstruct the ancestral genome and thus are not concerned with whether a certain reversal travels backward or forward in time.

if a similar principle holds for reversals — are they occurring over and over again in the same genomic regions? A fundamental question in chromosome evolution studies is whether the **breakage points** of reversals (i.e., the ends of the inverted intervals) occur along "fault lines" called **rearrangement hotspots**. If such hotspots exist in the human genome, we want to locate them and determine how they might relate to genetic disorders, which are often attributable to rearrangements.

Of course, we should rigorously define what we mean by a "rearrangement hotspot". Re-examining the seven-reversal scenario changing the mouse X chromosome into the human X chromosome in Figure 6.2, we record the endpoints of each reversal using vertical segments. Regions affected by multiple reversals are indicated by multiple vertical segments in the human X chromosome. For example, the region adjacent to the pointed side of block 3 in Figure 6.2 is used as an endpoint of both the fourth and fifth reversals. As a result, we have placed two vertical lines between blocks 3 and 4 in the human X chromosome. However, just because we showed two breakage points in this region does not imply that this region is a rearrangement hotspot, since the reversals in Figure 6.2 represent just one possible evolutionary scenario. Because the true rearrangement scenario is unknown, it is not immediately clear how we could determine whether rearrangement hotspots exist.

The Random Breakage Model of Chromosome Evolution

In 1973, Susumu Ohno proposed the **Random Breakage Model** of chromosome evolution. This hypothesis states that the breakage points of rearrangements are selected randomly, implying that rearrangement hotspots in mammalian genomes do not exist. Yet Ohno's model lacked supporting evidence when it was introduced. After all, how could we possibly determine whether rearrangement hotspots exist without knowing the exact sequence of rearrangements separating two species?

STOP and Think: Consider the following questions.

1. Say that a series of random reversals result in one huge synteny block covering 90% of the genome in addition to 99 tiny synteny blocks covering the remaining 10% of the genome. Should we be surprised?

2. What if random reversals result in 100 synteny blocks of roughly the same length? Should we be surprised?

The idea that we wish to impress on you in the preceding questions is that we can test the Random Breakage Model by analyzing the distribution of synteny block lengths. For example, the lengths of the human-mouse synteny blocks on the X chromosome vary widely, with the largest block (block 11 in Figure 6.2) taking up nearly 25% of the entire length of the X chromosome. Is this variation in synteny block length consistent with the Random Breakage Model?

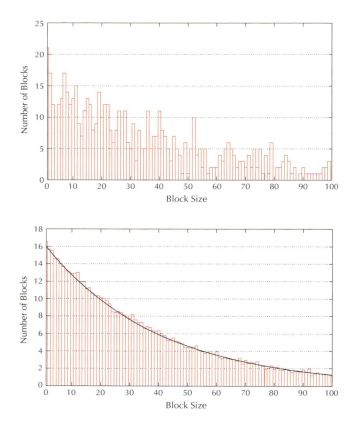

FIGURE 6.3 (Top) A histogram showing the number of blocks of each size for a simulated genome with 25,000 genes (an approximation for the number of genes in a mammalian genome) after 320 randomly chosen reversals. Blocks having more than 100 genes are not shown. (Bottom) A histogram of synteny block lengths averaged over 100 simulations, fitted by the exponential distribution.

In 1984, Joseph Nadeau and Benjamin Taylor asked what the expected lengths of synteny blocks should be after N reversals occurring at random locations in the genome. If we rule out the unlikely event that two random reversals cut the chromosome in exactly the same position, then N random reversals cut the chromosome in $2N$ locations and produce $2N + 1$ synteny blocks. Figure 6.3 (top) depicts the result of a computational experiment in which 320 random reversals are applied to a simulated chromosome consisting of 25,000 genes, producing $2 \cdot 320 + 1 = 641$ synteny blocks. The average synteny block size is $25,000/641 \approx 34$ genes, but this does not mean that all synteny blocks should have approximately 34 genes. If we select random locations for breakage points, then some blocks may have only a few genes, whereas other blocks may contain over a hundred. Figure 6.3 (bottom) averages the results of 100 such simulations and illustrates that the distribution of synteny block lengths can be approximated by a curve corresponding to an **exponential distribution** (see DETOUR: **PAGE 341** The Exponential Distribution). The exponential distribution predicts that there will be about seven blocks having 34 genes and one or two much larger blocks having 100 genes.

What happens when we look at the histogram for the real human and mouse synteny blocks? When Nadeau and Taylor constructed this histogram for the limited genetic data available in 1984, they observed that the lengths of blocks fit the exponential distribution well. In the 1990s, more accurate synteny block data fit the exponential distribution even better (Figure 6.4). Case closed — even though we don't know the exact rearrangements causing our genome to evolve over the last 75 million years, these rearrangements must have followed the *Random Breakage Model*!

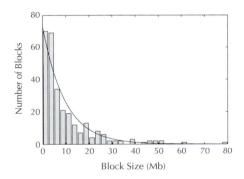

FIGURE 6.4 Histogram of human-mouse synteny block lengths (only synteny blocks longer than 1 million nucleotides are shown). The histogram is fitted by an exponential distribution.

STOP and Think: Do you agree with the logic behind this argument?

Sorting by Reversals

We now have evidence in favor of the Random Breakage Model, but this evidence is far from conclusive. To test this model, let's start building a mathematical model for rearrangement analysis. We will therefore return to a problem that we hinted at in the introduction, which is finding the minimum number of reversals that could transform the mouse X chromosome into the human X chromosome.

STOP and Think: From a biological perspective, why do you think we want to find the minimum possible number of reversals?

We ask for the minimum number of reversals in accordance with a principle called **Occam's razor**. When presented with some quandary, we should explain it using the simplest hypothesis that is consistent with what we already know. In this case, it seems most reasonable that evolution would take the "shortest path" between two species, i.e., the most **parsimonious** evolutionary scenario. Evolution may not always take the shortest path, but even when it does not, the number of steps in the true evolutionary scenario often comes close to the number of steps in the most parsimonious scenario. How, then, can we find the length of this shortest path?

Genome rearrangement studies typically ignore the lengths of synteny blocks and represent chromosomes by **signed permutations**. Each block is labeled by a number, which is assigned a positive/negative sign depending on the block's direction. The number of elements in a signed permutation is its **length**. As you can see from Figure 6.2, the human and mouse X chromosomes can be represented by the following signed permutations of length 11:

$$\textbf{Mouse:}\ (+1\ -7\ +6\ -10\ +9\ -8\ +2\ -11\ -3\ +5\ +4)$$
$$\textbf{Human:}\ (+1\ +2\ +3\ +4\ +5\ +6\ +7\ +8\ +9\ +10\ +11)$$

In the rest of the chapter, we will refer to signed permutations as **permutations** for short. Because we assume that each synteny block is unique, we do not allow repeated numbers in permutations (e.g., $(+1\ -2\ +3\ +2)$ is not a permutation).

EXERCISE BREAK: How many permutations of length n are there?

We can model reversals by inverting the elements within an interval of a permutation, then switching the signs of any elements within the inverted interval. For example, the cartoon in Figure 6.5 illustrates how a reversal changes the permutation $(+1\ +2\ +3\ \textbf{+4}$ $\textbf{+5}\ \textbf{+6}\ \textbf{+7}\ \textbf{+8}\ +9\ +10)$ into $(+1\ +2\ +3\ \textbf{-8}\ \textbf{-7}\ \textbf{-6}\ \textbf{-5}\ \textbf{-4}\ +9\ +10)$. This reversal can be viewed as first breaking the permutation between +3 and +4 as well as between +8 and +9,

$$(+1 +2 +3 \mid +4 +5 +6 +7 +8 \mid +9 +10).$$

It then inverts the middle segment,

$$(+1 +2 +3 \mid -8 -7 -6 -5 -4 \mid +9 +10),$$

and finally glues the three segments back together to form a new permutation,

$$(+1 +2 +3 -8 -7 -6 -5 -4 +9 +10).$$

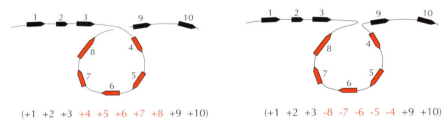

(+1 +2 +3 +4 +5 +6 +7 +8 +9 +10) (+1 +2 +3 -8 -7 -6 -5 -4 +9 +10)

FIGURE 6.5 A cartoon illustrating how a reversal breaks a chromosome in two places and inverts the segment between the two breakage points. Note that the reversal changes the sign of each element within the permutation's inverted segment.

EXERCISE BREAK: How many different reversals can be applied to a permutation of length n?

We define the **reversal distance** between permutations P and Q, denoted $d_{\text{rev}}(P, Q)$, as the minimum number of reversals required to transform P into Q.

Reversal Distance Problem:

Calculate the reversal distance between two permutations.

Input: Two permutations of equal length.
Output: The reversal distance between these permutations.

We represented the human X chromosome by $(+1 +2 +3 +4 +5 +6 +7 +8 +9 +10 +11)$; such a permutation, in which blocks are ordered from smallest to largest with positive directions, is called the **identity permutation**. The reason why we used the identity permutation of length 11 to represent the human X chromosome is that when comparing two genomes, we can label the synteny blocks in one of the genomes however we like. The block labeling for which the human X chromosome is the identity permutation automatically induces the representation of the mouse chromosome as

$$(+1 -7 +6 -10 +9 -8 +2 -11 -3 +5 +4).$$

Of course, as shown in Figure 6.6, we could have instead encoded the mouse X chromosome as the identity permutation, which would have induced the encoding of the human X chromosome as

$$(+1 +7 -9 +11 +10 +3 -2 -6 +5 -4 -8).$$

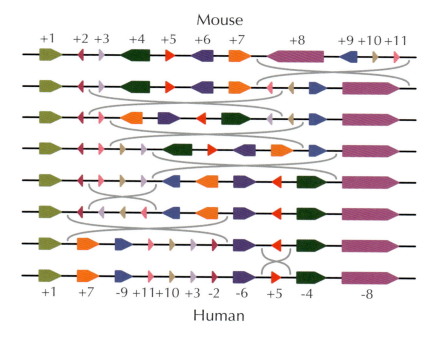

FIGURE 6.6 Encoding the mouse X chromosome as the identity permutation implies encoding the human X chromosome as $(+1 +7 -9 +11 +10 +3 -2 -6 +5 -4 -8)$.

Because we have the freedom to label synteny blocks however we like, we will consider an equivalent version of the Reversal Distance Problem in which permutation Q is the identity permutation $(+1\ +2\ldots +n)$. This computational problem is called **sorting by reversals**, and we denote the minimum number of reversals required to sort P into the identity permutation as $d_{\text{rev}}(P)$. The history of sorting by reversals is founded in a culinary application and involves two celebrities (see DETOUR: Bill Gates and David PAGE 342 X. Cohen Flip Pancakes).

Sorting by Reversals Problem:

Compute the reversal distance between a permutation and the identity permutation.

    Input: A permutation P.
    Output: The reversal distance $d_{\text{rev}}(P)$.

Here is a sorting of $(+2\ -4\ -3\ +5\ -8\ -7\ -6\ +1)$ using five reversals, with the inverted interval at each step shown in red:

$$(+2\ \ -4\ \ -3\ \ +5\ \ -8\ \ -7\ \ -6\ \ +1)$$
$$(+2\ \ +3\ \ +4\ \ +5\ \ -8\ \ -7\ \ -6\ \ +1)$$
$$(+2\ \ +3\ \ +4\ \ +5\ \ +6\ \ +7\ \ +8\ \ +1)$$
$$(+2\ \ +3\ \ +4\ \ +5\ \ +6\ \ +7\ \ +8\ \ -1)$$
$$(-8\ \ -7\ \ -6\ \ -5\ \ -4\ \ -3\ \ -2\ \ -1)$$
$$(+1\ \ +2\ \ +3\ \ +4\ \ +5\ \ +6\ \ +7\ \ +8)$$

STOP and Think: Can you sort this permutation using fewer reversals?

Here is a faster sorting:

$$(+2\ \ -4\ \ -3\ \ +5\ \ -8\ \ -7\ \ -6\ \ +1)$$
$$(+2\ \ +3\ \ +4\ \ +5\ \ -8\ \ -7\ \ -6\ \ +1)$$
$$(-5\ \ -4\ \ -3\ \ -2\ \ -8\ \ -7\ \ -6\ \ +1)$$
$$(-5\ \ -4\ \ -3\ \ -2\ \ -1\ \ +6\ \ +7\ \ +8)$$
$$(+1\ \ +2\ \ +3\ \ +4\ \ +5\ \ +6\ \ +7\ \ +8)$$

STOP and Think: Consider the following questions.

1. Is it possible to sort this permutation even faster?

2. During sorting by reversals, the intermediate permutations in the example above are getting more and more "ordered". Can you come up with a quantitative measure of how ordered a permutation is?

A Greedy Heuristic for Sorting by Reversals

Let's see if we can design a greedy heuristic to approximate $d_{rev}(P)$. The simplest idea is to perform reversals that fix $+1$ in the first position, followed by reversals that fix $+2$ in the second position, and so on. For example, element 1 is already in the correct position and has the correct sign $(+)$ in the mouse X chromosome, but element 2 is not in the correct position. We can keep element 1 fixed and move element 2 to the correct position by applying a single reversal.

$$(+1 \quad -7 \quad +6 \quad -10 \quad +9 \quad -8 \quad +2 \quad -11 \quad -3 \quad +5 \quad +4)$$
$$(+1 \quad -2 \quad +8 \quad -9 \quad +10 \quad -6 \quad +7 \quad -11 \quad -3 \quad +5 \quad +4)$$

One more reversal flips element 2 around so that it has the correct sign:

$$(+1 \quad -2 \quad +8 \quad -9 \quad +10 \quad -6 \quad +7 \quad -11 \quad -3 \quad +5 \quad +4)$$
$$(+1 \quad +2 \quad +8 \quad -9 \quad +10 \quad -6 \quad +7 \quad -11 \quad -3 \quad +5 \quad +4)$$

By iterating, we can successively move larger and larger elements to their correct positions in the identity permutation by following the reversals below. The inverted interval of each reversal is still shown in red, and elements that have been placed in the correct position are shown in blue.

$$(+1 \quad -7 \quad +6 \quad -10 \quad +9 \quad -8 \quad +2 \quad -11 \quad -3 \quad +5 \quad +4)$$
$$(+1 \quad -2 \quad +8 \quad -9 \quad +10 \quad -6 \quad +7 \quad -11 \quad -3 \quad +5 \quad +4)$$
$$(+1 \quad +2 \quad +8 \quad -9 \quad +10 \quad -6 \quad +7 \quad -11 \quad -3 \quad +5 \quad +4)$$
$$(+1 \quad +2 \quad +3 \quad +11 \quad -7 \quad +6 \quad -10 \quad +9 \quad -8 \quad +5 \quad +4)$$
$$(+1 \quad +2 \quad +3 \quad -4 \quad -5 \quad +8 \quad -9 \quad +10 \quad -6 \quad +7 \quad -11)$$
$$(+1 \quad +2 \quad +3 \quad +4 \quad -5 \quad +8 \quad -9 \quad +10 \quad -6 \quad +7 \quad -11)$$
$$(+1 \quad +2 \quad +3 \quad +4 \quad +5 \quad +8 \quad -9 \quad +10 \quad -6 \quad +7 \quad -11)$$
$$(+1 \quad +2 \quad +3 \quad +4 \quad +5 \quad +6 \quad -10 \quad +9 \quad -8 \quad +7 \quad -11)$$
$$(+1 \quad +2 \quad +3 \quad +4 \quad +5 \quad +6 \quad -7 \quad +8 \quad -9 \quad +10 \quad -11)$$
$$(+1 \quad +2 \quad +3 \quad +4 \quad +5 \quad +6 \quad +7 \quad +8 \quad -9 \quad +10 \quad -11)$$
$$(+1 \quad +2 \quad +3 \quad +4 \quad +5 \quad +6 \quad +7 \quad +8 \quad +9 \quad +10 \quad -11)$$
$$(+1 \quad +2 \quad +3 \quad +4 \quad +5 \quad +6 \quad +7 \quad +8 \quad +9 \quad +10 \quad +11)$$

This example motivates a greedy heuristic called **GREEDYSORTING**. We say that element k in permutation $P = (p_1 \ldots p_n)$ is **sorted** if $p_k = +k$ and **unsorted** otherwise. We call P **k-sorted** if its first $k-1$ elements are sorted, but if element k is unsorted. For every $(k-1)$-sorted permutation P, there exists a single reversal, called the **k-sorting reversal**, that fixes the first $k-1$ elements of P and moves element k to the k-th position.

In the case when $-k$ is already in the k-th position of P, the k-sorting reversal merely flips $-k$ around.

For example, in the sorting of the mouse X chromosome shown above, the 2-sorting reversal transforms $(+1\ -7\ +6\ -10\ +9\ -8\ +2\ -11\ -3\ +5\ +4)$ into $(+1\ -2\ +8$ $-9\ +10\ -6\ +7\ -11\ -3\ +5\ +4)$. In this case, an additional 2-sorting reversal flipping -2 was needed to make element 2 sorted. The idea of **GREEDYSORTING**, then, is to apply k-sorting reversals for increasing values of k. Here, $|P|$ refers to the length of permutation P.

GREEDYSORTING(P)
    approxReversalDistance ← 0
    for k ← 1 to $|P|$
        if element k is not sorted
            apply the k-sorting reversal to P
            approxReversalDistance ← *approxReversalDistance* + 1
            if the k-th element of P is $-k$
                apply the k-sorting reversal to P
                approxReversalDistance ← *approxReversalDistance* + 1
    return *approxReversalDistance*

In the case of the mouse X chromosome, **GREEDYSORTING** requires eleven reversals, but we already know that this permutation can be sorted with seven reversals, which causes us to wonder: how good of a heuristic is **GREEDYSORTING**?

EXERCISE BREAK: What is the largest number of reversals **GREEDYSORTING** could ever require to sort a permutation of length n?

Consider the permutation $(-6\ +1\ +2\ +3\ +4\ +5)$. You can verify that the greedy heuristic requires ten steps to sort this permutation, and yet it can be sorted using just two reversals!

$$(-6\ +1\ +2\ +3\ +4\ +5)$$
$$(-5\ -4\ -3\ -2\ -1\ +6)$$
$$(+1\ +2\ +3\ +4\ +5\ +6)$$

This example demonstrates that **GREEDYSORTING** provides a poor approximation for the reversal distance.

STOP

STOP and Think: Can you find a lower bound on $d_{rev}(P)$? For example, can you show that the mouse permutation $(+1 \ -7 \ +6 \ -10 \ +9 \ -8 \ +2 \ -11 \ -3 \ +5 \ +4)$ cannot be sorted with fewer than seven reversals?

Breakpoints

What are breakpoints?

Consider the sorting by reversals shown in Figure 6.7. We would like to quantify how each subsequent permutation is moving closer to the identity as we apply subsequent reversals. For the first reversal, at the right endpoint of the inverted interval, it changes the consecutive elements $(-11 \ +13)$ into the much more desirable $(+12 \ +13)$. Less obvious is the work of the fourth reversal, which places -11 immediately left of -10 so that at the next step, the consecutive elements $(-11 \ -10)$ can be part of an inverted interval, creating the desirable consecutive elements $(+10 \ +11)$.

												BREAKPOINTS(P)
|+3 +4	+5	|−12	|−8	−7	−6	|+1	+2	|+10	|+9	|−11	|+13	8
|+3 +4	+5	|+11	|−9	|−10	|−2	−1	|+6	+7	+8	|+12	+13	7
+1 +2	|+10	|+9	|−11	|−5	−4	−3	|+6	+7	+8	|+12	+13	6
+1 +2	+3	+4	+5	|+11	|−9	|−10	|+6	+7	+8	|+12	+13	5
+1 +2	+3	+4	+5	|+9	|−11	−10	|+6	+7	+8	|+12	+13	4
+1 +2	+3	+4	+5	|+9	|−8	−7	−6	|+10	+11	+12	+13	3
+1 +2	+3	+4	+5	+6	+7	+8	|−9	|+10	+11	+12	+13	2
+1 +2	+3	+4	+5	+6	+7	+8	+9	+10	+11	+12	+13	0

FIGURE 6.7 A sorting by reversals. The inverted interval of each reversal is shown in red, while breakpoints in each permutation are marked by vertical blue segments.

The intuition that we are trying to build is that consecutive elements like $(+12 \ +13)$ are desirable because they appear in the same order as in the identity permutation. However, consecutive elements like $(-11 \ -10)$ are also desirable, since these elements can be later inverted into the correct order, $(+10 \ +11)$. The pairs $(+12 \ +13)$ and $(-11 \ -10)$ have something in common; the second element is equal to the first element plus 1. We therefore say that consecutive elements $(p_i \ p_{i+1})$ in permutation $P = (p_1 \ldots p_n)$ form an **adjacency** if $p_{i+1} - p_i$ is equal to 1. By definition, for any positive integer $k < n$, both $(k \ k+1)$ and $(-(k+1) \ -k)$ are adjacencies. If $p_{i+1} - p_i$ is not equal to 1, then we say that $(p_i \ p_{i+1})$ is a **breakpoint**.

We can think about a breakpoint intuitively as a pair of consecutive elements that are "out of order" compared to the identity permutation $(+1 +2 \ldots +n)$. For example, the pair $(+5 -12)$ is a breakpoint because +5 and -12 are not neighbors in the identity permutation. Similarly, $(-12 -8)$, $(-6 +1)$, $(+2 +10)$, $(+9 -11)$, and $(-11 +13)$ are clearly out of order. But $(+10 +9)$ is also a breakpoint (even though it is formed by consecutive integers) because its signs are out of order compared to the identity permutation.

STOP and Think: The permutation $(-5 -4 -3 -2 -1)$ is clearly not the identity permutation, but where are its breakpoints?

We will further represent the beginning and end of permutation P by adding **0** to the left of the first element and $n + 1$ to the right of the last element,

$$(0 \; p_1 \ldots p_n \; (n + 1)) .$$

As a result, there are $n + 1$ pairs of consecutive elements:

$$(0 \; p_1), \; (p_1 \; p_2), \; (p_2 \; p_3), \; \ldots, \; (p_{n-1} \; p_n), \; (p_n \; (n + 1)) .$$

We use ADJACENCIES(P) and BREAKPOINTS(P) to denote the number of adjacencies and breakpoints of permutation P, respectively. Figure 6.7 illustrates how the number of breakpoints changes during sorting by reversals (note that 0 and $n + 1$ are placeholders and cannot be affected by a reversal).

Counting breakpoints

Because any pair of consecutive elements of a permutation form either a breakpoint or adjacency, we have the following identity for any permutation P of length n:

$$\text{ADJACENCIES}(P) + \text{BREAKPOINTS}(P) = n + 1.$$

STOP and Think: A permutation on n elements may have at most $n + 1$ adjacencies. How many permutations on n elements have exactly $n + 1$ adjacencies?

You can verify that the identity permutation $(+1 +2 \ldots +n)$ is the only permutation for which all consecutive elements are adjacencies, meaning that it has no breakpoints.

Note also that the permutation $(-n \ -(n-1) \ldots -2 \ -1)$ has adjacencies for every consecutive pair of elements except for the two breakpoints $(0 \ -n)$ and $(-1 \ (n+1))$.

EXERCISE BREAK: How many permutations of length n have exactly $n-1$ adjacencies?

Number of Breakpoints Problem:

Find the number of breakpoints in a permutation.

Input: A permutation.

Output: The number of breakpoints in this permutation.

STOP and Think: We defined a breakpoint between an arbitrary permutation and the identity permutation. Generalize the notion of a breakpoint between two arbitrary permutations, and design a linear-time algorithm for computing this number.

Sorting by reversals as breakpoint elimination

The reversals in Figure 6.7 reduce the number of breakpoints from 8 to 0. Note that the permutation becomes more and more "ordered" after every reversal as the number of breakpoints reduces at each step. You can therefore think of sorting by reversals as the process of breakpoint elimination — reducing the number of breakpoints in a permutation P from BREAKPOINTS(P) to 0.

STOP and Think: What is the maximum number of breakpoints that can be eliminated by a single reversal?

Consider the first reversal in Figure 6.7, which reduces the number of breakpoints from 8 to 7. On either side of the inverted interval, breakpoints and adjacencies certainly do not change; for example, the breakpoint $(0 \ +3)$ and the adjacency $(+13 \ +14)$ remain the same. Also note that every breakpoint within the inverted interval of a reversal remains a breakpoint after the reversal. In other words, if $(p_i \ p_{i+1})$ formed a breakpoint within the span of a reversal, i.e.,

$$p_{i+1} - p_i \neq 1,$$

then these consecutive elements will remain a breakpoint after the reversal changes them into $(-p_{i+1} \, -p_i)$:

$$-p_i - (-p_{i+1}) = p_{i+1} - p_i \neq 1.$$

For example, there are five breakpoints within the span of the following reversal on the permutation $(0 \; +3 \; +4 \; +5 \; \mathbf{-12} \; \mathbf{-8} \; \mathbf{-7} \; \mathbf{-6} \; \mathbf{+1} \; \mathbf{+2} \; \mathbf{+10} \; \mathbf{+9} \; \mathbf{-11} \; +13 \; +14 \; 15)$:

$$(-12 \; -8) \qquad (-6 \; +1) \qquad (+2 \; +10) \qquad (+10 \; +9) \qquad (+9 \; -11)$$

After the reversal, these breakpoints become the following five breakpoints:

$$(+11 \; -9) \qquad (-9 \; -10) \qquad (-10 \; -2) \qquad (-1 \; +6) \qquad (+8 \; +12)$$

Since all breakpoints inside and outside the span of a reversal remain breakpoints after a reversal, the only breakpoints that could be eliminated by a reversal are the two breakpoints located on the boundaries of the inverted interval. The breakpoints on the boundaries of the first reversal in Figure 6.7 are $(+5 \; -12)$ and $(-11 \; +13)$; the reversal converts them into a breakpoint $(+5 \; +11)$ and an adjacency $(+12 \; +13)$, thus reducing the number of breakpoints by 1.

STOP and Think: Can the permutation $(+3 \; +4 \; +5 \; -12 \; -8 \; -7 \; -6 \; +1 \; +2 \; +10 \; +9 \; -11 \; +13 \; +14)$, which has 8 breakpoints, be sorted with three reversals?

A reversal can eliminate at most two breakpoints, so two reversals can eliminate at most four breakpoints, three reversals can eliminate at most six breakpoints, and so on. This reasoning establishes the following theorem.

Breakpoint Theorem: $d_{\mathrm{rev}}(P)$ *is greater than or equal to* BREAKPOINTS$(P)/2$.

It would be nice if we could *always* find a reversal that eliminates two breakpoints from a permutation, as this would imply a simple greedy algorithm for optimal sorting by reversals. Unfortunately, this is not the case. You can verify that there is no reversal that reduces the number of breakpoints in the permutation $P = (+2 \; +1)$, which has three breakpoints.

EXERCISE BREAK: How many permutations of length n have the property that no reversal applied to P decreases BREAKPOINTS(P)?

It turns out that every permutation of length n can be sorted using at most $n + 1$ reversals and that the permutation $(+n +(n-1) \ldots +1)$ requires $n + 1$ reversals to sort. Since this permutation has $n + 1$ breakpoints, there is a large gap between the lower bound of $(n + 1)/2$ provided by the Breakpoint Theorem and the reversal distance.

EXERCISE BREAK: Prove that there exists a shortest sequence of reversals sorting a permutation that never breaks a permutation at an adjacency.

You will soon see that the idea of breakpoints will help us return to our original aim of testing the Random Breakage Model. For now, we would like to move from permutations, which can only model single chromosomes, to a more general multichromosomal model. You may be surprised that we are moving to a seemingly more difficult model before resolving the unichromosomal case, which is already difficult. However, it turns out that our new multichromosomal model will be easier to analyze!

Rearrangements in Tumor Genomes

As we move toward a more robust model for genome comparison, we need to incorporate rearrangements that move genes from one chromosome to another. Indeed, with the notable exception of the X chromosome, the genes from a single human chromosome usually have their counterparts distributed over many mouse chromosomes (and vice-versa). We hope that there is a nagging voice in your head, wondering: *How can a genome rearrangement affect multiple chromosomes?*

Although multichromosomal rearrangements have occurred during species evolution over millions of years, we can witness them during a much narrower time frame in cancer cells, which exhibit many chromosomal aberrations. Some of these mutations have no direct effect on tumor development, but many types of tumors display recurrent rearrangements that trigger tumor growth by disrupting genes or altering gene regulation. By studying these rearrangements, we can identify genes that are important for tumor growth, leading to improved cancer diagnostics and therapeutics.

Figure 6.8 presents a rearrangement involving human chromosomes 9 and 22 in a rare form of cancer called **chronic myeloid leukemia (CML)**. In this type of rearrangement, called a **translocation**, two intervals of DNA are excised from the end of chromosomes 9 and 22 and then reattached on opposite chromosomes. One of the rearranged chromosomes is called the **Philadelphia chromosome**. This chromosome fuses together two genes called ABL and BCR that normally have nothing to do with each other. However, when joined on the Philadelphia chromosome, these two genes create a single **chimeric gene** coding for the **ABL-BCR fusion protein**, which has been implicated in the development of CML.

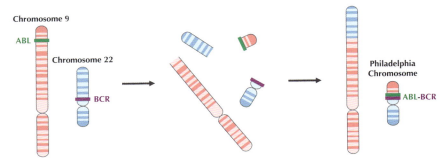

FIGURE 6.8 The Philadelphia chromosome is formed by a translocation affecting chromosomes 9 and 22. It fuses together the ABL and BCR genes, forming a chimeric gene that can trigger CML.

Once scientists understood the root cause of CML, they started searching for a compound inhibiting ABL-BCR, which resulted in the introduction of a drug called **Gleevec** in 2001. Gleevec is a **targeted therapy** against CML that inhibits cancer cells but does not affect normal cells and has shown great clinical results. However, since it targets only the ABL-BCR fusion protein, Gleevec does not treat most other cancers. Nevertheless, the introduction of Gleevec has bolstered researchers' hopes that the search for specific rearrangements in other forms of cancer may produce additional targeted cancer therapies.

From Unichromosomal to Multichromosomal Genomes

Translocations, fusions, and fissions

To model translocations, we represent a multichromosomal genome with k chromosomes as a permutation that has been partitioned into k pieces. For example, the genome $(+1 +2 +3 +4 +5 +6)(+7 +8 +9 +10 +11)$ is made up of the two chromosomes $(+1 +2 +3 +4 +5 +6)$ and $(+7 +8 +9 +10 +11)$. A translocation exchanges segments of different chromosomes, e.g., a translocation of the two chromosomes

$$(+1 +2 +3 +4 +5 +6) (+7 +8 +9 +10 +11)$$

may result in the two chromosomes

$$(+1 \ +2 \ +3 \ +4 \ +9 \ +10 \ +11) \ (+7 \ +8 \ +5 \ +6).$$

You can think about a translocation as first breaking each of the two chromosomes

$$(+1 \ +2 \ +3 \ +4 \ +5 \ +6) \quad (+7 \ +8 \ +9 \ +10 \ +11)$$

into two parts,

$$(+1 \ +2 \ +3 \ +4) \quad (+5 \ +6) \qquad (+7 \ +8) \quad (+9 \ +10 \ +11),$$

and then gluing the resulting segments into two new chromosomes,

$$(+1 \ +2 \ +3 \ +4 \ +9 \ +10 \ +11) \quad (+7 \ +8 \ +5 \ +6).$$

Rearrangements in multichromosomal genomes are not limited to reversals and translocations. They also include chromosome **fusions**, which merge two chromosomes into a single chromosome, as well as **fissions**, which break a single chromosome into two chromosomes. For example, the two chromosomes

$$(+1 \ +2 \ +3 \ +4 \ +5 \ +6) \quad (+7 \ +8 \ +9 \ +10 \ +11)$$

can be fused into the single chromosome

$$(+1 \ +2 \ +3 \ +4 \ +5 \ +6 \ +7 \ +8 \ +9 \ +10 \ +11).$$

A subsequent fission of this chromosome could result in the two chromosomes

$$(+1 \ +2 \ +3 \ +4) \quad (+5 \ +6 \ +7 \ +8 \ +9 \ +10 \ +11).$$

Five million years ago, shortly after the human and chimpanzee lineages split, a fusion of two chromosomes (called 2A and 2B) in one of our ancestors created human chromosome 2 and reduced our chromosome count from 24 to 23.

STOP and Think: *A priori*, it could just as easily be the case that the human-chimpanzee ancestor had an intact chromosome 2, and that a fission split these two chromosomes into chimpanzee chromosomes 2A and 2B. How would you choose between the two scenarios? Hint: gorillas and orangutans, like chimpanzees, also have 24 chromosomes.

From a genome to a graph

We will henceforth assume that all chromosomes in a genome are circular. This assumption represents a slight distortion of biological reality, as mammalian chromosomes are linear. However, circularizing a linear chromosome by joining its endpoints will simplify the subsequent analysis without affecting our conclusions.

We now have a multichromosomal genomic model, along with four types of rearrangements (reversals, translocations, fusions, and fissions) that can transform one genome into another. To model genomes with circular chromosomes, we will use a **genome graph**. First represent each synteny block by a directed black edge indicating its direction, and then link black edges corresponding to adjacent synteny blocks with a colored undirected edge. Figure 6.9 shows each circular chromosome as an **alternating cycle** of red and black edges. In this model, the human genome can be represented using 280 human-mouse synteny blocks spread over 23 alternating cycles.

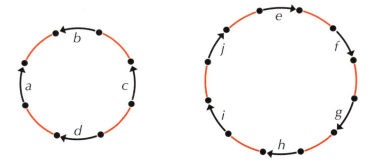

FIGURE 6.9 A genome with two circular chromosomes, $(+a -b -c +d)$ and $(+e +f +g +h +i +j)$. Black directed edges represent synteny blocks, and red undirected edges connect adjacent synteny blocks. A circular chromosome with n elements can be written in $2n$ different ways; the chromosome on the left can be written as $(+a -b -c +d)$, $(-b -c +d +a)$, $(-c +d +a -b)$, $(+d +a -b -c)$, $(-a -d +c +b)$ $(-d +c +b -a)$, $(+c +b -a -d)$, and $(+b -a -d +c)$.

STOP and Think: Let P and Q be genomes consisting of linear chromosomes, and let P^* and Q^* be the circularized versions of these genomes. Can you convert a given series of reversals/translocations/fusions/fissions transforming P into Q into a series of rearrangements transforming P^* into Q^*? What about the reverse operation — can you convert a series of rearrangements transforming P^* into Q^* into a series of rearrangements transforming P into Q?

2-breaks

We now focus on one of the chromosomes in a multi-chromosomal genome and consider a reversal transforming the circular chromosome $P = (+a -b -c +d)$ into $Q = (+a -b -d +c)$. We can draw Q in a variety of ways, depending on how we choose to arrange its black edges. Figure 6.10 shows two such equivalent representations.

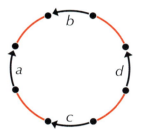 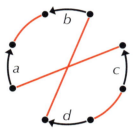

FIGURE 6.10 Two equivalent drawings of the circular chromosome $Q = (+a -b -d +c)$.

Although the first drawing of Q in Figure 6.10 is its most natural representation, we will use the second representation because its black edges are arranged around the circle in exactly the same order as they appear in the natural representation of $P = (+a -b -c +d)$. As illustrated in Figure 6.11, keeping the black edges fixed allows us to visualize the effect of the reversal. As you can see, the reversal deletes ("breaks") two red edges in P (connecting b to c and d to a) and replaces them with two new red edges (connecting b to d and c to a).

Figure 6.12 illustrates a fission of $P = (+a -b -c +d)$ into $Q = (+a -b)(-c +d)$; reversing this operation corresponds to a fusion of the two chromosomes of Q to yield P. Both the fusion and the fission operations, like the reversal, correspond to deleting two edges in one genome and replacing them with two new edges in the other genome.

A translocation involving two *linear* chromosomes can also be mimicked by circularizing these chromosomes and then replacing two red edges with two different red edges, as shown in Figure 6.13. We have therefore found a common theme uniting the four different types of rearrangements. They all can be viewed as breaking two red edges of the genome graph and replacing them with two new red edges on the same four nodes. For this reason, we define the general operation on the genome graph in which two red edges are replaced with two new red edges on the same four nodes as a **2-break**.

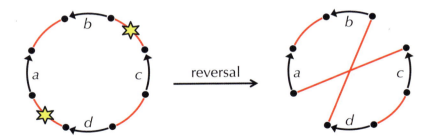

FIGURE 6.11 A reversal transforms $P = (+a\ -b\ -c\ +d)$ into $Q = (+a\ -b\ -d\ +c)$. We have arranged the black edges of Q so that they have the same orientation and position as the black edges in the natural representation of P. The reversal can be viewed as deleting the two red edges labeled by stars and replacing them with two new red edges on the same four nodes.

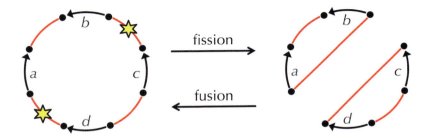

FIGURE 6.12 A fission of the single chromosome $P = (+a\ -b\ -c\ +d)$ into the genome $Q = (+a\ -b)(-c\ +d)$. The inverse operation is a fusion, transforming the two chromosomes of Q into a single chromosome by deleting two red edges of Q and replacing them with two other edges.

We would like to find a shortest sequence of 2-breaks transforming genome P into genome Q, and we refer to the number of operations in a shortest sequence of 2-breaks transforming P into Q as the **2-break distance** between P and Q, denoted $d(P, Q)$.

2-Break Distance Problem:

Find the 2-break distance between two genomes.

Input: Two genomes with circular chromosomes on the same synteny blocks.
Output: The 2-break distance between these genomes.

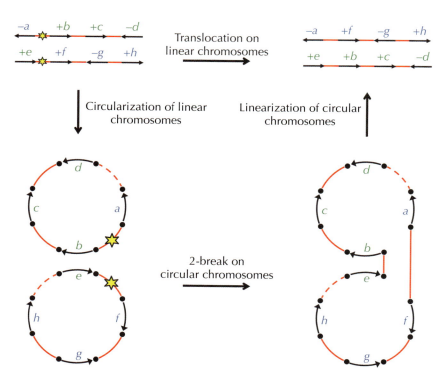

FIGURE 6.13 A translocation of linear chromosomes $(-a +b +c -d)$ and $(+e +f$ $-g +h)$ transforms them into linear chromosomes $(-a +f -g +h)$ and $(+e +b$ $+c -d)$. This translocation can also be accomplished by first circularizing the chromosomes (i.e., connecting the ends of each chromosome with a dashed red edge), then applying a 2-break to the new chromosomes, and finally converting the resulting circular chromosome into two linear chromosomes by removing the dashed red edges.

Breakpoint Graphs

To compute the 2-break distance, we will return to the notion of breakpoints to construct a graph for comparing two genomes. Consider the genomes $P = (+a -b -c +d)$ and $Q = (+a +c +b -d)$. Note that we have used red for the colored edges of P and blue for the colored edges of Q. As before, we rearrange the black edges of Q so that they are arranged exactly as in P (Figure 6.14, middle). If we superimpose the genome graphs of P and Q, then we obtain the tri-colored **breakpoint graph** BREAKPOINTGRAPH(P, Q), shown in Figure 6.14.

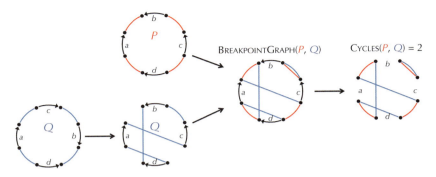

FIGURE 6.14 Constructing the breakpoint graph for the unichromosomal genomes $P = (+a -b -c +d)$ and $Q = (+a +c +b -d)$. After rearranging the black edges of Q so that they are arranged the same as in P, the breakpoint graph BREAKPOINTGRAPH(P, Q) is formed by superimposing the graphs of P and Q. As shown on the right, there are two alternating red-blue cycles in this breakpoint graph.

Note that the red and black edges in the breakpoint graph form P, and the blue and black edges form Q. Moreover, the red and blue edges in the breakpoint graph form a collection of red-blue alternating cycles.

STOP and Think: Prove that the red and blue edges in any breakpoint graph form alternating cycles. Hint: How many red and blue edges meet at each node of the breakpoint graph?

We denote the number of red-blue alternating cycles in BREAKPOINTGRAPH(P, Q) as CYCLES(P, Q). For $P = (+a -b -c +d)$ and $Q = (+a +c +b -d)$, CYCLES$(P, Q) = 2$, as shown on the right in Figure 6.16. In what follows, we will be focusing on the red-blue alternating cycles in breakpoint graphs and often omit the black edges.

Although Figure 6.14 illustrates the construction of the breakpoint graph for single-chromosomal genomes, the breakpoint graph can be constructed for genomes with multiple chromosomes in exactly the same way (Figure 6.15).

STOP and Think: Given genome P, which genome Q maximizes CYCLES(P, Q)?

In the case that P and Q have the same number of synteny blocks, we denote the number of their synteny blocks as BLOCKS(P, Q). As shown in Figure 6.16, when P and Q are identical, their breakpoint graph consists of BLOCKS(P, Q) cycles of length

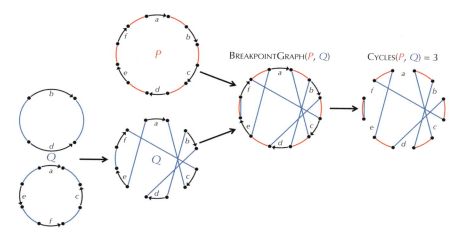

FIGURE 6.15 The construction of BREAKPOINTGRAPH(P, Q) for the unichromosomal genome $P = (+a +b +c +d +e +f)$ and the two-chromosome genome $Q = (+a -c -f -e)(+b -d)$. At the bottom, to illustrate the construction of the breakpoint graph, we first rearrange the black edges of Q so that they are drawn the same as in P.

2, each containing one red and one blue edge. We refer to cycles of length 2 as **trivial cycles** and the breakpoint graph formed by identical genomes as the **trivial breakpoint graph**.

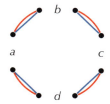

FIGURE 6.16 The trivial breakpoint graph BREAKPOINTGRAPH(P, P), formed by two copies of the genome $P = (+a -b -c +d)$. The breakpoint graph of *any* genome with itself consists only of length 2 alternating cycles.

EXERCISE BREAK: Prove that CYCLES(P, Q) is smaller than BLOCKS(P, Q) unless P is equal to Q.

You are likely wondering how the breakpoint graph is useful. We can view a 2-break transforming P into P' as an operation on BREAKPOINTGRAPH(P, Q) that yields BREAKPOINTGRAPH(P', Q) (Figure 6.17).

By extension, we can view a series of 2-breaks transforming P into Q as a series of 2-breaks transforming BREAKPOINTGRAPH(P, Q) into BREAKPOINTGRAPH(Q, Q), the trivial breakpoint graph. Figure 6.18 illustrates a transformation of a breakpoint graph with CYCLES$(P, Q) = 2$ into a trivial breakpoint graph with CYCLES$(Q, Q) = 4$ using two 2-breaks.

FIGURE 6.17 A 2-break (indicated by stars) transforming genome P into P' also transforms BREAKPOINTGRAPH(P, Q) into BREAKPOINTGRAPH(P', Q) for any genome Q. In this example, $P = (+a -b -c +d)$, $P' = (+a -b -c -d)$, and $Q = (+a +c +b -d)$.

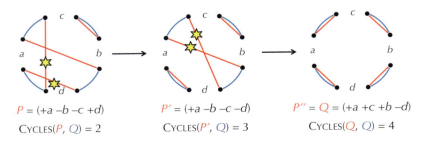

$P = (+a -b -c +d)$ $P' = (+a -b -c -d)$ $P'' = Q = (+a +c +b -d)$

CYCLES$(P, Q) = 2$ CYCLES$(P', Q) = 3$ CYCLES$(Q, Q) = 4$

FIGURE 6.18 Every 2-break transformation of genome P into Q corresponds to a transformation of BREAKPOINTGRAPH(P, Q) into BREAKPOINTGRAPH(Q, Q). In the example shown, the number of red-blue cycles in the graph increases from CYCLES$(P, Q) = 2$ to CYCLES$(Q, Q) = $ BLOCKS$(Q, Q) = 4$.

Since every transformation of P into Q transforms BREAKPOINTGRAPH(P, Q) into the trivial breakpoint graph BREAKPOINTGRAPH(Q, Q), any sorting by 2-breaks increases the number of red-blue cycles by

$$\text{CYCLES}(Q, Q) - \text{CYCLES}(P, Q).$$

STOP and Think: How much can each 2-break contribute to this increase? In other words, if P' is obtained from P by a 2-break, how much bigger can CYCLES(P', Q) be than CYCLES(P, Q)?

Computing the 2-Break Distance

The Breakpoint Theorem stated that a reversal applied to a linear chromosome P can reduce BREAKPOINTS(P) by at most 2. We now prove that a 2-break applied to a multichromosomal genome P can increase CYCLES(P, Q) by at most 1, i.e., for any 2-break transforming P into P', and for any genome Q, CYCLES(P', Q) cannot exceed CYCLES$(P, Q) + 1$.

Cycle Theorem: *For genomes P and Q, any 2-break applied to P can increase* CYCLES(P, Q) *by at most 1.*

Proof. Figure 6.19 presents three cases that illustrate how a 2-break applied to P can affect the breakpoint graph. Each 2-break affects two red edges that either belong to the same cycle or to two different cycles in BREAKPOINTGRAPH(P, Q). In the former case, the 2-break either does not change CYCLES(P, Q), or it increases it by 1. In the latter case, it decreases CYCLES(P, Q) by 1. ☐

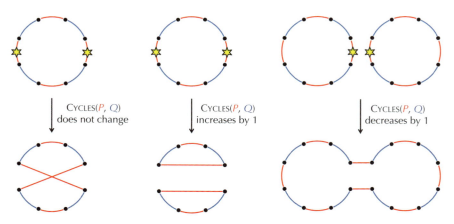

FIGURE 6.19 Three cases illustrating how a 2-break can affect the breakpoint graph.

Although the preceding proof is short and intuitive, it is not a formal proof, but rather an invitation to examine Figure 6.19. If you are interested in a more rigorous mathematical argument, please read the next proof.

Proof. A 2-break adds two new red edges and thus forms at most **2** new cycles (containing two new red edges) in BREAKPOINTGRAPH(P, Q). At the same time, it deletes two red edges and thus deletes at least **1** old cycle (containing two old edges) from BREAKPOINTGRAPH(P, Q). Thus, the number of red-blue cycles in the breakpoint graph increases by at most $2 - 1 = 1$, implying that CYCLES(P, Q) increases by at most 1. $\qquad\square$

Recall that there are permutations for which no reversal reduces the number of breakpoints, a fact that defeated our hopes for a greedy algorithm for sorting by reversals that reduces the number of breakpoints at each step. In the case of 2-breaks (on genomes with circular chromosomes), we now know that each 2-break can increase CYCLES(P, Q) by at most 1. But is it *always* possible to find a 2-break that increases CYCLES(P, Q) by 1? As the following theorem illustrates, the answer is yes.

2-Break Distance Theorem: *The 2-break distance between genomes P and Q is equal to* BLOCKS$(P, Q) -$ CYCLES(P, Q).

Proof. Recall that every sorting by 2-breaks must increase the number of alternating cycles by CYCLES$(Q, Q) -$ CYCLES(P, Q), which equals BLOCKS$(P, Q) -$ CYCLES(P, Q) because BLOCKS$(P, Q) =$ CYCLES(Q, Q). The Cycle Theorem implies that each 2-break increases the number of cycles in the breakpoint graph by at most 1. This immediately implies in turn that $d(P, Q)$ is *at least* BLOCKS$(P, Q) -$ CYCLES(P, Q). If P is not equal to Q, then there must be a **non-trivial cycle** in BREAKPOINTGRAPH(P, Q), i.e., a cycle with more than two edges. As shown in Figure 6.19 (middle), any non-trivial cycle in the breakpoint graph can be split into two cycles by a 2-break, implying that we can always find a 2-break increasing the number of red-blue cycles by 1. Therefore, $d(P, Q)$ is equal to BLOCKS$(P, Q) -$ CYCLES(P, Q). $\qquad\square$

Armed with this theorem, you should be ready to design an algorithm solving the 2-Break Distance Problem.

CHARGING STATION (From Genomes to the Breakpoint Graph): You may be wondering how the graph representation that we have been using for breakpoint graphs could be transformed into an adjacency list. After all, we haven't even labeled the nodes of this graph! Check out this Charging Station to see how to implement the genome graph.

We now know how to compute the 2-break distance, but we would also like to reconstruct a collection of 2-breaks making up a shortest path between two genomes. This problem is called **2-break sorting**, which we leave to you as an exercise.

2-Break Sorting Problem:

Find a shortest transformation of one genome into another by 2-breaks.

Input: Two genomes with circular chromosomes on the same synteny blocks.
Output: The sequence of genomes resulting from applying a shortest sequence of 2-breaks transforming one genome into the other.

PAGE 338

CHARGING STATION (Solving the 2-Break Sorting Problem): The Breakpoint Theorem guarantees that there is always a 2-break reducing the number of red-blue cycles in the breakpoint graph by 1. However, it does not tell us how to find such a 2-break. Check out this Charging Station to see how this can be done.

Having proved the formula $d(P, Q) = \text{BLOCKS}(P, Q) - \text{CYCLES}(P, Q)$ for the 2-break distance between genomes with multiple circular chromosomes, we wonder whether we can find an analogous formula for the reversal distance between single linear chromosomes.

EXERCISE BREAK: Compute the 2-break distance between the circularized human and mouse X chromosomes. Can you transform a series of 2-breaks for these chromosomes into a series of reversals sorting the linear X chromosomes?

It turns out that a polynomial algorithm for sorting permutations by reversals does exist, yielding an exact formula for the reversal distance! Although this algorithm also relies on the notion of the breakpoint graph, it is unfortunately too complicated to present **PAGE 343** here (see DETOUR: Sorting Linear Permutations by Reversals).

The breakpoint graph constructed on the 280 human-mouse synteny blocks contains 35 alternating cycles, so that the 2-break distance between these genomes is $280 - 35 = 245$. Again, we don't know exactly how many 2-breaks happened in the last 75 million years, but we are certain that there were *at least* 245 steps. Remember this fact, since it will prove important in the next section.

Rearrangement Hotspots in the Human Genome

The Random Breakage Model meets the 2-Break Distance Theorem

You have probably anticipated from the beginning of the chapter that we would eventually argue against the Random Breakage Model. But it may still be unclear to you how the 2-break distance could possibly be used to do so.

Rearrangement Hotspots Theorem: *There are rearrangement hotspots in the human genome.*

Proof. Recall that if the Random Breakage Model is correct, then N reversals applied to a linear chromosome will produce approximately $2N + 1$ synteny blocks, since the probability is very low that two nearby locations in the genome will be used as the breakage point of more than one reversal. Similarly, N random 2-breaks applied to circular chromosomes will produce $2N$ synteny blocks. Since there are 280 human-mouse synteny blocks, there must have been approximately $280/2 = 140$ 2-breaks on the evolutionary path between humans and mice. However, the 2-Break Distance Theorem tells us that there were at least 245 2-breaks on this evolutionary path.

STOP and Think: Is $245 \approx 140$?

Since 245 is much larger than 140, we have arrived at a contradiction, implying that one of our assumptions is incorrect! But the only assumption we made in this proof was *"If the Random Breakage Model is correct..."* Thus, this assumption must have been wrong. □

This argument, which is not a mathematical proof, is nevertheless logically solid. It offers an example of a **proof by contradiction**, in which we begin by assuming the statement that we intend to disprove and then demonstrate how this assumption cannot be true. As a result of the Rearrangement Hotspots Theorem, we conclude that there was breakpoint reuse on the human-mouse evolutionary path. This breakpoint reuse was extensive, as quantified by the large ratio between the actual 2-break distance and what the 2-break distance would have been under the Random Breakage Model ($245/140 = 1.75$).

Of course, our arguments need to be made statistically sound in order to ensure that the discrepancy between the Random Breakage Model's prediction and the 2-break distance is significant. After all, even though genomes are large, there is still a small chance that randomly chosen 2-breaks might occasionally break a genome more than once in a small interval. The necessary statistical analysis is beyond the scope of this book.

The Fragile Breakage Model

But wait — what about Nadeau and Taylor's argument in favor of the Random Breakage Model? We certainly cannot ignore that the lengths of the human-mouse synteny blocks resemble an exponential distribution.

STOP and Think: Can you find anything wrong with Nadeau and Taylor's logic?

The Nadeau and Taylor argument in favor of the Random Breakage Model exemplifies a classic logic fallacy. It is true that if breakage is random, then the histogram of synteny block lengths should follow the exponential distribution. But it is a completely different statement to conclude that just because synteny block lengths follow the exponential distribution, breakage must have been random. The distribution of synteny block lengths certainly provides support for the Random Breakage Model, but it does not prove that it is correct.

Nevertheless, any alternative hypothesis we put forth for the Random Breakage Model must account for the observation that the distribution of synteny block lengths for the human and mouse genomes is approximately exponential.

STOP and Think: Can you propose a different model of chromosome evolution that explains rearrangement hotspots and is consistent with the exponential distribution of synteny block lengths?

The contradiction of the Random Breakage Model led to an alternative **Fragile Breakage Model** of chromosome evolution, which was proposed in 2003. This model states that every mammalian genome is a mosaic of long solid regions, which are rarely affected by rearrangements, as well as short **fragile regions** that serve as rearrangement hotspots and that account only for a small fraction of the genome. For humans and mice, these fragile regions make up approximately 3% of the genome.

If we once again follow Occam's razor, then the most reasonable way to allow for exponentially distributed synteny block lengths is if the fragile regions themselves are distributed randomly in the genome. Indeed, *randomly* selecting breakpoints within *randomly* distributed fragile regions is not unlike randomly selecting the endpoints of a rearrangement throughout the entire genome. Yet although we now have a model that fits our observations, many questions remain. For example, it is unclear where fragile regions are located, or what causes genomic fragility in the first place.

> **STOP and Think:** Consider the following statement: "The exponential distribution of synteny block lengths and extensive breakpoint re-use imply that the Fragile Breakage Model must be true." Is this argument logically sound?

The point we are attempting to make by asking the preceding question is that we will never be able to prove a scientific theory like the Fragile Breakage Model in the same way that we have proved one of the mathematical theorems in this chapter. In fact, many biological theories are based on arguments that a mathematician would view as fallacious; the logical framework used in biology is quite different from that used in mathematics. To take an historical example, neither Darwin nor anyone else has ever proved that evolution by natural selection is the only — or even the most likely — explanation for how life on Earth evolved!

We have already given many reasons to biology professors to send us to Biology 101 boot camp, but now we will probably be rounded up and thrown into the Gulag alongside Intelligent Design proponents. However, the fact remains that not even Darwinism is unassailable; in the 20th Century, this theory was revised into Neo-Darwinism, and there is little doubt that it will continue to evolve.

Epilogue: Synteny Block Construction

Throughout our discussion of genome rearrangements, we assumed that we were given synteny blocks in advance. In this section, we will describe one way of constructing synteny blocks from genomic sequences.

Genomic dot-plots

Biologists sometimes visualize repeated k-mers within a string as a collection of points in the plane; a point with coordinates (x, y) represents identical k-mers occurring at positions x and y in the string. The top panels in Figure 6.20 present two of these **genomic dot plots**. Of course, since DNA is double-stranded, we should expand the notion of repeated k-mers to account for repeats occurring on the complementary strand. In the bottom left panel of Figure 6.20, blue points (x, y) indicate that the k-mers starting at positions x and y of the string are reverse complementary.

Finding shared k-mers

Recalling that a synteny block is defined by many similar genes occurring in the same order in two genomes, let's first find the positions of all *k*-mers that are shared by the human and mouse X chromosomes. If we choose *k* to be sufficiently large (e.g., $k = 30$), then it is rather unlikely that shared *k*-mers represent spurious similarities. A more likely explanation is that they come from related genes (or shared repeats) in the human and mouse genomes.

Formally, we say that a *k*-mer is **shared** by two genomes if either the *k*-mer or its reverse complement appears in each genome. Below are four pairs of 3-mers (shown in bold) that are shared by AAACTCATC and TTTCAAATC; note that the second pair of 3-mers are reverse complements of each other.

0	0	4	6
AAACTCATC	**AAA**CTCATC	AAAC**TCA**TC	AAACTC**ATC**
TTTC**AAA**TC	**TTT**CAAATC	TTT**CA**AATC	TTTCAA**ATC**
4	0	2	6

We can further generalize the genomic dot plot to analyze the shared *k*-mer content of two genomes. We color the point (x, y) red if the two genomes share a *k*-mer starting at respective positions x and y; we color (x, y) blue if the two genomes have reverse complementary *k*-mers at these starting positions. See Figure 6.20 (bottom right).

EXERCISE BREAK: Find all shared 2-mers of AAACTCATC and TTTCAAATC.

Shared *k*-mers Problem:

Given two strings, find all their shared k-mers.

> **Input**: An integer *k* and two strings.
> **Output**: All *k*-mers shared by these strings, in the form of ordered pairs (x, y) corresponding to starting positions of these *k*-mers in the respective strings.

EXERCISE BREAK: Answer the following questions regarding counting shared *k*-mers.

1. Compute the expected number of 30-mers shared by two random strings, each a billion nucleotides long.

2. How many shared 30-mers do the *E. coli* and *S. enterica* genomes share?

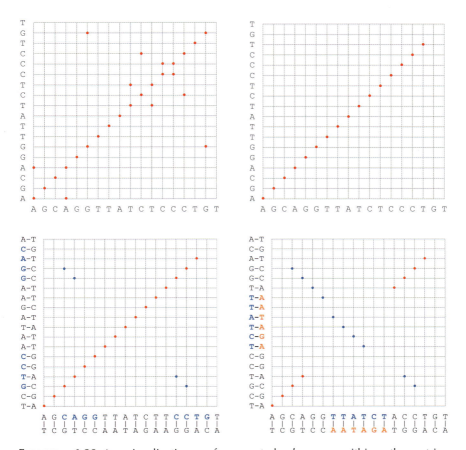

FIGURE 6.20 A visualization of repeated *k*-mers within the string AGCAGGTTATCTCCCTGT for *k* = 2 (top left) and *k* = 3 (top right). (Bottom left) We add blue points to the plot shown in the upper left corner to indicate reverse complementary *k*-mers. For example, CCT and AGG are reverse complementary 3-mers in AGCAGGTTATCTTCCTGT. (Bottom right): Genomic dot-plot showing shared 3-mers between AGCAGG**TTATCT**ACCTGT and AGCAGG**AGATAA**ACCTGT. The latter sequence resulted from the former sequence by a reversal of the segment **TTATCT**. Each point (x, y) corresponds to a *k*-mer shared by the two genomes. Red points indicate identical shared *k*-mers, whereas blue points indicate reverse complementary *k*-mers. Note that the dot-plot has six "noisy" blue points in the diagram: four in the upper left corner, and two in the bottom right corner. You will also notice that red dots can be connected into line segments with slope 1 and blue dots can be connected into line segments with slope −1. The resulting three synteny blocks (**AGCAGG**, **TTATCT**, and **CCCTGT**) correspond to three diagonals (each formed by four points) in the dot-plot.

The *E. coli* and *S. enterica* genomes are both about five million nucleotides long. It can be shown that the expected number of shared 30-mers between two random 5 million nucleotide-long sequences is approximately $2 \cdot (5 \cdot 10^6)^2 / 4^{30} \approx 1/20,000$.

Yet solving the Shared *k*-mers Problem for *E. coli* and *S. enterica* yields over 200,000 pairs (x, y) corresponding to shared 30-mers. The surprisingly large number of shared 30-mers indicates that *E. coli* and *S. enterica* are close relatives that have retained many similar genes inherited from their common ancestor. However, these genes may be arranged in a different order in the two species: how can we infer synteny blocks from these genomes' shared *k*-mers? The genomic dot-plot plot for *E. coli* and *S. enterica* is shown in Figure 6.21.

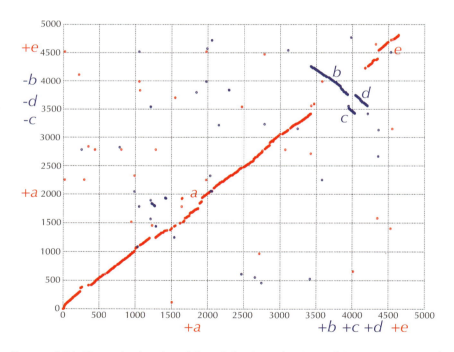

FIGURE 6.21 Genomic dot-plot of *E. coli* (horizontal axis) and *S. enterica* (vertical axis) for $k = 30$. Each point (x, y) corresponds to a *k*-mer shared by the two genomes. Red points indicate identical shared *k*-mers, whereas blue points indicate reverse complementary *k*-mers. Each axis is measured in kilobases (thousands of base pairs).

STOP and Think: Can you see the synteny blocks in the genomic dot-plot in Figure 6.21?

Constructing synteny blocks from shared k-mers

The genomic dot-plot in Figure 6.21 indicates five regions of similarity in the form of points that clump together into approximately diagonal segments. These segments are labeled by *a*, *b*, *c*, *d*, and *e* according to the order in which they appear in the *E. coli* genome. We ignore smaller diagonals such as the short blue diagonal starting around position 1.3 million in *E. coli* and around position 1.9 million in *S. enterica*. For example, while *a* corresponds to a long diagonal segment of slope 1 that covers approximately the first 3.5 million positions in both genomes, *b* corresponds to a shorter diagonal segment of slope −1 that starts shortly before position 3.5 million in *E. coli* and shortly after position 4 million in *S. enterica*. Although *b* appears small in Figure 6.21, don't be fooled by the scale of the figure; *b* is over 100,000 nucleotides long and contains nearly 100 genes.

The segments *a*, *b*, *c*, *d*, and *e* give us the synteny blocks that we have been looking for. If we project these blocks onto the *x*- and *y*-axes, then the ordering of blocks on each axis corresponds to the ordering of synteny blocks in the respective bacterium. The ordering of synteny blocks in *E. coli* (plotted on the *x*-axis) is $(+a +b +c +d +e)$, and the ordering in *S. enterica* (*y*-axis) is $(+a -c -d -b +e)$. Note that the blue letters in *S. enterica* are assigned a negative sign because these blocks were constructed from reverse complementary *k*-mers. Figure 6.21 also illustrates what the directions of blocks are — they respectively correspond to diagonals in the dot-plot with slope 1 (blocks with a "+" sign) and slope −1 (blocks with a "−" sign).

We have therefore represented the relationship between two bacterial genomes using just five synteny blocks. Of course, this simplification required us to throw out some points in the dot plot, corresponding to tiny regions of similarity that did not surpass a threshold length in order to be considered synteny blocks.

We are now ready to construct the eleven human-mouse synteny blocks originally presented in Figure 6.1 (page 294), but since the human and mouse X chromosomes are rather long, we will instead provide you with all positions (x, y) where they share significant similarities. Figure 6.22 (top left) presents the resulting genomic dot-plot for the human and mouse X chromosomes, where each point represents a long similar region rather than a shared *k*-mer. Our eyes immediately find eleven diagonals in this plot corresponding to the human-mouse X chromosome synteny blocks — problem solved! We state this problem as the Synteny Blocks Problem.

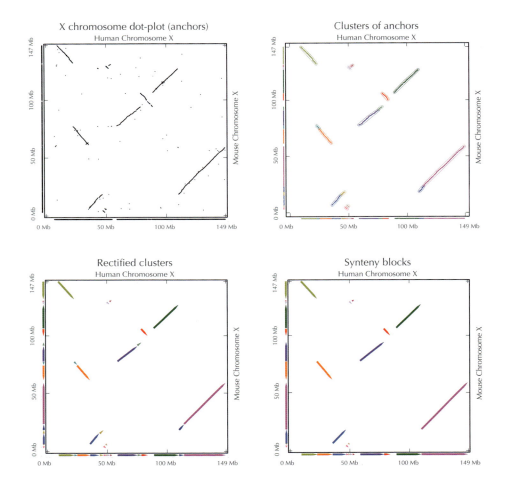

FIGURE 6.22 From local similarities to synteny blocks. (Top left) The genomic dot-plot for the human and mouse X chromosomes, representing all positions (x, y) where they share significant similarities. In contrast with Figure 6.21, we do not distinguish between red and blue dots. (Top right) Clusters (connected components) of points in the genomic dot-plot are formed by constructing the synteny graph. (Bottom left) Rectified clusters from the synteny graph transform each cluster into an exact diagonal of slope ± 1. (Bottom right) Aggregated synteny blocks. Projection of the synteny blocks to the x-and y-axes results in the arrangements of synteny blocks in the respective human and mouse genomes ($+1\ +2\ +3\ +4\ +5\ +6\ +7\ +8\ +9\ +10\ +11$) and ($+1\ -7\ +6\ -10\ +9\ -8\ +2\ -11\ -3\ +5\ +4$).

Synteny Blocks Problem:

Find diagonals in the genomic dot-plot.

> **Input**: A set of points *DotPlot* in the plane.
> **Output**: A set of diagonals in *DotPlot* representing synteny blocks.

Unfortunately, it remains unclear how to write a program to do what our eyes found to be so easy; we hope you have already noticed that the Synteny Blocks Problem is not a well-formulated computational problem. As we have mentioned, the diagonals in Figure 6.22 (top left) are not perfect. Moreover, there are many gaps within diagonals that cannot be seen by the human eye but will become apparent if we zoom into the genome plot. It is therefore unclear what method the human brain is using to transform the dots into the eleven diagonals in the genomic dot-plot.

STOP and Think: How can we translate the brain's ability to construct the diagonals that you see in Figure 6.22 (top left) into an algorithm that a computer can understand?

Synteny blocks as connected components in graphs

The reason why you can easily see the synteny blocks in a genomic dot-plot is that your brain is good at *clustering* nearby points in an image. To mimic this process with a computer, we therefore need a precise notion of clustering. Given a set of points *DotPlot* in the plane as well as a parameter *maxDistance*, we will construct the (undirected) **synteny graph** SYNTENYGRAPH(*DotPlot*, *maxDistance*) by connecting two points in *DotPlot* with an edge if the distance between them does not exceed *maxDistance*.

Every graph can be divided into disjoint connected subgraphs called **connected components**. The connected components in SYNTENYGRAPH(*DotPlot*, *maxDistance*) represent candidate synteny blocks between the two genomes (Figure 6.23). When we construct the synteny graph for the human and mouse X chromosomes, we find a huge number of small connected components (the exact number depends on our choice of the *maxDistance* parameter). However, we will ignore these small connected components, since they may represent spurious similarities. We thus introduce the parameter *minSize* representing the minimum number of points in a connected component that we will consider as forming a synteny block. Our goal is to return all connected components having at least *minSize* nodes.

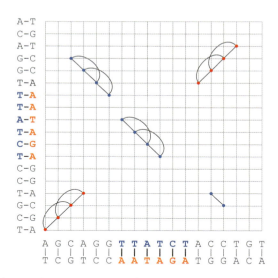

FIGURE 6.23 The graph SYNTENYGRAPH(*DotPlot*, 4) constructed from the genomic dot-plot of AGCAGG**TTATCT**CCCTGT and AGCAGG**AGATAA**CCCTGT for *k* = 3. Note that the three synteny blocks (all of which have four nodes) correspond to diagonals in the genomic dot-plot. We ignore the two smaller, noisy synteny blocks.

SYNTENYBLOCKS(*DotPlot, maxDistance, minSize*)
  construct SYNTENYGRAPH(*DotPlot, maxDistance*)
  find the connected components in SYNTENYGRAPH(*DotPlot, maxDistance*)
  output connected components containing at least *minSize* nodes as candidate synteny blocks

As Figure 6.22 (top right) illustrates, **SYNTENYBLOCKS** has the tendency to partition a single diagonal (as perceived by the human eye) into multiple diagonals due to gaps that exceed the parameter *maxDistance*. However, this partitioning is not a problem, since the broken diagonals can be combined later into a single (aggregated) synteny block.

STOP and Think: We have defined synteny blocks as large connected components in SYNTENYGRAPH(*DotPlot, maxDistance*) but have not described how to determine where these synteny blocks are located in the original genomes. Using Figure 6.22 as a hint, design an algorithm for finding this information.

You should now be ready to solve the challenge problem and discover that the choice of parameters is one of the dark secrets of bioinformatics research.

> **CHALLENGE PROBLEM:** Construct the synteny blocks for the human and mouse X chromosomes and compute the 2-break distance between the circularized human and mouse X chromosomes using the synteny blocks that you constructed. How does this distance change depending on the parameters *maxDistance* and *minSize*?

Open Problem: Can Rearrangements Shed Light on Bacterial Evolution?

Although there exist efficient algorithms for analyzing *pairwise* genome rearrangements, constructing rearrangement scenarios for *multiple* genomes remains an open problem. For example, we now know how to find a most parsimonious rearrangement scenario transforming the mouse X chromosome into the human X chromosome. However, the problem of finding a most parsimonious rearrangement scenario for the human, mouse, and rat X chromosomes — let alone for their entire genomes — is a more difficult problem. The difficulties further amplify when we attempt to reconstruct a rearrangement history for dozens of mammalian genomes. To address this challenge, we start from the simpler (but still unsolved) case of bacterial genomes.

Let *Tree* be a tree (i.e., a connected acyclic undirected graph) with nodes labeled by some genomes. In the case of bacterial genomes, we assume that every node (genome) is labeled by a circular permutation on n elements. Given an edge e connecting nodes v and w in *Tree*, we define $\text{DISTANCE}(v, w)$ as the 2-break distance between genomes v and w. The **tree distance** $\text{DISTANCE}(\textit{Tree})$ is the sum

$$\sum_{\text{all edges } (v,w) \text{ in } \textit{Tree}} \text{DISTANCE}(v, w).$$

Given a set of genomes $P_1, \ldots, P_n$ and an evolutionary tree *Tree* with n leaves labeled by $P_1, \ldots, P_n$, the Ancestral Genome Reconstruction Problem attempts to reconstruct genomes at the internal nodes of the tree such that $\text{DISTANCE}(\textit{Tree})$ is minimized across all possible reconstructions of genomes at internal nodes.

Ancestral Genome Reconstruction Problem:

Given a tree with leaves labeled by genomes, reconstruct ancestral genomes that minimize the tree distance.

> **Input**: A tree *Tree* with each leaf labeled by a genome.
> **Output**: Genomes *AncestralGenomes* assigned to the internal nodes of *Tree* such that DISTANCE(*Tree*) is minimized across all possible choices of *AncestralGenomes*.

In the case when *Tree* is not given, we need to infer it from the genomes.

Multiple Genome Rearrangement Problem:

Given a set of genomes, reconstruct a tree with leaves labeled by these genomes and minimum tree distance.

> **Input**: A set of genomes.
> **Output**: A tree *Tree* with leaves labeled by these genomes and internal nodes labeled by (unknown) genomes *AncestralGenomes* such that DISTANCE(*Tree*) is minimal among all possible choices of *Tree* and *AncestralGenomes*.

Although many heuristics have been proposed for the Multiple Genome Rearrangement Problem, they have mainly been applied to analyze mammalian evolution. However, there have been hardly any applications of the Multiple Genome Rearrangement Problem for analyzing bacterial evolution. The fact that bacterial genomes are approximately 1,000 times smaller than mammalian genomes does not make this problem 1,000 times easier. In fact, there are unique challenges and opportunities in bacterial evolutionary research.

Consider 100 genomes from three closely related bacterial genera, *Salmonella*, *Shigella*, and *Escherichia*, whose various species are responsible for dysentery, typhoid fever, and a variety of foodborne illnesses. After you construct synteny blocks shared by all these genomes, you will see that there are relatively few (usually fewer than 10) rearrangements between every pair of genomes. However, solving the Multiple Genome Rearrangement Problem even in the case of closely related genomes presents a formidable challenge, and nobody has been able to construct a rearrangement scenario for more than a couple dozen — let alone 100! — species yet.

After you solve this puzzle, you will be able to address the question of whether there are fragile regions in bacterial genomes. Answering this question for a pair of bacterial genomes, like we did for the human and mouse genomes, may not be possible because there are typically fewer than 10 rearrangements between them. But answering this question for 100 bacterial genomes may be possible if we witness the same breakage occurring independently on many branches of the evolutionary tree. However, you will need to develop algorithms to analyze fragile regions in multiple (rather than pairwise) genomes.

After you construct the evolutionary tree, you will also be in a position to analyze the question of what triggers rearrangements. While many authors have discussed the causes of fragility, this question remains open, with no shortage of hypotheses. Many rearrangements are flanked by **matching duplications**, a pair of long similar regions located within a pair of breakpoint regions corresponding to a rearrangement event. However, it remains unclear what triggers rearrangements in bacteria; can you answer this question?

Charging Stations

From genomes to the breakpoint graph

Our goal is to count the number of cycles in the breakpoint graph and therefore solve the 2-Break Distance Problem. First, however, we will need to obtain a convenient graph representation of genomes. In the main text, we represented a circular chromosome by converting each synteny block into a directed edge, and then connected adjacent synteny blocks in the chromosome with red edges. Although this provided us with a way of visualizing genomes, it is not immediately clear how to represent this graph with an adjacency list.

Given a genome P, we will represent its synteny blocks not as letters but as integers from 1 to $n = |P|$. For example, $(+a\ -b\ -c\ +d)$ will be represented as $(+1\ -2\ -3\ +4)$ (Figure 6.24 (left)). Then, we will convert the directed black edges of P into undirected edges as follows. Given a directed edge labeled by integer x, we assign the node at the "head" of this edge as x_h and the node at the "tail" of this edge as x_t. For example, we replace the directed edge labeled "2" in Figure 6.24 (left) with an undirected edge connecting nodes 2_t and 2_h (Figure 6.24 (middle)). This results in the cyclic sequence of nodes $(1_t, 1_h, 2_h, 2_t, 3_h, 3_t, 4_t, 4_h)$. Finally, to simplify analysis of this graph even further, instead of using x_h and x_t to denote the head and tail of synteny block x, we will use the integers $2x$ and $2x - 1$, respectively (Figure 6.24 (right)). With this encoding, the original genome $(+1 -2 -3 +4)$ is transformed into the cyclic sequence of nodes $(1, 2, 4, 3, 6, 5, 7, 8)$.

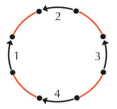 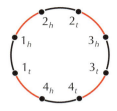 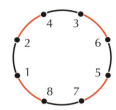

FIGURE 6.24 (Left) The circular chromosome $(+a -b -c +d)$ can be represented as $(+1 -2 -3 +4)$ using integers. (Middle) Representing this chromosome by replacing the black directed edges with undirected edges connecting "heads" and "tails" of each synteny block. (Right) Encoding head and tail nodes as integers. 1_t and 1_h are converted into 1 and 2; 2_t and 2_h are converted into 3 and 4; and so on. The original chromosome has been converted into the alternating cycle $(1, 2, 4, 3, 6, 5, 7, 8)$.

STOP and Think: Is the transformation illustrated in Figure 6.24 invertible? In other words, if we were to give you a cyclic sequence of nodes labeled from 1 to $2n$, could you reconstruct the chromosome with n synteny blocks from which it derives?

The following pseudocode bypasses the intermediate step in Figure 6.24 (middle) of assigning "head" and "tail" nodes in order to transform a single circular chromosome $Chromosome = (Chromosome_1, \ldots, Chromosome_n)$ into a cycle represented as a sequence of integers $Nodes = (Nodes_1, \ldots, Nodes_{2n})$.

CHROMOSOMETOCYCLE(*Chromosome*)
    for $j \leftarrow 1$ to $|Chromosome|$
        $i \leftarrow Chromosome_j$
        if $i > 0$
            $Node_{2j-1} \leftarrow 2i - 1$
            $Node_{2j} \leftarrow 2i$
        else
            $Node_{2j-1} \leftarrow -2i$
            $Node_{2j} \leftarrow -2i - 1$
    return *Nodes*

This process is in fact invertible, as described by the following pseudocode.

CYCLETOCHROMOSOME(*Nodes*)
    for $j \leftarrow 1$ to $|Nodes|/2$
        if $Node_{2j-1} < Node_{2j}$
            $Chromosome_j \leftarrow Node_{2j}/2$
        else
            $Chromosome_j \leftarrow -Node_{2j-1}/2$
    return *Chromosome*

CHROMOSOMETOCYCLE generates the sequence of nodes of a chromosome, but it does not explicitly add the edges. Any genome P with n synteny blocks will have the black undirected edges $\text{BLACKEDGES}(P) = (1,2), (3,4), \ldots, (2n-1, 2n)$.

We now define $\text{COLOREDEDGES}(P)$ as the set of colored edges in the graph of P. For the example in Figure 6.24, the set $\text{COLOREDEDGES}(P)$ contains the edges $(2,4)$, $(3,6)$, $(5,7)$, and $(8,1)$.

The following algorithm constructs $\text{COLOREDEDGES}(P)$ for a genome P. In this pseudocode, we will assume that an n-element array $(a_1, \ldots, a_n)$ has an invisible $(n+1)$-th element that is equal to its first element, i.e., $a_{n+1} = a_1$.

COLOREDEDGES(*P*)
    Edges $\leftarrow$ an empty set
    for each chromosome *Chromosome* in *P*
        Nodes $\leftarrow$ **CHROMOSOMETOCYCLE**(*Chromosome*)
        for $j \leftarrow 1$ to $|Chromosome|$
            add the edge $(Nodes_{2j}, Nodes_{2j+1})$ to *Edges*
    return *Edges*

The colored edges in the breakpoint graph of P and Q are given by $\text{COLOREDEDGES}(P)$ together with $\text{COLOREDEDGES}(Q)$. Note that some edges in these two sets may connect the same two nodes, which results in trivial cycles.

Although we are now ready to solve the 2-Break Distance Problem, we will later find it helpful to implement a function converting a genome graph back into a genome.

> GRAPHTOGENOME(*GenomeGraph*)
> *P* ← an empty set of chromosomes
> **for** each cycle *Nodes* in *GenomeGraph*
>   *Chromosome* ← CYCLETOCHROMOSOME(*Nodes*)
>   add *Chromosome* to *P*
> **return** *P*

Solving the 2-Break Sorting Problem

Note: This Charging Station uses some notation from **CHARGING STATION: From Genomes to the Breakpoint Graph**.

Figure 6.25 (top) illustrates how a 2-break replaces colored edges $(1, 6)$ and $(3, 8)$ in a genome graph with two new colored edges $(1, 3)$ and $(6, 8)$. We will denote this operation as 2-BREAK$(1, 6, 3, 8)$. Note that the order of the nodes in this function matter, since the operation 2-BREAK$(1, 6, 8, 3)$ would represent a different 2-break that replaces $(1, 6)$ and $(3, 8)$ with $(1, 8)$ and $(6, 3)$ (Figure 6.25 (bottom)).

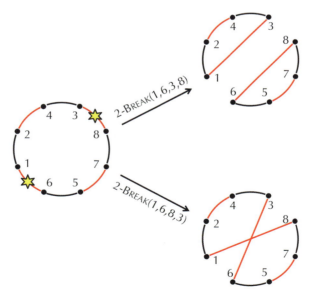

FIGURE 6.25 Operations 2-BREAK$(1, 6, 3, 8)$ (top) and 2-BREAK$(1, 6, 8, 3)$ (bottom) on the genome $(+1\ -2\ -3\ +4)$ from Figure 6.24.

The following pseudocode describes how 2-BREAK(i, i', j, j') transforms a genome graph.

> **2-BREAKONGENOMEGRAPH**(*GenomeGraph, i, i', j, j'*)
>   remove colored edges (i, i') and (j, j') from *GenomeGraph*
>   add colored edges (i, j) and (i', j') to *GenomeGraph*
>   **return** *GenomeGraph*

We can extend this pseudocode to a 2-break defined on genome P.

> **2-BREAKONGENOME**(*P, i, i', j, j'*)
>   *GenomeGraph* ← BLACKEDGES(*P*) and COLOREDEDGES(*P*)
>   *GenomeGraph* ← **2-BREAKONGENOMEGRAPH**(*GenomeGraph, i, i', j, j'*)
>   *P* ← **GRAPHTOGENOME**(*GenomeGraph*)
>   **return** *P*

We are now ready to find a series of intermediate genomes in a shortest transformation of P into Q by 2-breaks. The idea of our algorithm is to find a 2-break that will increase the number of red-blue cycles in the breakpoint graph by 1. To do so, as illustrated in Figure 6.26, we select an arbitrary blue edge in a non-trivial alternating red-blue cycle and perform the 2-break on the two red edges flanking this blue edge in order to split the red-blue cycle into two cycles (at least one of which is trivial).

> **SHORTESTREARRANGEMENTSCENARIO**(*P, Q*)
>   **output** *P*
>   *RedEdges* ← COLOREDEDGES(*P*)
>   *BlueEdges* ← COLOREDEDGES(*Q*)
>   *BreakpointGraph* ← the graph formed by *RedEdges* and *BlueEdges*
>   **while** *BreakpointGraph* has a non-trivial cycle *Cycle*
>   (j, i') ← an arbitrary edge from *BlueEdges* in a nontrivial red-blue cycle
>   (i, j) ← an edge from *RedEdges* originating at node j
>   (i', j') ← an edge from *RedEdges* originating at node i'
>   *RedEdges* ← *RedEdges* with edges (i, j) and (i', j') removed
>   *RedEdges* ← *RedEdges* with edges (j, i') and (j', i) added
>   *BreakpointGraph* ← the graph formed by *RedEdges* and *BlueEdges*
>   *P* ← **2-BREAKONGENOME**(*P, i, i', j, j'*)
>   **output** *P*

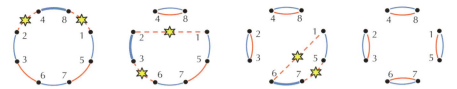

FIGURE 6.26 A shortest 2-break transformation (from left to right) of the breakpoint graph of $P = (+a -b -c +d)$ and $Q = (+a +b -d -c)$. The arbitrary blue edge selected by **SHORTESTREARRANGEMENTSCENARIO** at each step is shown in bold, and the red edges on either side of it are dashed (with stars indicating 2-breaks).

Detours

Why is the gene content of mammalian X chromosomes so conserved?

While mammalian X chromosomes are enriched in genes related to sexual reproduction, most of the approximately 1,000 genes on the X chromosome have nothing to do with gender. Ideally, they should be expressed (i.e., transcribed and eventually translated) in roughly the same quantities in females and males. But since females have two X chromosomes and males have only one, it would seem that all the genes on the X chromosome should have twice the expression level in females. This imbalance would lead to a problem in the complex cellular system of checks and balances underlying gene expression.

The need to balance gene expression in males and females led to the evolution of **dosage compensation**, or the inactivation of one X chromosome in females to equalize gene expression between the sexes. Because of dosage compensation, the gene content of the X chromosome is highly conserved between mammalian species because if a gene jumps off the X chromosome, then its expression may double, thus creating a genetic imbalance.

Discovery of genome rearrangements

After Sturtevant discovered genome rearrangements in *Drosophila* in 1921, another breakthrough occurred with the discovery that the salivary glands of *Drosophila* contain **polytene cells**. In normal cellular division, each daughter cell receives one copy of the genome. However, in the nuclei of polytene cells, DNA replication occurs repeatedly in the absence of cell division. The resulting chromosomes then knit themselves together into much larger "superchromosomes" called **polytene chromosomes**.

Polytene chromosomes serve a practical purpose for the fruit fly, which uses the extra DNA to boost the production of gene transcripts, producing lots of sticky saliva. But the human value of polytene chromosomes is perhaps greater. When Sturtevant and his collaborator, Theodosius Dobzhansky, looked at polytene chromosomes under a microscope, they were able to witness the work of rearrangements firsthand in tangled mutant chromosomes. In 1938, Sturtevant and Dobzhansky published a milestone paper with an evolutionary tree presenting a rearrangement scenario with seventeen reversals for various species of *Drosophila*, the first evolutionary tree in history to be constructed based on molecular data.

The exponential distribution

A **Bernoulli trial** is a random experiment with two possible outcomes, "success" (having probability p) and "failure" (having probability $1 - p$). The **geometric distribution** is the probability distribution underlying the random variable X representing the number of Bernoulli trials needed to obtain the first success:

$$\Pr(X = k) = (1 - p)^{k-1}p.$$

A **Poisson process** is a continuous-time probabilistic process counting the number of events in a given time interval, if we assume that the events occur independently and at a constant rate. For example, the Poisson process offers a good model of time points for passengers arriving to a large train station. If we assume that the number of passengers arriving during a very small time interval ϵ is $\lambda \cdot \epsilon$ (where λ is a constant), then we are interested in the probability $F(X)$ that nobody will arrive to the station during a time interval X. The **exponential distribution** describes the time between events in a Poisson process.

STOP and Think: Do you see any similarities between the Poisson process and the Bernoulli trials or between the exponential and geometric distributions?

The exponential distribution is merely the continuous analogue of the geometric distribution. More precisely, the Poisson process is characterized by a **rate parameter** λ, such that the number of events k in the time interval of duration ϵ follows the **Poisson probability distribution**:

$$e^{-\lambda \cdot \epsilon}(\lambda \cdot \epsilon)^k \big/ k!$$

The probability density function of the exponential distribution is $\lambda e^{-\lambda \cdot X}$ (compare with the geometric distribution shown in Figure 6.27).

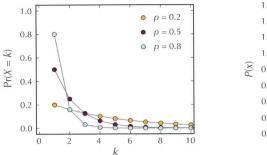 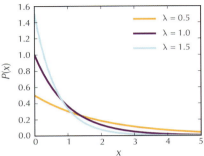

FIGURE 6.27 The probability density functions of the geometric (left) and exponential (right) distributions, each provided for three different parameter values.

Bill Gates and David X. Cohen flip pancakes

Before biologists faced genome rearrangement problems, mathematicians posed the **Pancake Flipping Problem**, arising from the following hypothetical waiter's conundrum.

> *The chef in our place is sloppy, and when he prepares a stack of pancakes they come out all different sizes. Therefore, when I deliver them to a customer, on the way to a table I rearrange them (so that the smallest winds up on top, and so on, down to the largest at the bottom) by grabbing several from the top and flipping them over, repeating this (varying the number I flip) as many times as necessary. If there are n pancakes, what is the maximum number of flips that I will ever have to use to rearrange them?*

Formally, a **prefix reversal** is a reversal that flips a prefix, or initial interval, of a permutation. The **Pancake Flipping Problem** corresponds to sorting unsigned permutations by prefix reversals. For example, the series of prefix reversals shown below ignores signs and represents the sorting of the **unsigned permutation**, (1 7 6 10 9 8 2 11 3 5 4), into the **identity unsigned permutation**, (1 2 3 4 5 6 7 8 9 10 11). The inverted interval is shown in red, and sorted intervals at the end of the permutation are shown in blue.

```
( 1   7   6  10   9   8   2  11   3   5   4 )
(11   2   8   9  10   6   7   1   3   5   4 )
( 4   5   3   1   7   6  10   9   8   2  11 )
(10   6   7   1   3   5   4   9   8   2  11 )
( 2   8   9   4   5   3   1   7   6  10  11 )
( 9   8   2   4   5   3   1   7   6  10  11 )
( 6   7   1   3   5   4   2   8   9  10  11 )
( 7   6   1   3   5   4   2   8   9  10  11 )
( 2   4   5   3   1   6   7   8   9  10  11 )
( 5   4   2   3   1   6   7   8   9  10  11 )
( 1   3   2   4   5   6   7   8   9  10  11 )
( 3   1   2   4   5   6   7   8   9  10  11 )
( 2   1   3   4   5   6   7   8   9  10  11 )
( 1   2   3   4   5   6   7   8   9  10  11 )
```

When we search for a shortest series of prefix reversals sorting a *signed* permutation, the problem is called the **Burnt Pancake Flipping Problem** (each pancake is "burnt" on one side, giving it two possible orientations).

STOP and Think: Prove that every unsigned permutation of length n can be sorted using at most $2 \cdot (n-1)$ prefix reversals. Prove that every signed permutation of length n can be sorted using at most $3 \cdot (n-1) + 1$ prefix reversals.

In the mid-1970s, Bill Gates, an undergraduate student at Harvard, and Christos Papadimitriou, Gates's professor, made the first attempt to solve the Pancake Flipping Problem and proved that any permutation of length n can be sorted with at most $5/3 \cdot (n+1)$ prefix reversals, a result that would not be improved for three decades. David X. Cohen worked on the Burnt Pancake Flipping Problem at Berkeley before he left computer science to become a writer for *The Simpsons* and eventually producer of *Futurama*. Along with Manuel Blum, he demonstrated that the Burnt Pancake Flipping Problem can be solved with at most $2 \cdot (n-1)$ prefix reversals.

Sorting linear permutations by reversals

In the main text, we defined the breakpoint graph for circular chromosomes, but this structure can easily be extended to linear chromosomes. Figure 6.28 depicts the human and the mouse X chromosomes as alternating red-black and blue-black paths (first and second panels). These two paths are superimposed in the third panel to form the breakpoint graph, which has five alternating red-blue cycles.

STOP and Think: Prove the following analogue of the Cycle Theorem for permutations: Given permutations P and Q, any reversal applied to P can increase $\text{CYCLES}(P, Q)$ by at most 1.

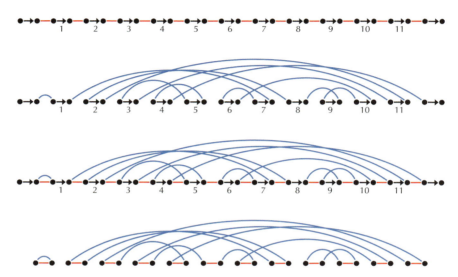

FIGURE 6.28 (1st panel) An alternating red-black path representing the human X chromosome $(+1 +2 +3 +4 +5 +6 +7 +8 +9 +10 +11)$. (2nd panel) An alternating blue-black path representing the mouse X chromosome $(+1 -7 +6 -10 +9 -8 +2 -11 -3 +5 +4)$. (3rd panel) The breakpoint graph of the mouse and human X chromosomes is obtained by superimposing red-black and blue-black paths from the first two panels. (4th panel) To highlight the five alternating red-blue cycles in the breakpoint graph, black edges are removed.

Whereas the number of trivial cycles is equal to $\text{BLOCKS}(Q, Q)$ in the trivial breakpoint graph of a circular permutation, the trivial breakpoint graph of a linear permutation has $\text{BLOCKS}(Q, Q) + 1$ trivial cycles. Since the Cycle Theorem holds for linear permutations, perhaps the reversal distance $d_{\text{rev}}(P, Q)$ is equal to $\text{BLOCKS}(P, Q) + 1 - \text{CYCLES}(P, Q)$ for linear chromosomes? After all, for the human and mouse X chromosomes, $\text{BLOCKS}(P, Q) + 1 - \text{CYCLES}(P, Q)$ is equal to $11 + 1 - 5 = 7$, which we already know to be the reversal distance between the human and mouse X chromosomes.

STOP and Think: Can you modify the proof of the 2-Break Distance Theorem to prove that $d_{rev}(P, Q) = \text{BLOCKS}(P, Q) + 1 - \text{CYCLES}(P, Q)$ for linear permutations P and Q?

You can verify that if $P = (+2\ +1)$ and $Q = (+1\ +2)$, then $d_{rev}(P, Q) \neq \text{BLOCKS}(P, Q) + 1 - \text{CYCLES}(P, Q)$. This makes it unlikely that we will be able to develop a simple algorithm for the computation of reversal distance.

However, the lower bound $d_{rev}(P, Q) \geq \text{BLOCKS}(P, Q) + 1 - \text{CYCLES}(P, Q)$ approximates the reversal distance between linear permutations extremely well. This intriguing performance raised the question of whether this bound is close to an exact formula. In 1999, Hannenhalli and Pevzner found this formula by defining two special types of breakpoint graph structures called "hurdles" and "fortresses". Denoting the number of hurdles and fortresses in $\text{BREAKPOINTGRAPH}(P, Q)$ by $\text{HURDLES}(P, Q)$ and $\text{FORTRESSES}(P, Q)$, respectively, they proved that the reversal distance $d_{rev}(P, Q)$ is given by

$$\text{BLOCKS}(P, Q) + 1 - \text{CYCLES}(P, Q) + \text{HURDLES}(P, Q) + \text{FORTRESSES}(P, Q).$$

Using this formula, they developed a polynomial algorithm for computing $d_{rev}(P, Q)$.

Bibliography Notes

Alfred Sturtevant was the first to discover rearrangements while comparing gene orders in fruit flies (Sturtevant, 1921). Together with Theodosius Dobzhansky, Sturtevant pioneered the analysis of genome rearrangements, publishing a milestone paper that presented a rearrangement scenario for many fruit fly species (Sturtevant and Dobzhansky, 1936). The Random Breakage Model was proposed by Ohno, 1973, further developed by Nadeau and Taylor, 1984, and refuted by Pevzner and Tesler, 2003b.

The notion of the breakpoint graph was proposed by Bafna and Pevzner, 1996. The polynomial algorithm for sorting by reversals was developed by Hannenhalli and Pevzner, 1999. The synteny block construction algorithm presented in this chapter was described by Pevzner and Tesler, 2003a. The 2-break operation was introduced in Yancopoulos, Attie, and Friedberg, 2005 under the name of "double cut and join".

The first algorithmic analysis of the Pancake Flipping problem was described by Gates and Papadimitriou, 1979. The first algorithmic analysis of the Burnt Pancake Flipping problem was described by Cohen and Blum, 1995.

The Multiple Genome Rearrangement problem was addressed by Ma et al., 2008 and Alekseyev and Pevzner, 2009. Zhao and Bourque, 2009 observed that matching duplications may trigger genome rearrangements.

Bibliography

Alekseyev, M. A. and P. A. Pevzner (2009). "Breakpoint graphs and ancestral genome reconstructions". *Genome Research* Vol. 19: 943–957.

Bafna, V. and P. A. Pevzner (1996). "Genome Rearrangements and Sorting by Reversals". *SIAM Journal on Computing* Vol. 25: 272–289.

Butler, J., I MacCallum, M. Kleber, I. A. Shlyakhter, M. Belmonte, E. S. Lander, C. Nusbaum, and D. B. Jaffe (2008). "ALLPATHS: *de novo* assembly of whole-genome shotgun microreads." *Genome Research* Vol. 18: 810–820.

Cohen, D. S. and M. Blum (1995). "On the Problem of Sorting Burnt Pancakes". *Discrete Applied Mathematics* Vol. 61: 105–120.

Conti, E., T. Stachelhaus, M. A. Marahiel, and P. Brick (1997). "Structural basis for the activation of phenylalanine in the non-ribosomal biosynthesis of gramicidin S". *The EMBO Journal* Vol. 16: 4174–4183.

Conti, E., N. P. Franks, and P. Brick (1996). "Crystal structure of firefly luciferase throws light on a superfamily of adenylate-forming enzymes". *Structure* Vol. 4: 287–298.

Cristianini, N. and M. W. Hahn (2006). *Introduction to Computational Genomics: A Case Studies Approach*. Cambridge University Press.

de Bruijn, N. (1946). "A Combinatorial Problem". In: *Proceedings of the Section of Sciences, Koninklijke Akademie van Wetenschappen te Amsterdam*. Vol. 49: 758–764.

Doolittle, R. F., M. W. Hunkapiller, L. E. Hood, S. G. Devare, K. C. Robbins, S. A. Aaronson, and H. N. Antoniades (1983). "Simian sarcoma virus onc gene, v-sis, is derived from the gene (or genes) encoding a platelet-derived growth factor". *Science* Vol. 221: 275–277.

Drmanac, R., I. Labat, I. Brukner, and R. Crkvenjakov (1989). "Sequencing of megabase plus DNA by hybridization: Theory of the method". *Genomics* Vol. 4: 114–128.

Euler, L. (1758). "Solutio Problematis ad Geometriam Situs Pertinentis". *Novi Commentarii Academiae Scientarium Imperialis Petropolitanque*, 9–28.

Gao, F. and C.-T. Zhang (2008). "Ori-Finder: A web-based system for finding *oriCs* in unannotated bacterial genomes". *BMC Bioinformatics* Vol. 9: 79.

Gardner, M. (1974). "Mathematical Games". *Scientific American* Vol. 230: 120–125.

Gates, W. H. and C. H. Papadimitriou (1979). "Bounds for sorting by prefix reversal". *Discrete Mathematics* Vol. 27: 47–57.

Geman, S. and D. Geman (1984). "Stochastic Relaxation, Gibbs Distributions, and the Bayesian Restoration of Images". *IEEE Transactions on Pattern Analysis and Machine Intelligence* Vol. PAMI-6: 721–741.

Good, I. J. (1946). "Normal Recurring Decimals". *Journal of the London Mathematical Society* Vol. 21: 167–169.

Grigoriev, A. (1998). "Analyzing genomes with cumulative skew diagrams". *Nucleic Acids Research* Vol. 26: 2286–2290.

Grigoriev, A. (2011). "How do replication and transcription change genomes?" In: *Bioinformatics for Biologists*. Ed. by P. A. Pevzner and R. Shamir. Cambridge University Press, 111–125.

Guibas, L. and A. Odlyzko (1981). "String overlaps, pattern matching, and nontransitive games". *Journal of Combinatorial Theory, Series A* Vol. 30: 183 –208.

Hannenhalli, S. and P. A. Pevzner (1999). "Transforming Cabbage into Turnip: Polynomial Algorithm for Sorting Signed Permutations by Reversals". *Journal of the ACM* Vol. 46: 1–27.

Harmer, S. L., J. B. Hogenesch, M. Straume, H. S. Chang, B. Han, T. Zhu, X. Wang, J. A. Kreps, and S. A. Kay (2000). "Orchestrated transcription of key pathways in *Arabidopsis* by the circadian clock". *Science* Vol. 290: 2110–2113.

Hertz, G. Z. and G. D. Stormo (1999). "Identifying DNA and protein patterns with statistically significant alignments of multiple sequences." *Bioinformatics* Vol. 15: 563–577.

Idury, R. M. and M. S. Waterman (1995). "A New Algorithm for DNA Sequence Assembly." *Journal of Computational Biology* Vol. 2: 291–306.

Ivics, Z., P. Hackett, R. Plasterk, and Z. Izsvák (1997). "Molecular reconstruction of Sleeping Beauty, a Tc1-like transposon from fish, and its transposition in human cells". *Cell* Vol. 91: 501–510.

Konopka, R. J. and S. Benzer (1971). "Clock mutants of Drosophila melanogaster". *Proceedings of the National Academy of Sciences of the United States of America* Vol. 68: 2112–2116.

Lawrence, C. E., S. F. Altschul, M. S. Boguski, J. S. Liu, A. F. Neuwald, and J. C. Wootton (1993). "Detecting subtle sequence signals: a Gibbs sampling strategy for multiple alignment". *Science* Vol. 262: 208–214.

Levenshtein, V. I. (1966). "Binary codes capable of correcting deletions, insertions, and reversals". *Soviet Physics Doklady* Vol. 10: 707–710.

Liachko, I., R. A. Youngblood, U. Keich, and M. J. Dunham (2013). "High-resolution mapping, characterization, and optimization of autonomously replicating sequences in yeast". *Genome Research* Vol. 23: 698–704.

Lobry, J. R. (1996). "Asymmetric substitution patterns in the two DNA strands of bacteria". *Molecular Biology and Evolution* Vol. 13: 660–665.

Lundgren, M., A. Andersson, L. Chen, P. Nilsson, and R. Bernander (2004). "Three replication origins in *Sulfolobus* species: Synchronous initiation of chromosome replication and asynchronous termination". *Proceedings of the National Academy of Sciences of the United States of America* Vol. 101: 7046–7051.

Lysov, Y., V. Florent'ev, A. Khorlin, K. Khrapko, V. Shik, and A. Mirzabekov (1988). "DNA sequencing by hybridization with oligonucleotides". *Doklady Academy Nauk USSR* Vol. 303: 1508–1511.

Ma, J., A. Ratan, B. J. Raney, B. B. Suh, W. Miller, and D. Haussler (2008). "The infinite sites model of genome evolution". *Proceedings of the National Academy of Sciences of the United States of America* Vol. 105: 14254–14261.

Maxam, A. M. and W. Gilbert (1977). "A new method for sequencing DNA." *Proceedings of the National Academy of Sciences of the United States of America* Vol. 74: 560–564.

Medvedev, P., S. K. Pham, M. Chaisson, G. Tesler, and P. A. Pevzner (2011). "Paired de Bruijn Graphs: A Novel Approach for Incorporating Mate Pair Information into Genome Assemblers." *Journal of Computational Biology* Vol. 18: 1625–1634.

Nadeau, J. H. and B. A. Taylor (1984). "Lengths of chromosomal segments conserved since divergence of man and mouse". *Proceedings of the National Academy of Sciences of the United States of America* Vol. 81: 814–818.

Ng, J., N. Bandeira, W.-T. Liu, M. Ghassemian, T. L. Simmons, W. H. Gerwick, R. Linington, P. Dorrestein, and P. A. Pevzner (2009). "Dereplication and *de novo* sequencing of nonribosomal peptides". *Nature Methods* Vol. 6: 596–599.

Ohno, S. (1973). "Ancient linkage groups and frozen accidents". *Nature* Vol. 244: 259–262.

Park, H. D., K. M. Guinn, M. I. Harrell, R. Liao, M. I. Voskuil, M. Tompa, G. K. Schoolnik, and D. R. Sherman (2003). "Rv3133c/dosR is a transcription factor that mediates the hypoxic response of Mycobacterium tuberculosis". *Molecular Microbiology* Vol. 48: 833–843.

Pevzner, P. and G. Tesler (2003a). "Genome rearrangements in mammalian evolution: lessons from human and mouse genomes". *Genome Research* Vol. 13: 37–45.

Pevzner, P. and G. Tesler (2003b). "Human and mouse genomic sequences reveal extensive breakpoint reuse in mammalian evolution". *Proceedings of the National Academy of Sciences of the United States of America* Vol. 100: 7672–7677.

Pevzner, P. A. (1989). "1-Tuple DNA sequencing: computer analysis". *Journal of Biomolecular Structure and Dynamics* Vol. 7: 63–73.

Pevzner, P. A., H Tang, and M. S. Waterman (2001). "An Eulerian path approach to DNA fragment assembly". *Proceedings of the National Academy of Sciences of the United States of America* Vol. 98: 9748–53.

Rosenblatt, J. and P. Seymour (1982). "The Structure of Homometric Sets". *SIAM Journal on Algebraic Discrete Methods* Vol. 3: 343–350.

Sanger, F, S Nicklen, and A. Coulson (1977). "DNA sequencing with chain-terminating inhibitors". *Proceedings of The National Academy of Sciences of The United States Of America* Vol. 74: 5463–5467.

Sedgewick, R. and P. Flajolet (2013). *An Introduction to the Analysis of Algorithms.* Addison-Wesley.

Sernova, N. V. and M. S. Gelfand (2008). "Identification of replication origins in prokaryotic genomes". *Briefings in Bioinformatics* Vol. 9: 376–391.

Smith, T. F. and M. S. Waterman (1981). "Identification of common molecular subsequences." *Journal of Molecular Biology* Vol. 147: 195–197.

Solov'ev, A. (1966). "A combinatorial identity and its application to the problem about the first occurence of a rare event". *Theory of Probability and its Applications* Vol. 11: 276–282.

Southern, E. (1988). "Analysing Polynucleotide Sequences". Patent (United Kingdom).

Stachelhaus, T., H. D. Mootz, and M. A. Marahiel (1999). "The specificity-conferring code of adenylation domains in nonribosomal peptide synthetases." *Chemistry & Biology* Vol. 6: 493–505.

Sturtevant, A. H. (1921). "A Case of Rearrangement of Genes in Drosophila". *Proceedings of the National Academy of Sciences of the United States of America* Vol. 7: 235–237.

Sturtevant, A. H. and T. Dobzhansky (1936). "Inversions in the Third Chromosome of Wild Races of Drosophila Pseudoobscura, and Their Use in the Study of the History of the Species". *Proceedings of the National Academy of Sciences of the United States of America* Vol. 22: 448–450.

Tang, Y. Q., J. Yuan, G. Osapay, K. Osapay, D. Tran, C. J. Miller, A. J. Ouellette, and M. E. Selsted (1999). "A cyclic antimicrobial peptide produced in primate leukocytes by the ligation of two truncated alpha-defensins". *Science* Vol. 286: 498–502.

Venkataraman, N., A. L. Cole, P. Ruchala, A. J. Waring, R. I. Lehrer, O. Stuchlik, J. Pohl, and A. M. Cole (2009). "Reawakening retrocyclins: ancestral human defensins active against HIV-1". *PLoS Biology* Vol. 7: e95.

Wang, X., C. Lesterlin, R. Reyes-Lamothe, G. Ball, and D. J. Sherratt (2011). "Replication and segregation of an *Escherichia coli* chromosome with two replication origins". *Proceedings of the National Academy of Sciences* Vol. 108: E243–E250.

Xia, X. (2012). "DNA replication and strand asymmetry in prokaryotic and mitochondrial genomes". *Current Genomics* Vol. 13: 16–27.

Yancopoulos, S., O. Attie, and R. Friedberg (2005). "Efficient sorting of genomic permutations by translocation, inversion and block interchange". *Bioinformatics* Vol. 21: 3340–3346.

Zerbino, D. R. and E. Birney (2008). "Velvet: Algorithms for *de novo* short read assembly using de Bruijn graphs". *Genome Research* Vol. 18: 821–829.

Zhao, H. and G. Bourque (2009). "Recovering genome rearrangements in the mammalian phylogeny". *Genome Research* Vol. 19: 934–942.

Image Courtesies

Figure 1.26: Ævar Arnfjörð Bjarmason
Figure 3.5: Dan Gilbert
Figure 3.45 (left): Royal Irish Academy
Figure 4.1: Open Clip Art
Figure 6.27: Wikimedia Commons user Skbkekas
Figure 6.1: Glenn Tesler
Figure 6.2: Glenn Tesler
Figure 6.3: Max Alekseyev
Figure 6.4: Max Alekseyev
Figure 6.5: Glenn Tesler
Figure 6.6: Glenn Tesler
Figure 6.22: Glenn Tesler